School Social Work

School Social Work

Theory to Practice

EDITED BY

Lynn Bye
University of Minnesota, Duluth

Michelle Alvarez
University of Southern Indiana

THOMSON

BROOKS/COLE

Australia • Brazil • Canada • Mexico • Singapore • Spain
United Kingdom • United States

THOMSON
™
BROOKS/COLE

School Social Work: Theory to Practice
Edited by Lynn Bye and Michelle Alvarez

Editor in Chief: Marcus Boggs
Executive Editor: Lisa Gebo
Assistant Editor: Alma Dea Michelena
Editorial Assistant: Sheila Walsh
Technology Project Manager:
   Inna Fedoseyeva
Marketing Manager: Caroline Concilla
Marketing Assistant: Rebecca Weisman
Senior Marketing Communications Manager:
   Tami Strang
Project Manager, Editorial Production:
   Christy Krueger
Creative Director: Rob Hugel

Art Director: Vernon Boes
Print Buyer: Judy Inouye
Permissions Editor: Robert Kauser
Production Service: Matrix
   Productions Inc.
Production Editor: Aaron Downey
Copy Editor: Dan Hays
Cover Designer: Roger Knox
Cover Image: Chad Johnson / Masterfile
Cover Printer: Webcom
Compositor: International
   Typesetting and Composition
Printer: Webcom

Library of Congress Control Number: 2005938652

ISBN 0-534-54797-4

Thomson Higher Education
10 Davis Drive
Belmont, CA 94002-3098
USA

For more information about our products,
contact us at:
**Thomson Learning Academic Resource
Center 1-800-423-0563**

For permission to use material from this
text or product, submit a request online at
http://www.thomsonrights.com.
Any additional questions about permissions
can be submitted by e-mail to
thomsonrights@thomson.com.

Contents

CHAPTER 2

School Social Work and Educational Reform   21
Joseph R. Gianesin, M.S.W., Ph.D.

CHAPTER 3

Ecological Perspective for School Social Work Practice   41
Kendra J. Garrett, D.S.W.

PART 3 | SCHOOL SOCIAL WORK: SMALLER SYSTEMS PRACTICE   121

CHAPTER 8
School Social Work With Families   122
Lynn Bye, M.S.W., Ph.D.

PART 4 | SCHOOL SOCIAL WORK: KEY ISSUES AND CONSIDERATIONS FOR PRACTICE   195

CHAPTER 15
Legal Issues in School Social Work   248
Gaylon J. Nettles, M.S.W., J.D.

CHAPTER 16
School Social Work Practice With Students With Disabilities 261
James P. Clark, M.S.W., and Charlene Thiede, M.S.W.

CHAPTER 19
International School Social Work 310
Marion Huxtable, M.S.W.

Introduction

The purpose of this book is to provide school social workers, students, and faculty with a comprehensive, practical, factual, and thought-provoking text that addresses the foundations of school social work practice. In preparation for this book a survey and content analysis were conducted on topics in school social work syllabi to ensure that the range of topics taught in school social work courses at universities throughout the United States was covered. Topics that appeared most frequently in the syllabi were the highest priority for inclusion in this book.

KEY THEMES

In addition to being comprehensive in the range of topics covered, we wanted our text to focus on a few key themes essential to school social work practice, such as **best practice, ecological perspective, strengths perspective,** and **cultural competence.** We were very intentional about how the book was structured so that these themes were woven throughout each chapter of the book. This book employs a multisystemic approach to providing school social work services that is aligned with generalist, advanced generalist, and clinical social work practice. This book is unique in that it emphasizes the importance of school social work at the larger system levels of policy/community (macro), and organizational (mezzo) by placing those chapters before the chapters on micro level school social work with families (Chapter 8) and individuals and small groups (Chapter 9). This ordering of content was done to place an emphasis on interventions that impact larger numbers of students and tend to be more preventative. A policy change has the potential to increase educational opportunities for many students and the organizational climate of a school affects everyone in that school. By reversing the typical order of how material is presented from micro, mezzo, macro to macro, mezzo, micro, we hope to highlight the importance of a more preventative approach.

PURPOSE OF BOOK

The goal of our book is to provide a straightforward, hands-on guide to new and evolving best practice in school social work using

- Tools that school social workers need to do their job in elementary, middle, and high schools
- Multisystemic approaches that address all levels of intervention including communitywide (macro), organizational (mezzo), and individual/small group/family (micro) from prevention to remediation
- Guidelines for utilizing an ecological and culturally sensitive approach

CULTURAL COMPETENCE

In every chapter of this book, we invite the reader to think about how cultural competence applies to school social work practice. To be effective, school social workers must continually improve skills in cultural competence. **Cultural competence** is defined as "a set of congruent behaviors, attitudes, practices, and policies that come together in a system or agency or among professionals and enable that system or agency or those professionals to work effectively together" (Isaacs-Shockley, Cross, Bazron, Dennis, & Benjamin, 1996, p. 25). Working toward cultural competence requires awareness of how values and beliefs shape behavior in ourselves and in people from other cultures. School social workers also need to be aware of white privilege, systems of oppression, and the largely Eurocentric structure of schools in the United States. The following cultural competence continuum developed by Cross, Bazron, Dennis, and Isaacs (1989, pp. 14–18) can be used by school social workers for self assessment and to assist schools in becoming increasingly safe and welcoming for all students:

1. *Cultural destructiveness,* where the intention is to destroy a culture
2. *Cultural incapacity,* where people believe their culture is superior
3. *Cultural blindness,* where people pretend there are no differences
4. *Cultural precompetence,* where there is a beginning awareness of the systemic oppression faced by some groups
5. *Basic cultural competence,* where differences are respected and action is taken to accommodate them
6. *Advanced cultural competence* or cultural proficiency, where culture is honored

School social workers can help the schools in which they work to develop a system for gaining the cultural knowledge needed to work with diverse families. The first step in this process is heightening awareness among school personnel for the need to better understand the history and culture of the families they serve. In addition to school social workers offering information related to cultural competence, people from cultures represented in the school population can serve as cultural guides and meet with the school staff to share their insight. School social workers can facilitate book clubs for teachers in which books on different cultures and videos depicting the strengths or history of a culture can be viewed and discussed. It is helpful to invite cultural guides into these discussions so that they can speak to the accuracy of what is portrayed. These learning experiences need to be continual and ongoing because cultural competence is "a process born of a commitment to provide quality services and to make a positive difference for clients and communities of color" and is not accomplished with a few events (Isaacs-Shockley et al., 1996, p. 28).

OVERVIEW AND STRUCTURE OF THE BOOK

To facilitate the learning experience, this book uses minimal jargon and, when used, defines special terms and concepts. Examples are frequently incorporated to clarify concepts, techniques, and strategies. The book is divided into the following five parts: Part 1: School Social Work: History and Contexts; Part 2: School Social Work: Policy, Community, and Organizational Practice; Part 3: School Social Work: Smaller Systems Practice; Part 4: School Social Work: Key Issues and Considerations for Practice; and Part 5: School Social Work: Emerging Trends and Looking Ahead to the Future.

Part 1, School Social Work: History and Contexts, includes Chapters 1–4, which provide the orientation and background necessary to understand the profession. Chapter 1, History of School Social Work, discusses how school social work began and has changed over the course of time. Chapter 2, Social Work and Educational Reform, covers the political, societal, and economic forces that influence educational reform and describes specific reform attempts such as the No Child Left Behind legislation. Chapter 3, Ecological Perspective for School Social Work Practice, explains the ecological framework on which this book is based. Although the ecological framework is used throughout the book, it is our intention that the information covered is more applied than theoretical. Chapter 4, The Many Facets in the Role of the School Social Worker, introduces the reader to the different roles school social workers perform.

Part 2, School Social Work: Policy, Community, and Organizational Practice, consists of Chapter 5–7. Chapter 5, School Social Work at the Policy and Community Level, makes a case for school social workers to become more involved in using their group work, community-organizing, and advocacy skills to implement policies that help students be successful. Chapter 6, School Social Work at the School Organizational Level, addresses schoolwide interventions and the importance of the school climate for student learning. Chapter 7,

Community Schools: New Roles for Social Work Practitioners, covers a major national trend toward community schools and provides information about a specific model.

Part 3, School Social Work: Smaller Systems Practice, includes Chapters 8–11. Chapter 8, School Social Work with Families, gives specific suggestions based on the literature for ways to partner with families in the education of their children. Chapter 9, School Social Work with Individuals and Small Groups, discusses the unique features of school-based assessment and practice, including classroom behavioral management and group work interventions. Chapter 10, School Social Work and Crisis Intervention, outlines a process for intervention at the scene of a trauma and describes methods for intervening at the small group and classroom level. Consultation is a skill used at every level of school social work practice and is so central to the work that school social workers perform that we decided to focus an entire chapter on it. Chapter 11, Consultation in School Social Work, shares helpful strategies for fulfilling this important role.

Part 4, School Social Work: Key Issues and Considerations for Practice includes Chapters 12–16. Everyday, school social workers must deal with the issue of confidentiality. Chapter 12, Confidentiality in the Schools, covers this important information. Chapter 13, Incorporating Best Practices, defines "best practice" and gives practice guidelines for how to achieve it. Chapter 14, Research and Evaluation of School Social Work Practice, makes a compelling case for all school social workers to get involved in research and explains ways to do it. Chapter 15, Legal Issues in School Social Work, defines the terms law, rule, policy, and ethical code and describes the access and due process issues for children who have special needs. Chapter 16, School Social Work Practice with Students with Disabilities, covers the role of school social workers in the special education process and equal educational opportunity for students with disabilities. Chapter 16 also provides information about the laws related to students with disabilities, assessments, goal development, and interventions.

Part 5, School Social Work: Emerging Trends and Looking Ahead to the Future, includes Chapters 17–19. Ideas presented in Chapter 17, Technology and School Social Work, will help practitioners use many novel technology-based approaches in their work with students. In our effort to create a truly practical book, Chapter 18, The Transition from Student to School Social Worker, was included to give information critical to professional development and obtaining employment in the field of school social work. Recent college graduates hoping to become school social workers will find this chapter particularly helpful. Chapter 19, International School Social Work, describes the primary mission of school social work throughout the world and compares the way services are delivered in different countries.

As noted previously, the chapters are organized with the policy/community and organizational content preceding the content on work with individuals. Because school social workers work at policy/community (macro), the organizational (mezzo), and individual, family, and small group (micro) levels, we have included chapters on each (Chapters 5, 6, 8, and 9).

When developing the book, we recruited authors from different areas in the United States to gain more of a national perspective. We are extremely fortunate that our contributing authors are all active in the field of social work at the state, regional, and/or national levels. Practicing school social workers and university faculty are represented among this talented group of contributing authors.

Our book has web-based assignments, quizzes, and online course curriculum modules. The goals of our web-based assignments, quizzes, and resources are varied. The web-based assignments will give the instructor an option to reinforce and apply the concepts learned in the chapters. The goal of the quizzes is to check the level of understanding of the material covered in the chapters. The goal of the web-based resources is to link the user with other opportunities to gain information at the national and international levels and also to connect with others in the field. Another goal of the web-based resources is to facilitate interactivity and the practical application of information learned in the text.

References

Cross, T., Bazron, B., Dennis, K., & Isaacs, M. (1989). *Towards a culturally competent system of care: A monograph on effective services for minority children who are severely emotionally disturbed.* Washington, DC: Georgetown University Child Development Center, National Technical Assistance Center for Children's Mental Health.

Isaacs-Shockley, M., Cross, T., Bazron, B. J., Dennis, K., & Benjamin, M. P. (1996). Framework for a culturally competent system of care. In B. A. Stroul (Ed.), *Children's mental health: Creating systems of care in a changing society* (pp. 23–40). Baltimore, MD: Brookes.

Acknowledgements

The editors would like to acknowledge those who supported the development of this school social work text. First, we would like to thank Douglas Bye and Marvin Alvarez for their patience and encouragement. We extend an additional thank you to family members who supported the editors and the chapter authors in their quest to create a school social work text that is engaging and scholarly.

The chapters in this book are written by dedicated leaders in the field of school social work who contribute to the literature about practice in the field. The field of school social work benefits greatly from these role models who move policy and theory into practice.

We are especially grateful to Phyllis Horgen and Karen Nichols for the long hours they spent helping to edit and format the text. Their skill and expertise added to the quality of this book.

Thanks also to Lisa Gebo, Brooks/Cole Publishing Executive Editor, for her assistance and guidance in the process of developing this book. It was our tremendous good fortune to work with such a talented publication editor. Sheila Walsh, Editorial Assistant to Lisa Gebo, was also very helpful.

We express our appreciation to those in the field who influenced us in our development as school social workers and school social work academics. Jim Clark, former Iowa State School Social Work Consultant and current Supervisor of School Social Work Services in the Iowa Heartland AEA 11, and Nic Dibble, School Social Work Consultant for Wisconsin, deserve special mention for their visionary thinking that challenges us to stretch what we know into what might be.

This book is dedicated to the Pinellas County, Florida and St. Cloud, Minnesota school social workers, school psychologists, school counselors, school nurses, teachers, attendance workers, administrative assistants, and administrators who exemplify the collaborative model by working as a team in the best interest of the student.

About the Editors

Lynn Bye, MSW, Ph.D., is an associate professor of social work at the University of Minnesota, Duluth, where she teaches the school social work course along with other practice courses. Prior to teaching at the college level, Bye was a school social worker and received recognition as Minnesota School Social Worker of the Year. She has a long and active involvement with the Minnesota School Social Worker's Association, serving as president and treasurer of the organization. Her involvement in the field of school social work continues through her work with the Minnesota School Social Work Summer Institutes and her current research on school social work outcomes.

Michelle Alvarez, MSW, Ed.D., LCSW, C-SSWS, is an assistant professor of social work at the University of Southern Indiana. She coordinates and teaches courses in the university's school social work specialization. In July 2003, she was appointed to the National Association of Social Workers (NASW) School Social Work Section Committee and was elected to the School Social Work Association of America board in October 2003. She is editor of NASW's *School Social Work Section Connection* newsletter and a consulting editor for the NASW journal, *Children & Schools*. Most important, she is an advocate for the field of school social work and the students served.

School Social Work: History and Contexts

1

CHAPTER

History of School Social Work

GARY LEE SHAFFER, Ph.D.
The University of North Carolina at Chapel Hill

CHAPTER OUTLINE

CHAPTER OVERVIEW

After completing this chapter, readers will be able to (1) identify educational, social, political, and economic trends that led to the development of school social work practice; (2) describe early school social work practice; (3) explain developments in the 1930s and 1940s that influenced school social work practice and progress; (4) describe survey findings that helped shape the profession's search for more effective roles and models; and (5) identify trends that will influence future school social work practice.

INTRODUCTION: ANTECEDENTS OF SCHOOL SOCIAL WORK SERVICES

Social work practice in public schools dates to 1906–1907 with the establishment of visiting teacher services in New York, Chicago, Boston, and Hartford, Connecticut. At its inception in the early 1900s, school social workers were known, among other things, as visiting teachers, school counselors, and home and school visitors. In 1945, a U.S. Office of Education survey identified 50 different titles used to designate social workers in the schools. A survey of North Carolina school social workers in the 1980s found more than 20 titles in use. Terminology remains varied in some localities today despite the National Association of Social Workers' (NASW) efforts to have the term **school social worker** adopted. **School social work services** and **school social worker** are used in this chapter except for historical accuracy.

Settlement workers, women's civic leagues, child welfare practitioners, and others who studied "child maladjustment" viewed the schools as an excellent environment for intervening with "problem children and youth." Even though these early programs began at approximately the same time, this field of practice did not spring up spontaneously but evolved from antecedent educational, social, political, and economic developments, such as the establishment of common schools, compulsory education, child labor legislation, and the onset of the Progressive Movement in the 1890s. School-age populations increased rapidly, fueled by the flood of immigrants from Southern and Eastern Europe combined with the migration of African Americans from the agrarian south to the industrialized north. Thus, the factors of the considerable ethnic, racial, and socioeconomic diversity of the public schools, coupled with the convergence of new knowledge in such fields as education, psychology, and mental heath, pressured schools to change and modify many long-held beliefs and practices.

The Common School Movement

Common School reformers of the 1830s and 1840s established a pattern of public education that continues to exist in many forms today. Horace Mann lent direction to this movement that replaced the "Charity Schools" for the poor and provided educational opportunities to the masses that previously had been accessible only to children of the wealthy. The common schools were publicly financed, conservative, bureaucratic, uniform in curriculum and method, and slow to change. The reformers "believed that education could be used to assure the dominance of Protestant Anglo-American culture, reduce tensions between social classes, eliminate crime and poverty, stabilize the political system, and form patriotic citizens" (Spring, 2001, p. 103). Public schools placed a premium on punctuality, standardization, and routinization—skills important for America's industrial revolution. Detractors demanded ethnic and religious school choice options and charged that secular public schools were non-Christian and ungodly (Cordasco, 1963; Nelson, 1987).

Compulsory Attendance

The first state compulsory attendance law was passed by Massachusetts in 1852 when children between 8 and 14 years of age were required to attend school at least 3 months out of the year for a minimum of 6 consecutive weeks. Exceptions were made for poor children, those with mental or physical disabilities, or those able to demonstrate previous mastery of the content. States were slow to require attendance because only three additional states enacted similar statutes before the 1870s. However, by 1900 more than two thirds of the states had compulsory attendance laws, and by 1918 compulsory attendance statutes existed in all states. Required ages for attendance, exemptions from attendance, and length of the school year lacked uniformity, and truant enforcement remained uneven for decades because staffing, credentials, administration, and services varied across jurisdictions (Peterson, 1985; Richardson, 1980).

Child Labor Legislation

Compulsory attendance was both opposed and ignored at times but generally proved to be simply ineffective without legislation that prohibited or severely limited the workforce participation of children and youth. Industry's demand for child workers was enormous and by 1900 18% of children 10–15 years old were employed. Control over who should socialize children and parents' right to the benefits of their child's labor were two hotly contested issues with racial, ethnic, and class overtones. In 1904, the National Child Labor Committee was organized to investigate and dramatize child labor dangers in concert with lobbying for protective legislation. Organized labor supported such legislation in part because it reduced job competition from the child labor force. Although numerous states outside of the South responded to this lobbying effort, other attempts to secure uniform federal child labor laws were stymied by conservative church and farm organizations as well as the U.S. Supreme Court until passage of the Fair Labor Standards Act of 1939. This legislation limited the number of working hours for school-age children and prohibited child employment in certain industries (Trattner, 1970).

Migration and Immigration

African American migration from the South to the cities of the north, combined with the flood of Southern and Eastern European immigrants to the cities of the East and Midwest, rapidly expanded the school-age population and exacerbated social unrest. Between 1880 and 1890, immigration increased by 5.25 million people (Cohen, 1958). The immigrants came primarily from Eastern and Southern Europe; many were Jewish victims of Czarist Russian pogroms. By 1890, two-thirds of the population of New York City lived in hastily constructed tenements that often lacked proper sanitation, utilities for lighting, and fire safety. Free western lands were scarce, and by 1900 50% of the nation lived in cities (Cohen, 1958).

It fell to the social settlements, private philanthropies, churches, and local civic authorities to address the urban filth and disease because state and federal governmental intervention was minimal. Congress and the courts objected to involvement in social reforms, and social Darwinism and laissez-faire philosophies were popular. Educational reformers tried to address the needs of the desperately poor, illiterate, and unskilled immigrants and migrants; however, their efforts proved both constructive and destructive. For example, immigrant children adapted quickly and were often required to interpret the new culture to their families; however, immigrant parents felt their parental authority and respect undermined by the schools' "Americanization" or "deculturalization" programs (Nelson, 1987; Spring, 2001). Ellwood Cubberly (1909), a prominent educator of the era, wrote,

> Our task is to break up these groups or settlements, to assimilate and amalgamate these people as a part of our American race, and to implant in their children, so far as can be done, the Anglo-Saxon conception of righteousness, law and order and popular government. (p. 15)

The Progressive Movement and the Social Welfare Efforts in the Schools

Similar to the earlier Common School reformers, the Progressives saw the schools as a means to address poverty and decrease crime, but their approaches to the situation differed significantly. Common School supporters sought these goals through education in the classroom, whereas the Progressives sought these ends by expanding the social welfare function of the schools. For example, Jacob Riis's widely read and influential muckraking exposés, *How the Other Half Lives* (1890) and *The Children of the Poor* (1892), called for "strengthening and more effective enforcement of compulsory education and child labor laws; municipal provision of truant schools, nurseries, kindergartens, manual skill training, school playgrounds, and the opening of the schools in the evening" (Cohen, 1964, p. 10).

Progressive "good government" organizations, philanthropic groups, neighborhood associations, and the budding American settlement house movement saw the schools as the panacea for a host of social ills, including bitter poverty, tenement slums, foreign influences, deplorable health conditions, delinquency, and inadequate welfare for children and youth. However, systems could not respond quickly enough to the rapidly expanding school-age population and thousands of students in urban settings were turned away as public schools were overcrowded, underfunded, and often in such poor physical repair as to endanger the inhabitants (Spring, 2001).

It became apparent that enforcement of compulsory attendance was not without "hidden" costs to local and state governments as they assumed the fiscal responsibility and authority for schooling. They faced a long list of new demands, including the following: school construction; increased teaching staff; additional truant officers; more truancy schools; development of programs for exceptional children; and a growing need for medical and nursing staff in addition to (not incidentally) a need for psychologists, psychiatrists, school vocational counselors, and school social workers. Julia Lathrope, first chief of the Federal Children's Bureau, raised concerns about the appropriateness of the demands being placed on the schools. She asked (1916), "Are we trying to establish standards of family life and income which render it possible for children to go to school equipped to learn, or are we increasingly shouldering off upon the schools the work of social welfare?" (p. 556).

Convergence of Education and Social Work

During most of the Common School era, children were required to "fit the school" and social services, if they existed, were provided by personnel from outside the school. As the concept of individual differences emerged from the field of psychology, there was greater recognition that individuals could adapt to their environment and that the environment could be altered to meet individual needs (Irwin & Marks, 1924). Social work began to employ new findings from psychology and psychiatry to better understand the mental and emotional life of the child and to emphasize prevention and early intervention in the schools. The mental hygiene movement took root and influenced practice for decades. Educators began to recognize that the home and community influenced the child's education and that academic success required attention to both the intellectual and the social development of the child. Collaboration between these professions was necessary if these dual goals were to be achieved (Culbert, 1929).

SCHOOLS AT THE TURN OF THE 20TH CENTURY

By 1900, 44% of the U.S. population was younger than 20 years of age. To best serve the burgeoning young populations, the majority of schools were reorganized into elementary schools with eight separate graded classrooms; however, one-room schoolhouses remained dominant in rural communities well into the 20th century. Urban schools were typically overcrowded, with class size, at times, approaching 50 students. Training for teachers was limited, with most teachers in the elementary grades having, at most, 2 years of training in what were called "normal schools." Public school enrollment reached 15.5 million children, equivalent to 72% of the population aged 5–17 years, and all but 519,000 of these children were in kindergarten though eighth grade. The average school year was 144 days and although 33 states had passed compulsory attendance statutes, truancy was an ongoing problem, with less than 70% of students in attendance on any given school day (Peterson, 1985; Tyack, 1967). Throughout the nation, only 7% of 17-year-olds were high school graduates. During the next decade, little changed and it was observed that two-thirds of the children who began elementary school dropped out before or by the time they were 13 years old (Harvey, 1914).

Tristram W. Metcalfe, school editor of the *New York Globe,* enumerated a list of problems needing remedy in the public schools, including the following (as cited in Denison, 1912, pp. 7–8):

Studies not made real to the pupil

Teaching much that is useless

Do not help increase earning power

Opposition to desirable changes

Lack of preparation

Neglect to meet pupils' needs

Discouraging outside cooperation

High schools inadequate

Results poor in English and arithmetic

School board acts without the facts

Dissatisfied teachers

Neglect to fit pupils for business or life

Misleading data of pupils' progress

A myriad of other problems could easily have been added to Metcalfe's list, including poor health and sanitation; structurally unsafe facilities; lack of space for the growing influx of students; inequitable distribution of resources among differing racial, religious, ethnic, and income groups; and insufficient finances.

VISITING TEACHERS—THE BEGINNING OF SCHOOL SOCIAL WORK

As noted previously, visiting teacher programs were introduced almost simultaneously in four cities in 1906–1907: New York, Chicago, Boston, and Hartford, Connecticut. The New York program was initiated in 1906 by two settlement houses seeking to serve the needs of their children and achieve closer cooperation between home and school. The social settlements had already demonstrated that physical care of children, recreation, and parent education promoted healthy child development; now they wanted to demonstrate that home and school teamwork could better serve pupils. The visiting teacher service was strongly supported by the Public Education Association (PEA), an organization of women interested in educational reform and a potent political force in the city. The PEA vigorously lobbied to have the board of education adopt the visiting teacher service and sought to establish high standards for visiting teachers that would employ "methods of social workers," consider needs of the individual child often lost in large classes and highly regimented curricula, and develop community centers in the schools (Oppenheimer, 1925). At approximately the same time, the University of Chicago Settlement and the Chicago Woman's Club placed a full-time social worker in a Chicago school (McCullagh, 2000).

In 1907, the Boston's Women's Education Association employed a "home and school visitor" to improve children's school performance by providing social services and liaison between the home and school. The need for this liaison was highlighted by a 1908 report to the district that stated (Oppenheimer, 1925),

> Lack of understanding between school and home often results in loss, sometimes in serious injustice to the child, but under the present conditions it is difficult for busy mothers to visit the school, and the large-sized classes make it almost impossible for teachers to know the homes. (p. 3)

The director of the Hartford district's Psychological Clinic established its program in 1907. A "special teacher" was employed to take social histories and to carry out clinic recommendations in regard to social service, physical treatment, or school adjustment (Oppenheimer, 1925). These school social work experiments were viewed as successful, which led other settlement houses and organizations to provide visiting teachers to the schools in their districts in order to create a better understanding between the home and school.

In February 1913, the New York City public school system became the first to fund a visiting teacher service when six staff members were assigned to graded and special needs classes. The board of education in Rochester, NY, hired a visiting teacher in September of the same year, although her services were restricted to girls (Oppenheimer, 1925). Mary Richmond (1922) eloquently noted the importance of the visiting teacher service: It "occupies that strategic ground between home and school over which there is still no well used path" (p. 197). The role of private groups and organizations hiring and financing the visiting teacher service was greatly diminished after 1913 because most school social services, where they existed, became an integral part of the public school system.

Formation of a National Association

The National Conference of Visiting Teachers and Home and School Visitors was organized and held its first conference in 1916, at which it discussed the use of visiting teachers to prevent delinquency and retardation. By 1919, a professional membership association was formed, and a second national conference was held in 1920 (Oppenheimer, 1925). *The New York Times* ("Visiting Teachers," 1920) reported the following about this meeting: "As a result of their visits the pupils are so improved that they are enabled to advance from grade to grade regularly, whereas if they were left alone they would in many instances fail to do so" (p. 14). Called the National Association of Visiting Teachers from 1919 to 1929, the organization published a journal and later became known as the American Association of Visiting Teachers (1929–1942) and subsequently the American Association of School Social Workers (1942–1945). From 1945 until the formation of the NASW, the organization was known as the National Association of School Social Workers (NASSW). In 1955, NASSW was one of the seven organizations that merged to form the NASW (Johnson, 1965).

The early school social work movement grew in legitimacy and strength but it was not without its critics. In *Helping School Children*, Denison (1912) argued that employing a visiting teacher to pay attention to the individual needs of a child was the route of least resistance. She asked,

> Shall the city pay for one, two or ten visiting teachers when it has employees supposed to be doing that work? What does the visiting teacher do that cannot be done by the combined force of efficient nurse, attendance officer, relief visitor, hospital physician, and grade teacher? (p. 172)

Skills Reflective of Early Social Work Practice

Visiting teachers drew heavily from the tools being defined in the new field of social work. In *What Is Social Case Work?*, a seminal book in the social work profession, Mary Richmond (1922) wrote about the qualifications and roles of the visiting teacher:

Case | **Case Study**

A visiting teacher is a social worker, preferably one with some classroom experience of teaching. She undertakes, for a given number of pupils reported to her by the school for poor scholarship, bad health, misconduct, lateness, irregular attendance, or for what appear to be adverse home conditions, to discover the causal factors in the difficulty and then tries to work out a better adjustment. It is not astonishing to find that, among the measures she most frequently employs, are the exercising of personal influence, winning the cooperation of parents, seeking the advice and assistance of medical and mental experts, seeking the aid of the various social agencies, utilizing recreational facilities, and changing the child's environment. We have seen repeatedly that these are the measures most frequently used by all social case workers. "Change of environment" may mean a change outside any school, within the present school, or to another school. Such changes within the present school as a promotion, a demotion, and a transfer to a special class, are based on information brought back to the teachers after a study of the individual child in his neighborhood environment and in that of his home. (pp. 198–199)

The Commonwealth Fund Expands Practice in the Schools

The activities of the Commonwealth Fund during the 1920s encouraged the greatest expansion of visiting teacher activities until after World War II. The Fund established a "Program for the Prevention of Delinquency" in 1921 that included demonstrations of visiting teacher services in 30 selected communities nationwide. Each community paid one third of the worker's salary and pledged to continue support if the demonstration proved valuable. When the Fund withdrew support in 1930, there were 244 school social workers employed in 31 states (Costin, 1969b; Fink, 1949; Poole, 1947). The Fund published reports of the program widely and offered courses to teachers and others to demonstrate the value of psychiatric study and treatment in serving children with problems. Additionally, the Fund provided consultation to other communities and school systems wishing to initiate school social work services.

PROMISING PRACTICES IN THE 1920s

In the period after World War I, social work reform and social action took a back seat to the development of methods, educational training, and professionalism. This trend was reflected in school social work as well. Publications of the Commonwealth Fund on the visiting teacher demonstration programs and on the Public Education Association of New York City's pioneering visiting teacher efforts provide rich documentation of promising practices during the 1920s (Culbert, 1921, 1929, 1930; Ellis, 1925; Glueck, 1924; Oppenheimer, 1925; Sayles & Nudd, 1925). Jane Culbert, the first president of the National Association of Visiting Teachers and Home and School Visitors, noted that the recommendations drawn from these studies were not meant to be "dogmatic conclusions" or "crystallized standards" but were based "upon careful observation of actual practice . . . not upon academic theory" (1929, p. 109).

The visiting teacher's knowledge of home and community provided a view of the student and family often poorly understood by school staff and yet essential to meet the evolving changes in educational philosophy and practice. Stationing the visiting teacher in the school, rather than in a school-linked agency, enabled her to follow cases on a daily basis, respond to emergencies, provide consultation to school personnel, and use her knowledge of home and community resources to assist individual students and the school. Studies recommended that the visiting teacher be assigned to one or a few small neighboring schools. This assignment would enable her to best represent the interests of the home, school, and the community. Howard Nudd, chairman of the National Committee of Visiting Teachers, noted, "It is important that the visiting teacher . . . not be required to scatter her efforts over too many cases or too wide an area" (Sayles & Nudd, 1925, p. 264). Because many of the visiting teachers served immigrants, foreign language skills were a great asset. Cultural sensitivity was also important: "The visiting teacher needs to know the nationalities of the children's parents, their customs, traditions, and interests so that she may have a sympathetic approach" (Culbert, 1921, p. 9).

The ratio of visiting teacher to students often defined the depth and breath of the services she could provide. Oppenheimer's (1925) studies found that the number of cases annually addressed by one visiting teacher

> ranged from 119 to 1,175; the most common number was 500. This means that a visiting teacher can do intensive work on less than half that number of cases and that the others receive short service, which requires but little time. (p. 54)

He found that service ratios for visiting teachers employed by private agencies in New York City and Philadelphia averaged 1:250. President Hoover's 1930 White House Conference on Child Health and Protection recommended a ratio of one visiting teacher for every 500 pupils. More typically, one visiting teacher served a school population of 1,500–3,000 students (Leonard, 1935).

Most visiting teachers served elementary schools, composed of first through eighth grades, but many noted that their services were just as needed with older students. Fewer than 30% of 17-year-olds were graduated from high school in 1930, and it was not until the late 1940s that graduation rates approached 50% (Tynack, 1967).

Even though half of her time was spent visiting homes, community agencies, and other areas outside of the school, it was considered essential that the visiting teacher have an office in the school where she could be easily approached by parents, students, and school staff. A phone or phone access and locked files were also deemed necessary. Her hours, while similar in duration to those of a teacher, varied considerably. Although time was always scheduled for meetings in the school, good diagnosis and casework planning required additional early morning, evening, Sunday, and even holiday home visits in order to see the whole family and to observe their interactions. Most schools provided little, if any, secretarial support for the visiting teacher (Culbert, 1921; Oppenheimer, 1925).

Visiting teachers were advised to maintain close contact and collaboration with the superintendent, principals, and teachers because the case plan and changes sought in the child, home, and school required the support and cooperation of these colleagues. Teachers were frequently asked to assist in case planning for students. Other student support personnel also played important roles in the change efforts. In small systems and rural communities, case intervention depended heavily on the visiting teacher's own skills. In larger districts, she collaborated with school-linked health bureaus, dental clinics, and programs for the gifted as well as special programs for the "physically defective" and "retarded" children. Vocational guidance personnel, truant officers, and the child study departments responsible for testing and placement of students were frequent referral sources. Testing and accurate placement of students were viewed as critical and most controversial at times (Sayles & Nudd, 1925):

> It became the fashion for one community to point with pride to the fact that it had fewer morons or more superior children in its school system than had another, or that its children "averaged" better in arithmetic, spelling or penmanship than those of another community. (pp. 268–269)

The superintendent, his designated representative, or a principal typically provided supervision for the work of the visiting teacher. In some of the larger systems, such as Minneapolis, Rochester, Philadelphia, and New York City, an experienced visiting teacher supervised a staff of 7–14 visiting teachers. Unfortunately, supervisors did not always possess the knowledge or skills needed for this role. Oppenheimer (1925) observed, "As has been the case in other auxiliary services, there is frequently a disposition on the part of boards of education to desire the appointment of people who *do not possess* the necessary qualifications for such positions" (p. 36). Financial support for the visiting teacher programs came primarily from the local school board.

Service was not limited to individual children, and community change resulted from the casework focus of the visiting teacher. Group study and community assessment also were encouraged. Culbert (1921) claimed, "Through individuals to the group is the approach of the visiting teacher" (p. 8). Visiting teachers occupied a unique role in the community because of their knowledge of both the neighborhood dynamics and the school system. The presence of the visiting teacher in the community acted as a catalyst for community change. In response to identified needs, members of the community were prompted to work together to provide scholarship funds, nurseries, homes for neglected children, better policing, playgrounds, and parks with lights. The impact of the visiting teacher on the school system led to adjustments in the school that encouraged the establishment of parents' clubs, school lunches, recreational programs, and new courses.

Not surprisingly, the typical visiting teacher was "spread thin" and not all objectives of the program could be achieved. Preventive services did not get the attention needed. Some observed that the visiting teacher's time was consumed by serving "children whose problems have become almost overwhelming because of past oversight or neglect" (Sayles & Nudd, 1925, p. 261). Administrators recognized that situations if attended to earlier might not need further service. It was observed that more time for prevention was afforded in those systems that clearly separated the efforts of attendance (truant) officers and visiting teachers.

The American Association of Visiting Teachers (AAVT) set high standards for the preparation and training of those wishing to serve as visiting teachers. In 1925, AAVT recommended the following: a B.A. or a normal (teacher) school certificate or its equivalent; at least 1 year of course work in the theory and practice of casework from a recognized school of social work or 2 years of "well-supervised training" in a recognized social casework agency; and at least 1 year of teaching and 1 year of practice in a family or psychiatric casework agency or one year of visiting teacher experience (Culbert, 1930). Not all, of course, met these high standards.

FROM THE DEPRESSION TO THE COLD WAR—1930 TO 1960

The 1930s were a period of retrenchment for school social work practitioners in function and method. Casework had little to say in response to the Great Depression and professionalism took a step back. Grace Abbott (1941), social worker and chief of the Children's Bureau in the U.S. Department of Labor, observed the following:

> The schools were the first to suffer because theirs was the largest item in the social welfare budget. The accounts of the closing of schools and shortening of terms, the increase in pupil–teacher ratios, and the elimination of kindergartens, health supervision, attendance officers, evening schools, continuation schools, opportunity schools or classes, and nursing services have made very discouraging reading. (p. 172)

During the Depression, children commonly lacked food, clothing, school supplies, and shelter. Malnutrition was common, public health problems surged, and students dropped out of school to become the primary breadwinners for their families because parents were unable to secure employment (Amidon, 1937). Private philanthropy failed, local governments went bankrupt, and public attitudes and legal statutes prohibited substantial federal intervention until passage of the Social Security Act in 1935. Thousands of children simply stopped attending school and sought low-paid, dead-end manufacturing jobs that were available to the untrained. School social work practitioners returned to their roots as distributors of relief. Health, hot lunches, and clothing shops took precedence (Lide, 1953). The length and depth of the Depression required the schools to cooperate with other community groups to meet the needs of their children and families (Lowry, 1939). Towle (1939) supported this call for community collaboration:

> We are coming not only to recognize the futility of persisting in situations which are beyond the scope of casework help, but to realize also our social responsibility for revealing the inadequacy of social casework in these instances, in order that interest and effort may be directed toward social action. (p. 525)

As the crisis of the Depression era began to recede, school social work services reemerged. A 1939 survey found school social work practice established in 150 school systems. Casework, not social action, continued to predominate, but examples of educational group work could also be found (Poole, 1947).

With the nation's approach and eventual entry into World War II, school social work was once again faced with circumstances little suited to casework practice. School social work literature of the period does not seem to reflect the immigration of refugees from abroad, the increase in racial and ethnic tensions, the huge migration of families to war industrial centers, or the social–emotional stresses children experienced as family members mobilized for war. Divorces more than doubled between 1940 and 1946, and out of wedlock births increased from 71 to 127 per 10,000. School years were shortened and school days compressed to permit children to work in fields, stores, and factories. Rates of school dropouts increased as opportunities to earn wages increased (Cohen, 1958, pp. 224–226).

However, amid this turmoil, legislators established school social work services in Louisiana, Georgia, Virginia, Maryland, Michigan, Illinois, and Puerto Rico. During this time, the National Association of School Social Workers had members in 34 states and Hawaii (Sikkema, 1949). The U.S. Office of Education found approximately 1,000 full-time visiting teachers in 266 different communities and visiting teacher services were provided by school personnel not classified as regular visiting teachers in another 102 locations. Other school districts expressed interest in exploring such programs (Poole, 1947).

At this time, Ruth Smalley (1947) defined school social work as "a specialized form of social casework. It is identified with and is a part of the program of the public school. It is a method of helping individual children use what the school offers them" (p. 51). While casework continued to prevail, changes of note did take place in the field during this period. There was a growing awareness that school social work could be as valuable for students in middle and secondary schools as for the elementary programs that were traditionally served. Although first employed to work primarily with the underprivileged, school social work services were now being requested in schools throughout the community. Consultation to principals, teachers, and parents continued to be an important function of the program, and prevention was gaining a foothold. Rather than focusing only on "problem children," some schools recognized that all children experienced stress and challenges as they developed socially, emotionally, and physically and school social workers might assist these children in recognizing the problems they were experiencing and what might be done to alle-viate their concerns (Fink, 1949). By 1950, the ranks of school social workers had grown to include an estimated 1,700 school social workers employed in 450 cities. The NASSW reported 650 members for this period (Sikkema, 1953). The stresses and strains of the period seemed to foster a resurgence of school social work practice.

Mildred Sikkema's *Report of a Study of School Social Work Practice in Twelve Communities* (1953) was completed in collaboration with the American Association of Social Workers and the NASSW and gives the most complete overview of school social work practice during this era. Almost one-fourth of the school social work practitioners participated in this research. Her study revealed that there continued to be wide variability in the training and prepa-ration for practice as a school social worker. Other findings in the study showed that informal teacher consultation was viewed as a critical role for the school social worker. Referrals made by the school social worker were most frequently related to student behavior, personality issues, nonattendance, academic prob-lems, home or neighborhood conditions, or parental neglect. Brief "limited service" interventions with students were frequently reported by the participating school social workers.

The merger of the NASSW into the NASW in 1955 marked the beginning of a new era for school social work. Greater political clout was achieved but visibil-ity of school social work practice was dimmed. Termination of the NASSW *Bulletin*, published since 1925, left this field without a prominent, national voice until NASW initiated *Social Work in Education* in 1978 (now titled *Children & Schools*).

A SEARCH FOR MORE EFFECTIVE PRACTICE ROLES AND MODELS—1960 TO THE PRESENT

School social workers in the 1960s met with racial and political unrest, war protest, and sexual revolution. Calls for educational reform in curriculum, lead-ership, structure, and funding became vociferous and remain so. Passage of the Education for All Handicapped Children Act (P.L. 94–142) in 1975 led to a sub-stantial increase in school social work practitioners because they were viewed as instrumental in the assessment and placement of children with disabilities and subsequent service delivery to the children and their families. The caseloads of children with disabilities expanded rapidly as well.

In response to a changing social and educational climate, school social work-ers initiated a search for new and more effective roles and models of practice that continues to the present. A 1969 National Workshop in School Social Work sup-ported by NASW and the National Institute of Mental Health was held to stim-ulate change and innovation in this practice arena (Sarri & Maple, 1972). State and regional conferences have also promoted new models, methods, and inno-vative projects. During this period, John Alderson (1972) described and analyzed four models of practice by which school social workers could examine and eval-uate their work: (1) the durable traditional–clinical model; (2) the school-change model, whose major focus was the dysfunctional conditions of the school; (3) the community school model, which urged school social workers to employ community organization methods; and (4) the social interaction model, which deemphasized a specific methodology and required the worker to intervene with the systems interacting with the target system.

To clarify prevalent practice and to guide practitioner training, a series of surveys, reminiscent of those conducted in the 1910s and 1920s by early school social workers, took place in the 1960s, 1970s, and 1980s (Alderson & Krishef, 1973; Allen-Meares, 1977, 1987, 1994; Chavkin, 1985; Costin, 1969a; Mintzies & Hare, 1985; Nelson, 1990). A close examination of these surveys will provide the reader with both a picture in time and a sense of the trends in the field. Only a few of the findings are noted here.

Costin's national survey in the mid-1960s reaffirmed the emphasis school social work practitioners placed on traditional casework services. The tasks respondents performed and preferred reflected a focus on individual children: "Little recognition was given to the impact of school conditions upon pupil or the total set of circumstances within the school which might be related to his poor adjustment" (Costin, 1969a, pp. 277–278). Costin asserted that changing times and problems required reassessment of even well-established practice and that practitioners could not ignore the impact of school policies and community conditions on pupils. In the early 1970s, she and colleagues at the University of Illinois at Urbana–Champaign demonstrated a "school–community–pupil relations model" that focused on situation rather than personality. The model gave attention to "(1) deficiencies in the school and the community and (2) the interaction between specific characteristics of the system and characteristics of groups of pupils at points of stress in the pupil life cycle" (Costin, 1975, p. 135).

Allen-Meares's (1977) replication of Costin's study found only modest evidence of change. However, many school social workers reported activities described as "transitional" between the polar extremes of traditional casework and Costin's approach. Chavkin's 1982 research found, once again, that traditional casework services predominated but that many were employing a wide range of individual, group, family, and community interventions. Chavkin (1985) asserted that greater emphasis was needed in the areas of group intervention, consultation to administrators and students, students' rights, and resource development; community change was needed if Costin's leadership challenge was to be met.

Barriers to education and recommendations to address these barriers were identified in a NASW study carried out in conjunction with its Third National Conference on School Social Work (Mintzies & Hare, 1985). Recommendations included (1) strengthening collaboration and coordination between the school and community, such as mental health and protective services; (2) strengthening pupil services and making services available to the entire school, not only to handicapped and "problem students;" (3) increasing parent involvement and reaching out to those detached from the school; (4) emphasizing early intervention and prevention; (5) expanding the use of school buildings by opening them to after-school programming and community organizations; (6) addressing family barriers by helping students deal with sexual abuse, child abuse, neglect, and family violence; (7) strengthening student self-esteem and increasing opportunities for success; and (8) developing special in-school and alternative programs for "at risk" groups.

The last national study of school social work practitioners, completed in 1989–1990 by NASW and the Educational Testing Service, used a modified version of Meares's 1974 survey (Allen-Meares, 1994; Nelson, 1990). Participants ranked 94 tasks and job responsibilities clustered into five job functions. Maintenance of records, confidentiality, and continuing education were given the highest priorities, followed by home–school liaison and educational counseling to students. Although some evidence of group and family counseling existed, the leadership and policy-making tasks advocated by Costin, Allen-Meares, and others received the lowest mean ranking. In the early 1990s, a national exam was developed from this study that became incorporated as part of NASW's Specialty Certification in School Social Work. It was administered to more than 3,000 practitioners before its use was discontinued in 1998.

School social workers continue to face the dilemma of practicing in a host setting. In the mid-1930s, Charlotte Towle commented on this challenge when she observed that while working in schools, the school social worker's identity is that of social worker, but there are few social work colleagues to provide support and identification with this profession. Job requirements demand knowledge of education, but while practicing as a social worker, she is not quite accepted in the role of educator. At times, the philosophy of the school conflicts with basic principles of social work (Lowry, 1939). Contemporary school social workers routinely face challenges to their professional ethics in areas such as privacy and confidentiality, informed consent, client self-determination, cultural competence, performance evaluation, and education and training. Towle also noted that the school, with which her clients identify her, is the very same milieu that needs to be modified at times. Dane and Simon (1991) suggested that practitioners in host settings encounter several problems, including (1) discrepancies between professional mission and values, (2) token status in a workplace employing few social workers, and (3) role ambiguity and strain.

NASW provides guidance to school social workers, school administrators, and the general public through its *Standards for School Social Work Services*, first published in 1978 and revised in 1992 and 2002. The knowledge, skills, and values in the *Standards* (2002) reflect best practice in this specialty area and the type of training required. Administrative structures and support necessary for effective school social work programs are also defined by the standards. The 2002 standards reinforce the use of the ecological perspective, evidence-based practice, and assessments based on data obtained through the use of multiple methods and sources. There is also an emphasis on health, resiliency, and protective factors that reflect practice advancements in social work over the past 15 years. Interdisciplinary planning and services delivered through school-based and school-linked programs are recognized as a requirement for effective needs assessment, prevention, early intervention, and responses to chronic and acute problems. NASW plans to update the standards every 5 years to reflect contemporary practice.

Effective child and family advocacy demands school social workers have considerable knowledge of educational legislation, Supreme Court decisions, and case law because they play a major role in defining practice. Additionally, it is of critical importance for school social workers to be informed about the following in order to be effective in their practice: knowledge of attendance and exceptional children policies and procedures, child abuse and neglect recognition and reporting, public health and public welfare statutes, the rights of undocumented minors and pregnant and parenting teens, and policies regarding students facing suspension and expulsion. Knowledge of Section 504 of the Rehabilitation Act of 1973 and federal laws such as the Individuals with Disabilities Education Act, the McKinney–Vento Homeless Education Act, the Family Education Rights and Privacy Act, and the No Child Left Behind Act are critical as well.

The field of school social work is currently being driven in multiple directions by the convergence of factors such as changes in federal legislation, shifts in demographics, persistent poverty, diminishing state and local financing, rising public expectations, and a growing emphasis within the social work profession for evidenced-based practice. In addition to being shaped by these factors, school social work is also shaped by other forces influencing U.S. schools, including mainstreaming of students with handicaps, ballooning migrant populations, urban and rural school decay, gangs, drugs, high teacher turnover, property-based financing, and weak curricula.

The restructuring of school-based and school-linked services has begun, and new models of student support and funding options are being proposed (Dryfoos & Maguire, 2002; UCLA, 2001). Four regional coalitions (representing school social workers in 29 states), the School Social Work Association of America, and the School Social Work Section of the National Association of Social Workers are lobbying for supportive legislation, regulation of practice, continuing education opportunities, better salaries, reduced school social worker–student ratios, and use of best practice principles.

SUMMARY

A review of the first 100 years of school social work demonstrates many parallels between the administration, policies, and practices of today and those of earlier periods. Wide variations in education and training, supervision, staffing patterns, and qualifications continue to exist, as does the struggle to establish an effective presence in a host setting. The home, school, and community liaison role remains a constant. Practice will continue to evolve in response to changes in social work practice, school funding, educational focus, and political demands. Fortunately and unfortunately, Norma Radin's (1975) words of a quarter century ago ring true today:

> The role of the school social worker is ambiguous; there is typically little supervision and often much misunderstanding by educators who fill the school system. Yet, it is in school social work that one effective worker can have an enormous impact. It is in schools that the otherwise hard-to-reach population abounds. It is in school

that children can be crippled psychologically for life or aroused to do great things. In spite of the many problems permeating the school, there is enough flexibility in the system today for one creative, energetic social worker to make a significant difference in the lives of thousands of children. It is a challenge that is irresistible to a particular kind of social worker, and that is the person that school social work needs. (p. 613)

School Social Work Companion Website

Please be sure to check out our companion website at www.thomsonedu.com/social_work/bye, where you will find relevant materials for each chapter, including flashcards, online practice quizzes, and PowerPoint slides.

References

Abbott, G. (1941). *From relief to social security: The development of the new public welfare services and their administration.* Chicago: University of Chicago Press.

Alderson, J. J. (1972). Models of school social work practice. In R. C. Sarri & F. F. Maple (Eds.), *The school in the community* (pp. 57–74). Washington, DC: National Association of Social Workers.

Alderson, J. J., & Krishef, C. H. (1973). Another perspective on tasks in school social work. *Social Casework, 54,* 591–600.

Allen-Meares, P. (1977). Analysis of tasks in school social work. *Social Work, 22*(3), 196–201.

Allen-Meares, P. (1987). A national study of educational reform: Implications for social work services in schools. *Children & Youth Services Review, 9,* 207–219.

Allen-Meares, P. (1994). Social work services in schools: A national study of entry-level tasks. *Social Work, 39,* 560–565.

Amidon, B. (1937, January). Children wanted. *Survey Graphic—Magazine of Social Interpretation, 26*(1), 10–15.

Chavkin, N. F. (1985). School social work practice: A reappraisal. *Social Work in Education, 8*(1), 3–13.

Cohen, N. E. (1958). *Social work in the American tradition.* New York: Holt, Rinehart & Winston.

Cohen, S. (1964). *Progressives and urban reform: The Public Education Association of New York City 1895–1954.* New York: Columbia University, Teachers College.

Cordasco, F. (1963). *A brief history of education: A handbook of information on Greek, Roman, medieval, renaissance, and modern educational practice.* Paterson, NJ: Littlefield, Adams.

Costin, L. B. (1969a). An analysis of the tasks in school social work. *Social Service Review, 43,* 274–285.

Costin, L. B. (1969b). A historical review of school social work. *Social Casework, 50*(8), 439–453.

Costin, L. B. (1975). School social work practice: A new model. *Social Work, 20,* 135–139.

Cubberly, E. P. (1909). *Changing conceptions of education.* Boston: Houghton.

Culbert, J. F. (1921). *The visiting teacher.* New York: Joint Committee on Methods of Preventing Delinquency. (Reprinted from the *Annals of the American Academy of Political and Social Science, 98*(187), November 1921)

Culbert, J. F. (1929). *The visiting teacher at work.* New York: Commonwealth Fund.

Culbert, J. F. (1930). Visiting teachers. In F. S. Hall (Ed.), *Social work year book 1929* (pp. 466–469). New York: Russell Sage Foundation.

Dane, B. O., & Simon, B. L. (1991). Resident guests: Social workers in host settings. *Social Work, 36*(3), 208–213.

Denison, E. (1912). *Helping school children: Suggestions for efficient cooperation with the public schools.* New York: Harper & Brothers.

Dryfoos, J., & Maguire, S. (2002). *Inside full-service community schools.* Thousand Oaks, CA: Corwin Press.

Ellis, M. B. (1925). *The visiting teacher in Rochester.* New York: Joint Committee on Methods of Preventing Delinquency.

Fink, A. E. (1949). *The field of social work* (2nd ed.). New York: Holt.

Glueck, B. (1924). *Some extra-curricular problems of the classroom* (Publication No. 3). New York: Joint Committee on Methods of Preventing Delinquency. (Reprinted from *School and Society, 19*(476), February 9, 1924)

Harvey, L. D. (1914). Systematic education for those pupils leaving school too soon. *National Education Association of the United States. Meeting: Journal of Proceedings and Addresses of the Annual Meeting, 52,* 119–122.

Irwin, E. A., & Marks, L. A. (1924). *Fitting the school to the child: An experiment in public education.* New York: Macmillian.

Johnson, A. (1965). Schools (Social work practice in). In H. L. Lurie (Ed.), *Encyclopedia of social work* (15th ed., pp. 672–679). New York: National Association of Social Workers.

Lathrop, J. C. (1916). Introductory statement by the chairman. *Proceedings of the National Conference of Charities and Correction, 43,* 555–556.

Leonard, S. (1935). Visiting teachers. In F. S. Hall (Ed.), *Social work year book 1935* (pp. 532–535). New York: Russell Sage Foundation.

Lide, P. (1953). A study of the historical influences of major importance in determining the present function of the school social worker. *Bulletin of the National Association of Social Workers, 29*(1), 18–33.

Lowry, F. (Ed.). (1939). *Readings in social case work 1920–1938. Selected reprints for the case work practitioner.* New York: Columbia University Press.

McCullagh, J. G. (2000, Fall). School social work in Chicago: An unrecognized pioneer program. *School Social Work Journal, 25*(1), 1–15.

Mintzies, P., & Hare, I. (1985). *The human factor: A key to excellence in education.* Silver Spring, MD: National Association of Social Workers.

National Association of Social Workers. (2002). *NASW standards for school social work services.* Washington, DC: Author.

Nelson, C. (1990). *A job analysis of school social workers.* Princeton, NJ: Educational Testing Service.

Nelson, F. C. (1987). *Public schools: An evangelical appraisal.* Old Tappan, NJ: Revell.

Oppenheimer, J. J. (1925). *The visiting teacher movement with special reference to administrative relationships* (2nd ed.). New York: Joint Committee on Methods of Preventing Delinquency.

Peterson, P. E. (1985). *The politics of school reform 1870–1940.* Chicago: University of Chicago Press.

Poole, F. (1947). Nationwide developments in school social work. *Bulletin of the National Association of School Social Workers, 22*(3), 4–8.

Radin, N. (1975). A personal perspective on school social work. *Social Casework, 56,* 605–613.

Richardson, G. (1980). Variation in date of enactment of compulsory school attendance laws: An empirical inquiry. *Sociology of Education, 53,* 153–163.

Richmond, M. E. (1922). *What is social casework? An introductory description.* New York: Russell Sage Foundation.

Sarri, R. C., & Maple, F. F. (Eds.). (1972). *The school in the community.* Washington, DC: National Association of Social Workers.

Sayles, M. B., & Nudd, H. W. (1925). *The problem child in school* (Publication No. 4). New York: Joint Committee on Methods of Preventing Delinquency.

Sikkema, M. (1949). An analysis of the structure and practice of school social work today. *Social Service Review, 23*(4), 447–453.

Sikkema, M. (1953). *Report of a study of school social work practice in twelve communities.* New York: American Association of Social Workers.

Smalley, R. (1947). School social work as part of the school program. *Bulletin of the National Association of Social Workers, 22*(3), 51–54.

Spring, J. (2001). *The American school: 1642–2000* (5th ed.). Boston: McGraw-Hill.

Towle, C. (1939). Discussion of Miss Hall's paper. In F. Lowry (Ed.), *Readings in social case work 1920–1939* (pp. 521–526). New York: Columbia University Press.

Trattner, W. I. (1970). *Crusade for the children: A history of the National Child Labor Committee and child labor reform in America.* Chicago: Quadrangle Books.

Tyack, D. B. (Ed.). (1967). *Turning points in American educational history.* Waltham, MA: Blaisdell.

UCLA Center for Mental Health in Schools. (2001). *Framing new directions for school counselors, psychologists, & social workers.* Los Angeles: Author.

Visiting teachers meet. (1920, June 29). *The New York Times,* p. 14.

School Social Work and Educational Reform

CHAPTER **2**

JOSEPH R. GIANESIN,
M.S.W., Ph.D.
Springfield College School of Social Work,
Springfield, Massachusetts

CHAPTER OUTLINE

Chapter Overview

Introduction

Understanding School Reform

Background: Four Waves of School Reform

No Child Left Behind Act (2001)

NCLB and the IDEA

School Reform From a School Social Work Perspective

School Social Work's Response to School Reform

The New School Social Worker

Best Practice in an Era of Reform

Summary

CHAPTER OVERVIEW

This chapter highlights how reform attempts progressed from raising graduation standards to requiring teachers to pass special examinations for certification, offering full-service schools and school-linked community agency services, offering school choice for parents and students through magnet and charter schools, and implementing school-based management or site-based management. After reading this chapter, readers will (1) be familiar with what is meant by "educational reform;" (2) learn the historical background that includes the political, societal, and economic forces that have influenced educational reform; (3) be able to discuss the four stages or waves of reform; (4) understand how school social workers responded historically to school reform; and (5) understand the skills and roles necessary to embrace and become full participants in future educational reform movements.

INTRODUCTION

The school reform movement has placed enormous pressure on educators to change and upgrade how schools achieve educational objectives. These developments, which began in the early 1980s and have progressed through the 1990s and the millennium, culminated in legislative mandates at the federal, state, and local levels. Since the *Nation at Risk* (National Commission on Excellence in Education, 1983) report was published, there have been numerous attempts to create an education system that produces students who can demonstrate academic achievement and critical thinking. Samuel Bacharach (1990) refers to these reform attempts as "waves of reform" (p. 10).

In this environment of high-stakes testing and assessment, acknowledging the importance of social and emotional variables and understanding how much emotion, motivation, and parental attitudes impact the student's ability to enter school willing and ready to learn are a major challenge for educators. School social workers need to become integral members of the reform movement, developing collaborative relationships with parents, administrators, and teachers to improve the educational outcomes for children. They can also be advocates for children who are often left behind. According to Hodgkinson (1991), "one third of the American children have the deck stacked against them before they enter school" (p. 10).

Demand for Educational Reform

Demand for educational reform in the 1980s and 1990s will be remembered as one of the most turbulent for this country's public schools. Changes in the social, political, and economic environments necessitate a reexamination of how schools educate children who have difficulty achieving academically and adapting to the school environment. Demands for school reform and change have been at the forefront of the political debate since the early 1980s when the *A Nation at Risk*, was released during the Reagan administration. It reported that U.S. students' scored lower than students from most other countries on science and math exams and that the U.S. dropout rate was far higher than those of all our competitors. It was a scathing report on the state of education throughout the country that blamed the educational establishment for the poor performance of students.

The response to the *Nation at Risk* report was immense. States throughout the country began to carefully examine their public schools. By May 1984, the U.S. Department of Education observed that the report issued in 1983 had "created a tidal wave of school reform which promises to renew American education" with an "extraordinary array of initiatives under discussion and underway" (p. 11). Schoolwide reform became an increasingly popular school improvement strategy, especially for low-performing, high-poverty schools.

UNDERSTANDING SCHOOL REFORM

Although school reform varies from state to state in approaches, all school reform models push teachers, principals, and parents to focus on redesigning curriculum, student assessment, professional development, governance, management, and other key functions around one schoolwide vision (Education Commission of the States [ECS], 1999). School reform often means restructuring teaching conditions, the delivery options for support services, and refining roles in school governance. Reform implies change, and change is difficult for individuals who invested time and energy into a particular method of delivering educational services.

The reform movement has been confusing in its focus and development, causing those engaged in the system to regard it suspiciously. Many schools aim their reforms at the relatively easy problems and avoid the difficult ones, the problems that result from changes in the demographics of society and schools. In some schools, 4 out of 10 students are absent on any given day. How is excellence possible when students are not even in the school building? The breakup of families, communities wretched by crime, poverty, and the loss of good teachers threaten to overwhelm our most vulnerable schools (Boyer, 1989). Little political rhetoric is heard about these factors, but much media coverage is given to the lack of academic achievement.

BACKGROUND: FOUR WAVES OF SCHOOL REFORM

To really understand how we got to this present state of affairs, it is important to comprehend the historical record of school reform. The reform movement is dynamic in nature and has undergone drastic changes during the past two decades. For school social workers to understand and meet the challenges of school restructuring, it is important to note the dynamics or, "waves of reform" that resulted in our present state (Passow, 1990, p.10). These include structural reform, service system reform, systemic reform, and comprehensive school reform.

Structural School Reform

Public school educators survived several waves of the school reform movement of the 1980s that initially focused on structural changes in areas of academic achievement, teacher and administrator certification requirements, and increased graduation standards (Passow, 1990). Reformers attempted to change public education from the top down with mandates to address problems with rules, procedures, and standards. Legislators believed that if they tinkered with the structural components of the educational system, they could institute change.

Educators who worked during that phase of the reform movement recall teachers having to pass state teacher certification tests before licenses were issued. Administrators, including principals, superintendents, and supervisors, were required to take special classes in the "art of teacher evaluation" to assist them in weeding out poor teachers. Graduation requirements were heightened and many high school classes that were thought frivolous were eliminated. School days and educational time on task were increased. Testing and assessment of teachers, administrators, and students became the norm. Academic achievement tests for students were increased and consolidated so that policymakers could compare schools and districts using the same assessment instruments. Legislators believed that if they changed the state and federal policy using this approach, schools and the children they served would improve under their new mandates.

In the 1980s and early 1990s, the debates over school funding, school choice, vouchers, and the function of teacher unions created a complex and adversarial environment that did little to foster collaboration among the major constituents of school reform. Not surprisingly, few changes occurred in the educational outcomes of the first waves of reform. Achievement scores continued to dip, and more students became disenfranchised with school. Five mistakes in the first wave of reform were (1) assuming that structural change from the top down will make significant impacts on educational outcomes; (2) not involving teachers, administrators, pupil personnel professionals, and parents, who are closest to the school and perform the most critical functions in public education; (3) expecting that complex social and economic problems remedy themselves when structural changes are made; (4) using a piecemeal approach to changing poor classroom practice; and (5) developing isolated programs that did not create schoolwide improvement.

Service System Reform

New reformers hoped that by "totally rethinking the very structure of the educational system," schools would be better prepared to meet the needs of all children and the communities in which they live (ECS, 1999, p. 1). The essential elements of system reform called upon those in education and other child service providers to rethink learning and service delivery from the ground up.

It was thought that if teaching and learning, educational relationships, and school-community relationships were well coordinated, then children and families could more easily navigate multiple systems. According to David Florio of the National Science Foundation (as cited in Lewis, 1992), common themes in system service reform include a greater emphasis on depth of knowledge, new relationships between people, more flexible physical arrangements in schools, and restructured time schedules.

New collaborative relationships between social service agencies that serve children were established. These collaborative arrangements were sometimes referred to as school-based services, wrap-around services, school-linked services, and service-centered schools. The rationale behind this movement was that a growing number of children and families developed problems related to learning, development, health, and legal involvements. The need for across-site information sharing, interprofessional collaboration, and service integration to coordinate and blend the interventions were key elements in this approach (Briar-Lawson, Lawson, Collier, & Joseph, 1997).

Initially, schools became sites for "one-stop shopping." A child and his or her family could go to the local school and find their caseworker from social services, their mental health therapist, the probation officer, and a community health clinic—all located at the school. The assumption was that all these agencies would coordinate with school personnel to meet the needs of the child, thus eliminating a duplication of services and saving the parent and child multiple visits to the agencies represented. Unfortunately, this assumption did not take into account professional jealousy, agency restrictions, school space issues, budget reductions, and transient client populations. Despite its great intentions, the approach has fallen short in many communities.

Collaborative partnerships with schools among mental and physical health-related agencies continue. For example, in Chicago and Hartford, Connecticut, there are high schools and nonprofit agency partnerships that provide both physical and mental health services. These programs offer promise that school reform can successfully involve community partnerships and change the school from within.

Systemic Reform

The third wave of reform, systemic, involved teachers and others through the use of school-based or site-based management. This approach offers school administrators and other educators flexibility to meet the challenge of bridging the school's decision making with the community members and parents.

Reformers hoped that by totally rethinking the very structure of the educational system, "schools will be better prepared to meet the needs of all children and communities in which they live" (ECS, 1991, p. 1). The restructuring of schools through school-based management (SBM) became the centerpiece for restructuring and reform efforts (Robertson & Buffett, 1991). This shift of formal decision-making authority away from central administration to a smaller decision-making arena had the endorsement of a wide range of educational practitioners, business leaders, and policymakers (Gibbs, 1989).

Many educators advocated for SBM, a method of decentralization in which the school, instead of the district office, is the primary unit of educational decision making (Lindelow, 1981). These advocates argued that school productivity will increase because decisions regarding the educational program would be made by those most closely affected by them: principals, teachers, students, and parents (Robertson & Buffet, 1991). Educational reformers contended that greater school autonomy is a prerequisite to school effectiveness and necessary for educational reforms to have sustained impact (Purkey & Smith, 1985).

In an effort to improve student achievement, some school districts began to examine whether changing the way educational decisions were made served as another tool to increase student achievement (American Association of School Administrators [AASA], 1988). According to the consortium referred to as the School-Based Management Task Force, SBM offered the promise that "by mobilizing and utilizing the resources at the school level, student and teacher performance can be affected" (AASA, 1988, p. 2).

School districts engaged in school-based management activities were involved in a major shift from traditional leadership roles to school-based management involving teachers and others in the decision-making activity. School administrators were "leaders only to the extent that others grant them cooperation and see them as leaders" (Bolman & Deal, 2002, p. 2). Thus, the relationship between principal, teacher, and student personnel workers underwent great scrutiny. Professionalization of teaching and empowerment of school social workers, counselors, and school psychologists are examples of how this new type of decentralized governance structure involved multiple personnel in the decision-making process.

The SBM movement influenced states throughout the country. Massachusetts and other states passed legislative mandates requiring schools to organize and govern themselves based on a SBM model. Efforts to involve both teachers and parents in the decision-making process were important but lacked a comprehensive approach to reform schools. Teachers found that they were not only being asked to become part of the decision-making process but also had to continue their role of teaching. Many teachers felt they could not participate in a meaningful manner without compromising their teaching responsibilities. Ultimately, schools and the personnel involved were being bombarded by a negative press and were experiencing a difficult and complex student body with many personal and social problems. High teacher involvement constituted high degrees of burnout. In addition, an aging teaching population of baby-boomers and a reduction of educational resources added to the lack of effectiveness of this reform effort.

Comprehensive School Reform

If educators have learned anything about school reform, it is that a piecemeal approach to changing poor classroom practice is a losing battle. A collection of isolated programs does not add up to schoolwide improvement. In recent years, attention has increasingly focused on a radically different approach to improving the quality and performance of schools—comprehensive school reform. Rather than layering one program on top of another, this approach focuses on redesigning and integrating all aspects of a school—curriculum, instruction, teacher training and professional development, school management, governance, assessment, and parent and community involvement (ECS, 1999, p. 2).

According to the ECS (1999), a national think tank on public education, this new generation of reform uses individual "models" that combine the best of what research has found to work in the classroom. These models emphasize high academic standards for all children, clear and consistent goals, coordinated district and school restructuring, and accountability. Some models emphasize technology, others focus on basic skills, and others center on team teaching. More than 20 models are truly comprehensive in scope (ECS, 1999).

Comprehensive school reform is rooted in the work of leading reformers such as Stanford University's Henry Levin, Harvard University's Ted Sizer, and Johns Hopkins University's Robert Slavin. Models such as Levin's (1987) Accelerated Schools Project, Slavin's (Slavin & Madden, 2001) Success for All, and Sizer's (1985) Coalition of Essential Schools laid the early groundwork for what was then—and sometimes still is—called "whole school reform." These models and others, such as High Schools That Work and Core Knowledge, have been adopted by more than 4,500 schools nationwide (ECS, 1999).

Since the mid-1980s, these promising models have been embraced by thousands of schools throughout the country. According to the ECS, the number of schools using such an approach is expected to grow substantially during the next few years due to the Comprehensive School Reform Development project enacted by Congress in 1997. The move reflects a growing belief that comprehensive school reform is a way to raise the academic achievement of all students and improve the school climate. It also recognizes that the hard work of reforming schools requires the entire school, not isolated efforts.

Does comprehensive school reform work? The answer is not simple. Schools are a microcosm of a larger society. The complex social problems of families and children underscore the challenges that public education faces when it tries to increase achievement scores and ignore the social consequences of poverty and the lack of a comprehensive child welfare system. For school social workers, there is little mention of student support services in any of the comprehensive school reform models. School social workers who are employed in schools undergoing reform movements need to be involved in the debate and implementation process in their schools, districts, and state levels of governance. Despite the urgency of responses created by this highly politicized environment, school social work has been slow to respond and participate effectively in the school reform debate that has permeated the public school arena.

NO CHILD LEFT BEHIND ACT (2001)

The No Child Left Behind Act (NCLB), signed into law in January 2002, is a revised version of the Elementary and Secondary Education Act passed in 1965. NCLB is a blend of new requirements, incentives, and resources, and it poses significant challenges for states and local schools.

According to the ECS (2002), the law sets deadlines for states to expand the scope and frequency of student testing, revamp their accountability systems, and guarantee that every teacher is qualified in his or her subject area. NCLB requires states to make demonstrable annual progress in raising the percentage of students proficient in reading and math and in narrowing the test score gap between advantaged and disadvantaged students. At the same time, the new law increases funding in several areas, including K-3 reading programs and before- and-after-school programs, and it provides states with greater flexibility to use federal funds as they see fit.

This new law significantly strengthens the federal government's role in elementary and secondary education. The signal feature of the new act is its focus on accountability and results aimed at raising academic achievement for all students and improving the performance of poorly performing schools (White House, 2005).

President George W. Bush kept education reform at the forefront of his agenda, frequently expressing disappointment over how U.S. students score on national reading and math tests. He lamented that high school seniors trail students from Cyprus and South Africa on international math tests, and that nearly

 ## Title I—Improving the Academic Achievement of the Disadvantaged

Elementary & Secondary Education
Sec. 101. Improving the Academic Achievement of the Disadvantaged
Title I of the Elementary and Secondary Education Act of 1965 (20 U.S.C. 6301 et seq.) is amended to read as follows:

Title I—Improving the Academic Achievement of the Disadvantaged
Sec. 1001. Statement of Purpose
The purpose of this title is to ensure that all children have a fair, equal, and significant opportunity to obtain a high-quality education and reach, at a minimum, proficiency on challenging State academic achievement standards and State academic assessments. This purpose can be accomplished by

1. ensuring that high-quality academic assessments, accountability systems, teacher preparation and training, curriculum, and instructional materials are aligned with challenging State academic standards so that students, teachers, parents, and administrators can measure progress against common expectations for student academic achievement;
2. meeting the educational needs of low-achieving children in our Nation's highest-poverty schools, limited English proficient children, migratory children, children with disabilities, Indian children, neglected or delinquent children, and young children in need of reading assistance;
3. closing the achievement gap between high- and low-performing children, especially the achievement gaps between minority and nonminority students, and between disadvantaged children and their more advantaged peers;

one third of college freshman find they must take a remedial course before they are able to even begin regular college-level courses.

The attack on the failings of public education continued through President Bush's first term, when he helped institute NCLB as a means of improving public education. The philosophy behind it was to transform the federal role in education so that (1) there is an increase in accountability for student performance, (2) there is a focus on research-based programs and practices that target and enhance teacher quality, (3) there is reduced bureaucracy and increased flexibility at the local level, and (4) parents are empowered by receiving more information about the quality of schools and having a choice to remove their children from underperforming schools.

Key components of the Bush administration's education reform have been implemented during the reauthorization of the Elementary and Secondary Education Act. The box starting on page 28 is a short section of NCLB that addresses improving the academic achievement of the disadvantaged under Title I. Notice that there are several areas that school social workers can impact the implementation of NCLB, including meeting the needs of impoverished children, coordinating services, and involving parents in the educational process of their children.

4. holding schools, local educational agencies, and States accountable for improving the academic achievement of all students, and identifying and turning around low-performing schools that have failed to provide a high-quality education to their students, while providing alternatives to students in such schools to enable the students to receive a high-quality education;

5. distributing and targeting resources sufficiently to make a difference to local educational agencies and schools where needs are greatest;

6. improving and strengthening accountability, teaching, and learning by using State assessment systems designed to ensure that students are meeting challenging State academic achievement and content standards and increasing achievement overall, but especially for the disadvantaged;

7. providing greater decision-making authority and flexibility to schools and teachers in exchange for greater responsibility for student performance;

8. providing children an enriched and accelerated educational program, including the use of schoolwide programs or additional services that increase the amount and quality of instructional time;

9. promoting schoolwide reform and ensuring the access of children to effective, scientifically based instructional strategies and challenging academic content;

10. significantly elevating the quality of instruction by providing staff in participating schools with substantial opportunities for professional development;

11. coordinating services under all parts of this title with each other, with other educational services, and, to the extent feasible, with other agencies providing services to youth, children, and families; and

12. affording parents substantial and meaningful opportunities to participate in the education of their children.

U.S. Department of Education (2003).

NCLB AND THE IDEA

The NCLB law has been praised by parents and educators as the most important piece of federal legislation to affect educational outcomes for students with disabilities since the 1975 passage of P.L. 94-142 (the Education for All Handicapped Children Act, now know as the Individuals with Disabilities Education [IDEA]), the original law mandating that students with disabilities have access to a free, appropriate education. Most advocates and parents of children with disabilities endorse the NCLB law for two reasons: (1) General educators must pay attention to the academic progress of their students, and (2) scores of children with disabilities are reflected in the overall accomplishments of each school and may determine whether or not a school makes adequate yearly progress (AYP) as required by NCLB (Reder, 2004).

Many families with children who have disabilities bear the burden of dramatically lower rates of high school completion, lower rates of success in the labor market, and lower rates of entry into postsecondary education. The failure of our public schools disproportionately affects those in disadvantaged and lower-income neighborhoods (National Council on Disability, 2004).

According to the National Center on Educational Outcomes (2003), the main difference between IDEA and NCLB is that the former specifically governs services that are provided to students with disabilities and provides individual accountability through the Individual Education Plan process. The National Center believes that NCLB complements the IDEA provisions by providing public accountability at the school, district, and state levels for all students with disabilities. NCLB builds on IDEA by requiring the participation of students with disabilities in state- and districtwide assessments.

Under NCLB, students with disabilities are required to make AYP comparable to their peers without disabilities. The Department of Education allows an exception for students with the most significant cognitive impairments. One percent of the student population can take an alternative assessment based on alternate achievement standards. Special educators and school social workers alike are extremely concerned about the expectation of requiring most special education students to make AYP. Reaching the same proficiency as the general population is often an unattainable goal because of their disability. Examples of this include students with moderate mental retardation, severe emotional disabilities, or autism.

Concern exists among local officials about how students with disabilities, especially those with significant or multiple disabilities, are included in the overall school count of AYP. School principals and other school leaders who have high impact schools believe they are being unjustly singled out because they house and educate high concentrations of students with disabilities in their buildings. They believe they are being punished by NCLB because district programs located in their buildings have a higher than normal distribution of special education students. These leaders have to count the AYP of all students who attend their schools. Schools and districts that fail to pass AYP over time are subject to "improvement, corrective action, and restructuring measures" (Pasternack, 2003, p. 1).

As IDEA goes through the process of reauthorization by Congress, there is a movement and awareness of the necessity to bring IDEA and NCLB into greater alignment. For many local administrators, NCLB is viewed as a broad requirement for groups and IDEA is built on individualization. Both have accountability measures, but for students with disabilities, AYP can be difficult to measure given the extent of their disabilities. Findings also show a great deal of concern about how educators will respond to poor performance of students with disabilities on standardized assessments and high-stakes tests. The pressure to meet AYP goals and the use of high-stakes tests to measure whether goals are being met are leaving states and districts with little time to constructively determine how best to accomplish these tasks. Fears exist that high-stakes tests may have a disproportionate impact on students with disabilities. Mitchell D. Chester, Assistant Superintendent for Policy Development in the Ohio Education Department, stated the following (as quoted in Education Week, 2004):

> We're very concerned about the unintended consequences of holding schools accountable for [the disability] population. We're sensitive to the potential for pushing students out, for scapegoating students, for identifying these students as the reason that a school or a district isn't measuring up. (p. 16)

Criticisms of NCLB and School Reform

The political stance on NCLB is that all these requirements are meant to force public schools to improve, and that requiring every state to test every student every year (from third through eighth grades and then again in high school) is intended to identify troubled schools. However, real reform is not going to come from high-stakes tests. According to Richard Elmore (2002) of the Harvard Graduate School of Education,

> The ability of a school to make improvements has to do with the beliefs, norms, expectations, and practices that people in the organization share, not with the kind of information they receive about their performance. Low-performing schools aren't coherent enough to respond to external demands for accountability. The work of turning a school around entails improving the knowledge and skills of teachers, changing their knowledge of content and how to teach it, and helping them to understand where their students are in their academic development. (p. 5)

For school social workers interested in promoting social justice within the education system, the high-stakes tests demonstrate the inequalities of resources available to the low-performing schools. Low-performing schools generally do not have the financial and human capital internally or externally to improve their test scores. As Elmore (2002) relates, "Most high-performing schools simply reflect the social capital of their students; they are primarily schools with students of high socioeconomic status. Most low-performing schools also reflect the composition of their student populations" (p. 6).

Criticisms of NCLB include the movement of resources away from needy children and schools; the transfer of governance and control from local to federal and state governments; lack of appropriate funding; and, most important, the consequence of the standards and testing movement in the United States that has led to more students being pushed out of school, more retentions of students, more dropouts, a narrowing of the curricula, and dissatisfaction on the part of teachers, students, and parents. Critics contend that NCLB has created a narrow and inaccurate measure of school performance that has made public education worse rather than better.

On a broader scale, NCLB has what some authors refer to as "selective equality." Under NCLB, all schools are required to reach 100% passing rates for all student groups on state tests by 2013–2014. The declared goal is to have all students meet state standards and to eliminate academic achievement gaps. AYP refers to the formulas that NCLB uses to evaluate schools on the basis of standardized test scores. This mandate has been severely under-funded and impacts those schools and students who have the greatest need. According to Meier and Wood (2004), "Under NCLB the children of the poor will receive even more limited instruction, curriculum, and school experiences because their schools will be the first to be reported in need of improvement" (p. xii). The disparity in funding public schools exists throughout the country, where the wealthiest U.S. public schools spend at least 10 times more than the poorest schools. It is not surprising that this disparity and inequality contributes to a wider achievement gap and results in many students being pushed out or encouraged to leave school to improve the results of high-stake tests. Federal statistics often show that schools serving large numbers of low-income students and students of color have larger class sizes, fewer teachers and counselors, and lower-quality academic courses (Meier & Wood, 2004).

Improving a school's performance or the performance of any teacher or student in it without increasing the investment in teachers' knowledge, peda-gogical skills, and understanding of students is not realistic. NCLB is an exter-nal accountability system that does not take into account these important variables.

It is not difficult to identify poor performing schools. Teachers, adminis-trators, and parents alike can identify the schools that are not meeting academic expectations. After identifying the schools and districts that are obviously struggling, how many received the resources they need, at least without a court order? From the very beginning, NCLB has never been fully funded. In January 2005, President Bush's proposed budget for the year included significant cuts in NCLB, further hampering the financial resources of education. Reducing the education budget does not foster smaller classrooms, assist in the recruit-ment of quality teachers, and create incentives for nonperforming schools. Many critics believe that NCLB has created more problems for public edu-cation than it has helped. Unless it is adequately funded and more appropri-ate measures for school accountability are used, public education will continually be in crisis. The unfortunate outcome is that many children get left behind in the process.

SCHOOL REFORM FROM A SCHOOL SOCIAL WORK PERSPECTIVE

School reform has been a response to increased public awareness that many children are not being successful at school. In an ever-changing society, public schools are pressed to cope with children who often are not prepared to enter the classroom ready to learn. Many children find that their personal, home, and community problems overwhelm their ability to get the most out of school. School social workers have long known that "after the family, the school is the important influence on the behavior and accomplishments of pupils. Its expectations, organizational structure, climate, and resources, both financial and human, all interact to determine the educational future of children" (Allen-Meares, 1996, p. 534). Despite this knowledge, school social workers have not been major contributors in the school reform discussion.

School social workers have recognized that schools and communities are intertwined since the early 1900s, when agencies external to the school intervened to address the problems immersed in the family and the community. Those problems external to the school are not left at the schoolhouse door but often brought into the classroom. School social work's historical role was to address these social problems by linking the school, family, and community together. Although they have long been associated with providing these linkages, new roles and services are being expanded to meet the challenge of increased "at-risk" student populations that are involved in gang activity, drug addiction, school violence, and have behavioral problems.

Traditional roles of school social workers have been in direct counseling services, diagnostic assessment for special education, and teacher consultation. Nontraditional and less publicized roles take the form of community networking: group consensus building, coordinating school-based services, and student advocacy. In recent years, school social workers have been attempting to expand their role by participating in school reform and restructuring efforts. Their knowledge about group dynamics, conflict resolution, and community organization techniques could be invaluable to principals, teachers, and communities seriously trying to reform schools.

School Reform and School Social Work

America's pursuit of effective schools is also an appeal for educational reform. Many Americans who are dissatisfied with the current state of education believe strong school reform is a major key in addressing the restructuring of public education. As the demands from the public for improved quality and broader services increase, the leaders of public schools need to be at the forefront of the reform movement (National Association of Secondary School Principals [NASSP], 1992). Those leaders within the school need not just include the traditional school administrator but also school social workers, teacher leaders, school counselors, and psychologists.

Although social workers in schools have been working diligently with children and their families to help them get the most out of school, social workers have had small if not barely audible voices in the educational reform movement in the past two decades. Like their professional teacher counterparts, the educational reform movements have taken the school social workers for granted and treated them as "classroom furniture rather than as thinking possibly disputatious human beings" (Ravitch, 1985, p. 19).

The National Association of Social Workers and other organizations concerned with provision of services to schoolchildren have been actively engaged in promoting an advocate voice in lobbying congressional support for inclusion of social work services in schools. Under the guise of "pupil personnel services," "related services," and "coordinated services," school social workers have been written into federal education legislation. Their voices, along with those of other pupil personnel service providers, have been secured to be among many in the education reform discussion. The challenge for practicing school social workers is to be more assertive and make their voices loud enough to be heard and taken seriously. A forceful voice is required to advocate for children and families, and facilitate meaningful links with agencies and other concerned citizens in the community.

Although the past decades will be remembered as some of the most turbulent for this country's public schools, changes in the social, political, and economic environments have necessitated a reexamination of how schools deal with children who have difficulty adapting to the school environment. In an ever-changing society, schools are pressed to deal with children who often enter classrooms not ready to learn. Frequently, personal, family, and neighborhood problems overwhelm students' capability to reach their potential academically and socially. Dropouts and push-outs tend to be the norm in urban areas. Coinciding increases are noted in the number of children with special needs. Violent acts in the neighborhood are now invading the schools. Political leaders at the federal, state, and local levels have shown major concern regarding the problems of education and youth and have offered differing solutions and remedies that are instituted in the name of school reform.

SCHOOL SOCIAL WORK'S RESPONSE TO SCHOOL REFORM

School social work has responded inadequately, if at all, to the educational reform movement. For a profession that emerged in response to the inabilities of communities and families to deal with poverty, disease, disability, discrimination, and oppression (Specht & Courtney, 1994), school social work falls short of these same challenges in the present educational arena. This is not entirely the fault of individual school social workers, who are often treated as auxiliary and expendable partners in education. Often, school social workers have been excluded from reform discussions because they are not considered vital contributors to improving teaching and learning environments. In fact, an examination of the leading educational reform writers reflects little discussion about student support services, let alone school social work (Sirotnik & Soder, 1999). The closest they come to recognizing social work services are general references to family involvement, character education, and community and parent participation in school governance.

Additionally, school social work has not wholeheartedly endorsed the reform movement because of school social workers' close affiliation with teachers who have been under attack for almost two decades now. Adversaries in the conservative movement and other politically motivated challengers have forced educators and school social workers to quickly assume defensive postures. The educational establishment has responded guardedly to criticism and has fought vigorously against the solutions that have been implemented so far (Gianesin & Bonaker, 2003). Teachers and their representative unions embraced school social workers as union members and partners in their struggle to maintain the educational status quo regarding educational reform and viewed restructuring with suspicion and resistance.

Conversely, the efforts of individual school social workers who are engaged in reform efforts often go unnoticed and undocumented. They, like many other practitioners and teachers, are busy trying to meet the needs of the children and families they serve, permitting the political rhetoric and school reform discussions to take place without their participation. They prioritize the immediate emotional needs of children as worthy of their time and energy, avoiding the often contentious and frustrating political debate on school reform.

THE NEW SCHOOL SOCIAL WORKER

To respond to these challenges and the changing demographics, a different set of skills and behaviors are needed for the new type of school social worker to deal with the changing world of education. The future breed of school social workers must combine the skills of both the generalist and the specialist. They must understand how to create client advocacy as well as engage clients using their clinical skills. With these new demands, schools and their leaders must adopt distinct missions, structures, and relationships to meet the changing environment (NASSP, 1992). The change that school social workers must face will require skills to manage and create collaborative action among a variety of interest groups. This means they will need to take on leadership roles in educational systems.

Educational leadership skills are being refined and molded by the latest set of standards and organizational structures. Leadership in the education and business environments is being redefined from the traditional U.S. management perspective. The traditional top-down model of management and leadership is being discarded and replaced with the decentralized models that encourage leadership from many stakeholders. Research on effective schools is likely to be focused on organizational models that encourage leadership from many quarters (Bolman & Deal, 2002; Murphy, 1990). Educational policymakers have made efforts to change the organization of schools to accommodate this leadership approach. This restructuring is sometimes referred to as school-based management or SBM.

Research supports the fact that the most essential element for effective schools and educational change is a strong and committed principal (Cuban, 1988; Greenfield, 1987). Establishing an influential association between the principal and the school social worker can be an effective strategy in becoming an integral part of the reform movement. School social workers offer a valuable set of skills that range from micro to mezzo and macro. School leaders need the voice of an advanced generalist social worker to assist them in setting policy and for establishing collaborative relationships among staff, parents, and community members.

School social workers can establish a vital link between the principal and teaching personnel. Often, school social workers can act as mediators and buffers when principals and others are implementing unpopular school reform changes. As expert change agents, they can use their clinical skills with both principals and teachers to better understand the process of change, the importance of communication, and the motivations behind resistance. School social workers are in an influential position not only to help teachers and others see the benefits of school reform but also to demonstrate empathy regarding the everyday concerns of teachers who deal with students who are not always ready and willing to learn.

The professionalization of teaching, the empowerment of teachers, the creation of teacher leadership, the involvement in decision making, and the restructuring of the conditions for teaching and school governance under the banner of school reform can be complicated and confounded by issues of power and control. As schools and school systems deal with these critical issues, school social workers should use their group work and advocacy skills to be significant contributors to these discussions. This will assist the schools in bringing about meaningful change with teachers and staff.

Many schools aim their reforms at the relatively easy problems and avoid the difficult ones—the problems that result from changes in demographics of society and schools. Cultural competence is important for school social workers because they work with diverse and vulnerable populations who are often suspicious of school personnel. School social workers can develop cultural competence by actively learning about the norms, customs, and values of the groups they serve. This cultural competence can assist in making vital connections between marginalized groups and facilitate communication between families and the school.

In the area of cultural competence, school social workers can often act as the conscience of the school. They can provide advocacy for populations who are overlooked when the school's focus is primarily on test scores and achievement levels. School social workers can remind teachers and administrators that special education students have difficulties taking achievement tests that have high-stakes consequences to them. They can be advocates for disenfranchised populations who constitute the majority of the drop-out population. School social workers can be effective change and reform agents by helping school personnel understand that all parents and students have a stake in school reform.

BEST PRACTICE IN AN ERA OF REFORM

For many school social workers who are engaged in school reform activities, the individual student becomes the primary focus for assessing the outcomes of school reform. The National Council on Disability (2004) notes that a major thrust for teachers and support personnel engaged in NCLB and IDEA is improving educational outcomes for students with disabilities. For many years, students with disabilities have been separated from their peers not just physically but also through different types of instruction, assessment, special teachers, and accountability systems. NCLB requires that students with disabilities be included in the performance assessment of all children. Although there are drawbacks, NCLB does refute the belief that students with disabilities cannot meet rigorous standards. School social workers must help schools and teachers to assist disabled students toward mastery and academic achievement along with identifying those students who have serious cognitive or emotional disabilities that impair their ability to master academic curriculums. Alternative assessments and appropriate accommodations recommended by the school social worker should be a common practice.

NCLB's focus on data and evidence-based practice research has led to a growing awareness of the importance of thorough research and evaluations. There is a great need for evidence-based practice to inform school social workers and others on developing high-quality programs in schools. The use of evidence-based practices in special education is a fairly new initiative largely due to language authorized during the 1997 reauthorization of IDEA. Practitioners often have difficulty finding practices that are based on rigorous evaluation methods. Few school social workers engage in research that can be reported as evidenced-based practice. More school social workers need to engage in research while they practice. Their positive interventions often go unnoticed and lack the written documentation that is so critical to expanding the profession's impact on children in schools.

For example, many school social workers are involved in drop-out prevention programs. Even though there have been positive decreases in the percentage of students dropping out of high school, one third of all students with disabilities drop out (American Youth Policy Forum & Center on Education Policy, 2002). School social workers should be engaged in research and evidenced-based practice that prevents students with disabilities from dropping out. Drop-out prevention strategies for students with disabilities typically include counseling services, remediation, tutoring, attendance monitoring, mentoring, and after-school clubs.

Other services that school social workers often perform besides counseling are sustaining and monitoring interventions that include support groups and staff mentors focused on school completion. The research literature on effective drop-out strategies is very limited. Although there is an abundance of anecdotal evidence of success of programs and strategies, only a few have an empirical basis for success (National Council on Disability, 2004). The need for empirical evidence on the value of intervention strategies and school social work services is important in the context of the school reform movement.

SUMMARY

People in the field of education are searching for ways to improve student achievement and school climate and reduce student alienation and incidences of violence. Early on, education reformers thought mandating structural reforms and attacking the educational establishment would bring about major changes in the way schools functioned. They tried other approaches that included involving community agencies and businesses. They conceived the notion of school-based services, changed their organizational environments, and encouraged teachers and others closest to the problem to have a greater voice in the decision-making process. Currently, a comprehensive approach is being touted as the new wave of reform that will improve our public schools.

Many questions remain as to how school social workers and the interventions they do on a daily basis increase the academic achievement of students to whom they provide services. The assumption that school social workers make is that decreasing emotional turmoil or assisting students in coping with their environments will allow the students to focus and put more cognitive energy into learning and school work. This assumption does not always get translated into research. Social work practitioners see the correlations between receiving social work services and the outcome measures of grades, attendance, work completion, and academic achievement. However, they need to demonstrate their usefulness by conducting research and evaluative studies.

Despite all the waves of educational reform, achievement standards have remained the easiest method for reformers and politicians to measure the effectiveness of our public education system. The results are not in yet, but many school social workers concur that a comprehensive social policy on child welfare, mental health, and education is needed along with adequate funding. Without them, NCLB, initiated by President George W. Bush, has little meaning to those students and their families who were left behind many years ago.

School Social Work Companion Website

Please be sure to check out our companion website at www.thomsonedu.com/social_work/bye, where you will find relevant materials for each chapter, including flashcards, online practice quizzes, and PowerPoint slides.

References

Allen-Meares, P. (1996). The new federal role in education and family services: Goal setting without responsibility. *Social Work, 41*(5), 533–540.

American Association of School Administrators, National Association of Elementary School Principals, and National Association of Secondary School Principals. (1988). *School based management: A strategy for better learning.* Arlington, VA: National Association of Elementary School Principals.

American Youth Policy Forum & Center on Education Policy. (2002). *Educating children with disabilities.* Washington, DC: Author.

Bacharach, S. B. (Ed.). (1990). *Education reform: Making sense of it all.* Boston: Allyn & Bacon.

Bolman, L., & Deal, T. (2002). *Reframing school leadership: A guide for principals and teachers*. Thousand Oaks, CA: Corwin Press.

Boyer, E. L. (1989). What teachers say about America's children. *Educational Leadership, 46*(8), 73–75.

Briar-Lawson, K., Lawson, H., Collier, C., & Joseph, A. (1997). School-linked comprehensive services, promising beginnings, lessons learned, and future challenges. *Social Work in Education, 19*(3), 136–148.

Cuban, L. (1988). The managerial imperative and the practice of leadership in schools. New York: State University of New York Press.

Education Commission of the States. (1999). *Comprehensive school reform: A promising approach for today's schools*. Retrieved February 22, 2005, from http://nclb2 .ecs.org/Projects_Centers/index.aspx?issueid=gen&IssueName=General

Education Commission of the States. (2002). *No Child Left Behind Project Center*. Retrieved February 22, 2005, from http://nclb2.ecs.org/Projects_Centers/ index.aspx? issueid=gen&IssueName=General

Education Week. (2004). *Quality counts 2004: Count me in. Special education in an era of standards. A special report by Education Week*. Bethesda, MD: Editorial Projects in Education.

Elmore, R. (2002, Spring). Unwarranted intrusion. *Education Next*. Retrieved February 24, 2005, from www.educationnext.org/20021/30.html

Gianesin, J., & Bonaker, P. (2003). Understanding conservative challenges to school social work and public education. *Children and Schools, 25*(1), 49–62.

Gibbs, G. (1989). *Effective schools research: The principal as an instructional leader*. (ERIC No. ED308587)

Greenfield, W. (1987). Moral imagination and interpersonal competence: Antecedents to instructional leadership. In W. Greenfield (Ed.), *Instructional leadership: Concepts, issues, and controversies* (pp. 56–73). Boston: Allyn & Bacon.

Hodgkinson, H. (1991). Reform versus reality. *Phi Delta Kappan, 73*, 8–16.

Lewis, A. (1992). *Leadership styles*. Arlington, VA: American Association of School Administrators.

Levin, H. M. (1987). Accelerated schools for disadvantaged students. *Educational Leadership, 44*(6), 19–21.

Lindelow, J. (1981). School-based management. *School Management Digest, 1*(23), 1–72.

Meier, D., & Wood, G. (Eds.). (2004). *Many children left behind: How the No Child Left Behind Act is damaging our children and our schools*. Boston: Beacon.

Murphy, J. (1990). *Improving the education of at risk students: A system of checks and balances*. Paper presented at the International Conference on the Effective Education of At-Risk Children and Youth, Washington, DC.

National Association of Secondary School Principals. (1992). *Developing school leaders: A call for collaboration. A special report of the NASSP Consortium for the Performance-Based Preparation of Principals*. Reston, VA: Author.

National Center on Educational Outcomes. (2003). *Accountability for assessment results in the No Child Left Behind Act: What it means for children with disabilities*. Minneapolis: University of Minnesota, National Center on Educational Outcomes.

National Commission on Excellence in Education. (1983). *A nation at risk. The imperative for educational reform*. Washington, DC: U.S. Government Printing Office.

National Council on Disability. (2004). *Improving educational outcomes for students with disabilities*. Retrieved February 23, 2005, from www.educationalpolicy.org/ pdf/NCD.pdf

Passow, A. H. (1990). How it happened, wave by wave. In Bacharach, S. B. (Ed.), *Education reform: Making sense of it all.* Boston: Allyn & Bacon.

Pasternack, R. (2003). *No Child Left Behind. A PowerPoint presentation.* Washington, DC: U.S. Department of Education, Office of Special Education and Rehabilitative Services.

Purkey, S. C., & Smith, M. S. (1985). School reform: The district policy implication of the effective schools literature. *Elementary School Journal, 85,* 352–389.

Ravitch, D. (1985). *The schools we deserve.* New York: Basic Books.

Reder, N. (2004). *The intersection of the No Child Left Behind Act and the Individuals with Disabilities Act or can you fit a round peg into a square hole?* Retrieved February 23, 2005, from www.ctredpol.org/pubs/Forum14September2004/NCL Bpaper_Sep14.doc

Robertson, P. J., & Buffett, T. M. (1991, April). *The move to decentralize: Predictors of early success.* Paper presented at the annual meeting of the American Educational Research Association, Chicago.

Sirotnik, K., & Soder, R. (1999). *The beat of a different drummer: Essays on educational renewal in honor of John I. Goodlad.* New York: Lang.

Sizer, T. R. (1985). Common sense. *Educational Leadership, 42*(6), 21–22.

Slavin, R. E., & Madden, N. A. (2001). *One Million Children: Success for All.* Newbury Park, CA: Corwin.

Specht, H., & Courtney, M. (1994). *Unfaithful angel: How social work has abandoned its mission.* New York: Free Press.

U.S. Department of Education. (1984). *Nation at risk—A nation responds: Recent efforts to improve education.* Washington, DC: U.S. Government Printing Office.

U.S. Department of Education. (2003). *No Child Left Behind.* Retrieved November 6, 2003, from www.ed.gov/nclb/landing.jhtml

White House. (2005). White House web page (p. 1). Retrieved February 22, 2005, from www.whitehouse.gov/news/reports/no-child-left-behind.html

Ecological Perspective for School Social Work Practice

CHAPTER 3

KENDRA J. GARRETT, D.S.W.
School of Social Work, College of St. Catherine and
University of St. Thomas, Minnesota

CHAPTER OUTLINE

CHAPTER OVERVIEW

This chapter presents a rationale for organizing school social work practice according to ecology theory. Specifically, it (1) explains the rationale for use of a conceptual framework, (2) defines the principles of ecological theory, (3) summarizes research supporting ecological theory, and (4) identifies ways in which ecological theory can guide school social work practice.

INTRODUCTION: WHAT IS A CONCEPTUAL FRAMEWORK?

Theories help practitioners comprehend and explain the way the world functions by providing frameworks for understanding events, concepts, and behavior. Conceptual frameworks are broad-based, overarching theoretical perspectives that organize various observations and perspectives of reality and provide explanations of the how and why of happenings (Monette, Sullivan, & DeJong, 2002). In addition to a knowledge base, a conceptual framework is built on the values and ethics of the social worker and of the profession. Without such a framework to guide one's thinking about any situation, the worker may respond in a fragmented or even biased manner (Caple, Salcido, & Di Cecco, 1995).

The fact that social work has been guided by a theoretical orientation inclusive of both the person and the encompassing environment has quite literally shaped the entire profession, provided it with identity, and distinguished it from others that are more individually focused. It is the school social worker who attends not only to the student but also to the family, the teachers, and the administrators, as well as the classroom, school, and community environments. No other school professional shares the person-in-environment theoretical orientation; no other professional is as holistic as the social worker. Although a person-in-environment orientation has been a constant in the social work profession, there are a number of conceptual frameworks that have been used to supplement it. Throughout the years, social work has often used a problem-solving approach. Recently, there has been a push to identify client pathology through diagnosis as a prerequisite for insurance reimbursement. This trend has been countered by another theoretical perspective that emphasizes strengths and competence as a guiding force. The theoretical framework that guides a social worker's thinking, then, guides every practice decision a social worker makes. Nothing is more useful in planning practice than a good theory that provides explanations for the relationships between and among many concepts and constructs.

ECOLOGY THEORY

The National Association of Social Workers' *Standards for School Social Work Services* (2002) promotes an ecological conceptual framework for school social work. Ecology theory is a less abstract and biologically-based form of general systems theory. As such, it is concerned with the reciprocal relationships, often called transactions, and adaptive fit between and among living systems and between those systems and their surrounding environments (Germaine, 1979). The ecological framework suggests that a change in one part of a system (either the organism or the environment) leads to a corresponding, reciprocal change in the other, as a system works to maintain balance to remain intact and maintain a steady state (homeostasis) (White, 1974). Stress results from social or developmental transitions and any other life issues that disturb the existing equilibrium or person–environment fit. Stressors may come from poor fit with the immediate environment, traumatic life events, or natural transitions due to growth and development (Germaine & Gitterman, 1995).

CONCEPTS IN THE ECOLOGICAL FRAMEWORK

Many constructs borrowed from biological sciences are applicable in the ecological framework. Adaptation or "striving towards acceptable compromise" with the environment can take one of three forms: mastery, coping, or defense (White, 1974, p. 52). **Mastery** is a successful effort to overcome frustrations and find an acceptable fit with the environment. **Coping** is an ongoing, dynamic effort to adjust to changes in the environment when old behavior patterns are no longer effective. **Defense** is a response to danger or attack. An organism adapts to its environment by the use of three strategies: (1) obtaining information regarding the environment; 2) becoming alert, organizing to process information, and acting; and (3) maintaining autonomy and freedom of movement for either making decisions or taking action (White, 1974).

When the organism in question is human, the ecological framework becomes considerably more complex. The concept of the environment must include the home, school, workplace, neighborhood, community, state, nation, and planet. Each of these environmental systems influences values, beliefs, and behaviors. There are many transactions and relationships between and among the various environmental systems in a person's life (Bronfenbrenner, 1977).

The capacity for memory and emotion in humans makes an ecological framework more complex than for simpler life-forms. For example, people are able to anticipate stressors and adapt in advance by obtaining information, organizing and remaining alert, and maintaining autonomy. Coping, then, can be a proactive strategy as well as a reaction to an actual or threatened danger. The concept of defense is also more complicated in humans. In addition to developing ways to defend against physical attack, people find ways to defend against emotional danger, such as anxiety. Psychological defense mechanisms may serve such a purpose in the short term by helping individuals protect against emotional stressors (White, 1974).

Positive fit between individuals and the environment happens when successful adaptation takes place and the person and environment are in balance (Germaine, 1979). This balance can be difficult to maintain because individuals are constantly changing and developing over the life span. These natural individual changes lead, in turn, to changes in environmental systems (Germaine, 1979). Environmental systems are also in constant flux (Bronfenbrenner, 1977). Thus, person–environment transactions are ever changing and reciprocal; change in one produces a corresponding change in the other.

The term **habitat** is used in the ecological perspective to refer to the physical environment. Human habitats are homes, the physical layout of neighborhoods, workplaces, schools, and communities. Space plays an important part in the concept of habitat. **Niche** refers to an individual's place or status in the social environment (Germaine & Gitterman, 1995).

Culture is an environmental variable that can have a considerable effect on the individual (Maluccio, 2000). Differing cultural environments also make human coping and adaptation more complex. Change and maintenance of cultural patterns are affected by the physical environment, social networks of mutual interaction, traits internal to a given culture, and interaction between and among differing cultural groups. Cultural systems evolve, with patterns being maintained or modified over time (Cohen, 2001).

Poverty, power differentials, oppression, and institutionalized racism within society also affect coping and adaptation patterns. When white, middle-class Americans are considered a norm, other cultures may look different in contrast. Dominant cultural groups may perceive these differences negatively. People who do not fit such a cultural norm may develop coping strategies to adapt to the dominant society. These strategies may, in turn, be assessed as deviant by the dominant society. For example, African Americans living in U.S. society have used humor, music, and language to cope with life in a racist society (Draper, 1979).

In contrast to frameworks that dwell on pathology, an ecological framework emphasizes competence, adaptation, and the innate capacities and strengths each individual holds (Germaine, 1973). Competence comes from the interaction of an individual's innate skill, potential, motivation, talent, and hopes with the opportunities and demands of the surrounding environment (Maluccio, 2000). The goal of work with clients is to support environmental conditions that foster growth and development of individuals to maximize potential (Germaine, 1979). Intervention in the ecological framework is based on the assumption that all people have innate strengths and competencies. They grow and develop throughout life and have a natural tendency to become healthy. Interventions include both developing peoples' strengths and changing environmental systems to maximize the potential of individuals, families, groups, and communities. Social workers and clients collaborate to identify and resolve problems in the client's life situation and obtain a better fit between the person and the environment. Successful action is empowering to the client and reinforces a sense of self-competence. Interventions often strive toward increasing the client's ability to relate to others by developing connections to social networks and other support systems, as well as improving self-direction through active decision making and problem solving (Germaine & Gitterman, 1995).

CULTURE IN AN ECOLOGICAL FRAMEWORK

The ecological perspective is particularly helpful in framing discussions about cultural issues. **Culture** is a dynamic, ever-changing environmental condition that is constantly shaping individuals who both come from and into contact with a culture, and the culture, in turn, is shaped by contact with individuals (Caple et al., 1995). Children must adapt to school culture, whether it is similar to or different from that of their families of origin. When the cultural group is quite different from that of the school, there will be more stress and more need for adaptation by both student and school to improve the fit. The greater the discrepancies between two cultures, "the more dynamic the process of acculturation becomes" (Caple et al., 1995, p. 162).

Complete competence in a culture other than one's own is perhaps not possible because of the ever-changing nature of any culture (Dean, 2001), but social workers can strive toward competence through affirmation of a client's culture as a potential strength in resolving problems. While working to understand any cultural group, the worker must walk a fine line between learning about cultural influences and remaining aware of the many individual differences in any group (Caple et al., 1995).

In working to understand cultural differences, school social workers should be alert to the degree of acculturation of the student and family to the dominant culture of the school, economic concerns of the group, history of oppression of members of the cultural group, racism and prejudice (both from without and from within), the different uses of language and art, political issues affecting the group, child-rearing factors, family structure, cultural values, and traditions (Locke, 1992). An ecological framework is quite useful in analyzing a culture because of its holistic perspective in looking at environmental influences, the coping nature of behaviors, and the goal of improving goodness of fit between a student and the environment (Caple et al., 1995).

BEST PRACTICES AND THE ECOLOGICAL PERSPECTIVE

Verification through empirical research is the most important consideration in choosing a theoretical perspective (Monette et al., 2002). Empirical evidence to support the ecological perspective is often presented in terms of risk, assets, and resiliencies. For example, Sameroff, Bartko, Baldwin, Baldwin, and Seifer (1998) studied 20 environmental risk factors in six categories (family process, parent characteristics, family structure, community involvement, peers, and community climate). They found that as the number of environmental risk factors increased (regardless of the severity of individual factors and which factors were present), adolescents' psychological adjustment, self-competence, involvement in activities, and academic performance decreased. As numbers of environmental risks increased, problem behaviors increased.

Positive personal characteristics such as resourcefulness, as measured by the ability to solve problems and recover from setbacks, have been associated with greater competence on the outcome measures of psychological adjustment, self-competence, problem behavior, activity involvement, and academic performance. However, "the negative effects of a disadvantaged environment seem to be more powerful contributors to child achievement at every age than the personality characteristics of the child" (Sameroff, Gutman, & Peck, 2003, p. 384).

Factors that promote health and well-being are the opposite end of the continuum from risk factors. Parents with poor mental health are a risk; parents with good mental health promote positive outcomes (Sameroff et al., 2003). Research by the Search Institute (2002) identified 40 developmental assets. Half of these assets were categorized into external categories (support, community resources, expectations by important others, and constructive use of time). Protective internal asset categories were commitment to learning, positive values, social competencies, and positive identity. The institute found that the more assets adolescents reported, the more likely they were to exhibit leadership, maintain good health, value diversity, and succeed in school. As the number of assets increased, a student was less likely to abuse alcohol and drugs, engage in violent behavior, and be sexually active.

Best practices using the ecological framework include empirically validated programs that increase coping and competence. For example, Harvey and Hill (2004) found that a strength-based, holistic intervention for at-risk African American youths led to significant gains in self-esteem and accurate knowledge about drug use, although the parent component of the program noted no significant gains. The interventions used were based on an ecological foundation and included use of Afrocentric principles, peer support, a rite of passage program, after-school activities, and family empowerment and counseling. Similarly, Jones (2004) found that a group experience aimed at enhancing psychosocial competence for female African American college students significantly lowered participants' stress levels compared to those who did not participate in the group.

Comprehensive research on the ecological framework should not only examine individual responses to environmental conditions but also focus on the power of individuals to change encompassing social systems. Researchers should also investigate the relationship of several simultaneous subsystems and the indirect influences of the physical environment on social processes. Research based on the ecological perspective should also include such contextual variables as work, health, neighborhood, school, and community. Such research would also evaluate interventions that restructure some social systems, while monitoring subsequent changes (Bronfenbrenner, 1977). Because of the complex nature of ecological theory, much research on ecological principles remains undone.

THE ECOLOGY OF SCHOOL SOCIAL WORK

School social work practice based on an ecological framework is concerned not only with students but also with the environmental systems that interact in school settings. The ecological framework charges school social workers to be concerned with prevention (Maluccio, 2000) as well as remediation.

The habitat of students includes the school building, the neighborhood, the community, access to libraries, and spaces available for play and study. Such physical characteristics may have profound effects on student activities. The physical layout of neighborhoods can affect safety and the availability of after-school day care and youth centers. Students who live in homes and apartments that are overcrowded, poorly heated, and without adequate places to rest, read, and study are presumably at a disadvantage compared to students who have access to more conducive environments. Students must find a niche in their social environments and a peer group that is supportive and accepting. They need classrooms in which they feel respected and able to succeed. They also need to feel valued in their families, neighborhoods, and communities.

Assessment

Assessment is holistic; it involves more than talking with the student to determine his or her perspective, areas of success, and strength. The school social worker observes the student in as many of the school settings as possible, including classrooms, hallways, playgrounds, and the lunchroom. Teachers and other school staff who know and interact with the student are consulted. School records are reviewed to ascertain information about the student's functioning in other settings. The worker uses the ecological framework to not only study the student in several environments but also to assess how the student impacts the environment and vice versa. School social workers also need to meet with family members to obtain their perspective and learn the interactions between the student and family. How does the home support student learning, and how does this student affect the family? Naturally, the social worker evaluates other systems that affect the student (and that are affected by him or her), such as the day care setting, the neighborhood, the workplace, and the church. The social worker also evaluates the social setting, noting peer interactions, the student's social niche, the presence or absence of supportive social interactions, and the way the student affects others. In other words, assessment focuses on the goodness of fit between the student and his or her many environmental systems.

Behavior in the ecological perspective is viewed in the context of adaptation to the environment, so the purpose of activity is assessed (White, 1974). The worker would not assess the behavior alone but also the situation in which the behavior takes place, working to determine why behaviors occur, assuming that they are responses to either personal or environmental stressors. So behavior should be viewed as purposeful. Some behaviors that appear dysfunctional or counterproductive might be reframed as adaptive or even as strengths to survive in a difficult environment.

In assessing a student using an ecological perspective, the school social worker would be aware of cultural factors and values that might affect student interactions with others. Caple et al. (1995) suggest that an ecological perspective is particularly useful in considering the importance of cultural factors on students.

Finally, an ecological assessment focuses on the effect the student has on his or her various environments and the reciprocal interactions between and among them. What is the effect of the student on the classroom, his or her peer group, and family? How do dynamics in these areas change when the student is not present? How is the student perceived by others, and how do they react to him or her? How are these reciprocal relationships affecting and being affected by the student?

Interventions

Interventions from an ecological perspective may focus on helping the student change to improve the fit with any of the surrounding environmental systems (classroom, peer, home, etc.). As such, the worker might help improve a student's

Case	**Case Example**

One school social worker was concerned that students were rushing through lunch in an effort to get to recess quickly. She recommended changing the schedule so that lunch recess took place before students ate. When this change was implemented, students ate more slowly and consumed more food. They seemed less in a rush to get back to the classroom than they had previously been to get to the playground. Not only was there less waste in the lunchroom but also students were more alert in their afternoon classes.

ability to relate to others, increase his or her sense of competence, build self-esteem, or improve self-direction (Germaine & Gitterman, 1995). Building on White's (1974) conceptualization of ways of gaining mastery, interventions could include helping students gain information about their environments, organizing that information and developing appropriate responses, and maintaining autonomy and freedom of movement. For example, a student who is having difficulty in the classroom might be helped to understand the expected classroom structure and why his behavior is annoying to the teacher or peers. He can be helped to find other actions that would meet his needs without upsetting others and to understand that he has choices as to what actions to take in the school setting. Raines and Ahlman (2004) suggest that students benefit from such strength-oriented interventions as setting clear and measurable goals, identifying resources and opportunities available in the environment, anticipating obstacles to change, and highlighting successes.

In addition to intervening directly with the student, an intervention using the ecological perspective might involve working with others in an effort to change an environmental system. For example, a worker may decide not to work with a student directly but might instead help parents set limits at home, help classmates understand a student's situation, or help the teacher rearrange the seating in the classroom. One of the great advantages of school social work is the location of workers in the school, which allows them to observe and interact with several of the major environmental settings. Not only do school social workers have relatively easy access to teachers and other staff but also they have the ability to observe students in daily interaction within the school environment.

The school social worker may be involved in helping larger environmental systems change as well. As schools embrace site-based management, increasingly school governance issues are being handled at the building level. This means that decisions regarding scheduling, discipline, and staffing are often determined locally. In some instances, the school social worker is able to be involved in helping make changes to better reflect the needs of students.

SUMMARY

The ecological theoretical perspective has great utility in guiding the work of the school social worker. Unlike frameworks that are based on pathology and problem solving, ecological theory emphasizes strengths. The theory is derived from biological sciences and emphasizes the reciprocal interactions among individuals and between people and their physical, social, and cultural environments. People strive for adaptive fit with their environment, and there is a natural push for competence and mastery. Systems become out of balance as a result of changes in the environment, individual development, and life events. Behavior and emotions are viewed as ways to cope with, defend against, change, or adjust to stressors and a poor fit with the environments. Students are viewed holistically as participants in their many surrounding environments, in the context of their cultural and religious traditions. Assessment is holistic and focuses on both the effect of the environmental systems on the student and the effect of the student on those systems. Intervention can be individual, environmental, or both.

Although there are a number of challenges to empirical verification of the ecological perspective, there is much evidence to support it. Cumulative environmental risk factors have been found to have a negative effect on psychological adjustment, whereas increasing personal and environmental assets have increased positive outcomes. Programs using ecological tenets that address problems holistically have been shown to have positive results.

School Social Work Companion Website

Please be sure to check out our companion website at www.thomsonedu.com/social_work/bye, where you will find relevant materials for each chapter, including flashcards, online practice quizzes, and PowerPoint slides.

References

Bronfenbrenner, U. (1977). Toward an experimental ecology of human development. *American Psychologist, 32*(7), 513–531.

Caple, F. S., Salcido, R. M., & Di Cecco, J. (1995). Engaging effectively with culturally diverse families and children. *Social Work in Education, 17*(3), 159–170.

Cohen, D. (2001). Cultural variation: Consideration and implications [Electronic version]. *Psychological Bulletin, 127*(4), 451–471.

Dean, R. G. (2001). The myth of cross-cultural competence. *Families in Society, 82*(6), 623–630.

Draper, B. J. (1979). Black language as an adaptive response to a hostile environment. In C. B. Germaine (Ed.), *Social work practice: People and environments* (pp. 267–281). New York: Columbia University Press.

Germaine, C. B. (1973). An ecological perspective in social casework practice. *Social Casework, 54*(6), 323–330.

Germaine, C. B. (1979). Introduction: Ecology and social work. In C. B. Germaine (Ed.), *Social work practice: People and environments* (pp. 1–22). New York: Columbia University Press.

Germaine, C. B., & Gitterman, A. (1995). Ecological perspective. In R. L. Edwards & J. G. Hopps (Eds.), *Encyclopedia of social work* (pp. 816–824). Washington DC: National Association of Social Workers.

Harvey, A. R., & Hill, R. B. (2004). Africentric youth and family rites of passage program: Promoting resilience among at-risk African-American youths. *Social Work, 49*(1), 65–74.

Jones, L. V. (2004). Enhancing psychosocial competence among black women in college. *Social Work, 49*(1), 75–84.

Locke, D. C. (1992). *Increasing multicultural understanding: A comprehensive model.* Newbury Park, CA: Sage.

Maluccio, A. N. (2000). A competence-centered perspective on child and family welfare. In J. G. Hopps & R. Morris (Eds.), *Social work at the millennium: Critical reflections on the future of the profession* (pp. 160–174). New York: Free Press.

Monette, D. R., Sullivan, T. J., & DeJong, C. R. (2002). *Applied social research: Tool for the human services* (5th ed.). Fort Worth, TX: Harcourt.

National Association of Social Workers. (2002). *NASW standards for school social work services.* Washington DC: Author.

Raines, J. C., & Alhman, C. (2004). No substitutes for competence: How to survive and thrive as an interim school social worker. *School Social Work Journal, 28*(2), 37–52.

Sameroff, A., Bartko, W. T., Baldwin, A., Baldwin, C., & Seifer, R. (1998). Family and social influences on the development of child competence. In M. Lewis & C. Feiring (Eds.), *Families, risk and competence* (pp. 177–192). Mahwah, NJ: Lawrence Erlbaum.

Sameroff, A., Gutman, L. M., & Peck, S. C. (2003). Adaptation among youth facing multiple risks: Prospective research findings. In S. S. Luthar (Ed.), *Resilience and vulnerability: Adaptation in the context of childhood adversity* (pp. 364–391). New York: Cambridge University Press.

Search Institute. (2002). *The asset approach: 40 elements of healthy development.* Minneapolis, MN: Author.

White, R. W. (1974). Strategies of adaptation: An attempt at systematic description. In G. V. Coehlo, D. A. Hamburh, & J. E. Adams (Eds.), *Coping and adaptation* (pp. 47–68). New York: Basic Books.

The Many Facets in the Role of a School Social Worker

CHAPTER **4**

WILLIAM C. LEE, M.S.W.
Fremont County School District, Wyoming

CHAPTER OVERVIEW

This chapter introduces roles that school social workers fulfill as they work with individual students, families, school personnel, community agencies, and policymakers to help students succeed in school. After reading this chapter, readers will (1) understand the many roles school social workers perform within a

Case	**Case Example**

David attends a day treatment school and has begun to transition back to his high school. He attends high school two periods a day with the hope of transitioning fully by the end of the first semester. He is nervous about being back with the students with whom he had problems but tries not to let it show. To ease the transition, classes have been picked to facilitate his success. He has also signed up for the high school speech and debate team as a way to develop more friends and as an appropriate outlet for his argumentative personality. Things go well until he begins to have grand mal seizures. David has a history of petite mal seizures. His neurologist recommends that he discontinue medication prescribed for his attention deficit disorder, which is thought to be contributing to the seizures. However, discontinuing the medication leaves David more susceptible to impulsive behaviors. After having a good start in his transition, he struggles with the old issues of authority, inappropriate comments, and poor quality of work. The school social worker, who has worked with David since junior high and during his time at the day treatment school and return to part days at the high school, is assessing the situation. It appears that David has had a setback in his transition as a result of a medical issue that has affected his emotional stability, impulse control, and argumentativeness.

school setting, (2) be able to describe how school social work services address specific academic standards required of students, (3) understand that school social work interventions and programs are driven by student needs, (4) be able to explain the use of clinical and community organizational skills in the application of school social work roles, (5) understand the role of the school social worker in reducing internal and external barriers to student learning, (6) develop an awareness of the role of a school social worker as part of a multidisciplinary team, and (7) know how to access the National Association of Social Workers (NASW) national standards for school social work practice. Other chapters in this book elaborate on the ways school social work roles are carried out at the community, organizational, and individual levels. As you read this chapter, you will learn how complicated situations such as the example above are handled and the many roles school social workers perform to help students learn by reducing barriers to that learning.

INTRODUCTION: "ART AND SCIENCE"

Schools are institutions of learning—places to prepare the next generation of citizens to be independent, self-supporting, and employable. Schools are expected to prepare students "to function as citizens" (Allen-Mears, Washington, & Welsch, 1986, p. 11). However, not all students come prepared to learn. Many face internal and external barriers that make education difficult. To help students overcome these barriers and make the most of their education, school social workers assume a wide variety of roles, including clinician, collaborator, consultant, multidisciplinary team member, educator, case manager advocate, liaison, broker, change agent, and policymaker.

The education that school social workers receive equips them with the ability to fulfill the roles required and assess, identify, and collaborate, as well as perform, a range of other tasks required to assist students and their families to overcome educational barriers. School social workers perform roles at the micro, mezzo, and macro levels. The specific school social work role that is applied is directly related to the need of the student and his or her family. This wide variety of roles, interventions, and services on behalf of the students and their families showcases the art and science of the profession of school social work.

NASW's (2002) *Standards for School Social Work Services*, originally developed in 1978 and revised in 2002, details 42 standards regarding the ethical principles, professional preparation, competencies, services, and responsibilities expected of school social workers. Standard 17 describes the body of knowledge practitioners are expected to have and represents the "science" of school social work. The "art" of the profession is the application of that knowledge.

The school social worker's role in the educational process is providing services to students and their parents or guardians to help the students be successful in school and life. This role definition allows for greater creativity on the part of the school social worker to develop services, interventions, policies, and strategies to support the success of the student. School social workers apply the science and art of the profession within services, interventions, policies, and strategies.

The role of the school social worker is evolving, driven by the current needs of students whose educational process is affected by internal and external barriers. This is as true today as it was at the turn of the 20th century, when social workers were called visiting teachers and helped link the school and home. This link assisted students and families in working together to overcome living conditions that adversely affected the students' education. Since Jane Addams' time in the early 1900s, we have seen a change in the role of the school social worker from a community-based approach to a more individual clinical focus in the 1950s and 1960s. The clinical school social work role emphasized individual work with students and did not address the need for a broader approach in the provision of services (Allen-Meares et al., 1986).

ECOLOGICAL FRAMEWORK AND THE ROLE OF THE SCHOOL SOCIAL WORKER

In recent years, the ecological framework has increasingly shaped the role of the school social worker and placed the emphasis on the child in relationship to all the factors impacting him or her both positively and negatively. The ecological perspective used by school social workers combines community organization and clinical skills in a blend unique to the profession. Using the ecological framework, "school social workers target not only the psychosocial deficits of students, but also work with transactions between subsystems of students and teachers, home and school, teacher and administrators and transactions with the external environment" (Early, 1992, p. 208).

There are many factors that affect the child's ability to learn, including abuse, neglect, divorce, alcoholism, death of a sibling or parent, parental unemployment, truancy, drug or alcohol abuse, educational disabilities, gangs, poor nutrition, harassment, violence, and racism. Each person's life is made up of interconnected relationships and experiences similar to a mobile. The student is at the center of the mobile, and his or her social supports (family, friends, and community members) are what hold it in the balance required for it to be functional. The balance of the mobile is disrupted when one or more of these supports fail. This lack of balance can create multiple problems for students who must attempt to regain it, often using their own individual strengths. The role of the school social worker is to assist students in identifying these strengths as well as the elements that cause problems for them. School social workers embrace the ecological perspective by working with the families, teachers, and community resources in the student's environment to provide sufficient support for the student to maintain the balance necessary to function. Once assets and limitations are known, an ecological plan can be developed with the parents, teachers, community resources, and the student.

The needs of the student are met by the many roles a school social worker performs to remove barriers to student learning. These roles are represented by the work school social workers do as clinicians, collaborators, advocates, case managers, educators, transition planners, and policymakers.

CLINICAL ROLES

School social workers are often the first line of defense to provide clinical services to students and their families in a school setting. The clinical role of the school social worker includes diagnostician, counselor, and group facilitator. Assessment of the student's problem involves the diagnostician role. The counselor role is performed with follow-up services such as individual or family counseling. The group facilitator role can be applied in social skills groups, grief groups, anger management groups, parent groups, and staff team groups.

Early identification is very important according to the *Report of the Surgeon General's Conference on Children's Mental Health* (U.S. Department of Health and Human Services, 2001) because children who do not receive the services they need suffer negative life outcomes. The student's problems can take the form of nonattendance, poor peer relationships, challenging authority, depression, fighting, and substance abuse. In the role of the diagnostician, the school social worker's assessment of the problem can include an interview with parents or the student as well as a visit with the different agencies and services that are providers involved in that student's life. Often in this process, the school social worker will obtain permission from the legal guardian to collaborate with other professionals (youth service worker, family services, and public and mental health worker) who have or have had contact with the student to assist in the assessment and provide a more comprehensive view of the child.

During the assessment phase, the school social worker determines which clinical interventions will help with the student's problem. Social work assessments include social histories, adaptive behavior rating scales, observation in the classroom or on the playground, and communication fact-finding with others in the community. See Chapters 9 and 16 for more information on student assessment. Initially, the school social worker may work individually with the student to build trust and better understand the problem, and this may be the extent of the school social worker's intervention.

In cases in which it appears the student needs more support at school, the school social worker may invite the student to be part of a group to address social skills, resolve personal issues, or to address other concerns. It is possible for students to work individually with the school social worker and also be in a group. The school social worker can use the structured group setting for the student to practice or express behaviors, which surface in individual work, in a safe environment and controlled setting. During the individual or group intervention, familial problems may arise that can be addressed through family sessions or by meeting separately with the parents.

Interventions with the family may be brief, or the family may need to be referred to other professionals in community agencies. Local mental health centers or private practitioners can collaborate with school social workers on the student's and family's mental health needs.

In the following case example, the school social worker assumed several roles, such as diagnostician, individual counselor, and group facilitator, to help address the behavioral and emotional difficulties that were creating barriers to

---

Case | **Case Example**

Ellen, a 13-year-old seventh-grader at a junior high, was referred to the school social worker for her loud inappropriate comments, defiant nature, and distractible behavior in class and in the hallways. The school social worker noticed this girl in the hallway because she was loud and seeking attention. Ellen was a very bright girl, yet her impulsiveness and need for control interfered with her learning.

The principal and teachers referred Ellen to the school social worker to be "fixed." The school social worker assessed the student through interviews with the student and parent and an observation in the classroom. During the parent interview, the school social worker learned that Ellen was seeing a psychiatrist and was on medication for attention deficit hyperactive disorder. A family history was also taken that identified some areas of unresolved loss.

An intervention plan was developed with the teachers, Ellen's mother, and the principal, with input from Ellen and her psychiatrist. Her team regularly reviewed the clinical plan. During the next 2 years, the plan unfolded and was changed as needed. Ellen received individual and group counseling through the school, follow-up medication reviews with the doctor, and was placed for a short time at an inpatient psychiatric facility to stabilize her behavior and deal with her anger and disclosure of a sexual assault at a young age.

the student's learning. This clinical approach also involved the role of consultant with the student's mother and psychiatrist. The school is a great microcosm of society. School social workers are in a unique position because they are allowed the opportunity to see a student's life in school and in the family and yet have the clinical privacy of their office to provide counseling services when needed.

MULTIDISCIPLINARY TEAM MEMBER AND BROKER ROLES

School social workers do not work in isolation and often take the multidisciplinary team member and broker roles. Effectiveness in these roles derives from how well they interact and work with other professionals in the school and in the community. In the multidisciplinary team member role, school social workers work closely with nurses, occupational therapists, physical therapists, speech/language therapists, school psychologists, guidance counselors, and principals as well as other school staff. These professionals frequently meet with the school social worker, parents, and student to create a team to assist the student's learning and development. Serving in the broker role, the school social worker often links with community agencies and professionals when the student's issues call for additional resources outside the school. Community resources frequently used by the school social worker include vocational rehabilitation workers, counselors, public health workers, family service providers, probation officers, doctors, and other professionals in the community. Representatives from these community agencies join with the school social worker to develop a wraparound service approach as well as to provide case planning and interventions to reduce barriers to the student's learning. The term **wraparound services** refers to a system in which services are family-based and coordinated so that the family does not have to go from agency to agency to track down the help it needs.

Using the ecological systems approach is one way for school social workers to distinguish themselves because it provides a framework for collaboration with other helping professionals and parents. The school social worker often works with people in the student's environment to connect the different systems in the student's life and bring others together to collaborate on assessments and interventions to reduce the barriers to learning.

EDUCATOR AND BEHAVIORAL COACH ROLES

School social workers often function in the role of an educator sharing information with teachers, administrators, parents, and legislators. This role involves instructions through in-service training and workshops for school staff in the areas of mental health interventions, behavioral strategies, accessing community resources, and cultural competences. School social workers provide behavioral strategy coaching to teachers and similar assistance to staff when working with

Case Example

Mark was a 16-year-old who had been diagnosed by his psychiatrist as having a bipolar disorder with schizoid tendencies. The school qualified him for special education services due to his emotional disability. He was medicated for both diagnoses. He also had an allergy to certain foods that the mother believed could exaggerate his diagnosed symptoms.

Mark had a tough transition to high school from junior high. His attendance the first semester was spotty. He often slept in and his mother had difficulties getting him up for school. He relied on his mother to get his medication in the morning. In school, he was drowsy, yet his skills were not far below average.

The school social worker was called in to assist with the attendance problem, his sleepiness in class, and his inappropriate behavior in school. The school social worker used a team approach, collaborating with Mark's doctor, school nurse, special education teacher, and a clinical psychologist who Mark's mother had recently involved. It was apparent that Mark was going to need the coordinated interventions of all these people to help him and his mother manage. The ultimate goal was to help Mark become more independent by interrupting his avoidance behaviors and helping him successfully manage himself and his condition.

The school social worker collaborated with Mark's mother and encouraged her not to enable him to stay home. This led to Mark and the school social worker meeting with the assistant principal to discuss truancy and explain to him that he is truant when his mother tries to get him up for school and he refuses. There was also ongoing collaboration between the school social worker and the psychologist who was working with the mother and Mark on his independence. The school social worker reinforced the work that the clinical psychologist was doing with the mother and Mark regarding his responsibility and independence. The psychologist in turn reinforced the school social worker's efforts to develop age-appropriate behavior and reduce Mark's school avoidance behavior.

Mark's attendance behavior improved as a result of the combined efforts of the assistant principal, who explained the consequences of Mark's nonattendance; the clinical psychologist, who reinforced his independence and responsibility; the school social worker, who addressed avoidance behaviors; and Mark's mother, who followed through with recommendations. The team met and exchanged ideas about the best way to get Mark more involved in his education and help him achieve greater independence. The discussion of his future vocation goals (transition planning) was also reviewed. The school social worker linked the importance of Mark's on-time attendance, self-reliance, and lack of avoidance behavior to his transition plan and future employment.

---

emotionally/behaviorally disabled students in the school setting. This training can be done by the school social worker alone or jointly with other helping professionals from community agencies in a collaborative effort to bring additional resources from the community into the school to support the academic progress of the student.

School social workers help educate administrators and legislators about unmet needs and the impact of those needs. A new and emerging area in public education is the standards-based education movement, in which students must

| Case | **Case Example** |

Sally was an emotionally disabled seventh-grader who had an Individual Education Plan goal for interpersonal communication skills, a statewide academic standard. Sally had considerable difficulty expressing her emotions appropriately in school. Instead of using words to express her needs, she often became aggressive, swearing, yelling at teachers, and getting into physical fights with peers.

Fortunately, a school social worker was able to help Sally master the required standard in the area of interpersonal skills. After conducting an assessment, the school social worker met with Sally to establish specific goals in conflict management and effective verbal and nonverbal communication skills. Sally and the school social worker agreed upon how many times each day and each week she would exhibit the new conflict management and communication skills she was learning in their work together. Sally worked on this statewide standard with the school social worker in individual and group counseling. The school social worker also worked with the classroom teachers, giving them ideas about how they could help increase Sally's ability to express her needs in appropriate ways.

show a proficient level of academic mastery in subject areas required for graduation. There are two forms of testing used throughout the United States that evaluate academic mastery. The first form is called "high-stakes" testing, in which one test is administered by states to assess mastery. The second form of testing is called "body of evidence," which examines multiple sets of evaluative information to judge a student's level of knowledge according to the academic standards (Lee, 2002, p. 59).

School social workers have been working on academic standards for a long time in the area of behavioral standards. School social workers work on these standards during social skills groups as well as during individual and group counseling. Content areas in the behavioral standards include eye contact, respecting diversity, cooperative behaviors, personal and social responsibility, decision making, listening skills, taking turns, etc. These behavioral standards can be found in such classes as language arts, physical education, social studies, and health.

CASE MANAGER ROLE

School social workers perform the case manager role when they coordinate services for students and their families. In this role, school social workers keep the communication open between everyone involved and monitor to determine if the students' and their families' needs are being met (Lourie, Katz-Leavy, & Stroul, 1996). They also check with the family, school personnel, and community agencies involved to monitor and adjust intervention plans. They call meetings so that all the service providers can talk face-to-face with the family and with each other, and they encourage and reinforce people to follow through on the treatment plan.

Case	## Case Example

Mary had been skipping school often. She had little contact with the police and no contact with the community youth service program. Her first behavioral issues appeared in junior high with truancy. The school social worker worked with the family and Mary, yet she continued to be truant from school. A meeting was set up with the family and youth service by the school social worker to develop a plan to redirect Mary's behavior. Mary's behavior improved for approximately 1 month before she started skipping school again.

The school social worker called a meeting to bring in youth service and family services to expand the plan to address Mary's truancy with the family. Out of fear, Mary improved her behavior for approximately 1 month but eventually fell back into old patterns of skipping school. During this noncompliance time, Mary was involved with some car burglaries. During the presentencing phase of the juvenile court proceedings, the school social worker brought the deputy county attorney together with the parents and a representative from the Department of Family Services and Youth Services to explain all the interventions that had been tried with little success.

The case management by the school social worker resulted in a juvenile delinquency petition being signed by the court. The petition placed Mary in a group home for girls, with family and individual counseling ordered. The case management efforts of the school social worker after many attempts finally reached a level of intervention by the court that helped Mary confront her behavior.

ADVOCATE ROLE

Often, school social workers find themselves in the advocate role, working to help students and parents have a voice in the school setting and at the different levels of government. Educational systems can appear large, inflexible, and unresponsive to the needs of students and their families. The purpose of advocacy is to ensure that the student is being represented and to develop support for that student and his or her family. School social workers advocate for students who lack the political clout to be heard. An example of this advocacy is speaking with congressional representatives or testifying at the national level about the conflicting education laws—the No Child Left Behind Act and the Individuals with Disabilities Education Act (IDEA). The former law mandates all students will be proficient in content areas by 2014, and the latter mandates that students in special education have their educational programs individualized to meet their educational needs. In addition to advocacy at the national level, school social workers advocate locally at school board meetings and through writing in local newspapers.

Advocacy for individual students can take the form of sharing information about that student with a teacher or principal in order to help them better understand that student's life. The teacher may not be aware that the student goes home from school to baby-sit and get a brother and sister to bed while facing the uncertainty of the parent's drinking. The purpose of individual advocacy is not to get students out of schoolwork or make excuses but to support them educationally and emotionally by coordinating efforts among the home, school, and community agencies. Many opportunities to advocate for students exist, such as during Individualized Education Plan (IEP) meetings, school intervention team meetings, and child protection team or youth service team meetings.

Shedlin (as cited in Klopf, Shedlin, & Zaret, 1988) argued that schools need to be more responsive to the total child to help that student prepare to learn. The message was that schools need to be a "locus of advocacy" for students. Sheldin observed that schools are a primary institution where problems in students' lives that affect their safety and learning can be identified. If schools were this locus of advocacy, they would advocate for community agencies that reduce barriers to the students' learning. Sheldon saw the advocate role of the school social worker accomplished by the act of joining with outside agencies to reduce these barriers to learning. This theme of advocacy through collaboration was reinforced by Allen-Meares et al. (1986) when they wrote, "School social work must remember that the primary purpose of the school is to educate, not to be a social service agency" (p. 11). In other words, the role of the school social worker is to connect the child and family with community services when needed.

Advocacy can present a unique problem not uncommon in the mental health field. Whom does the school social worker represent in his or her advocacy— the student, the parent, or the school? The student is the primary focus because our responsibilities are to prepare him or her for learning. Understanding that the school is our employer may, at times, result in ethical conflicts. School social workers have to balance what is best for the child and what is dictated by the school district. This is where skills at mediation and problem solving are best used. Being able to combine these skills is the art of school social work.

Since the time of Jane Addams, advocacy has been the role of a school social worker. The case example on the next page illustrates the advocate role of school social work practice.

TRANSITIONAL PLANNER ROLE

The ultimate in wraparound services is showcased in the transitional planning for students on IEPs. Until 1997, transition planning focused on school guidance counselors sitting down with students to plan for post-secondary education through a college, university, or vocational–technical school. The reauthorization of IDEA in 1997 outlined the requirement to start planning with special education students by the time of their 14th birthday. The reauthorization of IDEA in 2004 raised the initial age for transitional planning from 14 to 16 years. This plan, developed by the student's IEP team, starts the process of tailoring the student's educational path through middle and high school. The purpose of this plan is to help students develop abilities and employable skills to prepare them for post-secondary education or work. This plan is reviewed yearly, if not more often, by the student and his or her team to continuously assess the student's progress toward his or her ultimate goal of employment in a field of the student's choosing.

Case	**Case Example**

Charlie was a quiet and shy eighth-grader who had been bullied much of his life by class-mates. The autumn following the Columbine High School shootings, Charlie was begin-ning to make violent remarks toward the kids who were bullying him. Charlie learned that his violent talk was giving him a new sense of power.

That autumn, Charlie had multiple contacts with the principal because of threats he was making toward the students who were teasing him. He had been suspended due to his actions. He had threatened students off the school grounds with a knife and the new sense of power was difficult to give up. A final incident occurred when he threatened some students after school, telling them he was going to shoot them. A risk assessment was done with Charlie's grandmother, the chief of police, his mental health worker, family service worker, and the school social worker. At this point, Charlie had not physically harmed anyone. Yet, all believed that the potential was great. This potential for violence was based on the fact that Charlie, when pushed too far, may have felt like he had to back up this new sense of power with more violent behavior or lose face with his peers.

The school needed to protect the other students and Charlie needed an education. The dilemma was do the "adults" wait for an incident to trigger an explosion in which students might be seriously harmed or killed, or do the adults act in a preventive way to deescalate the situation and provide for Charlie's needs and the safety of the other stu-dents? The school social worker met with Charlie's grandmother and the principal to help broker a solution that would be fair to all. It was a difficult compromise to balance both these needs.

What finally occurred to break the impasse was that Charlie was home schooled by the school district, provided a tutor, and received mental health services. This allowed Charlie to continue his education at home, allowed the situation to cool down, provided mental health services to help Charlie learn to regulate his anger, and reduced the risk of violence. It also allowed the school social worker time to work with those in Charlie's class who chose to bully him and help them learn how their actions contributed to this inci-dent. In addition, it allowed Charlie the opportunity to attend high school the following fall if he completed his work with his mental health counselor.

In the early stages of the plan's development, the student's IEP team is usu-ally made up of educational personnel from the school. As the student advances toward graduation, professionals from vocational rehabilitation services, group homes, adult developmental disability programs, colleges, or vocational–technical schools and other community resources will aid in the student's transition into post-secondary life and work. The plan becomes a "living, breathing" docu-ment that spells out the steps and who will provide services to help the student gain his or her greatest independence vocationally and in life. This document is not static but is reviewed often as skills develop and work experiences are gained.

The role of the school social worker in this process as a member of the IEP team is varied depending on the needs of the student and what the local district has outlined in the school social work job description. As a member of the IEP team, school social workers assess the social and emotional development of a student toward work. They develop, with the team, training opportunities to maximize the student's social skills to handle interactions with the public and other employees. This training occurs in classroom settings where students role-play demands of the workplace, and with job coaches in the school setting and on the job. It may also be part of a specific group counseling program provided by the school social worker to work on behaviors interfering with employment.

There are times when the school social worker coordinates the activities of the IEP team to facilitate planning and execution of the plan. This may include accompanying parents who are unsure of their child's future after high school on visits to community-based adult programs that provide supportive employment and housing.

POLICYMAKER ROLE

Schools are systems governed by policies that direct how educational services will be delivered and who will receive them. School district policies dictate who graduates, the role the school social worker plays, the definition of sexual harassment, the numbers of credits needed for graduation, and how much money is spent on vocational education. Policies of a school district determine whom the school social worker can work with and the scope of his or her services outside of counseling and other duties as assigned. Policies developed by the school board need to be reviewed and compared with state and federal standards to understand how the new policies affect students. Policies should support the

Case | **Case Example**

A need arose on a community child protection team, of which the school social workers were members, to develop more primary prevention programs for the community. Each month when the team met, they continued to deal with the frustration of the aftermath of abuse and neglect. The community child protection team saw that all their efforts were focused on service after the abuse had occurred (tertiary prevention) instead of efforts to educate students and families about protective behaviors to prevent child abuse (primary prevention). The team wanted to focus equally on primary prevention strategies to prevent the victimization of children.

In an effort to reduce incidents of sexual abuse in the community among school-age students, a primary prevention strategy was developed through the school's health program on sexual abuse titled "Personal Safety." The school social workers, along with a school nurse, worked with the Committee for Children of Seattle, Helen Swam (school social worker from Kansas), and the Kemp Center on the curriculum development.

For the personal safety unit to become part of the school's health curriculum, it had to be reviewed and accepted by the curriculum coordinating and administrative councils. Finally, it was presented in a public meeting for acceptance before the school board. The school social worker established the need and presented a solution to address the need. After lengthy discussion by parents and the school board, the curriculum became part of the school curriculum, setting into motion a policy to prevent sexual abuse through a preventive education program.

educational process of the students. Knowingly or unknowingly, policies may come in conflict with the needs of students. School social workers can help school boards learn the negative impact of certain policies. Policies are important governing tenants that can affect students and create barriers. As part of the educational community, the school social worker needs to be alert to new policies and modifications on current policies to monitor their impact on students. The case example on page 62 demonstrates the policymaker role of the school social worker.

SUMMARY

The essence of our profession is the art and science that we combine to perform the multiple roles required to help students experience success in school. The roles of the school social worker open up a multitude of opportunities to affect change, reduce barriers to learning, and help students become independent employable citizens. As clinicians, we work with students and families on emotional and behavioral problems that affect their ability to function in school and life. We collaborate as multidisciplinary team members to develop a comprehensive wraparound approach to help students to grow and gain independence. Our role in the school setting allows us to help students become ready for learning and to teach skills that are imbedded in educational standards. As issues develop in school with students, we find ourselves coordinating services as case managers that help students reduce barriers to learning so they are ready to function in school. As advocates, we find ourselves representing students and their families to the school and, occasionally, representing the school to the student and family. To effectively influence policy, we need to keep a watchful eye on issues that may interfere with the best interest of the students we serve. We must be alert to policies at the local, state and federal levels of government because they can all have an impact on the quality of education.

School Social Work Companion Website

Please be sure to check out our companion website at www.thomsonedu.com/social_work/bye, where you will find relevant materials for each chapter, including flashcards, online practice quizzes, and PowerPoint slides.

References

Allen-Meares, P., Washington, R., & Welsch, B. (1986). *Social work services in schools.* Englewood Cliffs, NJ: Prentice Hall.

Early, B. (1992). An ecological-exchange model of social work consultation within the work group of the school. *Social Work in Education, 14*(4), 207–214.

Individuals with Disabilities Education Act. (1997). Retrieved March 17, 2005, from www.ed.gov/offices/OSERS/Policy/IDEA/index.html

Individuals with Disabilities Education Act. (2004). Retrieved March 17, 2005, from edworkforce.house.gov/issues/109th/education/idea/ideafaq.pdf

Klopf, G., Shedlin, A., Jr., & Zaret, E. (1988). *The school as locus of advocacy for all children*. New York: Elementary School Center.

Lee, W. C. (2002). Let's not get lost in the standards! *Children and Schools, 24*(1), 59–64.

Lourie, I., Katz-Leavy, J., & Stroul, B. (1996). Individualize services in a system of care. In B. A. Stroul (Ed.), *Children's mental health: Creating systems of care in a changing society* (pp. 429–452). Baltimore: Brooks.

National Association of Social Workers. (2002). *NASW standards for school social work practice*. Retrieved May 17, 2004, from www.socialworkers.org/sections/credentials/school_social.asp

U.S. Department of Health and Human Services. (2001). *Report of the Surgeon General's conference on children's mental health: A national action agenda*. Washington, DC: Author. Retrieved February 7, 2003, from www.surgeongeneral.gov/topics/cmh/child report.htm

School Social Work: Policy, Community, and Organizational Practice

5 CHAPTER | # School Social Work at the Policy and Community Level

JAN WILSON, M.S.W., Ed.D.
St. Louis University, St. Louis, Missouri

CHAPTER OVERVIEW

This chapter presents the case for school social workers being involved in policy-level work. After reading this chapter, you will be able to (1) understand why school social work has tended to mostly have a micro-level focus, (2) explain how social work values and the code of ethics support school social work at the policy level, (3) describe the importance of cultural competence in policy work,

(4) be aware of macro-level social work methods, and (5) identify issues related to best practice policy-level work.

INTRODUCTION

Daily school social workers witness the impact of national, state, and local policy in the family poverty, homelessness, high rates of crime, and environmental hazards in their communities. The risks posed to children's academic success from exposure to these conditions are well documented (Dupper, 2003; Hare & Rome, 2002; Jozefowicz-Simbeni & Allen-Meares, 2002). School social workers must be involved at the policy level to address these and other systemic problems that create barriers to learning for students. Unfortunately, some school social workers may not feel prepared to work at the policy level. The majority of school social workers have limited knowledge and expertise in creating and changing policies because the social work profession historically emphasized direct interpersonal practice over macro approaches (Bombyk, 1995; Domanski, 1998; Figueira-McDonough, 1993; Weismiller & Rome, 1995). Although the Council on Social Work Education altered its curriculum policy statement by 1994 to give more support to empowerment and advocacy training, many social workers remain unfamiliar or uncomfortable with macro practice perspectives and methods (Abramovitz, 1998; Bombyk, 1995; Figueira-McDonough, 1993; Hayes, 1998; Vodde & Gallant, 2002; Weismiller & Rome, 1995; Witkin, 1998).

A commitment to the welfare of both individuals and society has inadvertently dichotomized the social work profession since the 1940s (Abramovitz, 1998; Domanski, 1998; Figuiera-McDonough, 1993; Iatridis, 1995; Weismiller & Rome, 1995). The result is that social workers often think of practice as a mutually exclusive choice between micro and macro orientations rather than integrating practice across the two levels. Although macro orientation and practice are described as an essential part of social work practice, many social workers do not share this holistic perspective or recognize macro practice as an essential part of their practice.

In *Unfaithful Angels: How Social Work Has Abandoned Its Mission*, Specht and Courtney (1995) accused social workers of upholding the social status quo and taking a laissez faire attitude toward vulnerable populations and social and economic injustice in their almost uniform preference for careers in psychotherapy and private practice. Weismilller and Rome (1995) noted a values conflict within the profession, finding that some social workers in direct practice believe that political activism is incompatible with the practice standard of being nonjudgmental.

Clancy (1995) called attention to the limitations of clinically oriented school social work in public schools:

> If school social workers' practice focuses only on counseling and treatment of students and families, they are maintaining the status quo because their practice defines the locus of the problem within the micro system. This type of school social work

practice views the students and families as deficient. . . . The actual problems in urban school communities are institutionalized racism, poverty, and the host of social problems these conditions create. (pp. 42–43)

Although school social workers address the immediate needs of students and their families through micro-level interventions, when larger social problems are ignored, school social workers are at risk of becoming "gatekeepers, helping to guard the social status of the dominant class by pacifying oppressed individuals" (Clancy, 1995, p. 42). This perspective is echoed by Dupper and Evans (1996), who noted that "reactive, individualistic practice approaches must give way to more preventive approaches that target systems rather than students for change" (p. 187).

Social Work Code of Ethics and Policy

The 1997 National Association of Social Workers' (NASW) *Code of Ethics*, Section 6, describes the social workers' ethical responsibilities to the broader society. It mandates that social workers engage in social justice practice to uphold the general welfare of society. Social workers are directed toward political action aimed at changing policies and institutions, educating and empowering people to act on their own behalf, and improving conditions to allow people equal access to resources and services to meet their basic needs and reach their potential.

Social Work Values and Policy

The values of the social work profession require school social workers to intervene not just with individual students and their families but also with the oppressive systems that prevent equal educational opportunities for all children. School social workers need to be concerned with major policy issues that target poverty, literacy, job training and employment, and community development (Allen-Meares, 2004b; Constable, McDonald, & Flynn, 2002; Dupper, 2003).

MACRO PRACTICE, SOCIAL JUSTICE, AND SCHOOL SOCIAL WORK

The *Social Work Dictionary* defines **macro practice** as "social work practice aimed at bringing about improvements and changes in general society" and includes "some types of political action, community action, community organization, public education, campaigning, and the administration of broad-based social services agencies or public welfare departments" (Barker, 2003, p. 257). Public education policy and legislation are recognized as aspects of macro practice (Allen-Meares, 2004b; Constable et al., 2002; Dupper, 2003). In the areas of policy analysis and legislative action, professional organizations have resources that help individual school social workers understand and respond to issues that affect professional standards, public education, and social conditions that affect the well-being of children.

Less attention has been paid to other macro practice approaches, such as community and organizational social work. Yet the role of the school social worker as school-home-community liaison is compatible with community and organizational development. During the past decade, macro social work practice has elevated the importance of community and organizational work, recognizing the strengths of community members and empowering their involvement in rebuilding neighborhoods and communities (Brueggemann, 2002). With research identifying parental involvement and community support as crucial to students' educational success, these macro practice methods could take on new importance for school social workers. Those who have a fuller understanding of macro practice methods may be able to establish and strengthen relationships between the school and community stakeholders. One of the weak links in school reform efforts is that school systems continue to have limited success in relationship building with outside constituents.

Social justice is an organizing value of the social work profession and a responsibility of all social workers (Swenson, 1998; Wakefield, 1988). Horejsi (2002) described the two types of justice important to social workers: economic justice (distributive justice), "the fair apportioning of material resources and economic opportunities and burdens," and social justice, "fairness and moral rightness of social and institutional structures" (p. 10). He defined social and economic injustice as "situations of basic unfairness and forms of exploitation, oppression, and discrimination, that are imbedded in social and economic systems such as legal codes, governmental and corporate policy, and societal norms" (p. 11).

Lack of fairness is evident when students who are denied access to equal educational opportunities find career paths closed to them. When public school systems do not provide adequate educational resources and opportunities, some students leave school without acquiring the education and skills needed to secure employment that provides a living wage. The prospect for stable employment and sufficient income to support families is diminished, perpetuating a cycle of poverty (Freire, 2001; Jozefowicz-Simbeni & Allen-Meares, 2002).

MACRO PRACTICE AND CULTURAL COMPETENCE

Culturally competent practice is necessary in macro social work practice in which social workers are likely to be working for the interests of marginalized groups, either directly in community development or coalition building or indirectly in policy analysis and legislative advocacy. NASW standards require social workers to be aware of the effects of social policies and programs on diverse client groups and to advocate for and with clients. Macro social work practice emphasizes the rights of minorities and disenfranchised groups to maintain their culture and heritage, to interpret their experiences of oppression and discrimination, to have their voices heard, and to be respected for their abilities and strengths. Consensus decision making is important because it reduces some of the dynamics of entitlement by establishing more of a part-nership as opposed to a hierarchical power-based relationship (Homan, 2004; NASW, 2001).

Two of the NASW standards for culturally competent social work practice are necessary starting points: (1) developing self-awareness of one's own cultural values and influences and (2) acquiring cross-cultural knowledge about specific groups—the history, traditions, values, ways of relating to other people, verbal and nonverbal communication patterns, family structure, gender roles, religious beliefs, coping mechanisms, patterns of adapting to the dominant culture, and experiences with trauma (Homan, 2004; NASW, 2001). In recognizing the cultural characteristics of diverse groups, it is also important to acknowledge within-group differences and individuals' rights to define their own unique identities, to avoid stereotyping, and to interpret behavior within cultural and situational contexts (Homan, 2004). Competence in these two skills would necessarily precede cross-cultural leadership, another NASW standard that applies to the organizational and societal levels of macro practice, in being able to communicate information about diverse client groups to other professionals (Homan, 2004; NASW, 2001).

Developing cultural competence for macro level work can best be accom-plished in dialogue in which learners exchange feedback with others and with facilitators who have experience and sensitivity (Van Soest & Garcia, 2003). Three national organizations provide cultural competence training and have spe-cific programs for training public school personnel: the Anti-Defamation League (ADL; www.adl.org) World of Difference program, the National Conference for Community and Justice (NCCJ; www.nccj.org), and the National Coalition Building Institute (NCBI; www.ncbi.org). All three organizations include under-standing oppression as an important part of cultural competence. ADL and NCCJ are organized into regional service areas, whereas NCBI is based in Washington, D.C. NCBI adds training on coping with intergroup conflict and building bridges between diverse groups. School social workers can take an important role in meeting the NASW cultural competence standard of profes-sional education by advocating for and implementing ongoing educational and training programs that help school faculty and staff understand and respect diversity (NASW, 2001).

MACRO SOCIAL WORK PRACTICE METHODS

Macro school social work practice has three main tasks: (1) changing social and economic systems that control the availability and access to needed resources, (2) developing resources that are needed but not available, and (3) assisting clients in using their abilities to exercise civil and economic rights (Kirst-Ashman & Hull, 1993). These tasks grow out of the basic commitment to equitable dis-tribution of resources for groups that have historically faced barriers to wealth and power due to gender, race, ethnicity, social class, religion, ability, and sexual orientation. Macro social work takes place at three different levels: community, organizational, and societal/global.

Community Social Work

Community school social work focuses on building and using collective power for change, and strengthening bonds between community members to identify and address the needs of the community. Community workers help individuals in impoverished communities work together to make changes that improve the quality of life, or they help local groups develop and carry out plans to ensure that services are available to those who are in need. Groups meet to plan a course of action for developing social polices and providing social services. Community workers also bring together neighborhood organizations to form coalitions and challenge elements of larger power structures in order to affect systemwide improvement and gain political power (Brueggemann, 2002).

School social workers who want to work in communities need to understand how communities work. Communities have five major social functions: (1) production, distribution, and consumption of goods and services; (2) socialization; (3) social control; (4) social participation; and (5) mutual support. **Community efficacy** is a term that denotes how well a community is functioning on these five dimensions (Kirst-Ashman & Hall, 1993). For community workers, increasing socialization, participation, and mutual support among community members sets off the processes of consciousness raising and critical thinking, the necessary steps to identifying needs for improving social control, addressing inequities in the distribution of goods and services, and increasing civic consciousness and citizen participation.

School social work recognizes the association between characteristics of community efficacy and educational outcomes. The relationship between poverty, community disorganization, and risk of school failure has been well established. For example, Nash (2002) found an association between neighborhood informal social control and the school behavior, attendance, and grades of middle and high school students identified as being at risk for school failure. School coherence, a feeling that the school is a safe and predicable environment, had a strong association with educational behavior, but levels of school coherence were affected by the degree of neighborhood social control and could be negatively impacted by crime and negative peer culture. Nash suggested that neighborhood residents be brought together to reach consensus on goals and to develop strategies for affecting neighborhood social control.

School social workers who intervene in conditions outside of the school environment can apply their skills to the type of efforts recommended by Nash (2002). If the local school district is perceived as part of the community, then it needs to make connections with neighborhood residents as well as with business and professional people. School social workers are generally the only professionals in the school system with the skills to take on grassroots community outreach. Relationships between professionals and community residents need to be collaborative, mutually beneficial, and strengths based (Anderson-Butcher & Ashton, 2004).

School social workers have to address three issues to do community work. First, they have to advocate for changing their role to include regular community

School social workers can assist schools in connecting with the community in the following ways:

- Bringing community residents together to discuss needs, goals, and strategies for improving student achievement
- Working with other grassroots community groups, including churches, recreation centers, women's support groups, block clubs, and business associations, to help residents identify and develop needed services, such as after-school programs, job development programs, and health and mental health services
- Helping community groups to form goal-oriented coalitions to force larger changes in the community, such as reducing crime and obtaining funds for new housing

Nash (2002)

outreach. Educating school administrators about the association between community efficacy and improved educational outcomes may help to accomplish this goal. Second, school social workers need to understand that community approaches must respect the rights of youth and families to become full partners in identifying needs, setting goals, and carrying out social change processes to improve community efficacy (Anderson-Butcher & Ashton, 2004; Brueggemann, 2003; Rubin & Rubin, 2001). For example, school social workers might view youth as competent community builders. When low-income, culturally diverse youth were given opportunities to become involved in decision making, programming, and hands-on community change, they experienced growth and direction in their own lives that led to positive advancements. Many of the youth developed skills in leadership and consensus building (Finn & Checkoway, 1998).

School social workers are encouraged to involve parents in policy advocacy for services that have shown promising results in helping children and families succeed, such as early childhood intervention and after-school and youth development programs (Jozefowicz- Simbeni & Allen-Meares, 2002). Suggestions for family–school–community involvement include having parents and youth serve on local nonprofit agency boards, with youth providing support to peers through community youth councils and peer courts; parents acquiring work experience by serving as tutors, Title I aides, and family support workers; and parents serving on school boards and curriculum committees (Anderson-Butcher & Ashton, 2004). Third, school social workers can help administrators understand that the school district needs to accept a partnership role in community planning and development, sharing power with community residents. The process is not an opportunity for the school system to push its own agenda, impose a top-down hierarchical governance structure, or assume control, even if meeting space is offered on school grounds.

School social workers could take the lead on collaboration efforts, expanding beyond their traditional micro practice role in the schools to include organizational and social change: "School social workers are excellent candidates to encourage the formation of school-based action groups comprising parents and staff and aiming to explore whether proposed legislative changes support the best interests of the school community" (Thorne-Beckerman, 1999, p. 184).

Organizational Social Work

Organizational social workers can be involved with social service or governmental organizations in different ways and at different levels, for example,

- initiating new organizations or programs, starting with the individuals who have identified a service need or concern;
- overseeing personnel, finances, and decision making in established organizations, as well as the mission and quality of service; and
- consulting with administrators of governmental, social service, or corporate organizations to improve organizational functioning (Brueggemann, 2003).

Because school social workers are in a host agency, they are seldom in administrative positions, although they may take on some administrative tasks. There are no statistics on the number of school social workers who go on to work in state departments of education or hold administrative positions in local school districts. However, the few who have done so are in positions to influence policy and practice, as well as advocate for school social work (Clark, 2003; Dibble, 2004).

In 1976, NASW organized Political Action for Candidate Election (PACE) to support national political candidates who endorse the organization's social policies and to educate members about candidates' positions on issues that are important to social workers. By 1998, all NASW state chapters had a PACE network to support candidates for state offices. NASW's efforts have paid off, and a number of social workers have been elected to political offices. As of 2004, six MSW social workers were serving in the U.S. Congress; 12 BSWs, 46 MSWs, 3 DSWs, and 3 social workers (credentials unknown) were holding positions in state legislatures (Colby & Dziegielewski, 2004).

According to NASW (2006), of the 170 social workers elected to public office, 2 serve as senators and 4 serve as representatives. Social workers have also taken an interest in state and local school governance. For example, several serve on state boards of education and local school boards (NASW, 2006). School social workers may also take appointed positions in state departments of education, as liaisons between the government and school districts, or as policy consultants on a variety of issues that affect students, their families, and school social work practice. School social workers are frequently part of school-linked or school-based service arrangements in which schools and community agencies establish formal working relationships to enhance family functioning and support students' educational progress. Franklin and Streeter (1995) outlined five main administrative models for linking public schools and human service agencies: informal relations, coordination, partnerships, collaboration, and integration.

The models vary along eight dimensions of increasingly formal system reform: commitment, planning, training, leadership patterns, resources, funding, scope of change, and impact. The most complex arrangement is the integrated school-linked services model, which has a high degree of formal commitment from both the school and the human services agencies, comprehensive planning on the state level with local input, interdisciplinary teamwork, leadership shared between state and local levels of education and human services, significant system change with new resources and shared initiatives, additional funds for restructuring, total reform of structure and process, and maximum benefit and improved service systems (Franklin & Streeter, 1995). Assessments of needs and resources, mediation, collaborative goal setting, and political action are all social work skills involved in establishing school-linked services agreements.

Public school systems and child welfare agencies experience administrative problems typical of large bureaucracies when they work together to meet children's social, emotional, and educational needs. Educators and social welfare caseworkers may not communicate well or understand the needs and demands of each other's jobs, resulting in confusion and misunderstanding of role expectations that ultimately impact foster children. School social workers have the skills to consult with child welfare agency staff to develop administrative procedures to improve communication, clear up misconceptions, and formalize roles so that goals, objectives, and responsibilities are clarified (Altshuler, 2003; Zetlin, Weinberg, & Kimm, 2003).

Societal Social Work

Social workers who engage in macro practice at the societal or global level are involved in politics, policy development, and social movements with the common purpose of becoming agents for social change.

Policies are "operating principles by which governmental systems carry out their goals in domestic and foreign affairs" (Brueggemann, 2002, p. 349). Most policy analysis is carried out by a professional analyst or an independent policy research group working within government, universities, large businesses, social institutions, professional associations, or special interest groups. Policy analysis

Ways for school social workers to get involved in policy formation:

- Become a candidate for elected office or manage political campaigns.
- Write legislation.
- Lobby.
- Give testimony to legislative bodies.
- Work in regulatory organizations to monitor laws.
- Analyze existing policy and develop proposals.
- Become an activist with a large social change movement.

Brueggemann (2002)

comprises a complex set of procedures for gathering and assessing information on a policy issue. Common methods of inquiry are needs assessments, cost-benefit analysis, cost-effectiveness analysis, outcome studies, case studies, and meta-analysis (Einbinder, 1995). Policy analysis can be undertaken at the community level by people who are directly affected by a social policy. School social workers can help people in their own neighborhoods to define policy issues, gather necessary factual information, develop potential solutions, and communicate recommendations to government. Local policy recommendations can be combined with those from other neighborhoods and sent to regional and national organizations (Brueggemann, 2002).

The Internet has made it possible for the average person to get current information on social policy issues. Websites for various advocacy groups provide policy analysis, position papers, and updates on funding and voting records. It is possible to access full text copies of pending legislation and updates on a bill's progress from state and federal government websites. Generally, World Wide Web sites for professional organizations (such as NASW or the School Social Work Association of America [SSWAA]) and official government offices are the most reliable. Because there are no quality controls on the web, the information from other sites should be carefully evaluated for accuracy and biases. Criteria for evaluating websites can be found in *Social Work and the Web* (Vernon & Lynch, 2000).

NASW and SSWAA are well organized to promote and guide members' involvement in policy analysis and legislative advocacy. Both organizations employ lobbyists and encourage social action by keeping members informed of policy issues through national and state chapter newsletters, websites, and e-mailed action alerts. SSWAA engages in social policy advocacy on national legislative issues relevant to school social work, employing a lobbyist, organizing to communicate information and action alerts to its membership, publicizing voting records of those in Congress, and holding a legislative forum each summer in Washington, D.C. SSWAA has primarily focused on legislation that affects education funding and quality, such as the reauthorizations of the Elementary and Secondary Education Act and the Individuals with Disabilities Education Act, and the regulations that define the role of the school social worker. The organization is concerned with standards of performance and possible national credentialing of school social workers.

Despite the information and action alerts provided by professional organizations such as NASW and SSWAA, not all social workers are committed to legislative advocacy and policy practice. Few social workers are involved in organized political action, participating in public hearings and contacting government officials to express personal views on social policies (Domanski, 1998). For this reason, some social work educators suggest that all social workers should be trained in macro practice skills so that the profession can have more influence on social policy change (Figueira-McDonough, 1993; Weil, 1996).

The first step in political advocacy is to be fully informed about the particular legislative process at the level (school board, city, county, state, or federal) or locality of concern because rules and procedures for introducing, reviewing, and voting on legislation or social policies differ on these dimensions.

Policy activists need to know how to

- get an idea written into a bill and sponsored by a legislator;
- determine whether a companion bill should be introduced;
- identify the key sources of support and then determine whether they will back efforts;
- get legislation referred to the appropriate committee; and
- get a bill on a committee's agenda and then through the committee process.

Ezell (2001)

Suggestions for successful lobbying:

- Be specific and know what you want to convey–sponsorship, support, or opposition to a proposed bill.
- Remember to ask for the legislator's decision or when a follow-up inquiry would be appropriate.
- Give positive feedback to legislators for their support, and make courtesy contacts with those that oppose the legislation or policy.

Ezell (2001)

Establishing good working relationships with elected officials and their staff members is a worthwhile effort. They can be helpful in monitoring progress and offering consultation on successful resolution. When action increases near the end of the process, information can be difficult to track because it is not updated quickly enough. Also, budget bills are difficult for the average person to understand and monitor. Advocating through coalitions increases the number of individuals to cover the work involved in getting legislation passed and provides social workers with important information that is not readily available (Ezell, 2001). Lobbying and giving legislative testimony are two advocacy activities that are accessible to most school social workers. Even though school social workers may not be directly involved in introducing legislation, they can lobby. Lobbying consists of "efforts made to persuade legislators to offer legislative proposals or amendments or to sway their votes for, against, or in favor of modifying a proposal. Lobbying involves persuasion, negotiation, and compromise" (Ezell, 2001, p. 81). School social workers are lobbying when they contact their legislators or other government officials to express their opinions, either of their own volition or in response to legislative alerts from professional organizations, such as NASW and SSWAA.

Advocates have the opportunity to inform lawmakers about client needs by testifying at public hearings, budget hearings, before committees, and at other meetings. Although testimony is not regarded as the best way to influence lawmakers, it has benefits of publicizing an issue and drawing attention

Suggestions for testifying:

- Prepare a two-page summary of arguments, data, research findings, and analysis of proposed policy.
- The statement should be limited to three or four major points.
- Make sure the statement is clearly written, with strongest points at the beginning.
- Include factual data and cites sources.
- Include real-life case examples, if possible.
- Practice the oral presentation before attending the forum.
- Arrive at the forum early in order to watch others testify.
- Give a copy of the written statement to the committee members before speaking.
- Bring a symbol, poster, or slogan that expresses the cause.

Schneider and Lester (2001)

to a particular bill, especially if covered by the media. The time allotted for each party to testify is very brief, ranging from 1 to 5 minutes.

The protocol for addressing the forum is to introduce oneself and include a sponsoring organization; recognize the chairperson and express appreciation for the opportunity to speak; and make a brief statement that establishes the position on the issue, a summary of recommendations, a review of the benefit or harm that will result from the bill, and suggested alternatives. When finished, ask the committee for questions and use the response time to briefly reiterate the major points of the testimony. Advocates are advised to avoid debate with the committee members and to honestly admit when they do not know the answer to a question but offer to get the information to the committee as soon as possible (Schneider & Lester, 2001).

Having clients or community residents testify before committee members carries greater weight with legislators than testimony from service providers, and it has the bonus of empowering clients to testify in their own voices and to participate in the political process. Stories told from personal experiences have more emotional impact than those told from secondary sources. Because the questions from committee members can sometimes be hostile or intimidating, clients will have to be prepared for what to expect and coached on how to respond (Schneider & Lester, 2001).

There is a need for school social workers to engage in social policy advocacy that addresses the larger social and economic systems that impact students' educational progress. Although it is important to understand and intervene in the structural issues affecting achievement in particular school systems or individual schools, there is some question as to whether these efforts really get at the root causes of academic failure. Poverty, parents' educational background, race, and ethnicity persist as the factors that most threaten children's academic success (Jozefowicz-Simbeni & Allen-Meares, 2002; Sipple, 2004).

For example, two issues outside of the school system that school social workers should support are family literacy and Even Start. Programs that improve adult literacy are important to raise family income and support for education within the home. In President Bush's 2004 budget proposal, Even Start, which funds projects that combine early childhood education, parenting instruction, and adult education into family literacy programs, lost a significant amount of fiscal support, and funding for before- and after-school projects was cut approximately 30%.

BEST PRACTICE AND SCHOOL SOCIAL WORK MACRO PRACTICE

A few trends are mentioned in this chapter that may be regarded as best practices for school social work at the macro level. The first is the social work profession's increased focus on social justice. The second is cultural competence. The third is the role of the social worker in client system relationships. For years, social work has been moving toward a partnering relationship with clients and away from a hierarchical expert stance, and this includes sharing power and decision making with clients. This last point may be most difficult for schools to accommodate due to their entrenched bureaucratic, top-down, hierarchical power structure.

Profession building (Reisch & Wenocur, 1986) may be part of the emphasis on the search for best practices, and more research is needed that demonstrates the effectiveness of macro system interventions on children's educational achievement. This is a long-term process; best practice interventions are likely to come from understanding the complex interaction of several variables over time. Studies that use qualitative methods, action research, and case studies should be performed to increase the knowledge base of school social work in macro practice. An example is Altshuler's (2003) study of collaboration between public schools and child welfare agencies, in which focus groups were used to draw suggestions from all constituent groups for improving services to children.

If macro system social work interventions can be shown to have an effect on student grades, test scores, attendance, or other educational indicators, then schools may become more interested in community work and school social workers may become more interested in working, quite literally, outside of the box. More needs to be done to train social workers in school systems to be more proficient in research skills, to avoid relying solely on the academic community to document intervention methods.

The ability of school social workers to engage in macro practice is dependent on the extent to which they have the power to negotiate their role in the school system. Social work responsibilities in public schools are defined in federal legislation and regulations as well as in guidelines set by the state departments of education. They are subject to variance across local districts and even within individual schools, depending on whether administrators understand, value, and grant autonomy to the social workers under their supervision.

School social workers can always engage in legislative advocacy through professional organizations on their own time. It is time for school social workers to promote practice changes that incorporate the larger vision and mandate of macro social work practice, one that includes grassroots organizing, administrative duties, policy analysis, and social action methods within public education systems and government institutions.

SUMMARY

School social workers need to actively address policies that create barriers to learning for students. By collaborating with families, school personnel, community stakeholders, and legislators, school social workers can help create and maintain policies that prevent problems and allow every child the support necessary to succeed in school. School social workers can use their group work, advocacy, and organizing skills to bring community members and local organizations together to define policy issues, gather information, and make recommendations to local school boards as well as state and national legislators. It is important that school social workers reassess their role in the public schools and place more emphasis on community- and policy-level work.

School Social Work Companion Website

Please be sure to check out our companion website at www.thomsonedu.com/social_work/bye, where you will find relevant materials for each chapter, including flashcards, online practice quizzes, and PowerPoint slides.

References

Abramovitz, M. (1998). Social work and social reform: An arena of struggle. *Social Work, 43*(6), 512–526.

Allen-Meares, P. (2004a). School social work: Historical development, influences, and practices. In P. Allen-Meares (Ed.), *Social work services in schools* (4th ed., pp. 23–51). Boston: Allyn & Bacon.

Allen-Meares, P. (Ed.). (2004b). *Social work services in schools* (4th ed.). Boston: Allyn & Bacon.

Altshuler, S. J. (2003). From barriers to successful collaboration: Public schools and child welfare working together. *Social Work, 48*(1), 52–63.

Anderson-Butcher, D., & Ashton, D. (2004). Innovative models of collaboration to serve children, youths, families, and communities. *Children & Schools, 26*(1), 39–53.

Barker, R. L. (2003). *The social work dictionary* (5th ed.). Washington, DC: National Association of Social Workers.

Bombyk, M. (1995). Progressive social work. In R. L. Edwards (Ed.), *Encyclopedia of social work* (19th ed., Vol. 3, pp. 1933–1942). Washington, DC: National Association of Social Workers.

Brueggemann, W. G. (2002). *The practice of macro social work.* Belmont, CA: Wadsworth/Thomson Learning.

Clancy, J. (1995). Ecological school social work: The reality and the vision. *Social Work in Education, 17*(1), 40–47.

Clark, J. (2003). *Iowa's non-categorical special education model: Implications for school social work practice*. Paper presented at the 36th annual Midwest School Social Work Conference, Cedar Rapids, IA.

Colby, I., & Dziegielewski, S. (2004). *Introduction to Social work: The people's profession* (2nd ed.). Chicago: Lyceum.

Constable, R., McDonald, S., & Flynn, J. P. (Eds.). (2002). *School social work: Practice, policy, and research perspectives* (5th ed.). Chicago: Lyceum.

Dibble, N. (2004, Spring). Revenues generated for school districts by school social work services. *School Social Work Section Connection, 1*, 11–12.

Domanski, M. D. (1998). Prototypes of social work political participation: An empirical model. *Social Work, 43*(2), 156–167.

Dupper, D. R. (2003). *School social work: Skills and interventions for effective practice*. New York: John Wiley.

Dupper, D. R., & Evans, S. (1996). From Band-Aids to putting out fires to prevention: School social work practice approaches for the new century. *Social Work in Education, 18*(3), 187–192.

Einbinder, S. D. (1995). Policy analysis. In R. L. Edwards (Ed.-in Chief), *Encyclopedia of social work* (19th ed., Vol. 3, pp. 1849–1855). Washington, DC: National Association of Social Workers.

Ezell, M. (2001). Legislative advocacy. In M. Ezell (Ed.), *Advocacy in human services* (pp. 74–97). Belmont, CA: Brooks/Cole Thomas.

Figueira-McDonough, J. (1993). Policy practice: The neglected side of social work intervention. *Social Work, 38*(2), 179–188.

Finn, J. L., & Checkoway, B. (1998). Young people as competent community builders: A challenge to social work. *Social Work, 43*(4), 335–345.

Franklin, C., & Streeter, C. (1995). School reform: Linking public schools with human services. *Social Work, 40*(6), 773–782.

Freire, P. (2001). *Pedagogy of the oppressed* (M. B. Ramos, Trans.). New York: Continuum.

Hare, I., & Rome, S. H. (2002). The developing social, political, and economic context for school social work. In R. Constable, S. McDonald, & J. P. Flynn (Eds.), *School social work: Practice, policy, and research perspectives* (5th ed., pp. 101–121). Chicago: Lyceum.

Hayes, K. S. (1998). The one hundred-year debate: Social reform versus individual treatment. *Social Work, 43*(6), 501–509.

Homan, M. (2004). *Promoting community change: Making it happen in the real world* (3rd ed.). Belmont, CA: Brooks/Cole.

Horejsi, C. R. (2002). Social and economic justice: The basics. *The New Social Worker, 9*(3), 10–12.

Iatridis, D. S. (1995). Policy practice. In R. L. Edwards (Ed.-in-Chief), *Encyclopedia of social work* (19th ed., Vol. 3, pp. 1855–1866). Washington, DC: National Association of Social Workers

Jozefowicz-Simbeni, D. M. H., & Allen-Meares, P. (2002). Poverty and schools: Intervention and resource building through school linked services. *Children & Schools, 24*(2), 123–136.

Kirst-Ashman, K. K., & Hull, G. H. (1993). *Understanding generalist practice*. Chicago: Nelson-Hall.

Nash, J. K. (2002). Neighborhood effects on sense of school coherence and educational behavior in students at risk of school failure. *Children & Schools, 24*(2), 73–89.

National Association of Social Workers. (1997). *Code of ethics.* Washington, DC: Author.

National Association of Social Workers. (2001). *NASW standards for cultural competence in social work practice.* Washington, DC: Author.

National Association of Social Workers. (2006). *General fact sheet: Social work profession.* Retrieved January 30, 2006, from www.naswdc.org/pressroom/features/general/profession.asp

Reisch, M., & Wenocur, S. (1986, March). The future of community organization in social work: Social activism and the politics of profession building. *Social Service Review,* 70–93.

Rubin, H. J., & Rubin, I. S. (2001). *Community organizing and development* (3rd ed.). Needham Heights, MA: Allyn & Bacon.

Schneider, R. U., & Lester, L. (2001). *Social work advocacy.* Stamford, CT: Brooks/Cole Thomson Learning.

Sipple, J. (2004). Major issues in American schools. In P. Allen-Meares (Ed.), *Social work services in schools* (4th ed., pp. 1–21). Boston: Pearson.

Specht, H., & Courtney, M. (1995). *Unfaithful angels: How social work has abandoned its mission.* New York: Free Press.

Swenson, C. R. (1998). Clinical social work's contribution to a social justice perspective. *Social Work, 43*(6), 527–537.

Thorne-Beckerman, A. (1999). Postmodern organizational analysis: An alternative framework for school social workers. *Social Work in Education, 21*(3), 177–188.

Van Soest, D., & Garcia, B. (2003). *Diversity education for social justice: Mastering teacher skills.* Alexandria, VA: Council on Social Work Education.

Vernon, R., & Lynch, D. (2000). *Social work and the Web.* Belmont, CA: Wadsworth.

Vodde, R., & Gallant, J. P. (2002). Bridging the gap between micro and macro practice: Large scale change and a unified model of narrative–deconstructive practice. *Journal of Social Work Education, 38*(3), 439–458.

Wakefield, J. C. (1988). Psychotherapy, distributive justice, and social work. *Social Service Review, 62*(2), 187–210.

Weil, M. O. (1996). Community building: Building community practice. *Social Work, 41*(5), 481–499.

Weismiller, T., & Rome, S. H. (1995). Social workers in politics. In R. L. Edwards (Ed.-in-Chief), *Encyclopedia of social work* (19th ed., Vol. 3, pp. 2305–2313). Washington, DC: National Association of Social Workers.

Witkin, S. L. (1998). Is social work an adjective? *Social Work, 43*(6), 483–486.

Zetlin, A., Weinberg, L., & Kimm, C. (2003). Are the educational needs of children in foster care being addressed? *Children & Schools, 25*(2), 105–119.

6

CHAPTER

School Social Work at the School Organization Level

A N D Y F R E Y , M . S . W . , P h . D .
University of Louisville

H I L L W A L K E R , P h . D .
University of Oregon

CHAPTER OUTLINE

CHAPTER OVERVIEW

School social work at the organization level provides an important vehicle to address a wide range of school safety and socioeconomic and cultural issues. This chapter addresses (1) school social work practice at the school organization level; (2) adoption, implementation, coordination, and evaluation of schoolwide interventions; (3) teaching practices designed to improve students' academic and behavioral success; and (4) integration of interventions at the individual, family, and community levels.

INTRODUCTION

A dramatic increase in the number of sensationalized mass school shootings and studies exploring students' perceptions of school violence (Kingery, Coggeshall, & Alford, 1998) and victimization (Furlong, Chung, Bates, & Morrison, 1995) during the mid- to late 1990s resulted in a heightened awareness among educators, the general public, policymakers, and legislators regarding the various adjustment problems children face at home, school, and in community contexts. These developments suggest that children today are more at risk than they have been at any time in the recent past, and they are more likely to follow a developmental trajectory that ends in delinquency, violence, school failure, and a host of other negative outcomes (Sprague & Walker, 2000). The national spotlight on school safety and poor outcomes for at-risk youth have broadened the definition of school violence to include lower level acts of violence (peer pressure, put-downs, verbal intimidation, teasing, bullying, and harassment) that may escalate to physical intimidation and assault.

In addition to school safety, a number of schooling issues suggest the educational community is systematically failing when it comes to educating certain subgroups of children. During the past 30 years, the average national test scores in reading, math, and science have remained stable. However, when the subgroup of students eligible for free/reduced lunch is compared to the group of students who do not qualify, profound differences between these students' academic performance emerge. Although mild gains have occurred for both groups, the gap between students in high poverty and those who are not remains relatively high (Sadovnik, Cookson, & Semel, 2001).

The research related to school-based mental health services clearly indicates that intervening at the school organization level constitutes a best practice. For example, research demonstrates that the ecology of schools is highly germane to student success because behavior and academic problems are both context specific (McEvoy & Welker, 2000) and that a positive and open school climate increases student achievement (Cummings, 1986; Fine, 1991; Hoy, Hannum, & Tschannen-Moran, 1998; Kagan, 1990; Reyes, 1989) as well as ratings of a school's effectiveness (Hoy, Tarter, & Kottkamp, 1991). School climate is the most important variable in schools exceeding their academic expectations based on the percentage of poor children enrolled (Glidden, 1999). Positive school and peer cultures increase school bonding, which is a key protective influence for children (Hawkins, Farrington, & Catalano, 1998). The use of proactive classroom management strategies reduces classroom disruption and increases learning (Gettinger, 1988; Jones, 1996). Finally, school and classroom factors significantly reduce antisocial forms of behavior, improve attendance, decrease dropouts and suspensions, increase time spent on homework assignments, and facilitate cooperation and positive social relations among students and staff (Mayer et al., 1993). Therefore, school organization-level interventions and teaching practices are an important vehicle for addressing school safety, academic achievement, and socioeconomic and cultural issues. School social workers have important contributions to make toward creating positive school climates, peer cultures, and classroom environments.

SCHOOL-BASED ORGANIZATIONAL-LEVEL INTERVENTIONS

This section reviews several recommended interventions at the school organization level. School organization-level interventions are distinct from other intervention types because they are implemented across the entire school setting and for a substantial period of time (at least 1 year). Although some of the interventions and teaching practices discussed in this section can be implemented in individual classrooms or on a time-limited basis, doing so is not recommended. The goal of many schoolwide interventions is to reduce or eliminate problem behavior and maximize prosocial behavior (via primary prevention) for as many students as possible and to implement well-established procedures for addressing problematic behavior when it occurs (via secondary and tertiary prevention), with the ultimate goal of improving students' academic and social competence performance. Other interventions also attempt to create an atmosphere that eliminates racism and homophobia, celebrates diversity, and increases student involvement in decision making and school governance. Excluded from this section are interventions that focus primarily on parents or families, which are the focus of Chapter 8. Table 6.1 offers some examples of effective programs in this regard. School social workers need to advocate for organizational-level programs that limit or prevent problems.

Table 6.1 | Examples of School Organization-Level Intervention Programs

Program; Author/ Website	Type/Program Components	Description
Early Screening Project (pre-K); www.nekesc.org/kids/esp .html The Systematic Screening for Behavior Problems (K-2); www.sopriswest.com/swst ore/product.asp?sku=102	Early screening	The procedures for both of these efficient and low-cost mass-screening procedures involve three stages, or "gates." In the first stage, teachers rate the three highest students in their class on internalizing and externalizing behavioral dimensions. For these students, the teacher completes brief rating scales. Children who exceed normative criteria pass

Program; Author/ Website	Type/Program Components	Description
		through the second gate and are observed in the classroom and on the playground. Children who again exceed normative criteria are referred for intervention or to the Child Study Team.
School Wide Information System (SWIS); Rob Horner, Ph.D., College of Education, University of Oregon, www.swis.org	Early screening	SWIS is a web-based software program for entering, organizing, and reporting office discipline referrals in schools. This system computerizes discipline referrals within archival school records and provides valuable information to teachers and administrators. Schools that adopt SWIS must pay an annual fee of $200 and meet a series of eight requirements to access SWIS's staff development training and program reports.
Effective Behavioral Support (EBS); contact George Sugai at (541) 346-1642 or Rob Horner at (541) 346-2460 or http://cecp.air.org/ resources/success/ebs.htm	Schoolwide discipline	EBS approaches (1) target all students in the school; (2) coordinate the implementation of universal, targeted, and selected interventions; and (3) focus on positive, proactive approaches. EBS is a popular intervention approach that has been adopted in more than 400 schools nationwide, and it will likely be adopted by many more in the years to come. This program teaches behavioral expectations to all students and requires buy-in from all school personnel. Implementation takes at least 2 years.

continued

Table 6.1 | Examples of School Organization-Level Intervention Programs *continued*

Program; Author/ Website	Type/Program Components	Description
*Peace Builders; wwwkel.lkwash.wednet .edu/html/Peacebldrs.htm	Schoolwide discipline	Teaches five universal principles: (1) praise people, (2) avoid put-downs, (3) seek wise people as advisors and friends, (4) notice and correct hurts we cause, and (5) right wrongs.
Building Effective Schools Together (BEST); contact Jeff Sprague at (541) 726-0512 or www.calstat.org/BEST_ guidelines.pdf	Schoolwide discipline	BEST provides a highly recommended approach for schools to use to create orderly, positive, and well-managed school environments.
*Second Step; available from the Committee for Children, Seattle, WA, 1-800-634-4449, www.cfchildren.org/ program_ss.shtml	Conflict resolution/social problem solving	Second Step is another highly recommended curriculum-based intervention for creating a positive peer culture and for teaching individuals to resolve conflicts peacefully. Second Step teaches social skills, including empathy, impulse control, and anger management. This program was rated by an expert panel of the Safe and Drug Free Schools Division of the U.S. Department of Education as the most effective program of its kind.
*Promoting Alternative Thinking Strategies (PATHS); contact Carol A. Kusche at (206) 323-6688 or ckusche @attglobal.net	Conflict resolution/ social problem solving	131-lesson curriculum designed to build self-esteem and improve communication. Generalization of skills to the home setting is emphasized.
Positive Adolescents Choices Training; www.hamfish.org/ programs/id/53	Conflict resolution/social problem solving	Targets high-risk youth who have serious behavior problems or a history of violence, victimization, or

Program; Author/ Website	Type/Program Components	Description
		exposure to violence. Twenty 1-hour group sessions focus on social skills training, violence awareness, and anger management for African American youth.
Gang Resistance Education and Training; www.atf.gov/great/	Conflict resolution/ social problem solving	Designed to reduce youth violence and gang membership through a nine-lesson curriculum.
School Survival Group; Dupper (2002)	Conflict resolution/ social problem solving	Group intervention for middle/junior high school students with school behavior problems. Changing students' perceptions about the extent to which they have control over their school behavior.
*I Can Problem Solve: An Interpersonal Cognitive Problem-Solving Program (ICPS); www.hamfish.org/pro grams/id/52	Conflict resolution/social problem solving	ICPS serves as an effective violence prevention program by helping children think of nonviolent ways to solve everyday problems.
*Aggression Replacement Training; www.researchpress.com /scripts/product.asp?item =5004	Conflict resolution/social problem solving	A comprehensive intervention for aggressive youth combining anger management, moral education, and social skills training.
Students for Peace	Conflict resolution/social problem solving	Coordinated curriculum (from Second Step) and organized "peace-related" activities.
Character Counts!; www.charactercounts.org	Peer mediation (also has peer counseling and parent outreach components) Character education	The program teaches and develops consensus regarding values that cut across race, creed, politics, gender, and wealth. The curriculum I program is designed for students aged 4–19.
*Child Development Project; www.cdp.auburn.edu	Character education	Focuses on the long-term development of prosocial

continued

Table 6.1 │ Examples of School Organization-Level
Intervention Programs *continued*

Program; Author/ Website	Type/Program Components	Description
		behavior while deemphasizing extrinsic control of rewards and punishers. Emphasizes constructivist strategies for developing social responsibility, intrinsic motivation, and prosocial behavior.
*Bullying Prevention Program; www.state.ma.us/ccj/bully.htm	Bullying prevention (also considered school reform)	Increases the awareness of bullying and develops protection for victims.
Steps to Respect; www.cfchildren.org/program_str.shtml	Bullying prevention (also considered school reform)	Increases adult awareness of bullying and teaches them to respond to it appropriately.
*Seattle Social Development Project; depts.washington.edu/ssdp	School reform (also has conflict resolution/social problem solving and classroom management components)	Designed to develop children's communication, conflict resolution, and problem-solving skills. Teachers are trained in classroom management, interactive teaching, and cooperative learning.
School Development Program; http://info.med.yale.edu/comer	School reform (culture/climate)	Transforms school culture (primarily for low-income, African American youth) by restructuring school governance and management to include students, administrators, teachers, parents, and support staff.
Success for All; www.successforall.com/resource/research/everychild.htm	School reform (culture/climate)	Schoolwide reform effort for serving disadvantaged students. Provides individual academic assistance, family support, and addresses institutional racism in schools.
*School Transitional Environment Project;	School reform (culture/climate)	Transforms school culture and climate to enhance the

Program; Author/ Website	Type/Program Components	Description
www.colorado.edu/cspv/ publications/factsheets/ blueprints/FS-BPP12.html		transition from elementary to middle or middle to high school.
Project ACHIEVE; www.projectachieve.info	School reform (also has conflict resolution/social problem solving and classroom management components)	Comprehensive school reform project that includes classroom management techniques; social skills training, social problem solving, and self-control management; problem-solving consultation; remedial instruction; and a home–school collaboration component.
Project 10; www.project10.org	School reform	Provides on-site educational support services to gay, lesbian, bisexual, and questioning youth; workshops to train counselors, teachers, and other staff regarding sexual orientation issues; and codes of behavior with regard to name calling.
CoZi Model; www.yale.edu/21c/ affiliated.html info.med.yale.edu/comer	School reform	Combines Edward Zigler's School of the 21st Century (on-site preschool, after-school care, and family support services) and James Comer's School Development Program (school management and collaborative decision making).

*Recognized as a model, exemplary, or promising program by the Surgeon General (www.surgeongeneral.gov/ library/youthviolence/chapter5/sec3.html#PrimaryPrevention), the Center for the Study and Prevention of Violence (www.colorado.edu/cspv), or the Safe, Disciplined, and Drug Free School Expert Panel (www.ed.gov/offices/OERI/ORAD/KAD/expert_panel/drug-free.html).

Early Screening

School social workers can encourage systematic screening to identify students whose current behavior places them at elevated risk for serious behavioral difficulties later in their schooling. Such screening procedures must first monitor all students at the point of school entry and refer possible at-risk students for early intervention services or more intensive assessments (Scott & Nelson, 1999). Standardized instruments or archival school records can provide valuable screening information. The latter data source can be used to profile an entire school, small groups of students, and selected individuals within a school. School discipline records are an inexpensive yet extremely valuable source of information that can not only identify student adjustment problems but also help schools better understand their own responses to adjustment problems (Feil, Walker, & Severson, 2001).

Violence Prevention

Although the ultimate goal of schooling is improved student achievement, most violence prevention interventions also address school culture/climate and connectedness. As previously mentioned, positive school and classroom climates are associated with "effective schools" or schools in which students, especially those from disadvantaged backgrounds, excel academically (Griffith, 1999). Schools with positive school cultures are characterized by leaders who instill in students a sense of fairness, belongingness, and empowerment to affect change and also establish an atmosphere in which students and staff members respect each other's rights (Hyman & Snook, 2000). Payne, Conroy, and Racine (1998) suggest that evidence of positive school climate includes community involvement; high daily attendance; positive attitudes of teachers, students, and parents; a sense of ownership and pride in the school; and high levels of participation in schoolwide and systemwide activities. Another common theme among violence prevention efforts is the creation of a sense of connectedness between youth and peers, family, school, and community, which school social workers are skilled at fostering. School connectedness has been identified as an important protective factor in several studies, and evidence suggests the relationship may be causal (Catalano & Hawkins, 1996; Resnick et al., 1997).

Schoolwide Discipline/Rules and Behavioral Expectations

Universal interventions designed for schoolwide application are a proven vehicle for establishing a school climate that is positive, inclusive, and accepting of all cultures and types of diversity. Walker, Colvin, and Ramey (1995) described discipline as an instrument that allows instruction and learning to take place, whereas Scott and Nelson (1999) defined schoolwide discipline as "an extension of traditional discipline to the entire school building, implemented by agreement across all school staff" (p. 57). Several programs advocate that discipline procedures must be positive, consistently followed, and communicated clearly to all parties (students, parents, teachers, and other school staff).

Conflict Resolution and Social Problem Solving

Conflict resolution curricula teach children to use alternatives to violence and often rely on instruction and discussion to alter their perceptions, attitudes, and skills relating to violence and conflict resolution. These programs often provide knowledge about violence and conflict, increase students' awareness and understanding of their own and others' feelings, and teach the strategies and skills necessary to avoid violence (Peterson & Skiba, 2001). Conflict resolution curricula emphasize understanding conflict and are negotiation based. A similar type of violence prevention strategy, cognitive social problem solving, teaches students to understand others' feelings and instructs students to use problem-solving strategies for resolving interpersonal problems. Lessons typically include information on the prevalence of violence or conflict, identifying and expressing feelings, managing anger, using conflict resolution, appreciating diversity, and coping with stress. Problem-solving programs are based on the assumption that, as a group, aggressive children do not think about the consequences of their behavior prior to acting (Peterson & Skiba, 2001).

Content for curriculum-based programs is delivered through lectures, class meetings, or discussions, and most programs also have a role-play component. Conflict resolution and problem-solving curricula are generally one component of a broader program that also includes peer mediation, school discipline, and/or classroom management components. Since curriculum-based, schoolwide violence prevention programs are fairly recent, few large-scale evaluations of them have been completed. However, one review of the literature found that the most successful programs include emotion-focused strategies such as relaxation, increased awareness of self and others, cognitive strategies such as problem solving and self-regulation, and specific skills in communication and assertiveness (Smith, Larson, DeBaryshe, & Salzman, 2000).

Peer Mediation

Negotiation-based, peer mediation programs teach student mediators strategies to help settle disputes among their peers. As a result, mediators and disputants learn alternative skills to use when resolving conflicts. The peer mediator serves as an objective third party whose goal is to help peers find a solution that is "win-win" rather than "win-lose" through the use of an interest-based negotiation procedure along with communication and problem-solving strategies (Fisher & Ury, 1991). Some programs train the entire school in the negotiation procedures, whereas other programs train the peer mediators, who in turn train the students as conflicts arise (Peterson & Skiba, 2001). Although peer mediation programs can be implemented as stand-alone programs, they are best used as one piece of a broader violence prevention or conflict resolution intervention.

The popularity and use of peer mediation programs are clearly disproportionate to the research on their effectiveness (Peterson & Skiba, 2001). Despite this limitation, students appear to be able to learn the negotiation steps, use them as designed, and sustain their involvement over several months. Peer mediation programs also alter the climate of the school and change how students approach and resolve peer conflicts. The planning and fidelity of peer mediation programs appear extremely important to their success.

Character Education

Character education programs provide guidance to youth by teaching them prosocial values to guide their lives in and outside school. Character education includes two primary components: (1) education in civic virtue and in the qualities that teach children the forms and rules of citizenship in a just society and (2) education in personal adjustment, or the qualities that allow them to become productive and dependable citizens. Character education programs involve many components, such as instruction in social skills, moral development, values clarification, and school values (Peterson & Skiba, 2001). School social workers can deliver or help others deliver these components together or as stand-alone instructional units. Although not always classified as character education, programs that incorporate cooperative learning strategies, participatory decision making, and service learning can be thought of as character education. Many elementary schools have developed schoolwide values statements that provide a foundation for behavioral expectations within the school (Peterson & Skiba, 2001). These statements are displayed throughout the school and on official school documents, such as stationary, newsletters to parents, and even official codes of conduct. These values can be reinforced by recognizing students whose behavior is consistent with them via publicly posting their names in the office, presenting certificates, providing special privileges, or giving tangible rewards.

No large-scale studies have examined the use of character education programs to prevent violence or reduce behavior problems. However, the Institute of Education Sciences has funded scientific research to test its effectiveness at the elementary school level.

Anti-Bullying Interventions

Peterson and Skiba (2001) stated that "a student is being bullied when exposed, repeatedly over time, to intentional injury or discomfort inflicted by one or more other students" (p. 173). **Bullying** is recognized as an ongoing form of harassment or abuse (Olweus, 1991); it is a special category of school violence that involves an imbalance of power or strength between the perpetrator(s) and victim, wherein the incidents are repeated over time, and there is the intention of doing harm to the victim. Bullying is a pervasive problem in U.S. schools, impacting between 15 and 20% of school-aged children (Nasel et al., 2001; Olweus, 1993).

Bullying has short- and long-term effects on not only victims but also bullies and bystanders (Dupper, 2002). Bullying negatively impacts the school's climate by creating an environment in which students are intimidated and less than satisfied with school (Olweus, Limber, & Mihalic, 1999). Bully prevention programs generally involve schoolwide efforts designed to change the climate of the school with regard to peer-based harassment. Effective programs combine a number of components, such as improved supervision, classroom rules prohibiting bullying, consequences for not following rules, and debriefing discussions with victims and bullies.

There is substantial research indicating that well-designed and implemented bullying prevention programs can reduce, eliminate, and/or prevent bully-victim problems and also help improve overall school climate (Peterson & Skiba, 2001). The essential elements of bullying prevention programs appear to be awareness and adult involvement. Thus, many successful programs have lengthy assessment phases in which parents, children, and school faculty share experiences with and beliefs about bullying. This information is often gathered through anonymous student surveys. Bullying prevention programs include schoolwide components, classroom components, and individual components. The focus on changing norms governing peer-directed behavior requires systematic efforts over time.

SCHOOL REFORM

Whole school reform efforts involve comprehensive programming to alter the culture and climate of the school; reform efforts often include some of the violence prevention strategies previously discussed. However, whole school reform efforts have additional intervention components, such as restructuring of the cultural inclusiveness of the curriculum and/or family support. A number of whole school reform interventions are designed specifically for vulnerable groups of students, such as those with known or presumed gay or lesbian orientation, children of color, and students being integrated into school from residential and juvenile justice settings.

Cultural Inclusiveness

School social workers can raise awareness of the importance of an inclusive school environment and curriculum. Currently, education curriculum and teaching practices are overwhelmingly Eurocentric. These practices have subverted other ways of knowing and marginalize the experiences and backgrounds of children of color. In culturally inclusive schools, the diversity of the student population is reflected in the school's physical environment and the educational materials used (Baskin, 2002). For example, holistic learning methodologies that include storytelling, drama, song, and experiential activities are consistent with Aboriginal culture. Incorporating the cultural history of American Indians, Mexican Americans, African Americans, Asian Americans, and other people of color into the curriculum is of critical importance for creation of an inclusive, culturally competent school setting and climate.

CLASSROOM MANAGEMENT PRACTICES

Classroom management teaching practices become school organization-level interventions when similar policies and procedures govern all classrooms within a school and when all teachers share similar knowledge and skills with regard to classroom management. With classroom management, teachers are the primary implementation agents and the school social worker provides the support that allows teachers to manage classrooms effectively.

Preventative Classroom Management

In a classic study by Kounin (1970), the primary factor that distinguished effective from ineffective teachers was their ability to prevent discipline problems in the classroom and their handling of minor problems immediately. Once minor discipline problems fester and require direct intervention, they have the potential to disrupt the classroom and pull the teacher away from the teaching-learning process. Despite the overwhelming consistency in the research regarding what constitutes effective classroom management, teachers are more likely to rely on punitive strategies, especially with children who exhibit externalizing behavior problems (Bear, 1998; Brophy, 1996).

Effective classroom management begins by developing caring relationships with students (Phelan, Davidson, & Cao, 1992). Simple strategies that school social workers can encourage teachers to incorporate into their daily classroom management plan include greeting students as they enter their classrooms (try to say something of a personal nature), joining in playground/extracurricular games, going to school and community events, writing personal notes to students on tests and quizzes, and providing a suggestion box in class (Pigford, 2001). Developing a democratic classroom is another strategy to foster positive relationships between teachers and students. In democratic classrooms, teachers emphasize cooperation, mutual goal setting, and shared responsibility (Hyman & Snook, 2000). Ideally, students behave out of a sense of social responsibility and because they respect the rights of others.

Next, classroom rules should be clearly defined and communicated to students and parents. Rules must be rational and easily understood, stated positively, fit within the structure of the school code of conduct, not be excessive in number, and address performance expectations as well as ethical or moral behavior. Often, teachers assume students enter their classrooms with the skills necessary to follow classroom rules, which can be a risky assumption. Teachers need to provide direct instruction for expected behaviors that are not immediately or acceptably performed, and classrooms should also have regular parent-teacher communication systems. The presence of effective incentives and motivational systems for following the rules is also essential. These motivational systems require extensive knowledge regarding operant learning strategies, which are addressed briefly next.

Operant Learning Strategies

School social workers must have a working knowledge of operant learning strategies, whose effectiveness in increasing desirable student behavior and decreasing undesirable behavior is well documented. Extensive research has identified which interventions are likely to lead to behavioral and academic improvements for children with emotional and behavioral problems and which interventions do not (Dunlap & Childs, 1996; Gresham, Sugai, & Horner, 2001; Quinn, Kavale, Mathur, Rutherford, & Forness, 1999; Skiba & Casey, 1985; Stage & Quiroz, 1997). Behaviorally based interventions involving reinforcement, cooperation, cognitive behavioral strategies, group contingencies, self-management, and behavioral consultation are consistently found to be more effective than interventions based on other theoretical orientations.

The most commonly used operant learning strategies involve privileges (e.g., extra recess), social rewards (e.g., teacher praise, peer recognition, and notes home to parents), and tangible rewards (e.g., stickers, prizes, and certificates). The limitations of operant strategies, especially with regard to their lack of attention to emotion and cognition in motivation and behavior, are also well documented (Lepper, Keavney, & Drake, 1996). Thus, operant learning strategies need to be balanced with the use of social cognitive and problem-solving strategies for developing self-discipline. The most highly effective teachers use these strategies in combination to promote the long-term goals of self-discipline and self-regulation.

ROLES FOR SCHOOL SOCIAL WORKERS AT THE ORGANIZATIONAL LEVEL

Using a strengths-based perspective, diverse skills sets at both the micro and macro levels, and the knowledge base outlined in the previous section, school social workers can work effectively with school administrators who have generally been open to, but skeptical about, investing in comprehensive, positive, behavioral support approaches that address the needs of all students. School social workers can adopt several roles to be effective at the school organization level, including schoolwide service coordinator, assessor, advocate, consultant, trainer, intervention coordinator, and evaluator. Other chapters in this book address the consultant and evaluator roles; therefore, these are not discussed here. The remaining roles, although not new to school social work, are discussed in relation to the assessment and intervention process at the school organization level. All of these roles put the social worker in the position of a change agent who primarily attempts to alter student perceptions, behavior, and performance by changing the attitudes and beliefs of school faculty and staff or by changing the school environment. These roles also ensure the school social worker's efforts will be perceived as central to the mission and goals of the school. Assuming these roles is likely to result in systemic school organizational change.

Schoolwide Service Coordinator

Walker, Sprague, and Severson (2003) described the essential components of a comprehensive approach for attending to the mental health needs of all students within a school. Their conceptualization of an integrated prevention model is based on the U.S. Public Health Service's classification of prevention approaches: primary (prevent onset), secondary (reduce emerging problems), and tertiary (reduce or reverse ongoing damage). Figure 6.1 illustrates these prevention approaches and the approximate proportion of students who are likely to need and respond to each type of prevention within school populations.

There is generally a lack of coordination among prevention efforts because no comprehensive strategic plan exists for coordinating and linking behavioral supports at the school or district level (Walker et al., 1996). Perhaps this is because there is rarely one person whose job description devotes sufficient emphasis to coordination. A service coordinator must be skilled at both micro and macro level changes, have excellent collaboration and mediation skills, and have the time to plan and coordinate with and among all school staff and administrators. Administrators have too many other responsibilities, school psychologists generally do not have much flexibility in their schedules (because they have so many

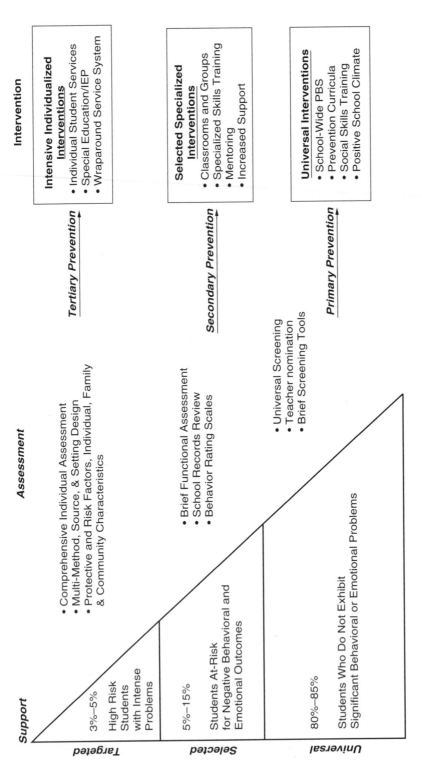

Figure 6.1 A Triangle of Support for Students with Behavioral and Emotional Problems

Case Example: Schoolwide Service Coordinator/Advocate/Intervention Coordinator

Ms. Graven, a school social worker at Rock Springs Elementary, identified lack of coordination among intervention efforts as a barrier to intervention effectiveness. She organized a team composed of the assistant principal, a regular education teacher, a special education teacher, the school psychologist, the resource teacher, a therapist from the local mental health center, and a parent from the school's site-based council. She presented the model in Figure 6.1 and discussed her concerns that led to the formation of the team. The group's goal was to create a cohesive and integrated schoolwide behavioral support plan that includes strategies, interventions, personnel, curricula, and in-service training to ensure a safe, respectful, and fair learning environment that offers the greatest chances for removing barriers to learning. The team met weekly for 3 months and began to achieve this goal by examining current school policy and drafting a written behavior support plan that took into consideration all the interventions that were currently in place for children at the primary, secondary, and tertiary levels. Ms. Graven then conducted a comprehensive literature search examining what intervention strategies are most effective at ensuring a safe, respectful, and fair learning environment. The team used her search results and the knowledge base outlined in this chapter to reflect on the evidence available for several of the interventions in place. A weakness of the plan was the lack of systematic screening for young children with behavior problems. The team decided to administer the Systematic Screening for Behavior Problems in all kindergarten classrooms at the beginning of each year and place children identified as at risk for school adjustment problems on individualized behavior plans, whether they were already identified as special education or not. The plan was presented at a faculty meeting so all faculty understood the referral process and options available to students for whom they had concerns. The plan was connected to and supported by the school's staff and linked to the needs, mission, and goals of the school, district, and state. The team agreed to continue to meet monthly to reflect on the strengths and limitations of the plan.

demands on their time from testing), and school counselors' training is grounded primarily in individual student change strategies. School social workers are the logical choice to fill this need for coordination because they often have flexible job descriptions and are skilled at consensus building, negotiation, mediation, and group facilitation, and they are comfortable working with families.

Assessor

School social workers must be knowledgeable about strategies to maximize intervention acceptability and the buy-in of key stakeholders; implementing systemwide change requires one to detect the existing school culture, obtain faculty and staff input on what is needed (Bulach, 2001), and identify and effectively deal with possible barriers to implementation effectiveness.

Interventions at the school organization level should be selected based on the school's need, the available evidence base, the match between program solution and problem, and the willingness of the school faculty and community to embrace the intervention. McEvoy and Welker (2000) suggest school climate assessments provide a basis for knowing which prevention and intervention programs are likely to be effective in addressing academic failure and behavior problems.

School climate includes all aspects of the school environment that affect learning and discipline, and it is impacted by communities, parents, students, teachers, and the physical structure of the school building. However, the school administrator has the most direct influence on school climate (Hyman & Snook, 2000). **School culture** is defined as a relatively enduring quality of the entire school that describes the collective perceptions of participants for routine behavior and affects their attitudes and behavior in the school (Hoy et al., 1991).

Every school, classroom, and district has a climate ranging from authoritarian to democratic. School climate can be assessed using surveys, questionnaires, or interviews. Prior to assessment, there needs to be open and clear commitment from the school administration to target school climate and openly seek feedback from students, parents, teachers, and the community. In addition to assessing the perceived strengths constituents have of the school, the assessment instrument should focus on problem identification.

Hyman and Snook (2000) identify several possible areas of consideration: discipline codes and policies; staff morale; availability of professional support services, such as social workers, school psychologists, and counselors; teacher-parent communication; teacher-administrator communication; administrator-parent communication; availability of resources; staff to help with discipline problems; and adequacy of libraries. Aspects of school/classroom climate that are most strongly associated with academic achievement and should therefore be assessed include expectations among school staff, students, and parents for academic achievement; orderliness of the school and classroom environments; morale (school staff and students); treatment of students; bonding and engagement of students; and social relationships among students (Stockard & Mayberry, 1992).

Concerning discipline, one should assess whether school rules are made clear to parents each year, as well as the perceived effects of diversity in discipline policies and practices. A thorough assessment of school climate will reveal which interventions specifically targeting racism, homophobia, or cultural diversity are warranted. It will also indicate if increasing students' voices in decision making and school governance is an important goal of intervention. Articles and documents that discuss standardized surveys or processes for assessing school climate can be found in Table 6.2. Carefully observing existing school programs (Turnbull et al., 2002) and using school archival records (e.g., referrals, suspensions, and attendance) also assist in determining the focus of prevention interventions.

Assessment of school climate outcomes can be analyzed and disseminated to constituents with a listing of the highest priority areas and steps to be taken. This process can take 1 year to complete (Hyman & Snook, 2000). Some suggest school climate assessment should be an ongoing process and must occur annually (McEvoy & Welker, 2000). After key target areas have been identified, the behavior support planning team is ready to select programs that would be a good fit for the goals and objectives of the school. When a school social worker leads the assessment process, he or she is positioned to become the intervention coordinator as well.

Table 6.2 | School Climate and Culture Assessment Tool

Assessment Tool	Reference
Instructional Climate Inventory	Braskamp and Maeher (1988)
Effective Schools Student Survey	San Diego County Office of Education (1984)
Effective Schools Project Student Survey	University of Washington, College of Education (1988)
Classroom Environment Scale	Trickett and Moos (1995)
School Discipline Survey	Mayer and Sulzer-Azaroff (1991)
Contextual Factors Contributing to Antisocial Behavior Checklist	Mayer (2001)

Advocate

When school social workers identify gaps in service delivery or weaknesses in the overall behavioral programming within a school, they can use their influence with administrators and influential teachers to ensure the necessary programming is implemented. Within the advocacy role, school social workers should be familiar with Greenberg, Domitrovich, and Bumbarger's (1999) work, which demonstrates that the most effective school-based interventions (1) have multiple components, (2) involve multiple social agents (parents, teachers, and peers), (3) are implemented across several settings (classroom, home, and playground), and (4) are in place for substantial periods of time–generally a minimum of 1 year. Consistent with these findings, it is widely known that add-on or supplemental programs, or multicomponent programs that are designed for the entire school but are only implemented partially or in a few classrooms, are generally not effective. Knowledge and skill regarding group dynamics and change are essential for any effective school organization-level intervention. Inattention to these areas often results in poor intervention fidelity or partially implemented programs. One way to advocate for services and generate support and buy-in from administrators, faculty, staff, parents, and community members is to conduct a school culture or climate assessment.

Trainer

Interventions at the school organization level generally require training of administrators, faculty, and staff. Being an effective trainer requires the knowledge and skills associated with adult learning principles, which many school social

| Case | **Case Example: Advocate/Trainer/ Intervention Coordinator** |

Mr. Jolivet is a school social worker in an urban middle school. His job description, developed by the former administrator in collaboration with the school social worker 12 years ago, identified his major role as that of a counselor to provide emotional support and problem-solving strategies for children who are referred by classroom teachers. Mr. Jolivet quickly realized the students were not the only problem contributing to their difficulties in the classroom. He conducted a comprehensive literature review to determine what school-based interventions are most and least effective for providing emotional support and problem-solving strategies for children. He learned that any effective intervention would need to target both individuals and the classroom environments contributing to the children's struggles, and he found substantial literature suggesting that when teachers possess some basic preventative classroom management skills, referrals within schools are minimized. He discussed his concern with the principal and they jointly structured three in-service trainings, which he facilitated. Each teacher was required to complete a written classroom management plan that could be implemented by a substitute teacher if they were absent. Mr. Jolivet collected pre- and post-test data regarding the number and type of referrals received both in his office and in the principal's office. The data were presented and reflected upon by faculty at the end of the year, and they collaboratively discussed what components of the plans were most and least effective and how the process could be altered for the next school year.

workers possess. Serving as a trainer increases visibility of the school social worker and also minimizes marginalization of students.

Intervention Coordinator

Many, if not all, of the interventions discussed in the previous section require advocacy. Similar to the skills required of the schoolwide service coordinator, interventions that are implemented at the school level require someone skilled in collaboration and mediation skills and someone who is able to coordinate with and among all school staff and administrators. School social workers are in an excellent position to coordinate schoolwide interventions; they have the knowledge and skills required to work with the school organization to implement comprehensive programs successfully. As an intervention coordinator, the school social worker can facilitate regular meetings with a core group of key stakeholders (students, parents, teachers, staff, and administrators) to discuss strengths and challenges to the implementation effort.

SUMMARY

Throughout this chapter, we have made the case that (1) schoolwide and classroom-level interventions hold great promise for improving school safety and narrowing the achievement gap, (2) these interventions must be coordinated and integrated with interventions at the individual and community levels, (3)

 **Case**

Case Example: Intervention Coordinator/Evaluator

After being identified as a school failing to make adequate yearly progress for three consecutive years, the new principal at Foster Elementary School decided to implement the School Transitional Environment Program. This comprehensive school reform model is designed to transform school culture and climate to enhance the transition from elementary to middle school. The school social worker, Ms. Gwen, first conducted a comprehensive literature review to determine what intervention would work best to improve the achievement of children from a school with a high proportion of low-income families. Once she discovered the School Transitional Environment Program was a good fit for the goals of the school, Ms. Gwen convinced the principal that the goals of the program were consistent with her role within the school and offered to serve as the lead intervention coordinator and spearhead the evaluation effort. The intervention was implemented for 1 year and a comprehensive evaluation effort monitored the program's impact on the school. Results suggested there was higher parent and community participation in the school compared to that in a similar school. Foster Elementary also had significantly higher parent and teacher school climate scores than the comparison group.

intervention approaches should be selected and implemented in accordance with the available research regarding effective schools and interventions, and (4) school social workers can be instrumental in intervening at the school organization level. There are numerous roles a school social worker can assume within a school. However, we believe the need for school social workers to approach student behavioral and academic problems from an organizational and ecological perspective is paramount. Although comprehensive behavior and academic support plans require multidisciplinary teams to execute, the school social worker, with training in ecological systems theory and broad clinical and research skills, is ideally positioned to provide leadership in the assessment and intervention process of schoolwide interventions and teaching practices.

School Social Work Companion Website

Please be sure to check out our companion website at www.thomsonedu.com/social_work/bye, where you will find relevant materials for each chapter, including flashcards, online practice quizzes, and PowerPoint slides.

References

Baskin, C. (2002). *Re-generating knowledge: Inclusive education and research*. Paper presented at the Annual Conference of the Canadian Indigenous and Native Studies Association, Toronto, Canada, May 29–31.

Bear, G. G. (1998). School discipline in the United States: Prevention, correction, and long-term social development. *School Psychology Review, 27*(1), 14–32.

Braskamp, L. A., & Maeher, M. L. (1988). *Instructional climate inventory: Form S*. Champaign, IL: MetriTech.

Brophy, J. E. (1996). *Teaching problem students*. New York: Guilford.

Bulach, C. R. (2001). A 4-step process for identifying and reshaping school culture. *Principal Leadership, 1*(8), 48–51.

Catalano, R. F., & Hawkins, J. D. (1996). The social development model: A theory of antisocial behavior. In J. D. Hawkins (Ed.), *Delinquency and crime: Current theories* (pp. 149–197). New York: Cambridge University Press.

Cummings, J. (1986). Empowering minority students: A framework for intervention. *Harvard Educational Review, 56*, 18–36.

Dunlap, G., & Childs, K. E. (1996). Intervention research in emotional and behavioral disorders: An analysis of studies from 1980-1993. *Behavioral Disorders, 21*(2), 125–136.

Dupper, D. R. (2002). *School social work: Skills and interventions for effective practice*. Hoboken, NJ: John Wiley.

Feil, E. G., Walker, H., & Severson, H. H. (2001). Screening and early intervention to prevent the development of aggressive, destructive behavior patterns among at-risk children. In M. K. Shinn, H. Walker, & G. Stoner (Eds.), *Interventions for achievement and behavior problems II*, National Association of School Psychologists Monograph Series. (pp. 143–166) Bethesda, MD: National Association of School Psychologists.

Fine, M. (1991). *Framing dropouts: Notes on the politics of an urban public high school*. New York: State University of New York Press.

Fisher, R. A., & Ury, W. (1991). *Getting to yes* (2nd ed.). New York: Penguin.

Furlong, M. J., Chung, A., Bates, M., & Morrison, R. L. (1995). Who are the victims of school violence? A comparison of student non-victims and multi-victims. *Education and Treatment of Children, 18*, 282–298.

Gettinger, M. (1988). Methods of proactive classroom management. *School Psychology Review, 17*, 227–242.

Glidden, H. G. (1999). Breakthrough schools: Characteristics of low-income schools that perform as though they were high-income schools. *ERS Spectrum, 17*(2), 21–26.

Greenberg, M. T., Domitrovich, C., & Bumbarger, B. (1999). *Preventing mental disorders in school-age children: A review of the effectiveness of prevention programs*. State College: Pennsylvania State University, College of Health and Human Development, Prevention Research Center for the Promotion of Human Development.

Gresham, F. M., Sugai, G., & Horner, R. H. (2001). Interpreting outcomes of social skills training for students with high-incidence disabilities. *Exceptional Children, 67*(3), 331–344.

Griffith, J. (1999). The school leadership/school climate relation: Identification of school configurations associated with change in principals. *Educational Administration Quarterly, 35*(2), 267–291.

Hawkins, J. D., Farrington, D. P., & Catalano, R. F. (1998). Reducing violence through the schools. In D. S. Elliot, B. A. Hamburg, & K. R. Williams (Eds.), *Violence in American schools: A new perspective*. (pp. 188–216) Cambridge, UK: Cambridge University Press.

Hoy, W. K., Hannum, J., & Tschannen-Moran, M. (1998). Organizational climate and student achievement: A parsimonious and longitudinal view. *Journal of School Leadership, 8*, 336–359.

Hoy, W. K., Tarter, C. J., & Kottkamp, R. (1991). *Open school/healthy schools: Measuring organizational climate*. Newbury Park, CA: Sage.

Hyman, I. A., & Snook, P. A. (2000). Dangerous schools and what you can do about them. *Phi Delta Kappan, 81*(7), 489.

Jones, V. (1996). Classroom management. In J. P. Sikula, T. J. Buttery, & E. Guyton (Eds.), *Handbook of research on teacher education*. New York: Simon & Schuster Macmillan.

Kagan, D. M. (1990). How schools alienate students at risk? A model for examining proximal classroom variables. *Educational Psychologist, 25*, 105–125.

Kingery, P. M., Coggeshall, M. B., & Alford, A. A. (1998). Violence at school: Recent evidence from four national surveys. *Psychology in the Schools, 35*, 247–258.

Kounin, J. S. (1970). Discipline and group management in classrooms. *Journal of Research and Development in Education, 4*(1), 62–72.

Lepper, M. R., Keavney, M., & Drake, M. (1996). Intrinsic motivation and extrinsic rewards: An attributional perspective: A commentary on Cameron and Pierce's meta-analysis. *Review of Educational Research, 66*, 5–32.

Mayer, G. R. (2001). Antisocial behavior: Its causes and prevention within our schools. *Education and Treatment of Children, 24*(4), 414–429.

Mayer, G. R., Mitchell, L., Clementi, T., Clement-Robertson, E., Myatt, R., & Bullara, D. T. (1993). A dropout prevention program for at-risk high school students: Emphasizing consulting to promote positive classroom climates. *Education and Treatment of Children, 16*, 135–146.

Mayer, G. R., & Sulzer-Azaroff, B. (1991). Interventions for vandalism. In G. Stoner, M. K. Shinn, & H. M. Walker (Eds.), *Interventions for achievement and behavior problems*. Washington, DC: National Association of School Psychologists.

McEvoy, A., & Welker, R. (2000). Antisocial behavior, academic failure, and school climate: A critical review. *Journal of Emotional & Behavioral Disorders, 8*(3), 130–140.

Nasel, T., Overpeck, M., Pilla, R., Ruan, W., Simmons-Morton, B., & Scheidt, P. (2001). Bullying behavior among US youth: Prevalence and association with psychological adjustment. *Journal of the American Medical Association, 285*, 2094–2100.

Olweus, D. (1991). Bully/victim problems among schoolchildren: Basic facts and effects of a school based intervention program. In D. J. Pepler & K. H. Rubin (Eds.), *The development and treatment of childhood aggression* (pp. 411–448). Hillsdale, NJ: Lawrence Erlbaum.

Olweus, D. (1993). *Bullying at school, what we know and what we can do*. Malden, MA: Blackwell.

Olweus, D., Limber, S., & Mihalic, S. F. (1999). *Blueprints for violence prevention, Book Nine: Bullying prevention program*. Boulder, CO: Center for the Study and Prevention of Violence.

Payne, M., Conroy, J., & Racine, L. (1998). Creating positive school climates. This we believe and now we must act. *Middle School Journal, 30*(2), 65–67.

Peterson, R. L., & Skiba, R. L. (2001). Creating school climates that prevent school violence. *Social Studies, 92*(4), 155–163.

Phelan, P. A., Davidson, A., & Cao, H. (1992). Speaking up: Students' perspectives on school. *Phi Delta Kappan, 73*, 695–704.

Pigford, T. (2001). Improving teacher-student relationships: What's up with that? *Clearing House, 74*(6), 337–339.

Quinn, M. M., Kavale, K. A., Mathur, S. R., Rutherford, R. B., & Forness, S. R. (1999). A meta-analysis of social skill interventions for students with emotional or behavioral disorders. *Journal of Emotional & Behavioral Disorders, 7*(1), 54–64.

Resnick, M., Bearman, P., Blum, R., Rauman, K., Harris, K. M., Jones, J., et al. (1997). Protecting adolescents from harm: Findings from the National Longitudinal Study on Adolescent Health. *Journal of the American Medical Association, 278*, 823–832.

Reyes, P. (1989). Factors that affect the commitment of children at risk to stay in school. In L. M. Lakebrink (Ed.), *Children at risk* (pp. 18–31). Springfield, IL: Charles C Thomas.

Sadovnik, A., Cookson, P., & Semel, S. (2001). *Exploring education: Introduction to the foundations to education.* Needham Heights, MA: Allyn & Bacon.

San Diego County Office of Education. (1984). *San Diego County effective schools program.* San Diego: Author. (ERIC Document Reproduction Service No. ED 393526)

Scott, T. M., & Nelson, C. M. (1999). Universal school discipline strategies: Facilitating positive learning environments. *Effective School Practices, 17*(4), 54–64.

Skiba, R., & Casey, A. (1985). Interventions for behaviorally disordered students: A quantitative review and methodological critique. *Behavioral Disorders, 10*(4), 239–252.

Smith, D., Larson, J., DeBaryshe, B., & Salzman, M. (2000). Anger management for youth: What works and for whom? In D. S. Sandhu & C. Aspy (Eds.), *Violence in American schools: A practical guide for counselors* (pp. 217–230). Reston, VA: American Counseling Association.

Sprague, J., & Walker, H. (2000). Early identification and intervention for youth with antisocial and violent behavior. *Exceptional Children, 66*(3), 367–379.

Stage, S., & Quiroz, D. (1997). A meta-analysis of interventions to decrease disruptive classroom behavior in public education settings. *School Psychology Review, 26*(3), 333–368.

Stockard, J., & Mayberry, M. (1992). *Effective educational environments.* Newbury Park, CA: Corwin Press.

Trickett, E. J., & Moos, R. H. (1995). *Classroom Environment Scale.* Redwood City, CA: Mind Garden.

Turnbull, A., Edmonson, P. G., Sailor, R. F., Guess, D., Lassen, S., McCart, A., et al. (2002). A blueprint for school wide positive behavioral support: Implementation of three components. *Exceptional Children, 68*(3), 377–402.

University of Washington, College of Education. (1988). *Effective schools research.* Seattle: Author. (ERIC Document Reproduction Service No. ED 297 459)

Walker, H. M., Colvin, G., & Ramey, E. (1995). *Antisocial behavior in school—Strategies and best practices.* Pacific Grove, CA: Brooks/Cole.

Walker, H. M., Horner, R. H., Sugai, G., Bullis, M., Sprague, J. R., Bricker, D., et al. (1996). Integrated approaches to preventing antisocial behavior patterns among school-age children and youth. *Journal of Emotional & Behavioral Disorders, 4,* 193–256.

Walker, H. M., Sprague, J. R., & Severson, H. H. (2003). Schools and youth violence: What educators need to know about developing healthy students and safe schools. In R. H. Haslan & P. J. Vallenutti (Eds.), *Medical problems in the classroom: The teacher's role in diagnosis and management* (4th ed., pp. 655–694). Austin, TX: PRO-ED.

Community Schools: New Roles for Social Work Practitioners

CHAPTER 7

JANE QUINN, M.A.
The Children's Aid Society, New York City

CHAPTER OUTLINE

Chapter Overview

Introduction

Community Schools From a National Perspective

One Community School Model (The Children's Aid Society, New York City)

Implications for Social Work Practice Nationally

Summary

CHAPTER OVERVIEW

This chapter describes a growing movement throughout the country, community schools, that is creating new opportunities for social work practitioners to promote the learning and healthy development of children and their families. The chapter complements other chapters by integrating several of the themes explored in the text, including the importance of innovation, the evolution of practice (skills and settings), and the idea of both building on and contributing to the ever-growing knowledge base. Readers will (1) learn about a major national trend and movement as well as about a specific model of community schools, (2) become acquainted with the knowledge base that underlies this approach, (3) develop an awareness of the rewards and challenges of working in this more integrated and interdisciplinary way, and (4) discover the multiple roles played by social work practitioners in these complex settings.

INTRODUCTION

Community schools are public schools that work together with community resources to integrate the schools' core instructional program with a wide array of supports, services, and opportunities designed to enrich the learning environment and remove barriers to learning. These additional programs and services may include medical, dental, mental health and social services; before- and after-school programs; summer camps; early childhood programs; parent involvement; community celebrations and other events; and community and economic development. This chapter describes community schools from a national and local perspective and analyzes new and expanded roles played by social work practitioners in their design, implementation, and assessment.

COMMUNITY SCHOOLS FROM A NATIONAL PERSPECTIVE

Basic Definitions

A **community school** is a public school that combines the best quality educational practices with a wide range of vital in-house health and social services to ensure that children are physically, emotionally, and socially prepared to learn. Open early mornings, afternoons, evenings, weekends, and summers, the community school serves as a true center of community life—a place where children attend classes; receive medical and dental care; speak to a counselor about a problem; stay after school to build reading skills, play chess, work on a computer, take art and music lessons, get help with homework, and practice sports; and attend summer camp.

Parents and community leaders play active roles in the school. Parents are welcomed and encouraged to get involved in their children's education, as well as take adult education classes, get advice and support, learn how to help their children succeed in school, meet other parents, and create their own programs, support groups, and activities.

A committed partnership between the school and school district, a community organization, and parents is essential to a community school's success. This new relationship shifts the responsibility for student and family outcomes to a shared responsibility between partners. Partners come together to surround young people with three key sets of supports and opportunities: (1) a strong, coherent core instructional program during the regular school day; (2) supports and services that address and seek to remove barriers to learning; and (3) enrichment opportunities during nonschool hours that build students' motivation and capacity to succeed in school. This conceptual approach is sometimes called a "developmental triangle," with the three core components serving as the legs of a triangle surrounding students with research-based elements that promote school success.

Underlying Research Base

The idea of community schools is not new; in fact, in the early 20th century, during the Progressive Era, educational philosopher John Dewey (1902) championed the cause of "the school as social centre," and his social work colleague, Jane Addams, wrote extensively about the importance of connecting education to the work of settlement houses and other institutions designed to foster child and family well-being (Lagemann, 1985). Since that time, several professional disciplines—including education, social work, health, mental health, and parent involvement—have contributed a broad base of knowledge that points to the wisdom of the Dewey–Addams vision. This research base can be summarized as follows:

- **All young people need ongoing supports and opportunities on the road to successful adulthood.** Extensive research on child and adolescent development indicates that young people need ongoing guidance and support in all the developmental domains (cognitive, social, emotional, physical, moral, and vocational) if they are to achieve productive adulthood—defined as having competencies that will allow them to participate in the labor economy, in responsible family life, and in active citizenship (Eccles, 1999).
- **Children do better in school when their parents regularly support, monitor, and advocate for their education.** Multiyear research at Johns Hopkins University Center for Law and Education documented the importance of parental involvement in children's education as a key factor in promoting academic achievement (Epstein, 1995; Henderson & Berla, 1995).
- **Constructive learning activities during non-school hours are essential to children's school success.** Clark (1988) found that low-income children who spent 20–35 hours of their free time each week in engaged learning (such as reading for pleasure and playing strategy games) got better grades in school than their more passive peers.
- **Children's participation in high-quality after-school programs results in several important learning and development outcomes.** A variety of studies spanning more than a decade documented a host of positive benefits from children's participation in high-quality after-school programs, including better grades, work habits, emotional adjustment, and peer relations (Vandell & Shumow, 1999).
- **Community-based youth development programs promote positive academic and social outcomes among teenagers.** Stanford education professor McLaughlin (2000) found that adolescents who participate regularly in community-based youth development programs (including arts, sports, and community service) have better academic and social outcomes, as well as higher education and career aspirations, than other similar teens.

- **Consistent adult guidance and support promote positive youth development.** Resilience theory indicates that children who have consistent access to adult guidance and support have better outcomes, such as higher education and career aspirations and a lower incidence of at-risk behaviors (Benard, 1991).
- **Where key developmental influences work together, positive youth outcomes are enhanced.** A 13-year study in 10 varied communities found that child and adolescent outcomes were enhanced in communities where the key developmental influences (home, school, and community resources) combined to provide consistent messages, opportunities, and supports for young people (Ianni, 1990).
- **Fragmentation among educational and social services hinders effectiveness.** Several studies have documented the fragmentation that characterizes much of the service delivery system for children and families in the United States as well as how such fragmentation limits effectiveness (Hodgkinson, 1989).
- **Community schools show great promise as the best way to promote children's learning and development.** Researcher Dryfoos (1994) synthesized a complex body of research on reducing risk and promoting resilience among children and adolescents and concluded that the single most effective intervention was the development and implementation of schools that integrate the delivery of quality education with needed health and social services.

National Influences

Of the many influences on the proliferation of community schools during the past 15 years, the Dryfoos (1994) analysis has probably been the most significant. Dryfoos began advocating community schools as a strategy for addressing youth needs after spending several years researching the issue of high-risk behaviors during adolescence. As a long-time researcher in the field of adolescent pregnancy, during the late 1980s she became interested in the question of whether or not the other major high-risk behaviors—substance abuse, juvenile crime, and school failure—shared common antecedents and common intervention strategies with the problem of adolescent pregnancy. Her findings are summarized in a masterful book titled *Adolescents at Risk: Prevalence and Prevention* (Dryfoos, 1990), in which she argues that these major high-risk behaviors do indeed have common antecedents and that effective interventions across all four preventive arenas also have common features. Another major finding of her analysis was that approximately 25% of American youth are at high risk of not achieving productive adulthood because of the hazards they face during adolescence (including poverty, inadequate parenting, and growing up in dangerous neighborhoods). Given the prevalence of high-risk environments and circumstances documented in her research, Dryfoos concluded that the best approach to reducing adolescent risk was to embed supports, services, and developmental opportunities into public schools—the institutions that serve the greatest number of the nation's youth.

Based on this work, Dryfoos (1994) went on to write something of a sequel—a text devoted to the idea and practice of "full-service" or community schools. In describing the full-service vision, Dryfoos noted that one in four public school students are at high risk for failure due to handicapping conditions. She advocates strongly for schools and community agencies to join together to help these students overcome the social, emotional, and health problems that stand in the way of their success.

This notion of shaping powerful new institutions lies at the heart of community schools. Throughout the country, many innovative models have emerged during the past 15 years. Some of the best known and most widely adapted models include the Beacons Schools in New York City (developed and funded by the city's Department of Youth and Community Development), Bridges to Success (developed by the United Way of Central Indiana and subsequently adopted as a national model by United Way of America), Communities in Schools (a national organization with approximately 180 local affiliates that bring case management and other services into schools to promote students' school success), Community Schools (developed by The Children's Aid Society in New York City and described more fully later in this chapter), Schools of the 21st Century (developed by Edward Zigler of Yale University), and the West Philadelphia Improvement Corps (a university-assisted model developed by the University of Pennsylvania). Several states have developed community school initiatives during this same period, including California (Healthy Start), Florida (Full-Service Schools), Kentucky (Family Resource and Youth Service Centers), and New Jersey (School-Based Youth Services Program). These and other programs work together to share information and promote the community schools' approach through a national Coalition for Community Schools, developed by several community school leaders in 1997 and funded initially by the Charles Stewart Mott Foundation and the DeWitt Wallace–Reader's Digest Fund.

Since its inception, the coalition has taken a "big tent" approach to convening the field and publicizing its work. Led by Marty Blank of the Institute for Educational Leadership, the coalition has developed several important publications (Blank, Melaville, & Shah, 2003), convened national and regional conferences, and advocated steadily for increased understanding of and support for community schools. The coalition's membership consists of 170 national and regional education and human service organizations, including the American Federation of Teachers, National Education Association, American Association of School Administrators, National Association of Elementary School Principals, National Association of Secondary School Principals, National School Boards Association, National Collaboration for Youth, Boys & Girls Clubs of America, and United Way of America.

Differences Between the Various Community Schools Models

The coalition's success in convening, publicizing, and advocating for community schools rests largely on its inclusive approach that emphasizes the commonalities across the various models, including extended hours, extended services, and partnerships between schools and community resources. Despite these basic similarities, there are many differences between and among the several models of community schools that currently exist. Key variables that distinguish the several models include the following:

Goals   This is probably the key difference—the one that informs all others. Some models seek explicitly to address fundamental school reform issues, including academic achievement, school climate, and school culture, whereas others seek primarily to expand services and opportunities for children and families. Some have explicit goals around community development, whereas others do not.

Nature of Partnerships   There are many courtship and marriage analogies in the community schools' literature, and they are generally quite apt. Some models represent long-term, committed relationships (similar to marriage), whereas others are more like roommates—you share space but do not necessarily have the same goals and probably do not pool your financial resources. Some of these models are like arranged marriages, in which the partners may not choose each other and they may or may not eventually fall in love. The nature of the partnership is related to another key difference, the point and method of entry.

Point and Method of Entry   Some of these models start as an after-school youth development program and may or may not grow into something larger. Most models, even if they are initially envisioned as full service, start small and grow. One of the key differences between the Beacons and The Children's Aid Society (CAS) models in New York has to do with point and method of entry. The CAS model, which is described more fully in the next section, is initiated with agreements at three levels of the school system—central board of education, local school district, and principal—whereas the Beacon model was initiated and is funded by the city's Department of Youth and Community Development, with a great deal of variation from site to site regarding principal involvement, investment, and leadership.

Program Components   Naturally, differences in goals, partners, and funding sources will lead to differences in program components. An evaluation conducted by Public/Private Ventures and the Manpower Demonstration Research Corporation of four extended-service schools models—Beacons, Bridges to Success, CAS, and West Philadelphia Improvement Corps (WEPIC)—found more emphasis programmatically on sports, recreation, and the arts in Beacons than in the other models; more emphasis on community service in the WEPIC model; and more focus on academics in the CAS model. However, the researchers believed that these differences were more a matter of relative emphasis than of core differences because all models offered some programming in all these areas (Grossman et al., 2002).

Role of Lead Agency   In some of the models, including the Beacons and the CAS community schools, the lead agency provides the majority of the youth development and after-school (or wraparound) services, whereas in the Bridges to Success model, the United Way as lead agency plays the role of services broker.

Cost   The costs both within and among the different models vary considerably, depending on hours of services, kinds of staffing, and types of services and programs offered. Some programs calculate costs on a per child basis, whereas others use the program's annual budget as the basis. For example, the After-School Corporation in New York City calculates its costs for a 3-hour per day, 5 days per week school year program to be $1,000 per child. The core budget for each Beacon program in New York City is approximately $450,000. These figures provide little basis for comparison. Whole school interventions may use the program's annual budget as the basis and calculate a per student cost by dividing the total annual budget by the number of students in the school. Using this approach, the CAS community schools calculated their per student costs to be approximately $1,000 per year, a different figure than that calculated by the After-School Corporation. The current state of knowledge indicates two things: in general, you get what you pay for, and few definitive cost studies have yet been conducted.

The evaluation of the Wallace–Reader's Digest Extended-Services Schools Program is one of the best studies, although it examined primarily the costs of running after-school programs rather than the more comprehensive set of services found in many community schools. This study found that the cost of providing a 3-hour after-school program was approximately $15 per day per child (Grossman et al., 2002), a figure that is very comparable to costs cited by Halpern (1999) in an earlier study of after-school programs in Boston, Chicago, and Seattle.

Funding   Every program struggles with funding issues, and every program draws from multiple funding streams. However, the mix is different from model to model. The major funding stream for the Beacons comes from general municipal tax revenues, the major funding stream for Bridges to Success is private, and the CAS model relies on a balance between public and private funding streams. The best source of funding for community schools is the federal 21st Century Community Learning Centers program, a part of the Elementary and Secondary Education Act (No Child Left Behind), which provides $1 billion for state-administered grants that support after-school and summer enrichment programs for young people and education (especially literacy) programs for parents.

Governance   Most community and full-service schools have developed a new form of governance that addresses such issues as crafting a shared vision, delineating the roles and responsibilities of the partners, and outlining procedures for communications, problem solving, and resolving conflicts. These governance structures may include school-based leadership teams that meet monthly or even weekly, or community-wide planning groups that involve key stakeholders.

Comprehensiveness   Some community schools seek to take a comprehensive or full-service approach, whereas others take an extended service approach. For example, a full-service approach is likely to include health, dental, and mental health services in addition to a full array of before-school, after-school, and parent involvement programs, whereas an extended service school might have only one or two of these offerings.

Scale   It is easier to go to scale with a more limited model and a dedicated and permanent (or even relatively permanent) funding stream. In New York City, the Beacons, the After-School Corporation, and the Virtual Y are each in more than 75 schools—with this success due to at least one of these two factors. Similarly, the federal 21st Century Community Learning Centers program is in thousands of schools nationwide, after only 7 years, because of the exponential growth in funding (from $40 million in 1997 to $1 billion in 2002 and beyond).

Integration Between School Day and After-School Programs   A major difference among the existing models is the extent to which they seek to integrate what happens during the regular school day with what happens in the other program components, especially the after-school program. This work represents the cutting edge in community schools' efforts throughout the country, with the more integrated approaches gaining favor from school districts, principals, and funders. Some after-school program curricula, including those created by the Developmental Studies Center in Oakland and Foundations, Incorporated, in Philadelphia, deliberately seek to enrich and extend children's learning opportunities while taking into account the new higher academic standards to which students and teachers are being held accountable.

In short, the major issue regarding the various models of community schools is the following: Several proven or promising models exist; all models have to be adapted to local needs and resources; and these models have key features in common, but they also have key differences. To understand how one of these models is initiated in a local community and also to understand the role of social agencies and social workers in community schools, let's examine one model that is sponsored by a social service organization—CAS in New York City.

ONE COMMUNITY SCHOOL MODEL (THE CHILDREN'S AID SOCIETY, NEW YORK CITY)

Overview and Goals

In 1989, CAS—New York City's oldest and largest youth-serving organization—joined in an unprecedented partnership with the New York City Board of Education, the city's Community School District 6, and other community-based partners to develop a comprehensive response to the pressing needs of children and families in the northern Manhattan neighborhood of Washington Heights. After 3 years of citywide planning, the first CAS community school, Intermediate School 218, opened in 1992. CAS currently operates 13 community schools in New York City—5 elementary schools, 7 intermediate schools, and

The CAS model is characterized by the following:

Comprehensiveness: Its full-service approach is designed to address the multiple needs of children and families.
Coherence: Joint planning and decision making involves the major partners (school, CAS, and parents) and intentionally seeks to integrate all aspects of the community school, particularly the school day academic program and the before- and after-school enrichment program.
Commitment: CAS and its partner schools make a long-term commitment to work together with and on behalf of students and their families.

1 high school. At these schools, children and parents have numerous services available to them, including adult education; immigration assistance; extended academic, sports, arts, and development programs; child health insurance enrollment; medical and dental services; mental health services; early childhood programs; and community development.

The overarching goal of the CAS model of community schools is to promote children's learning and development in ways that prepare them for productive adulthood. Recognizing that children's learning and development is influenced by their ongoing experiences in their families, schools, and communities, CAS community schools work to integrate the efforts of all three of these major influences through a partnership approach that addresses five outcome domains: students, families, school, community, and education policy.

The work at each school is guided by a school leadership team, which consists of board of education staff (principal, assistant principals, and teachers), CAS staff, and parents. These teams meet at least monthly for joint planning and decision making. In addition, CAS has explicit written agreements with the New York City Board of Education and with the local community school districts in which its partnership schools are located (the New York City Board of Education is divided into 32 local school districts).

Each CAS community school has a full-time director who works closely with the school's principal. Other key staff are a full-time program director (CAS staff member), an education coordinator (board of education employee who works part-time for CAS), and a parent coordinator (employed by CAS). At each site, the program staff is composed of teachers, youth workers, program specialists (such as dance teachers and artists), and high school and college students. Professional development activities include orientation for new staff; monthly Community Schools Work Group meetings for site directors and other key staff; and workshops offered through CAS, Boys and Girls Clubs of America (of which CAS is a member), the Partnership for After-School Education, and the After-School Corporation.

Parents, youth, and other community residents are actively involved in all aspects of the community school, starting with the needs assessment process that initiates each school. For example, at one of the newer CAS sites (public school

[PS] 50 in East Harlem), the initial needs assessment included focus groups with parents, students, and other community residents. Central to the CAS community school model is a Parent Resource Center—a place in the school where parents can socialize, get help, and participate in workshops; also central are CAS model community-wide celebrations and events, such as the Dominican Heritage Celebration that annually draws hundreds of community residents to intermediate school (IS) 218 in Washington Heights.

Results to Date

The two initial CAS community schools—PS 5 and IS 218 in Washington Heights—have been the focus of a 6-year process and outcome evaluation conducted by researchers from Fordham University (Brickman, 1996; Brickman & Cancelli, 1997; Brickman, Cancelli, Sanchez, & Rivera, 1998; Cancelli, Brickman, Sanchez, & Rivera, 1999). The first 3 years primarily addressed formative issues, whereas during the next 3 years the evaluation addressed a variety of outcome issues using a comparison design involving two other New York City public schools that were not community schools. Overall, key findings from these evaluations include improvements in attendance and academic achievement, increases in parental involvement, reductions in suspensions, and improvements in attitudes toward school.

Specifically, students at both PS 5 and IS 218 showed improvement in math and reading scores. This was true for students who graduated in 1997 and for a cohort that followed between 1996 and 1999, although 1998–1999 test scores were not examined. There was evidence that participation in the before- and after-school program correlated with improved test scores, but this was not fully investigated. Students' self-perception ratings improved in both schools and were particularly strong at PS 5 in terms of self-ratings of behavior and appearance. Attitudes toward school were more positive among community school students than among students attending comparison schools.

In relation to school environment and climate, interviews and observations consistently revealed that the schools were different in their ambience from traditional school buildings. Parents and students felt welcome and the physical environment contributed to a sense of safety, order, and cheerfulness. Both schools exhibited little or no violence or graffiti. Teachers, students, and parents considered the schools "special" and felt they were safe places for children. Teachers in the community schools spent more time on class preparation and working with students than teachers in the comparison schools. Student attendance rates were slightly higher at PS 5 and much higher at IS 218 than the average for comparable New York City schools. Teachers at community schools also had improved attendance rates.

Finally, according to the Fordham researchers, the dramatic levels of parent involvement were among the most significant findings. Parent involvement was 78% higher at PS 5 than at a comparable elementary school, and it was 147% higher at IS 218 than at a comparable middle school. At the community schools, parents took more responsibility for their children's school work and felt welcome and were observed to be a presence in the schools more than in the comparison schools. Parents also received many social services, attended adult education workshops, and received medical services.

Expansion Strategy

In New York City, CAS's strategy has been to expand gradually, moving from an initial site in 1992 to eight sites in 2000, adding a ninth site (PS 50) in 2001, a 10th school (CS 61/IS 190) in 2002, and three schools at the start of the 2003–2004 school year. The major expansion strategy has been a national approach of providing technical assistance and training to schools and community groups throughout the country that want to learn from and adapt the CAS model to their own local needs and circumstances. Since 1994, CAS has operated a Community Schools' Technical Assistance Center, which received initial financial support from the Carnegie Corporation of New York. More than 6,000 visitors have come to see and learn from the Washington Heights schools since that time. To date, more than 200 other community schools nationally and internationally have adapted the CAS model. Other expansion strategies have included an Ad Council campaign cosponsored by the Coalition for Community Schools and designed to educate the public about the value of the community schools' approach and partnerships with national organizations—including the Boys & Girls Clubs of America, the Public Education Network, and the Milton Eisenhower Foundation—to use their national reach to increase the number and quality of school–community partnerships nationally.

The Critical Role of Social Workers in CAS Community Schools

This model utilizes social work skills in a variety of traditional and nontraditional roles. Perhaps the most innovative role is that of the community school director, who serves as the lead partner with the school principal. CAS generally hires social workers with 5–15 years of experience for these positions. These full-time directors work long hours because the schools are open 12–15 hours per day, year-round, and need to have a complex set of administrative, programmatic, clinical, and interpersonal skills. Flexibility is essential to this work, as is a commitment to lifelong learning. For example, community school directors read *Education Week* as well as National Association of Social Workers newspapers and journals, and they are well versed in the New York State academic standards for students in grades K–12. Most community school directors find it important to stay open to changing their practice—adapting their skills to an extremely dynamic environment in which they are interacting regularly with diverse constituencies and multiple professional disciplines.

The most important ingredient of the CAS community school model is joint planning and assessment. Directors work side-by-side with their principals, both literally and figuratively. In negotiating for office space, CAS tries to locate the director right next to the principal to facilitate the kind of daily interaction needed if the school and agency are going to truly integrate the core components of the work. All CAS community school directors serve on their school leadership teams and most also serve on the principals' cabinet and the schools' pupil personnel committees. Participation in these formal structures ensures that CAS social workers are "at the table" when important decisions are made, such as developing the school's comprehensive education plan.

On a daily basis, the directors supervise large staffs, including full-time program directors, parent coordinators, and clinical social workers. Implementing this kind of new role for social workers is complicated by the fact that most practitioners are underprepared in one or more of the areas required by the demands of the position. Schools of social work have generally not caught up with this part of practice. Instead, they continue to prepare clinical, community organizing, or administrative specialists—not recognizing that, in these new roles, social workers combine and apply all these skills. To compensate for this lack of professional preparation, CAS has instituted a series of staff orientation and staff development opportunities for new and seasoned staff. However, clearly, our experience has implications for the social work field as a whole, particularly with regard to professional preparation.

In addition to serving as community school directors, social workers fulfill many other roles in CAS community schools, including mental health specialists, family counselors, and preventive service workers. This latter role is a specialized service that is contracted through the New York City government and targets services to families referred for child abuse or neglect.

IMPLICATIONS FOR SOCIAL WORK PRACTICE NATIONALLY

The work at CAS is hardly an anomaly. In fact, the Coalition for Community Schools estimates that there are between 3,000 and 5,000 community schools nationally, and a current project of the coalition, the development of a community school directory, will help to define and organize the field in useful ways. In the meantime, several thousand new jobs are being created as schools open their doors to social welfare and other community agencies and extend their services to address the needs of children and families. Several leading schools of social work are taking note of this trend and opportunity. For example, the School of Social Service Administration (SSA; 2004) at the University of Chicago announced plans to develop a program to prepare social workers for leadership roles in community schools. This program is designed to prepare graduates to work nationally and locally, where the Chicago Public Schools have publicly committed themselves to the development of 100 community schools during the next 5 years. The first cohort of 20 such schools has already been selected.

Nationally, the exponential growth of the 21st Century Community Learning Centers' program has spurred the demand for community school directors because federal legislation requires that eligible schools partner with community agencies and allocate funding for planning and coordination as well as for a wide array of direct services for children and families.

Another major trend creating demand for community school directors is the influx of new students entering the nation's schools. The 2000 Census confirmed what many educators and planners already knew from experience—that the United States is undergoing the largest wave of immigration in the nation's history. Many schools are struggling to catch up with this reality, including the fact that more of their students are English as a second language learners, many of the students' parents may not be literate in their native languages, and some students arrive in middle school with no prior formal education. At the institutional level, schools have such challenges as underprepared teachers and staff who do not speak the languages of the recent arrivals. The community schools' strategy represents a viable approach for addressing many of these issues. Many community agencies are skilled at welcoming new Americans and building on their many strengths, and they may have more flexibility than schools in hiring community residents who speak the language and understand the culture of their neighbors.

A third major trend creating demand for community schools (and new types of professionals to staff them) is new school construction. For a variety of reasons, the United States is involved in an educational building boom—by most accounts, the largest in recent memory. As new schools are built in communities throughout the country, many community-based organizations are exploring joint use agreements and other promising ways to make the best use of public facilities and reach more young people with youth development services. Several factors have contributed to this wave of new school construction. Policymakers project that by 2008, public school enrollment will increase by 1.4 million—to a total of 48 million. Furthermore, inattention to the physical infrastructure of schools during the past several decades is catching up with many districts. Also, a spate of court decisions mandating equitable financing of public education has compelled some state governments to make needed investments in their low-income schools, including the physical facilities.

These trends do not appear temporary or ephemeral. Rather, they are changing the landscape of public education and require commensurate changes in social work practice. Professional preparation programs should acquaint students with the theory and practice of community schools and encourage more field placements in community school settings. In-service courses should be developed to build the skills of current practitioners—not just social workers but also community school directors from a variety of backgrounds. SSA Dean Edward Lawlor observes that social work schools can teach the requisite skills (SSA, 2004). Both pre-employment and in-service courses can prepare community school staff to conduct community needs assessments, forge effective partnerships, engage parents and communities, develop responsive programs, secure human and financial resources, and evaluate results. These are essential tools in community schools' practice, but too few practitioners are schooled or skilled in these critical areas.

SUMMARY

Based on 12 years of experience partnering deeply with schools, CAS has developed three mantras that guide its daily work:

- It is all about relationships.
- Everything has to be negotiated, all the time.
- To make partnerships really work, you have to have the word "yes" written in your heart.

Social workers' commitment to social change and their ability to deal with ambiguity provide a solid basis for working in public schools through the community schools strategy. The future is likely to bring more opportunities for the kinds of partnerships described in this chapter—as schools and policymakers alike discover that if we are serious about leaving no child behind, our society is going to have to create more responsive institutions that address children's nonacademic as well as academic needs. As leaders of our nation's public schools increasingly come to recognize that they "cannot do it alone," we as social workers should prepare ourselves to respond affirmatively to these new opportunities to promote children's learning and development in the most effective ways possible.

School Social Work Companion Website

Please be sure to check out our companion website at www.thomsonedu.com/social_work/bye, where you will find relevant materials for each chapter, including flashcards, online practice quizzes, and PowerPoint slides.

References

Benard, B. (1991). *Fostering resiliency in kids: Protective factors in the family, school and community.* Portland, OR: Northwest Regional Educational Laboratories, Western Regional Center for Drug-Free Schools and Communities.

Blank, M. J., Melaville, A., & Shah, B. (2003). *Making the difference: Research and practice in community schools.* Washington, DC: Coalition for Community Schools.

Brickman, E. (1996). *A formative evaluation of P.S. 5: A Children's Aid Society/Board of Education Community School.* New York: Fordham University Graduate School of Social Services.

Brickman, E., & Cancelli, A. (1997). *Washington Heights Community Schools evaluation: First year findings.* New York: Fordham University Graduate School of Social Services and Graduate School of Education.

Brickman, E., Cancelli, A., Sanchez, A., & Rivera, G. (1998). *The Children's Aid Society/Board of Education Community Schools: Second-year evaluation report.* New York: Fordham University Graduate School of Social Services and Graduate School of Education.

Cancelli, A., Brickman, E., Sanchez, A., & Rivera, G. (1999). *The Children's Aid Society/Board of Education Community Schools: Third-year evaluation report.* New York: Fordham University Graduate School of Education and Graduate School of Social Services.

Clark, R. M. (1988). *Critical factors in why disadvantaged children succeed or fail in school.* New York: Academy for Educational Development.

Dewey, J. (1902). *The school as social centre.* Reprinted in Boydston, J. A. (1976). *John Dewey: The middle works, 1899–1924, Volume 2.* Carbondale: Southern Illinois University.

Dryfoos, J. G. (1990). *Adolescents at risk: Prevalence and prevention.* New York: Oxford University Press.

Dryfoos, J. G. (1994). *Full-service schools: A revolution in health and social services for children, youth, and families.* San Francisco: Jossey-Bass.

Eccles, J. (1999). The development of children ages 6 to 14. *The Future of Children: When School Is Out, 9*(2), 30–44.

Epstein, J. L. (1995). School, family, community partnerships: Caring for the children we share. *Phi Delta Kappan, 77*(9), 701–712.

Grossman, J. B., Price, M. L., Fellerath, V., Jucovy, L. Z., Kotloff, L. J., Raley, R., & Walker, K. E. (2002). *Multiple choices after school: Findings from the Extended-Service Schools Initiative.* Philadelphia: Public/Private Ventures.

Halpern, R. (1999). After-school programs for low-income children: Promise and challenges. *The Future of Children: When School Is Out, 9*(2), 81–95.

Henderson, A. T., & Berla, N. (1995). *A new generation of evidence: The family is critical to student achievement.* Washington, DC: Center for Law and Education.

Hodgkinson, H. L. (1989). *The same client: The demographics of education and service delivery systems.* Washington, DC: Institute for Educational Leadership.

Ianni, F. A. J. (1990). *The search for structure.* New York: Free Press.

Lagemann, E. C. (Ed.). (1985). *Jane Addams on education.* New York: Teachers College Press.

McLaughlin, M. W. (2000). *Community counts: How youth organizations matter for youth development.* Washington, DC: Public Education Network.

School of Social Service Administration. (2004, March). Bank One donates $1 million to create community schools leadership program at SSA. *News & Notes SSA Chicago* 1–3.

Vandell, D. L., & Shumow, L. (1999). After-school child care programs. *The Future of Children: When School Is Out, 9*(2), 64–80.

School Social Work: Smaller Systems Practice

8 CHAPTER | School Social Work With Families

LYNN BYE, M.S.W., Ph.D.
University of Minnesota, Duluth

CHAPTER OUTLINE

CHAPTER OVERVIEW

This chapter describes the critical role school social workers play in helping families overcome barriers that interfere with the education of their children. After reading this chapter, the reader will (1) be able to give several reasons for involving families in the education of their children, (2) be able to describe promising strategies to help families and schools work together in the best interest of the students, (3) be aware of cultural issues that must be considered in working with families, and (4) have an understanding of how best to support the home–school connection. This chapter uses the ecological and strengths perspective described in Chapter 3.

INTRODUCTION: IMPORTANCE OF FAMILY INVOLVEMENT

> The importance of a strong family and caring parents in a child's life can't be overstated. Parents are the child's first and most influential teachers.
>
> Kemthorne (2005, p. 23)

Family involvement in a child's education is important for many reasons. First, families are influential; children pick up attitudes about education from adults in the home before their first day at school. Second, children tend to do better academically when their families are involved (National Governor's Association Task Force on School Readiness, 2005). Third, the law requires schools to involve families in the education of their children.

Families Are Influential

In this chapter, the term **family** is used to represent parents, grandparents, legal guardians, and others with whom the child may live. Families, be it kinship, foster, or adoptive, provide a major life context and generally have far more influence over their children than do school personnel. Because families are so influential, it is important to partner with them in the education of their children. This partnership requires effort and sensitivity on the part of the school personnel. If the family views school as a hostile environment or a waste of time, it will be difficult to convince the children otherwise. On the other hand, if families and schools have a strong partnership, they can work together and support each other in providing the highest quality education for the students.

Case | Case Example

Sam, a first-grade student, was falling behind his classmates in reading. He told his teacher that his father said school was a waste of time and that reading was not important. Sam lived alone with his father, Fred, who dropped out of school at an early age. Fred had several bad experiences with schools, avoided dealing with school personnel, and frequently made negative comments to his son about the value of school. When the school social worker called Fred and asked if he could visit with him about his son's education, Fred reluctantly agreed. The school social worker spent the first visit asking Sam's father about his hopes and dreams for his son and explaining how school could possibly help his son achieve those dreams. The social worker also explained that the school needed his advice on how best to work with Sam. At the end of the visit, Fred told the school social worker that he was not able to practice reading with his son because he could not read. The social worker informed Fred about a free program in which volunteer tutors came to school to practice reading with students 3 days a week. Fred agreed to allow Sam to be in the program. The school social worker kept in touch with Fred, updating him on Sam's progress in reading and thanking him for his willingness to let Sam participate. On the second home visit, the school social worker told Fred about an adult literacy program in the community and how he was not alone in not being able to read as an adult. Fred attended the adult literacy program. Both Fred's and Sam's reading improved that year.

Children Do Better in School When Families Are Involved

Parent involvement in school was identified by the Search Institute (1998) as one of the developmental assets young people need to do well in life. A large body of research supports the idea that children do better in school when families are involved. For example, achievement in math and reading increases (Henderson & Mapp, 2002; Jeynes, 2003; Lopez & Cole, 1999; Starkey, & Klein, 2000; Wang & Wildman, 1994), there is less need for special education services (Miedel & Reynolds, 1999), behavior problems decline (Fischer, 2003), students are more likely to complete 4 years of college (Eagle, 1989), and there is a reduction in posttreatment substance abuse (Latimer, 2003).

The Law Requires Family Involvement

National legislation such as the Title I: Improving the Academic Achievement of the Disadvantaged Act (2002) and the No Child Left Behind Act of 2001 (House–Senate Education Conference Report, 2001) require parent involvement. Title I funding mandates that schools receiving these funds have a policy on parent involvement and spend a minimum of 1% of the funds to build on the parents' capacity to help their children (Federal Register, 1994). The Goals 2000: Educate America Act passed into law by Congress in 1994 requires that every school promote partnerships that increase parental involvement and participation in promoting the social, emotional, and academic growth of children (Federal Register, 1994). See Chapter 15 for a detailed discussion of the laws related to accessing education.

SCHOOL SOCIAL WORK AND FAMILY INVOLVEMENT

School social workers have a strong history of fostering partnerships between families and the schools their children attend (see Chapter 1 for more information about the history of school social work).

Services School Social Workers Provide to Families

1. Interviewing the family to obtain their perspective of problems that disrupt their child's education and their ideas about how to resolve those problems
2. Recognizing and affirming family strengths
3. Helping the family to understand academic and behavioral expectations at school and the services available to them
4. Providing families with information on resources in the community and assisting them in connecting with these resources when needed
5. Conducting parent/caregiver groups on a variety of topics
6. Organizing special events and other outreach efforts that help families learn what is happening at school and feel welcome there
7. Consulting with families about how they can help their child learn new skills and become more successful at school
8. Advocating for families to have a voice in decisions about their child's education

School Social Work Association of America (n.d.)

School social workers are a resource for families. In turn, families are a resource for their children, for the people at school who work with their children, and for other families in the community. School social workers mobilize this important resource by helping families connect with community agencies, teachers, and other families.

Connecting With Community Agencies

School social workers know whom to contact; they know the services available. I had a student who had a terrible, oozing infection in his mouth. The school social worker was able to help his family find a health care provider they could afford.

Barbara Bennett, Minneapolis Public School Teacher (personal communication, May 15, 2004)

Families are responsible for housing, clothing, feeding, caring for the medical needs of their children, and keeping them safe in the neighborhood so that they can come to school prepared to learn. Meeting this responsibility to have children ready for school is a difficult job for many families when simply obtaining food and shelter are major accomplishments. The U.S. Census Bureau reported that 16.7% of children in the country live in poverty (Proctor & Dalaker, 2003) and more than 12 million families with children have insufficient food (Nord, Andrews, & Carlson, 2002). In high-crime and gang-infested neighborhoods, the difficult task of keeping children safe and getting them to school is an important step in the educational process (Lawson, 2003). Families generally know what they need. School social workers help them meet that need by addressing financial, medical, and mental health issues and by linking them with appropriate community agencies. When no agencies are available to meet a family's need, school social workers must work with others in the community to develop the necessary resources (see Chapter 5 on school social work at the policy level).

| Case | Case Example |

It was late afternoon, in the dead of winter in Minnesota, on the last day of school before a long holiday break, when the phone rang in the school social worker's office. The mother on the end of the line said that her family had run out of propane gas used to heat their trailer home and had no money to purchase more. It was 25 degrees below zero and the forecast was for colder weather during the next 2 weeks of the holiday break. The family had no place to go and no friends or family to help; with three elementary age children, they were frantic. The mother asked the school social worker to see if there was any assistance for them in the community. The school social worker started to work down the list of the many contacts she had with different community agencies. On the sixth phone call she located an agency that had emergency funding and could help the family. The school social worker contacted the mother and connected her with the agency. The family was able to stay warm in their home over the holiday and the children's lives were not disrupted, which helped them to return to school ready to learn.

Connecting Families With Teachers

Research generally shows that children do better in school when their family is involved in their education (Henderson & Berla, 1995). School social workers serve as liaisons facilitating communication between the student's home and school. The goal of this facilitative work is to help the family and the school work together to enable the student's educational success. School social workers provide a direct link between the family and the school by contacting the family with regular updates. They also enable families and teachers to communicate directly with each other by taking teachers with them on home visits or arranging transportation so a family can come to school. In addition, they set up home–school notebooks in which teachers and family members can write short daily or weekly notes back and forth to each other. They also translate school jargon for the family and gather information on the family's strengths, hopes, culture, and concerns. This information about the family helps teachers better understand and work with the child. Likewise, information from school assists families in knowing what is expected and how they can reinforce academic skills at home (Henderson & Berla, 1995).

School social workers use a variety of techniques to involve families in the education of their children. They often foster the connection between the home and school through home visits, phone calls, and information sessions on topics such as "helping your child start kindergarten." Other methods of contact include newsletters, phone calls, notes sent home, conferences, and social events such as open houses. They can also ask school administrators to allow that computers at school be made available for families after school and on weekends, an effective approach in bringing families into the school environment (Brockett, 1998).

Connecting Families With Other Families

Perhaps one of the most important services school social workers offer families is helping them connect with other families for mutual support and exchange of information. The Parent to Parent (Santelli, Turnbull, Marquis, & Lerner, 1995) program is one example of how parents can be valuable resources for other parents. School social workers can work with parents to implement similar programs. Support groups and socioeducational groups are additional ways to assist families. Other innovative methods have also been used to help families communicate with each other about effective strategies for dealing with different situations. Ingemar Eckstrom, a school social worker in Minnesota, helped parents connect with each other by routinely offering a "family pizza night" with door prizes and a magician to entertain the children for 40 minutes after the meal while the parents met. He also regularly offered a series of four parent education group meetings on effective discipline, building self-esteem, encouraging responsibility, and building family strengths. Other school social workers organized a "cooperative game" night at school for families and "family fun" nights at which personnel from community agencies staffed booths at school with prizes and information about community resources for the families.

MODELS OF FAMILY INVOLVEMENT

Montemayor and Romero (2000) identified two models of family involvement that have relevance for school social workers. The deficit model focuses on changing the family and views the family as in need of repair. In contrast, the families as leaders model values the family as important stakeholders. The first model calls for change in the family; the second model requires schools to make accommodations for families. The deficit model "accepts school culture as normative, without questioning basic educational goals, processes, or norms," basically maintaining a system of exclusion based on middle class, Euro-American norms (Boethel et al., 2003, p. 16). The families as leaders model invites families to participate in the process of goal and policy development and program evaluation. This leadership model requires that efforts to connect with families be done in a way that they feel valued and respected. School social workers must challenge the deficit model whenever it is used.

In their role as family advocates, school social workers need to raise questions with school administrators and personnel about how families are treated. Without addressing these issues, it is easy for families and school personnel to blame each other for communication problems. When families feel attacked or they "lack the resources, social standing, and capital to make their voices and opinions heard," it is easier to withdraw or become confrontational (Lawson, 2003, p. 120).

CULTURAL COMPETENCE

School social workers and other school personnel must strive for cultural competence to work effectively with families. Cultural competence, which is defined in the introduction of this book, is necessary to address the racism and cultural ignorance families may face at school (Henderson, Jacob, Kernan-Schloss, & Raimondo, 2004). It is important to respect the knowledge about child-rearing practices that comes from community elders, natural social networks such as extended family, and ethnic and cultural traditions (Cochran & Dean, 1991).

To provide culturally competent school social work service, it is necessary to recognize that trust between the school and the family may be an issue, especially for families who have experienced oppression (Byrk & Schneider, 2002). Studies show that students do better in school when there is a strong level of trust between the teachers and the parents (Scribner, Young, & Pedroza, 1999). This trust can be developed by keeping families informed about what their children are learning, and how they are doing, in a way that respects cultural differences.

Working With Culturally Diverse Families

The number of students classified as limited English proficient has been increasing in U.S. schools, with a 105% increase between 1991 and 2001 (Hood, 2003). Approximately one in five students has at least one parent who was born in another country (U.S. Census Bureau, 2001). Language, lack of familiarity with the U.S. educational system, perceptions of discrimination at school, fear of being deported, and lack of cultural competence by school personnel create challenges for families who have immigrated to the United States (Collingnon, Men, & Tan, 2001; Levine & Trickett, 2000).

Other challenges come from families feeling pressure to acculturate and adjust to the dominant culture while maintaining their own culture. In essence, acculturation requires the ability to walk in two worlds and be bicultural. Assimilation, on the other hand, involves giving up one's culture to blend into the dominant society (Lum, 1999). Acculturation and assimilation take a toll on a person's identity and can create many problems for families. For example, children may want to fit in with their peers from the dominant culture regarding the way they dress and talk, creating a source of conflict in the family. Because school culture in the United States has been predominantly Euro-American, families from other cultures have been pressured to acculturate or assimilate for their children to do well in school.

The school social worker can tackle some of these challenges by acknowledging cultural differences and helping families understand what school personnel expect of them and by working with school administrators and personnel to adopt better procedures to work with diverse families (Leistyna, 2002). Sharing inspiring success stories about what teachers have done to work effectively with diverse families is one way to encourage faculty to be more understanding and inclusive (Franklin & Soto, 2002). Also, curricula are available that encourage students to take pride in their cultural heritage, potentially reducing some of the pressure to acculturate and, in turn, reducing conflict between students and their families. One such curricular example is the American Indian History, Culture and Language Curriculum Framework (Minnesota Department of Children, Families & Learning, n.d.).

The Seattle, Washington, school district uses a variety of approaches to involve the large immigrant population in the schools (Brockett, 1998). For example, it distributes copies of the student welcome letters, policies on attendance/behavior, student handbooks, and school newsletters in the family's primary language. On Friday nights, it invites the families for dinner at school. It also has interpreters at school events. The school provides a case manager and instructional assistants to help families find housing, job training, and make sure they know about resources for food and clothing in the community. School social workers can help their school districts implement similar services for families.

Working With Homeless Families

An estimated 1.35 million children are homeless in the United States (Urban Institute, 2000). The demand for shelters has increased significantly in the past two decades (National Coalition for the Homeless, 2002). The McKinney-Vento Act, described in Chapter 15, has implications for school social workers and the roles they play in ensuring homeless children have access to education.

Homelessness is traumatic, and for most families in this situation, getting their children to school is one of their focal problems. Approximately 33% of homeless children do not attend school on a regular basis (U.S. Department of Education, 2000). School social workers can work with other agencies in the community to coordinate services families who are homeless need to keep their children in school. Hicks-Coolick, Burnside-Eaton, and Peters (2003) noted that families who are homeless need before- and after-school care, help getting children to school, mentoring, tutoring, transportation, survival skills training, support groups, case management, advocacy, food, clothing, school supplies, and job counseling. In addition to connecting families with resources to meet their needs, school social workers can also make sure that teachers have information about how best to work with families who are homeless. Transportation is the major barrier to education for homeless children (U.S. Department of Education, 2000). At a minimum, the school social worker should advocate to ensure that children who are homeless are not moved from school to school based on the location of their temporary shelter but, instead, are provided transportation to a continuous school placement.

ASSESSMENT

The initial request for assessment can be anxiety producing for families because it can create fear about their child being labeled or not being successful in school. School social workers can work to reduce some of this anxiety by meeting with the family to discuss the referral for assessment, explain the assessment process, and learn how the family views the situation. Information from the family can help school personnel better understand the life circumstances of the student and work more effectively with them at school. In these initial contacts regarding the request for assessment, school social workers assist family members in learning how they can be involved in the assessment and decisions about strategies to help their child obtain the best education possible. Chapter 16 addresses policies related to parent involvement in special education assessment. It also provides an excellent description of information that should be included about the family in the school social worker's written report.

Problem-Solving and Solution-Focused Approaches to Assessment

The problem-solving approach has been widely used by social workers when doing family assessments.

Steps in the Problem-Solving Model

1. Identifying the problem
2. Obtaining the family's perspective on the problem, including the history
3. Reaching an agreement on the desired outcome
4. Generating ideas about how to achieve the desired outcome including cultural traditions
5. Developing a plan
6. Evaluating the progress toward the desired outcome

Hepworth, Rooney, and Larsen (2002)

The solution-building approach, also used by social workers, differs from the problem-solving approach in that less time is spent discussing the problem. The focus tends to be more on family strengths, resources, past successes in dealing with the problem, and desired outcomes.

Steps in the Solution-Building Approach

1. Asking the family how you can be helpful to them
2. Asking the family to describe what will be different when the problem is solved
3. Asking the family to describe a time when the problem was less severe and identify what was happening at that time
4. Complimenting the family on what they are already doing to improve the situation
5. Giving some suggestions about what the family could do that may be helpful
6. Asking them to rate on a scale of 0 to 10 how well the problem has been solved throughout the work with them

De Jong and Berg (2002)

School social workers are often asked to conduct social and developmental histories or other types of evaluation as part of the overall assessment (see Chapter 16). Occasionally, school social workers may use other family assessment tools, and there are several to choose from.

Creating a **genogram** with a family is a way to map the structure of the family tree dating back three generations (Guerin, 1976). Names and ages of family members are recorded along with the type of relationship (sister, brother, aunt, etc.). Significant events, such as death and divorce, as well as medical history, cultural identity, religion, and occupation are recorded. A genogram may allow a family to identify patterns, or the lasting impact of certain events, for the first time.

Ecomaps provide a method for examining the type and strength of the family's social connections (Hartman, 1978). In an ecomap, the family members are represented by writing the names of each person in the family inside a circle in the middle of a piece of paper. The people or agencies that have a relationship with the family are each drawn as additional circles outside the family circle. Lines and arrows are drawn between the family and the outer circles to show the strength of the relationship, the type of relationship, and if support is coming into or going out from the family.

Several questionnaires and rating scales can also be used when assessing families. The Family Assessment Device is a self-report, 60-item questionnaire that measures problem solving, communication, roles, affective responsiveness, affective involvement, and behavioral control (Epstein, Baldwind, & Bishop, 2000). The Family Adaptability and Cohesion Evaluation Scale IV (Olson, Tiesel, & Gorall, 1996) is a self-report questionnaire that allows people to rate their family interaction regarding their level of cohesion (enmeshed or disengaged) and adaptability (chaotic or rigid). The *Handbook of Family Measurement Techniques* (Touliatos, Perlmutter, Strauss, & Holden, 2000) provides comprehensive information on many other family assessment tools. It consists of three volumes of information on more than 900 different measurement instruments that can be used with families.

BEST AND PROMISING STRATEGIES FOR INVOLVING FAMILIES

Families and Schools Together

The Families and Schools Together program (McDonald, 2005) was developed in 1988 by a social worker. Many studies document the effectiveness of this program in improving academic and behavioral performance of the children, increasing parent involvement in school, and reducing family conflict (McDonald & Frey, 1999). The program has been implemented throughout most of the United States as well as in several other countries. Goals of the program are to enhance family functioning, decrease family stress, and prevent school failure. To accomplish these goals, a multifamily group intervention is used for families with children 4–12 years of age. Components of the program include a recruitment process; 8–12 weekly multifamily support group sessions with a family meal, games, parent support group, time for parents to play individually with their child, a family lottery, and opening and closing rituals; and ongoing monthly follow-up multifamily meetings.

Multisystemic Therapy

Multisystemic therapy has been successful in treating violent and chronic juvenile offenders and their families (Henggeler, Melton, & Smith, 1992). This form of therapy is intensive, with a therapist making several visits to the family's home each week. Specific aspects in the young person's life that create problems are targeted for change, such as contact with a negative peer group, poor academic performance, or how discipline or emotions are handled in the home. School social workers work closely with the multisystemic therapist regarding school and family issues.

School Development Program

Comer and Haynes's (1992) School Development Program was highly effective at increasing reading and math scores and decreasing suspensions, absences, and rates of punishment in low-income elementary and middle schools. The principles that guided this program focused on accomplishing goals rather than assigning blame, cooperation among the adults involved in a child's life, consensus rather than majority rule decision making, regular meetings, and parent involvement in the decision-making process. School social workers are in an excellent position to encourage use of these principles in the schools they serve. It is important that these principles be implemented in a way that ensures representation of the minority view in program planning and that gives families flexibility and choice as part of the decision-making process (Friesen & Huff, 1996).

Home Visits

Of the strategies that school social workers use to engage families in the education of their children, home visits stand out as one of the most effective (Sanders, 2000). Home visits have been more successful at involving low-income families in the educational system than requiring them to visit school (Toomey, 1986). Meeting in the home is convenient because it does not require families to make arrangements for transportation or child care. Home visits also allow the family to meet with school personnel in an environment that is familiar and comfortable.

To explore parent perception of the effectiveness of home visitation, Reglin (2002) conducted a study of 80 primarily African American families who had fourth- or fifth-graders at a school in Florida. More than half (63%) of the students changed residence during the school year, primarily because of the family's inability to pay rent. School involvement was defined as (1) providing assistance with school assignments, (2) providing the time and space for study, (3) having regular home visits, and (4) staying in regular communication with teachers and school personnel. The majority of parents surveyed (91.3%) reported that home visits by school personnel would help them better support their child's education and would increase their involvement in school. Reglin concluded that home visits can foster communication, reinforce the family's involvement, and help "address any unusual circumstances that may affect the child's performance" (p. 156).

Families and Homework: Teachers Involve Parents in Schoolwork

Families need information about what their children will be learning in advance of when the lessons are taught at school. It is best when homework directions are clear and include the amount of time that should be spent on any given task (Reglin, 2002). School social workers can coordinate with teachers to develop methods for keeping the parents informed about specific skills that need review at home. Additionally, families often need guidance on how to help their children with homework, and without this guidance homework can be a negative experience (Cooper, Lindsay, & Nye, 2000).

School social workers can help set up programs similar to Teachers Involve Parents in Schoolwork (TIPS) (Epstein et al., 1995), in which students are given homework twice a month that requires conversations and activities with family members. Students in the TIPS program had more accurate schoolwork and earned higher grades than did students from a similar background not in the program (Van Voorhis, 2003). Hoover-Dempsey et al. (2001) identified six ways families can help with homework: (1) encourage the student to do homework, (2) monitor the homework, (3) praise the effort put into the homework, (4) help explain the homework, (5) break tasks into smaller steps, and (6) demonstrate how to do the task required in the homework. School social workers can find ways to share this information with parents, such as publishing "How to Help Your Child with Homework" information in the school newspaper or tip sheets that can be handed out at conferences, during home visits, and at parent information sessions. School social workers may also work with teachers to create a video for parents that demonstrates the six techniques described previously.

Family Group Conferencing

School social workers need to be able to facilitate techniques such as family group conferencing (FGC) that encourage family involvement in their child's education. The FGC approach provides a means for involving extended family, friends, elders, and others the family can draw upon for support. FGC is a strategy borrowed from the Maori culture (Love, 2000) that brings family, friends, and anyone else the family wants to involve into a problem-solving session. Once the goals of the conference session are established by the family and the agency personnel, the family and the people they have invited go into a conference room and develop a plan to accomplish the goals. The beauty of FGC is that it gives families an "opportunity to tap into their own resources to rebuild and strengthen existing social support networks" (Merkel-Holguin, 2004, p. 156). Although it has mostly been used in child welfare agencies, FGC has been applied in some schools. For example, a suburban Pennsylvania school district used it to address incidents of misconduct and violence (Taylor & Kummery, 1996).

The FGC approach has the potential to increase family involvement in the schools because it shifts the power dynamics. A typical school meeting without the FGC approach may have one or two family members and several school professionals represented. In this situation, it is easy for family members to feel outnumbered and intimidated. Using FGC, there will likely be more representatives from the family's support network than school personnel because family members have the power to decide who goes into the conference room. Relinquishing power can provoke anxiety for school personnel, who have been taught that they are the experts, and as a result, school social workers may face some resistance when suggesting strategies such as FGC. When schools do not offer family-based approaches, school social workers need to build in as much support as possible for families. One way to do this is to encourage families to bring relatives or friends with them to school meetings so they will have someone with whom they can talk outside of the school to process the meeting. Parents can also be encouraged to join parent advocacy groups and bring a member from that group with them to meetings at school.

RELATIONSHIP BUILDING WITH FAMILIES

Relationship building is critical and necessary because many families have not had a positive experience with schools. The level of openness schools have toward families likely influences the home–school relationship and their level of involvement with the educational system. Henderson et al. (2004) provide a series of questions that school social workers can use with school personnel to determine openness to parents; depending on the answers, schools fall into one of the following four categories: "fortress school," "come if we call school," "open-door school," or "partnership school" (p. 12). School social workers need to be strong advocates for partner relationships between families and schools. Part of that advocacy involves raising questions about the ways families are regarded and treated. Fortunately, there are many resources that school social workers can share to assess the level of the family–school partnership. For example, the National Network of Partnership Schools offers the Measure of School, Family, and Community Partnership (Salinas, Epstein, Sanders, Davis, & Douglas, 2001) free on their website.

School social workers must work with school personnel to show family members that they will not be blamed, shamed, or coerced but, rather, they will be treated with dignity and respect and their voice will be heard. School social workers can use the following checklist with school personnel to guide relationship-building efforts. If schools are missing components on the checklist, they can take action to improve in those areas. For example, if the school does not have cultural guides who visit on a regular basis to help the personnel learn about the culture and history of the families they serve, then this is an area to target for change. The additional cultural knowledge could help the school personnel build stronger relationships with families.

Relationship-Building Checklist for Schools

- Work with cultural guides to learn more about the cultures represented at school.
- Decorate the school with art representative of the cultures of children attending.
- Recognize the expert knowledge of the family regarding their child.
- Recognize that all families want their children to do well in school.
- At least once a month, contact the family about the student's accomplishments.
- Thank families for making arrangements to meet.
- Serve beverages and food at meetings and events.
- Be willing to meet at night or other times.
- Offer transportation and child care for meetings and events.
- Provide information about specific skills required at each grade level.
- Share ideas about how families can help students gain skills.
- Have a translator available at events.
- Create a lending library for families and let them know about it.
- Host celebrations at school for small steps.
- Help families connect with resources in the community.
- Show interest in and respect for the family's culture and customs.
- Be honest and positive.
- Communicate respectfully and compassionately.
- Use words the families can understand and avoid acronyms (IIIP or SED).
- Honor the family members as important decision makers.
- Offer family literacy programs.

Adapted from Henderson and Mapp (2002)

School social workers can offer workshops for teachers that outline strategies for effective communication with family members and ways to encourage family involvement. They can also place family-friendly communication suggestions in teachers' mailboxes prior to conferences. Research shows that when teachers learn the importance of respecting the challenges families face and can communicate in a nonthreatening way, parents develop more positive attitudes toward school and feel more comfortable talking to teachers (Cochran & Dean, 1991).

Welcoming Environment

Welcoming practices are important in encouraging family involvement (Mapp, 1999). New security measures often require family members to pass through a security system and report to the office prior to going anywhere else in the school building. Once they arrive at the office, they may not always receive a warm greeting, and they may not understand the language spoken. Insensitive remarks by school personnel due to a lack of cultural competence are hurtful and can reinforce negative feelings toward the educational system (Collingnon et al., 2001). School social workers can work with personnel and administrators to make the school a more welcoming, friendly, and culturally inclusive place.

School social workers can help create a welcoming school environment in several ways. First, they can remind school personnel that a welcoming environment is important. Simple gestures, such as placing a welcome sign on the door, greeting family members with warmth and respect, and maintaining an environment that represents the culture of the families in the neighborhood, can ease the tension. School social workers can talk with school personnel and administration about recruiting families from each grade to assess the school environment and generate suggestions for making the school more welcoming. Videotapes of students interviewing the teachers, principal, support personnel, and parent organization leaders about the school can be given to new families. Parent associations can serve as a "welcome wagon" for new families. School social workers can help organize special welcoming events the first week of every month at which new families could be taken on school tours, meet the faculty, and receive information about services such as after-school programs. Door prizes for such an event could be solicited from local businesses.

SUMMARY

Much of the research on family involvement documents the influence that families have on their child's success in school. School social workers play a pivotal role in developing and maintaining family involvement in the education of their children.

School social workers need to work with faculty, staff, and administrators to develop a long-term commitment toward making the school a welcoming environment for everyone. Ideas such as warm greetings and a parent association welcome wagon for new families would not be costly and yet could set a positive first impression. The school social worker can help school personnel involve families in an assessment of barriers to family involvement and then develop, implement, and evaluate plans to eliminate those barriers. Families should be included as part of the decision-making team in this process. In their role as liaison, school social workers provide teachers with information that helps them communicate with families in a way that allows the family to feel valued and respected. The research on best practice shows home visits, developing a high level of trust between the family and the school, focusing on goals rather than blame, having families identify their successes, and family interactive homework are linked to positive outcomes regarding family involvement with the school.

Helping schools continually strive for increasing cultural competence is an important role of the school social worker. This can be done by raising the issue, self-assessment, linking schools with cultural guides, and having translators available for family events such as conferences. School social workers conduct family assessments with strengths-based, solution-focused, and problem-solving interviews. They also help families with children who have special needs deal with feelings, learn about their rights, and take an active role in developing and supporting educational program plans. Finally, school social workers organize activities and groups that help families connect with and support each other.

This chapter stressed the importance of family involvement in the education of their children and the supporting role that school social workers play. Families should be regarded as a valuable resource and full partner in the educational process. Their involvement should be encouraged not just for help with homework or when there are problems but also because they should be considered the constituents and decision makers in the educational system.

School Social Work Companion Website

Please be sure to check out our companion website at www.thomsonedu.com/social_work/bye, where you will find relevant materials for each chapter, including flashcards, online practice quizzes, and PowerPoint slides.

References

Boethel, M., Averett, A., Buttram, J., Donnelly, D., Jordan, C., Myers, M., Orozco, E., & Wood, L. (2003). *Diversity: School, family, & community connections annual synthesis*. Austin, TX: National Center for Family & Community Connections with Schools Southwest Educational Development Laboratory.

Brockett, D. (1998). Reaching out to immigrant parents. *Education Digest, 63*(8), 29–32.

Byrk, A., & Schneider, B. (2002). *Trust in schools: A core resource for improvement.* Chicago: Chicago University Press.

Cochran, M., & Dean, C. (1991). Home–school relations and the empowerment process. *Elementary School Journal, 91*(3), 261–269.

Collingnon, F. F., Men, M., & Tan, S. (2001). Finding ways in: Community-based perspectives on Southeast Asian family involvement with schools in a New England state. *Journal of Education for Students Placed at Risk, 6*(1–2), 27–44.

Comer, J., & Haynes, N. (1992). *Summary of school development program effects.* New Haven, CT: Yale Child Study Center.

Cooper, H., Lindsay, J. J., & Nye, B. (2000). Homework in the home: How student, family, and parenting-style differences relate to the homework process. *Contemporary Educational Psychology, 25,* 464–497.

De Jong, P., & Berg, I. K. (2002). *Interviewing for solutions* (2nd ed.). Pacific Gove, CA: Brooks/Cole Thomson Learning.

Eagle, E. (1989). *Socioeconomic status, family structure, and parental involvement: The correlates of achievement.* Paper presented at the annual meeting of the American Educational Research Association, San Francisco, March 27–31.

Epstein, J. L., Salinas, K. C., Jackson, V. E., & educators in Baltimore City Public School System. (1995). *TIPS (Teachers Involve Parents in Schoolwork) manual for teachers: Language arts, science/health, and math interactive homework in the middle grades.* Baltimore: Johns Hopkins University, Center on School, Family, and Community Partnerships.

Epstein, N., Baldwind, L., & Bishop, D. (2000). Family assessment device. In American Psychiatric Association (Ed.), *Handbook of psychiatric measures* (pp. 245–247). Washington, DC: American Psychiatric Association.

Federal Register. (March 31, 1994). *Goals 2000: Educate America Act* (Vol. 59, pp. 3633–3650). Washington, DC: U.S. Government Printing Office.

Fischer, R. L. (2003). School-based family support: Evidence from an exploratory field study. *Families in Society, 84*(3), 339–348.

Franklin, C., & Soto, I. (2002). Keeping Hispanic youths in school. *Children and Schools, 24*(3), 139–142.

Friesen, B., & Huff, B. (1996). Family perspectives on systems of care. In B. A. Stroul (Ed.), *Children's mental health: Creating systems of care in a changing society* (pp. 41–68). Baltimore: Brooks.

Guerin, P. J. (1976). *Family therapy: Theory and practice.* New York: Gardner.

Hartman, A. (1978). Diagrammatic assessment of family relationships. *Social Casework, 59,* 465–476.

Henderson, A., & Berla, N. (1995). Introduction. In A. Henderson & N. Berla (Eds.), *A new generation of evidence: The family is critical to student achievement* (pp. 1–20). Washington, DC: Center for Law and Education.

Henderson, A., Jacob, B., Kernan-Schloss, A., & Raimondo, B. (2004). *The case for parent leadership.* Arlington, VA: KSA-Plus Communications and the Center for Parent Leadership.

Henderson, A. T., & Mapp, K. L. (2002). *A new wave of evidence: The impact of school, family, and community connections on student achievement.* Austin, TX: Southwest Educational Development Laboratory.

Henggeler, S., Melton, G., & Smith, L. (1992). Family preservation using multisystemic therapy: An effective alternative to incarcerating serious juvenile offenders. *Journal of Consulting and Clinical Psychology, 60,* 953–961.

Hepworth, D. H., Rooney, R. H., & Larsen, J. A. (2002). *Direct social work practice: Theory and skills* (6th ed.). Pacific Grove, CA: Brooks/Cole Thompson Learning.

Hicks-Coolick, A., Burnside-Eaton, P., & Peters, A. (2003). Homeless children: Needs and services. *Child & Youth Care Forum, 32*(4), 197–210.

Hood, L. (2003). *Immigrant students, urban high schools: The challenge continues.* New York: Carnegie Corporation of New York.

Hoover-Dempsey, K. V., Battiato, A. B., Walker, J. M., Reed, R. P., DeJong, J. M., & Jones, K. P. (2001). Parental involvement in homework. *Educational Psychologist, 36*(3), 95–203.

House-Senate Education Conference Report. (2001, December 11). *No Child Left Behind.* Washington, DC: U.S. Department of Education.

Jeynes, W. H. (2003). A meta-analysis: The effects of parental involvement on minority children's academic achievement. *Education and Urban Society, 35*(2), 202–218.

Kemthorne, D. (2005). *National Governor's Association Task Force on School Readiness: Building the foundation for bright futures.* Washington, DC: National Governor's Association Center for Best Practices.

Latimer, W. W. (2003). Integrated family and cognitive–behavioral therapy for adolescent substance abusers: A stage efficacy study. *Drugs & Alcohol Dependence, 71*(3), 303–318.

Lawson, M. (2003). School-family relations in context: Parent and teacher perceptions of parent involvement. *Urban Education, 38*(1), 77–133.

Leistyna, P. (2002). Extending the possibilities of multicultural community partnerships in urban public schools. *Urban Review, 34*(1), 1–23.

Levine, E. B., & Trickett, E. J. (2000). Toward a model of Latino parent advocacy for educational change. *Journal of Prevention & Intervention in the Community, 20*(1–2), 121–137.

Lopez, A., & Cole, C. (1999). Effects of a parent-implemented intervention on the academic readiness skills of five Puerto Rican kindergarten students in an urban school. *School Psychology Review, 28*(3), 439–447.

Love, C. (2000). Family group conferencing: Cultural origins, sharing, and appropriations-A Maori reflection. In G. Burford & J. Hudson (Eds.), *Family group conferences: New directions in community centered child and family practice* (pp. 15–30). Hawthorne, NY: De Gruyter.

Lum, D. (1999). *Culturally competent practice: A framework for growth and action.* Pacific Grove, CA: Brooks/Cole.

Mapp, K. L. (1999). *Making the connection between families and schools: Why and how parents are involved in their children's education.* Unpublished doctoral dissertation, Harvard University, Cambridge, MA.

McDonald, L. (2005). *Families and Schools Together.* Retrieved February 17, 2005, from www.wcer.wisc.edu/fast/

McDonald, L., & Frey, H. (1999, November). Families and Schools Together: Building relationships. *Juvenile Justice Bulletin,* pp. 1–15.

Merkel-Holguin, L. (2004). Sharing power with the people: Family group conferencing as a democratic experiment. *Journal of Sociology and Social Welfare, 31*(1), 155–173.

Miedel, W. T., & Reynolds, A. J. (1999). Parent involvement in early intervention for disadvantaged children: Does it matter? *Journal of School Psychology, 37*(4), 379–402.

Minnesota Department of Children, Families & Learning, Office of Indian Education. (n.d.). *American Indian history, culture and language curriculum framework.* Roseville, MN: Author.

Montemayor, A., & Romero, A. (2000). Valued parent leadership. *IDRA Newsletter, 1–2,* 12–14.

National Coalition for the Homeless. (2002). *Why are people homeless? NCH fact sheet #1.* Retrieved February 20, 2005, from www.nationalhomeless.org/causes.html

National Governors Association Task Force on School Readiness. (2005). *Building the foundation for bright futures: Final report of the NGA Task Force on School Readiness*; and companion piece, *Building the foundation for bright futures: A governor's guide to school readiness.* Washington, DC: Author.

Nord, M., Andrews, M., & Carlson, S. (2002). *Household food security in the United States* (Research Report No. 35). Washington, DC: Department of Agriculture.

Olson, D., Tiesel, J., & Gorall, D. (1996). *Family Adaptability and Cohesion Evaluation Scale IV.* St. Paul: University of Minnesota, Family Social Science.

Proctor, B. D., & Dalaker, J. (2003). *United States Census Bureau current population: Report* (pp. 60–222). Washington, DC: U.S. Government Printing Office.

Reglin, G. (2002). Project reading and writing (R.A.W.): Home visitation and the school involvement of high-risk families. *Education, 123*(1), 153–161.

Salinas, K., Epstein, J., Sanders, M., Davis, D., & Douglas, L. (2001). *Measurement of school, family, and community partnership.* Northwest Regional Education Laboratory, National Network of Partnership Schools, Johns Hopkins University. Retrieved February 20, 2005, from www.nwrel.org/csrdp/mp.html

Sanders, M. G. (2000). Creating successful school-based partnership programs with families of special needs students. *School Community Journal, 10*(2), 37–56.

Santelli, B., Turnbull, A., Marquis, J., & Lerner, E. (1995). Parent to parent programs: A unique form of mutual support. *Infants and Young Children, 8,* 48–57.

School Social Work Association of America. (n.d.). *School social work: Connecting schools, families & communities.* Northlake, IL: Author.

Scribner, J. D., Young, M. D., & Pedroza, A. (1999). Building collaborative relationship with parents. In P. Reyes, J. D. Scribner, & A. Paredes-Scribner (Eds.), *Lessons from high-performing Hispanic schools: Creating learning communities* (pp. 36–60). New York: Teachers College Press.

Search Institute. (1998). *40 Developmental assets: Healthy Communities-Healthy Youth tool kit.* Minneapolis, MN: Author.

Starkey, P., & Klein, A. (2000). Fostering parental support for children's mathematical development: An intervention with Head Start families. *Early Education and Development, 11*(5), 659–680.

Taylor, B., & Kummery, G. (1996). Family group conferencing. *Educational Leadership, 54*(1), 44–46.

Toomey, D. (1986). Home-school relations and inequality in education. In A. T. Henderson & N. Berla (Eds.), *A new generation of evidence: The family is critical to student achievement* (pp. 138–139). Washington, DC: Center for Law and Education.

Touliatos, J., Perlmutter, B., Strauss, M., & Holden, G. (2000). *Handbook of family measurement techniques.* Thousand Oaks, CA: Sage.

Urban Institute. (2000). *A new look at homelessness in America.* Washington, DC. Author.

U.S. Census Bureau. (2000). *Current population reports* (Series P-25, No. 311). Retrieved May 11, 2004, from www.childstats.gov/ac2000/xpop3.asp

U.S. Census Bureau. (2001). Children of "baby boomer" and immigrants boost school enrollment to equal all-time high. *Census Bureau reports.* Retrieved May 11, 2004, from www.census.gove/Press-Release/www/2001/cb01-52.html

U.S. Department of Education. (2000). *Education for homeless children and youth report to Congress.* Washington, DC: Author.

Van Voorhis, F. L. (2003). Interactive homework in middle school: Effects on family involvement and science achievement. *Journal of Educational Research, 96*(6), 323–338.

Wang, J., & Wildman, L. (1994). The effect of family commitment in education on student achievement in seventh grade mathematics. *Education, 115*(2), 317–401.

School Social Work With Individuals and Small Groups

CHAPTER **9**

ELIZABETH TRACY,
M.S.W., Ph.D.
Case Western Reserve University

KATHLEEN USAJ, M.S.S.A.
Cleveland Heights–University Heights School District

CHAPTER OUTLINE

CHAPTER OVERVIEW

This chapter focuses on the knowledge, skills, and values needed to work with students individually and in groups. After reading this chapter, readers will be able to (1) identify the unique features of school-based assessment and practice;

(2) discuss the variety of individual assessments conducted within the school setting and individual and group interventions routinely used by school social workers; (3) understand the school-based team Intervention-Based Assessment model, behavioral observation, and data collection measurement strategies; (4) describe effective individual and classroom behavior management interventions; (5) explain group work in schools, including guidelines for group formation and key practice skills in facilitating groups with students; and (6) understand how these skills for individual student assessment and intervention are braided with macro school and districtwide behavioral intervention and supports. Although we recognize the important role of families in work with students, we are not specifically including content on families in this chapter because Chapter 8 is devoted to this topic.

INTRODUCTION

School social workers carry out multiple roles within a school, as other chapters have described. A primary role, however, is as a skilled direct service practitioner, providing services to students who experience academic and social difficulties in school. Even when working individually with students, school social workers approach assessment and intervention from a "person in environment" or "ecological" perspective. They recognize that what occurs (or does not occur) in the student's life before school and after school has tremendous impact on how the student behaves and performs during school (Allen-Meares, 2004). School districts are increasingly recognizing that until the nonacademic needs of students are met, it is very difficult to achieve academic goals. It has also become evident in recent years that school social workers provide services to many children and youth who would otherwise not receive any prevention or intervention services.

UNIQUE FEATURES OF SCHOOL-BASED SOCIAL WORK PRACTICE

School social work services are best understood in the context in which they are delivered. Working in a host setting, one in which social services are not the primary focus, there are several special practice considerations. To serve individual students, it is important for school social workers to (1) establish relationships with school personnel from other disciplines, (2) build rapport with the principal, (3) be clear about their role and who they serve, (4) be visible, and (5) provide prompt feedback (Berrick & Duerr, 1996). Additionally, determining who is the client—the student, family, classroom teacher, or entire school—is sometimes problematic in a school setting because any number of people and settings may be important to assessment or targets for intervention. For example, although a school social worker might work individually with a student who has been the victim of bullying, that worker may also simultaneously implement a schoolwide anti-bullying program and perhaps offer in-service education to teachers and parents about bullying (see Chapter 6 for more information on schoolwide bully prevention programs).

School social workers, drawing from the social work profession as a whole and the profession's **code of ethics**, apply an explicit set of values to their practice, including the worth and dignity of each person, respect for the individual, and the right to self-determination. These values are expressed within the school setting through the provision of culturally competent services, by building on student strengths and including students in planning their own learning experiences, by maintaining privacy and confidentiality of information, and through advocacy for students and families when policies or lack of services limit educational opportunities (National Association of Social Workers [NASW], 2002).

Social work assessments, whether conducted within a school or in other practice settings, are marked by a consideration of both person and environmental factors, gathered from a variety of sources and perspectives, and include strengths and resources as well as deficits and needs (Maluccio, Pine, & Tracy, 2002). The information collected in a school-based assessment should be "directly useful for designing interventions that address behaviors of concern" (NASW, 2002, p. 5). A functional approach to assessment (see Chapter 16) examines the purpose and effect of problematic behavior and provides information for intervention planning. The choice of assessment methods should be adapted to the situation being considered; it is unlikely that one assessment approach will be valid in all cases. Likewise, the choice of intervention should be based on an individualized accurate assessment of the situation or concern. As appropriate, school social workers collect information to assess developmental stage, social relations (Lucco, 1993), coping and self-regulation skills, internal and external assets (Search Institute, 2002), biological/medical conditions, cultural considerations, and emotional, legal, and environmental factors that affect student learning (NASW, 2002, standard 21). Cooper and Lesser (2005) suggest that an individual psychosocial assessment report include a section for each of the following: identifying information, referral source, presenting problem, history of the problem, previous attempts to resolve the problem, family background, developmental history, medical history, cultural history, spirituality, and current functioning.

INDIVIDUAL AND CLASSROOM-BASED ASSESSMENTS

School social workers need to be well versed in individual assessments for child development, child maltreatment; child mental health issues; school-based team assessments such as Intervention-Based Assessment (IBA), Functional Behavioral Assessment, Multi-Factored Evaluations, Manifestation Determinations; and school climate assessments/interventions (see Chapter 6). They must become experts in solution-focused assessments and interventions because their time is often limited by the large number of students for whom they are responsible. Sources of assessment information may include the student, classroom peers, family members, teachers, other educational staff members, and other community-based helping professionals. In addition, information may be gathered about the composition and resources within the classroom, school, and larger community environment (Allen-Meares, Washington, & Welsh, 1996). The source and type of data collection depend a great deal on the purpose of the assessment.

Child Maltreatment

School social workers are mandated by law to report a suspicion of child abuse or neglect to the child and family social services agency or the police. It is those agencies' responsibility to investigate the allegation. Most schools have policies and procedures whereby the school social worker informs the principal that a report was made to child protective services and also completes the necessary written documentation. School social workers have a key role in continuing to support students and families during and after the investigation. They often offer their ongoing assistance to parents who are struggling with appropriate parenting skills and provide linkages to supportive community agencies.

Suicidal Ideation

Suicide threats or ideation must always be addressed and should never be taken lightly (Bongar, 1992). The school social worker is often the clinician at the building who assesses a student's suicidal ideation. Be sure to follow the school's protocol for documenting and responding to suicide ideation.

Suicide Assessment Questions
1. How specific is the plan?
2. How lethal is the plan?
3. How readily available are the tools for carrying out the plan?
4. How likely is it that the person might be rescued by others?

Detailed plans, with greater lethality, more readily available tools, and less likelihood of rescue are higher in risk and warrant a direct safety plan. Questions about the emotional status include the following: Does the individual have plans for the future? How congruent is the affect shown? Is there tunneling or narrowing of the range of options? What is the emotional intensity? Inability to describe emotional states and extreme hopelessness present greater risk of suicide (Bongar, 1992).

In speaking with the student, do not act shocked or lecture on the value of life or whether suicide is right or wrong. Accept the student's feelings unconditionally. Be direct and nonjudgmental. Talk openly and matter-of-factly about suicide and show support. Offer hope that alternatives are available but do not offer glib reassurance. Tell the student that you care about him or her and that you will do all you can to keep the student safe until he or she feels like he or she can keep himself or herself safe again. Safety plans are made based on the risk assessment. The student must first agree that he will not commit suicide. If the student is unable to make that agreement, he must not be left alone, his parents must be contacted, and he must go immediately to an area hospital for an emergency assessment. Instruct the student's parents to remove means, such as guns or stockpiled pills. Give the parents a fact sheet on suicide. Tell the family you will accompany them to the hospital. If the level of risk is high and the family does not agree to take the student to the hospital, attempt to work with the family's resistance and denial. If you are unsuccessful, inform the parents that you must report the issue to the child protection agency.

Other Mental Health Assessments

The screening of mental health concerns can be conducted by the school social worker; there are many tools available (see Table 9.1) as well as observational assessments to determine if a student's mental health concern meets criteria for further assessment and linkage to community providers. Some mental health concerns include attention deficit hyperactivity disorder, posttraumatic stress disorder, obsessive–compulsive disorder, oppositional defiant disorder, anxiety, depression, grief reactions, and alcohol and/or drug abuse or dependency. In general, school social workers should consult with parents prior to screening, discuss the results of the screening with the parents, and assist parents in linking with community mental health agencies. School social workers must respect parents' decision to seek help for their child. The school social worker should work to build relationships with the family, continue to monitor the child's condition, and share continuing concerns with the family.

The most useful social work assessments employ a variety of sources and types of information, depending on the situation and setting (Gambrill, 1997). School social workers have a number of data collection methods available from which to choose.

Structured Interviews With Students, Teachers, Other School Staff, or Family Members

- Advantages: helpful in forming working relationships; direct means of gathering information; engages relevant people in the intervention; helps to identify antecedents and consequences to behavior; may provide home information
- Disadvantages: language, cognitive, or cultural barriers may limit the quality of information gathered; self-reports may not be accurate; there may be a bias toward reporting the situation as positive; requires good interview and recording skills; may require home visit to reach family members

Table 9.1 | Selected List of Assessment and Screening Tools

Instrument	Purpose and Format	Authors
Child Behavior Checklist	Screens for internalizing and externalizing emotional and behavioral problems	Achenbach (1979)
Semi-structured Clinical Interview for Children and Adolescents	Open-ended questions and tasks in eight areas; includes observation form	McConaughy and Achenbach (1994)
Behavior Assessment System for Children, Second Edition	Comprehensive set of rating scales and forms, including teacher, parent, and student self-report, observation and developmental history to assess adaptive behavior and to identify behavior problems	Reynolds and Kamphaus (1992) (available at www.agsnet.com)
Social Skills Rating System	Assesses social skills, problem behavior, and academic competence from the teacher, parent, and student perspective	Gresham and Elliot (1990)
Conners' Rating Scales—Revised	Screening instrument with forms for teachers and parents to rate problem behaviors related to attention deficit and hyperactivity	Conners (1997)
Coopersmith Self-Esteem Inventory	Student self-report checklist to assess how child/youth feels about self	Coopersmith (1981)
Borba Self-Esteem Tally	Teacher rating scale to identify student needs for security, selfhood, affiliation, mission, and competence	Borba (1989)
Child's Ecomap	Ecomap designed for use with children entering placement	Fahlberg (1991)
Child Sexual Behavior Inventory	Parent assessment of how frequently child engages in sexual behaviors	Faller (1993)
Recent Exposure to Violence	Questionnaire that asks children about violence experienced or witnessed	Singer et al. (1999); Flannery, Vazsonyi, Torquati, and Friedrich (1994)

Instrument	Purpose and Format	Authors
Parental Monitoring Scale	Questionnaire to determine extent to which parent monitors child's whereabouts	Singer et al. (1999); Flannery et al. (1994)
Culturalgram	Ecomap-like tool to gauge impact of different aspects of culture on the family (e.g., reasons for immigration and language spoken in home)	Hardy and Laszloffy (1995)
Ecomap	Visually depicts relationships between the family and the outside world	Hartman (1994)
Genogram	Diagram constructed by worker and family to depict family relationships extended over the past few generations	Hartman (1994)
Social Network Map	Gathers information about size and composition of personal social network, types of support available, and quality of network relationships	Tracy & Whittaker, 1990
School Success Profile	Survey instrument to collect information from students about schools, neighborhoods, families, peers, and physical and psychological well-being	Bowen, Woolley, Richman, and Bowen, (2001) (available from Jordan Institute for Families, UNC at Chapel Hill)
Australian Scale for Asperger's Syndrome	Rating scale to identify students at risk of Asperger's syndrome	Garnett and Attwood (1995)
Sexualized Behaviors Screening	Preschool through grade 4— chart of behavior that is normal, of concern, or needs professional assessment	Cavanaugh-Johnson (1999)
Burns Depression Checklist	Screening tools	Burns (1999)
Revised Children's Manifest Anxiety Scale	Measures anxiety	Reynolds and Richmond (1985)
Burns Anxiety Inventory	Screening tool	Burns (1999)
Student Self-Concept Scale	Measures self-concept	Gresham, Elliott, and Evans-Fernandez (1992)

Social and Developmental History

- Advantages: gathers information on developmental, environmental, health, and interpersonal relationships that may affect the student's ability to function in school; may be part of the psychosocial assessment for special education; may uncover environmental problems/needs; helps convey the student's social environment (real world) to teaching staff
- Disadvantages: may provide too much broad description and insufficient detail for developing interventions; needs to be individualized; less effective if used as an assessment battery approach in which the same tool is used with every student (Clark, 2002); may not gather data relevant to intervention design

Home Visit

- Advantages: provides a direct link between the school and home; allows for observation and assessment of the home environment; makes services more accessible to some families; may minimize power imbalance in the helping relationship; allows for teaching and modeling of parenting skills in the natural environment; capitalizes on the child's first teacher (Allen & Tracy, 2004)
- Disadvantages: time and travel costs; must make provisions for safety; may not be feasible with a team approach; home visits may not be desired by the family; may be subject to bias or misinterpretation by the home visitor

Classroom Observation

- Advantages: provides information on frequency, severity, and duration of behaviors as well as environmental triggers, antecedents, and consequences; consistent with an ecological approach to assessment; facilitates conversations with teachers; consistent with functional behavioral assessments
- Disadvantages: must be carried out in an unobtrusive manner; preconceptions may interfere with accurate observation; descriptions of behavior must be specific, not vague; behavior in one setting may not reflect behavior in another setting; may not be feasible due to time constraints

Standardized Self-Report Inventories or Screening Tools Completed by Child, Parent, and/or Teacher (See Table 9.1)

- Advantages: have uniform procedures for administration; may have known reliability, validity, norms; may be quick to use; include objective tests, projective tests, checklists and rating scales, and paper-and-pencil analogs
- Disadvantages: may not accurately measure what is intended; may not be appropriate with a particular population or age group; may be expensive or require prior training; may not yield information relevant to intervention design

Self-Recording/Monitoring

- Advantages: less intrusive than observation; puts client in control; begins to educate client about relevant factors and about the intervention approach; gathers information about the frequency and duration of a problem in more objectives terms; allows for information to be gathered about behavior in the home/community before and after intervention; can be used by students and parents
- Disadvantages: may be too time-consuming or too difficult to implement; may be inaccurate; client may need training and must understand purpose of the data collection

SCHOOL TEAM ASSESSMENTS

The school social worker is an important member of the school-based team. The team is usually composed of the building principal, school psychologist, school counselor, school social worker, school nurse, speech and language pathologist, a regular education teacher and a special education teacher, and, occasionally, an occupational and physical therapist. Collecting data and then considering and presenting a hypothesis about why a behavior is occurring is the first step for the school social worker considering a specific intervention, whether one is working on a team or performing an individual assessment.

Intervention-Based Assessment (IBA) is a collaborative, problem-solving process that focuses on a specific concern that affects the learner's educational progress. Individuals involved in this ongoing process include the learner, the learner's family, and school personnel, who mutually define and analyze the academic, social, emotional, or behavioral concerns; develop measurable goals; develop a hypotheses accounting for the problem; and design and implement interventions while evaluating the effectiveness of those interventions through the use of performance data (McNamara, Telzrow, & DeLamatre, 1999, p. 344). The IBA model is used to assess academic or behavioral concerns that arise for any student in the building and is not a "special education identification model." IBA begins with teacher observation and analysis of the student's behavior and development of a hypothesis regarding what might be causing the behavior. The intervention designed is in effect part of the assessment. If the intervention is successful, the hypothesis was correct and no further intervention may be required. If the desired results are not attained within 2–4 weeks, then the intervention is reviewed, a new hypothesis is developed, and another intervention is designed and/or the student may be suspected of having a disability and referred for collective assessment to the building Intervention Assistance Team (IAT). School social workers need to be well versed in the steps of the IBA process to be able to assist teachers to implement the model.

Description of the Problem   When a child is demonstrating difficulty with academics and/or behavior, the first step is to describe the behavior. The selection of behaviors for assessment and intervention is critical in remediating academic problems.

Case	**Case Example**

Jim is a new second-grade student. He enters the classroom every day in tears. His teacher, Mrs. Smith, has tried several interventions and yet Jim is still tearful for the first hour of the morning two months into the school year.

Developing a Hypothesis   With a description of the behavior and data gathering, a hypothesis begins to take shape to describe the problem. A **hypothesis** in this model is a tentative explanation that can be tested by further investigation. School social workers, whether working with a school-based team or individually, should always utilize hypothesis development when analyzing a student's behavior. The school social worker must address this process in an ecological framework, also taking into consideration mental health, disability, family, socioeconomic status, culture, gender, age, and other issues in developing a hypothesis and appropriate interventions. After the team members develop a hypothesis, they decide on an intervention to attempt to improve the targeted behavior. The intervention will become part of an ongoing assessment. The following are examples of environmental hypotheses: "Is the student being bullied?" "Is the student afraid to come to school and won't tell us?" "Is the student getting enough sleep (food, supervision) at night?" and "Are the child's behaviors meeting the *Diagnostic and Statistical Manual of Mental Disorders*, 4th edition, criteria for depression, anxiety, etc.?"

Case	**Case Example Continued**

The second-grade teacher consulted with Ms. Goodwin, the school social worker, about Jim. Ms. Goodwin and the teacher hypothesized that since Jim was a new student he might miss his former classmates or he might be not getting enough sleep at night and be tired in the morning.

Preintervention Data Gathering   Once the behavior has been described and targeted by the team, the next step is to gather preintervention data on that behavior, such as rating scale scores, frequency counts of how often the behavior occurs, and how often the student passes or fails pupil performance objectives. Data presented in graph form helps staff, parents, and students gain a realistic view with respect to the frequency, intensity, and duration of the behavior.

For behavioral performance, it is important to pinpoint the degree to which the student's targeted behavior is discrepant from other behaviors he or she exhibits (intrastudent variability) as well as the same behaviors exhibited by classroom peers (interstudent variability). When observing a student, one should compare him or her to a control student in the classroom. This way, one will be able to determine if the student's behavior is different from the norm of the classroom (which may indicate the need for teacher consultation versus student intervention).

Measurement Strategies for Behavioral Observation and Data Collection

- **Event recording** (e.g., raising a hand to get teacher's attention)—includes a tally of each time a behavior occurred, graphing over a period of time and preferably in different settings
- **Interval recording** (e.g., talking out of turn)—includes observing a student at a set interval (e.g., 30 seconds) and determining at that point if the behavior occurred
- **Duration recording** (e.g., crying)—record how long a behavior lasts
- **Latency recording** (e.g., following a direction)—record how long between a stimulus and a response.

Case Example Continued

Ms. Goodwin reviewed Jim's records to determine if there was a history of crying at his former school. She contacted his parents, who reported that Jim loved school last year and that he had not said anything at home about his crying in the morning. Ms. Goodwin observed him in the classroom and recorded the duration of his crying. She also observed him in the line before the morning bell rang and noticed that Jim was being teased by a known fourth-grade bully. She hypothesized that Jim did not feel safe.

Designing an Intervention   The next step is to design an intervention for the targeted behavior. Ideas for interventions can come from other teachers, support staff, and administrators and should be evidence based. In conjunction with designing or choosing an intervention, equally important is how the intervention will be monitored. Interventions can be monitored through various means: pre- and posttest measures, increase in percentages of accuracy in work, and decrease in frequency of undesired behavior. The school social worker will work with the teacher throughout the process to ensure the interventions are implemented and monitored with integrity. Typically, an intervention takes 2–4 weeks to be introduced, implemented, and monitored.

Case Example Continued

Ms. Goodwin shares her observational data with the teacher. They decide on a multilevel approach. First, Ms. Goodwin notifies the principal of the bullying observed in line and requests that he talk to the student who is bullying and also address the fourth-grade classroom regarding bullying issues. She conducts an all-classroom lesson on bullying for the second graders and, with parental permission, meets with Jim individually to make sure he knows he can trust the adults in the building to protect him. She role-plays appropriate ways to handle a bully. She monitors the line every morning and lets Jim know he is doing a good job standing up to the bully.

Reviewing the Results of the Intervention   After the intervention has been implemented, the success of that intervention in remediating the problem behavior will need to be assessed. Did the student show an increase in desired performance? If yes, the intervention was successful and should continue to be implemented. If yes, but only with the intense intervention of a special education teacher, school social worker, school psychologist, or speech language pathologist, then the student should be considered for referral to the IAT for a collective and more extensive assessment. If no, then a review of the entire process beginning with the description of the problem and the hypothesis should occur, which leads to the design and implementation of a different intervention.

| Case | **Case Example Concluded** |

Ms. Goodwin observes a marked change in Jim. He no longer cries in the morning. She observes that he has made a new friend in the second grade. Jim also talks to his teacher about his feelings and states that he feels safe.

Functional behavioral assessments are required by the reauthorized Individuals with Disabilities Education Act (1997) when the behavior of a student requiring special education services prompts disciplinary action. The school social worker advocates for and supports procedural safeguards to ensure that students who require special education continue to receive a free, appropriate public education. The procedural safeguards require that Individualized Education Program teams conduct a functional behavioral assessment and develop a behavioral intervention plan for students recommended for expulsion for more than 10 days in any school year. Functional behavioral assessment, now included in federal law, is consistent with sound social work practice. Assessment should take an ecological approach describing the function that behaviors serve for the student and generating information that leads to intervention. Positive behavioral interventions are specifically named in the law as the preferred method of intervention. School social workers should encourage parent participation in functional behavioral assessments and behavior intervention plans (Clark, 1998).

EVIDENCE-BASED INTERVENTIONS WITH INDIVIDUALS AND GROUPS

The following interventions are supported by research regarding their effectiveness for a variety of academic, social, emotional, and behavior problems. They can be modified for use with a range of issues and populations.

Self-Management Interventions

Self-management is a family of interventions intended to promote a student's ability to regulate his or her own behavior. The interventions are designed so that students can collect data about their own performance, deliver contingencies for such performance, guide their own work through self-instruction, and alter self-statements that have an impact on their psychological well-being and performance. Self-management skills can be taught individually or in small groups and practiced in a larger group setting, such as the classroom, lunchroom, or playground. The self-management skills addressed here are self-monitoring and self-instruction.

Self-Monitoring   Several important factors contribute to successful self-monitoring. The school social worker can assist the teacher in establishing a self-monitoring system for a student or for the entire classroom. The student must be instructed in and understand cueing and the procedures to be utilized.

Cueing Procedures

1. **Cueing** is a signal or indication from the teacher that the child should begin a self-monitoring procedure. Completion of a specific task can also prompt self-monitoring (e.g., academic: when student is finished with a worksheet he or she can evaluate and correct the answers. Behavioral: when the student raises his or her hand before asking question, he or she can put a hash mark on self-monitoring tally sheet). In many cases, visual, auditory, or physical prompts are used. These prompts are agreed upon with student and staff member prior to the beginning of the intervention.
2. Procedures: Using paper and pencil, the student can monitor a number of events or behaviors, including attention (on-task behavior) and productivity (summary record of work completed or expectations met).

Shapiro and Cole (1994)

Students must also be trained in self-monitoring procedures. A self-monitoring checklist can be created to enable students to monitor and review their own performance as they complete each step of the process they are trying to master, be it academic or social/behavioral. This method can be reinforced by posting problem-solving steps in the classroom.

Self-Monitoring Procedures

1. Define behavior to be recorded.
2. Model defined behavior.
3. Ensure that student understands behavior.
4. Observe student during self-monitoring behavior.

Self-Instruction   Once a student demonstrates success in self-monitoring his or her behavior, the student is taught self-instruction for academic and/or behavioral issues. The process of self-instruction training evolved from the early work of Meichenbaum and Goodman (1971).

The self-instruction procedure employs a series of questions that the child learns to ask himself or herself as he or she works; for example,

- What should I do here?
- Am I doing what I said I would do?
- What if I make a mistake, how will I fix it?
- Let me stop and think about what I am going to say/do next?

For self-instruction, a series of self-guiding statements specifying each step needed can be created for use by students. They can keep it on their desk or in their pocket if the problem is outside of the classroom. Students need to be supported in utilizing this process until they are able to internalize it and generalize it across the environment. The following are examples of self-guiding statements:

- I stand in line outside the door in the morning.
- I keep my hands and feet to myself.
- I greet my classmates by saying "Good morning! Did you do anything fun last night?"
- I walk in line to my class when the bell rings with no reminders.

The student places a check on each item he or she completed that morning and points are awarded for tasks achieved; additional points are awarded if all monitoring steps are correctly recorded.

Social–Emotional Behavioral Interventions

Differential Reinforcement   The behavioral management literature describes a number of strengths-based, differential reinforcement strategies, in which positive reinforcement is provided for behaviors other than the targeted misbehavior. In general, the purpose is to weaken undesired behavior by strengthening alternative behavior.

Types of Differential Reinforcement

- Differential reinforcement of incompatible behavior—reinforcing students for being "in their seat" rather than targeting them when they are "out of their seat."
- Differential reinforcement of alternative behavior—reinforcing appropriate alternative behavior, such as holding up a "HELP" card instead of talking out without being called on.
- Differential reinforcement of low rates of behavior—this is especially effective for behaviors that occur very frequently, such as talking out in class. Reinforcement is given for displaying fewer numbers of behaviors than agreed upon by the student and teacher in a specified interval. For example, a token is given to a student for interrupting fewer than five times during the morning.

Contracting

Contracting is a method for reaching an agreement with students about expected behavior or academic performance. It is effective in improving behavior among difficult to reach students and has a high degree of acceptance among teachers (Fuchs, 1991; Martens, Peterson, Witt, & Cirone, 1986). There are many variations on the use of contracts.

Elements of Contracting

1. Define specific behavior, such as "hand in homework first thing in the morning without being asked."
2. Specify criteria for success: Cumulative number of agreed upon specified behaviors adds up with each success, allowing for "bad days." For example, "hand in home work first thing in the morning without being asked 4 out of 5 days."
3. Select (with student participation) an appropriate positive consequence for satisfactory performance, and specify when and who will deliver the consequence.
   a. Consequences should be delivered soon after the desired behavior occurs, such as daily token and weekly choice from treasure box if the goal is met.
   b. A penalty clause can be included when the minimum agreed upon behavior is not attained and the child can lose tokens. But this approach should be used very cautiously.
4. Specify how the behavior/contract will be monitored. Utilizing the self-monitoring strategy with contracting can be a powerful reinforcement.
5. Put the agreement in writing and obtain signatures of all involved parties. Indicate whether the contract will be renegotiated upon its expiration.

Behavioral or performance requirements must be realistic and based on a student's current level of performance. The contract must be understandable and initially attainable. Standards for performance can be gradually raised. Keep frequent rewards small and use larger rewards as a bonus or "grand prize" for a series of successes. If the contract involves parent participation or monitoring such as homework completion, two sets of consequences can be specified—one set to be delivered at school and one delivered by parents at home.

Classroom Behavior Management Procedures

Effective commands gain and maintain the child's attention. The adult needs to use the child's or group's name and give a direction: for example, "Jim, put your name on the paper" and "Class, quiet voices." The adult uses a firm neutral tone and never yells or screams: for example, "Sarah, walk to the bench and sit down." The adult is specific and communicates exactly what he or she wants the student to do and pairs the command with a physical gesture if necessary: for example, "Class, stand against the wall in a single file." The adult uses positive phrasing, telling a student what to do rather than what to stop: for example,

"Walk down the hall" rather than "Stop running!" Finally, the adult states easy to manage steps with separate commands in each step: for example, "Jim, get out your spelling book. Turn to page 95." Most misbehavior can be prevented. Noncompliance with commands is one of the most salient problems of children with disruptive behavior disorders. Noncompliance can be reduced when adults issue effective commands.

Ineffective commands are easy to identify. They are not clear and concise. They can consist of multiple commands (e.g., "Sharpen your pencil, write your name and date in the right hand corner, get out your math book, do all the odds and skip problems 25–30"), vague commands (e.g., "Be good" or "Get organized"), question commands (e.g., "Will you get in line?" and "Why don't you listen all the time?"), unclear phrasing (e.g., "Let's get the books out now" or "Can you do that now?"), repeated commands without consequences (e.g., "Be quiet, I told you to be quiet ... I don't want to have to tell you again ... I meant it!"), or extended commands (e.g., "Never say that again" or "Don't ever do that again!").

Positive reinforcement is anything that is provided contingent upon the occurrence of a behavior that strengthens the behavior and increases the likelihood the behavior will occur in the future. Social reinforcers are one of the most common ways that adults provide reinforcement for student behavior. **Social reinforcement** consists of praise, smiles, hugs, and compliments. Appropriate use of social reinforcement can increase rates of attending, increase appropriate verbalizations to peers, and improve compliance; it can also decrease many negative behaviors that are in part inadvertently maintained by adult attention. Positive reinforcement is free and easy to use, no special equipment is required, parents and teachers are more likely to continue its use over time, and it is contagious.

Summarizing and providing feedback at the end of the day is important. Teachers should provide feedback to individual students regarding rule violations, homework, and time-outs. Students who meet certain criteria should earn a daily report card (positive note) and be recognized and praised for their efforts.

Cognitive Behavioral Therapy

Braswell and Bloomquist (1991) presented six stages of cognitive behavioral therapy (CBT) intervention for children and families. The first stage is assessment, which consists of a diagnostic assessment, a treatment-related assessment, and treatment planning that targets specific cognitions and behaviors of the child and parents/family. The assessment also considers the severity of child dysfunction, family dysfunction, developmental factors, and the extent of school involvement. The second stage in CBT is preparation for change, which includes forming a collaborative relationship and beginning to modify sources of resistance. The third stage, cognitive and/or behavioral skills training, has three foci—child, parent, and family. The fourth stage focuses on school consultation. The fifth stage involves termination, and the sixth stage is follow-up.

It is important to prepare the student and family for the change process that occurs with CBT by forming a collaborative relationship and dealing with resistance. The more clients know about the process in which they have agreed to engage, the more invested they will become in learning and practicing new skills. The skills taught will depend on the assessment. For example, if the student is found to have problem-solving deficits, then one would utilize a problem-solving therapy. If the parent was making negative comments about the child, then cognitive restructuring exercises for the parent would be warranted. If the assessment reveals that the family is exhibiting significant conflict, then conflict management training would be utilized.

Social Skills Training

School social workers provide a great deal of instruction in social and communication skills for students and families. Although there are a number of tested skills training models (McGinnis & Goldstein, 1997; McGinnis, Goldstein, Sprafkin, & Gershaw, 1984), most follow a structured approach as follows:

Social Skills Training Steps

1. Instruction: The child is taught to recognize social behaviors, such as participation, cooperation, communication, validation, and support.
2. Modeling: The child has an opportunity to observe the appropriate behaviors demonstrated.
3. Behavior rehearsal: The child has the opportunity to practice the behaviors that have been taught.
4. Coaching: Instructions are provided to the child during the behavior rehearsal. Focus on important concepts, and skills, providing specific behavioral examples in given situations and asking the child to evaluate his or her social behaviors in terms of the outcome.
5. Feedback: The child is given immediate reinforcement for appropriate behaviors during rehearsal (e.g., "Great job" and "That time you waited your turn").

National Mental Health and Education Center, www.naspcenter.org (2004)

A commonly used social skills curriculum is Skillstreaming the Elementary School Child: New Strategies and Perspectives for Teaching Prosocial Skills (McGinnis & Goldstein, 1997). The curriculum is divided into five skill groups: classroom survival skills, friendship-making skills, dealing with feelings, alternatives to aggression, and dealing with stress. Within these skill groups are strategies for teaching 60 specific prosocial skills, such as asking for help, saying thank you, using self-control, accepting consequences, making a complaint, and dealing with group pressure. An adolescent version is also available.

GROUP WORK WITH STUDENTS IN SCHOOLS

School social workers offer a variety of group approaches with children and adolescents in school settings in such areas as social skills training, grief and loss, separation and divorce of parents, peer mediation, and friendship skills. Groups

Advantages of Group Work

- Groups enable children and adolescents to form bonds with peers and to discuss feelings and ideas openly.
- Groups enable children and adolescents to understand that their concerns are not unique and that there is nothing wrong with them.
- Groups allow participants to articulate personal feelings and obtain feedback from their peers.
- Groups with children and adolescents enable social workers to serve more young people quicker.
- Groups often use play and art, which are a child's first language.

are often a developmentally appropriate way to offer support, provide information, and teach social and other life skills.

General Guidelines for Leading Small Groups

First, determine the need for a group and the group topic. Identify the students who will participate. Students may become a part of the group by referral or

Steps for Organizing Groups

1. Establish and prepare a meeting place: This involves finding the "best" place available and it may involve permission and cooperation from teachers and other staff members.
2. Number of participants and age ranges: The number of group members will be related to the kind of verbal interaction desired. The group size generally ranges from seven to nine students. Look for the complementarities of strengths and weaknesses from members so that they might learn from each other. A group of students who are shy will not generate interaction, and a group of students who are aggressive will be difficult to control. Age is another important variable. The leader should decide on the age the group will comprise.
3. Determine meeting time: Meeting at the same time each week provides needed consistency in the student's lives.
4. Duration of the group: Open-ended groups may meet for the length of the school term, or groups may have a definite duration. Six to 8 weeks is usually suggested.
5. Length and frequency of meetings: A general rule is that meetings need to be shorter for younger or immature group members. For elementary students, 30 minutes is suggested, and 45 minutes to 1 hour is suggested for adolescents. Groups generally meet once a week.
6. Group composition: The group leader should decide whether the group is to be composed of males only, females only, or both males and females. Among adolescents, mixed-sex groups tend to work better. At the lower grades, single-sex groups are usually preferable. However, group composition should be based on

assessments from the school social worker. It is helpful to meet with each potential member of the group individually before forming a group because this helps determine if a group is the appropriate modality. In practical terms, however, many school social workers do not get to choose who will be in their group. Careful planning and preparation are key elements in this situation.

In the early phases of working with a group, two process tasks must be addressed: confidentiality and group rules. Establishing confidentiality and the limits to confidentiality are essential to the free flow of thoughts within the group. An example of this follows:

- What is said in the group is confidential. That means things that are shared and discussed in groups should not be talked about outside of the group.
- The rules of confidentiality do not apply when
  - someone is being abused;
  - someone talks about suicide; or
  - the leader in the group judges a situation to be life-threatening.
- If the leader must tell someone outside the group, the student will in most cases be told what will be said and who will receive the information.

the problem area, the purpose of the group, and the personalities of those involved.

7. Notify parent and invite youth: Permission for membership in the group must be obtained from parents. Aside from legal and ethical reasons for obtaining permission, parental support of the group is important. When inviting students, persuade them that problems are an opportunity for change and growth. Stress the positive aspects of group membership.

8. Clarity of purpose: It is necessary to convey the purpose of the group to group members as well as the school administration and teachers. Goals and objectives with outcome criteria provide the framework for group sessions. Collaborate with teachers throughout the life of the group to examine the effect of the group experience on the classroom.

9. Evaluate outcomes: It is important to evaluate both the process and the outcomes of the group. An evaluation self-report questionnaire can be completed pre and post by the participants. Depending on the purpose of the group, participants might be asked about what they learned, how their behavior changed, how their feelings changed, or whether they would recommend this group to others. Teachers and/or parents can also be asked for their feedback on changes they have observed in the student.

10. End the group: End the group in such a way that significant achievements are recognized in a meaningful way. A certificate of completion may be appropriate. For some groups, a group presentation such as a skit about the group topic (e.g., anger management) to parents or other students may be a meaningful ending ritual. Always let students know whether and how additional help is available to them once the group is finished. Within the limits of confidentiality, it is often useful to provide some feedback in a general way to teachers, parents, or those who referred students to the group, once the group is finished.

Examples of Group Rules

- Uphold confidentiality about what is said in the group. This means whatever is said in the group stays in the group. Do not talk about things shared in the group outside of the group.
- One person speaks at a time while others use good listening skills (being quiet and showing interest).
- Students arrive on time to the group and are committed to working out their problems and helping others.
- Use constructive criticism—Treat others with respect.

Establishing group rules allows the group to work together with less conflict and confusion. Group rules provide the leader and the participants with guidelines for how to handle situations that occur with group members, such as not listening, laughing at other's comments, or put-downs.

POSITIVE BEHAVIORAL INTERVENTIONS AND SUPPORT

A major advance with regard to discipline is the emphasis on schoolwide systems of support that include strategies for teaching and supporting appropriate student behaviors to create positive school environments. A continuum of positive behavior support for all students within a school is implemented in areas including the classroom and nonclassroom settings (e.g., hallways and restrooms). Attention is focused on creating and sustaining primary (schoolwide), secondary (classroom), and tertiary (individual) systems of support that improve lifestyle results (personal, health, social, family, work, and recreation) for all children and youth (see Chapter 6 for more information).

MACRO PRACTICE SKILLS WITH INDIVIDUALS AND GROUPS

Direct practice tasks often achieve the best results when combined with other "indirect" helping services. We conclude this chapter with a discussion of key macro practice skills that help to support both our interventions in the school and our growth as professionals. These include involvement of volunteers and natural helping networks in support of case planning, such as linking a youth with a Big Brother or Big Sister or convening a family group to develop safety plans for the child. Advocacy efforts to change the physical environment for students is another important component—examples include helping a family either move into or move out of a shelter, establishing a study space at home, or even simply arranging for a bed, rather than a couch, for a child's nightly rest. For further information on macro level interventions, see Chapter 5.

SUMMARY

This chapter discussed the knowledge, skills, and values needed to work with students individually and in groups. School social workers often use home visits; social and developmental histories; structured interviews with students, teachers, school staff, and family members; as well as standardized assessment tools to conduct school-related assessments. The Intervention-Based Assessment model, behavioral observation, and data collection measurement strategies are also important tools used by school social workers in the assessment process. Data collected from these assessments can be used to set goals and implement effective individual and classroom behavior management interventions. It is important for school social workers to understand how the skills used for individual student assessment and intervention can be combined with school and districtwide positive behavioral intervention and supports. In addition to working with students and families individually, school social workers frequently facilitate groups. This chapter discussed the advantages of group work, guidelines for leading small groups, and steps for organizing a group.

Acknowledgments

The authors thank the following colleagues and students for contributing to this chapter: Kristine Balestra, Gwendoyln Howard, Tom O'Neil, and Jan Montgomery.

School Social Work Companion Website

Please be sure to check out our companion website at www.thomsonedu.com/social_work/bye, where you will find relevant materials for each chapter, including flashcards, online practice quizzes, and PowerPoint slides.

References

Achenbach, T. M. (1979). The child behavior profile: An empirically based system for assessing children's behavioral problems and competencies. *International Journal of Mental Health, 7*, 24–42.

Allen, S. F., & Tracy, E. M. (2004). Revitalizing the role of home visiting by school social workers. *Children Schools, 26*(4), 197–208.

Allen-Meares, P. (2004). *Social work services in schools* (4th ed.). Boston: Allyn & Bacon.

Allen-Meares, P., Washington, R., & Welsh, B. (1996). *Social work services in schools* (2nd ed.). Boston: Allyn & Bacon.

Berrick, J. D., & Duerr, M. (1996). Maintaining positive school relationships: The role of the social worker vis-a-vis full service schools. *Social Work in Education, 18*(1), 53–58.

Bongar, B. (1992). *Suicide: Guidelines for assessment, management, and treatment.* New York: Oxford University Press.

Borba, M. (1989). *Esteem builders: A K–8 self-esteem curriculum for improving student achievement, behavior and school climate.* Rolling Hills Estates, CA: Jalmar.

Bowen, G., Woolley, M., Richman, J., & Bowen, N. (2001). Brief intervention in schools: The school success profile. *Brief Treatment and Crisis Intervention, 1*, 43–54.

Braswell, L., & Bloomquist, M. L. (1991). *Cognitive–behavioral therapy with ADHD children: Child, family and school interventions.* New York: Guilford.

Burns, M. D. (1999). *The feeling good handbook.* New York: Penguin.

Cavanagh-Johnson, T. (1999). *Understanding your child's sexual behavior: What's natural and healthy.* Oakland, CA: New Harbinger.

Clark, J. (1998). *Functional behavioral assessment and behavioral intervention plan: Implementing the student discipline provisions of IDEA' 97—A technical assistance guide for school social workers.* Northlake, IL/Washington, DC: School Social Work Association of America/National Association of Social Workers School Social Work Section.

Clark, J. (2002). School social work assessment: Battery versus functional approaches. *Section Connection, 8*(1), 4–5.

Connors, C. K. (1997). *Connors' Rating Scales—Revised.* North Tonawanda, NY: Multi-Health Systems.

Cooper, M., & Lesser, J. (2005). *Clinical social work practice: An integrated approach* (2nd ed.). Boston: Allyn & Bacon.

Coopersmith, S. (1981). *Coopersmith Self-Esteem Inventory.* Palo Alto, CA: Consulting Psychologists Press.

Fahlberg, V. I. (1991). *A child's journey through placement.* Indianapolis, IN: Perspectives Press.

Faller, K. (1993). Child Sexual Behavior Inventory: Normative and clinical comparisons. *Psychological Assessment, 4,* 303–311.

Flannery, D., Vazsonyi, A., Torquati, J., & Friedrich, A. (1994). Ethnic differences in risk for early adolescent substance use. *Journal of Youth and Adolescence, 23,* 194–213.

Fuchs, D. (1991). Mainstream assistance teams: A prereferral intervention for difficult-to-teach students. In G. Stoner, M. Shinn, & H. Walker (Eds.), *Interventions for achievement and behavior problems* (pp. 241–267). Washington, DC: National Association of School Psychologists.

Gambrill, E. (1997). *Social work practice: A critical thinker's guide.* New York: Oxford University Press.

Garnett, M., & Attwood, A. (1995). *The Australian Scale for Asperger's Syndrome.* Paper presented at the 1995 Australian National Autism Conference, Brisbane, Australia.

Gresham, F. M., & Elliott, S. N. (1990). *Social skills rating system.* Circle Pines, MN: American Guidance Service.

Gresham, F. M., Elliott, S. N., & Evans-Fernandez, S. (1992). *Student Self-Concept Scale.* Circle Pines, MN: American Guidance Service.

Hardy, K. V., & Laszoloffy, T. A. (1995). The cultural genogram: Key to training culturally competent family therapists. *Journal of Marital and Family Therapy, 21*(3), 227–237.

Hartman, A. (1994). Diagrammatic assessment of family relationships. In B. R. Compton & B. Galaway (Eds.), *Social work processes* (pp. 153–165). Pacific Grove, CA: Brooks/Cole.

Lucco, A. (1993). Assessment of the school-aged child. In J. B. Rauch (Ed.), *Assessment: A sourcebook for social work practice.* Milwaukee, WI: Families International.

Maluccio, A., Pine, B. A., & Tracy, E. M. (2002). *Social work practice with families and children.* New York: Columbia University Press.

Martens, B., Peterson, R., Witt, J., & Cirone, S. (1986). Teacher perceptions of school-based interventions. *Exceptional Children, 53*(3), 213–223.

McConaughy, S. H., & Achenbach, T. M. (1994). *Manual for the semistructured clinical interview for children and adolescents.* Burlington: University of Vermont, Department of Psychiatry.

McGinnis, E., & Goldstein, A. P. (1997). *Skill-streaming the elementary school child: A guide for teaching prosocial skills.* Champaign, IL: Research Press.

McGinnis, E., Golstein, A., Sprafkin, R. P., & Gershaw, J. (1984). *Skill-streaming the elementary school child.* Champaign, IL: Research Press.

McNamara, K., Telzrow, C., & DeLamatre, J. (1999). Parent reactions to implementation of intervention-based assessment. *Journal of Educational and Psychological Consultation, 10*(4), 343–362.

Meichenbaum, D. H., & Goodman, J. (1971). Training impulsive children to talk to themselves: A means of developing self-control. *Journal of Abnormal Psychology, 77,* 115–126.

National Association of Social Workers. (2002). *NASW standards for school social work services.* Washington, DC: Author.

National Mental Health and Education Center. (2004). *Behavior problems: Teaching young children self control.* Retrieved December 30, 2004, from www.naspcenter.org

Reynolds, C., & Richmond, B. (1985). *Revised Children's Manifest Anxiety Scale (RCMAS) manual.* Los Angeles: Western Psychological Services.

Reynolds, C. R., & Kamphaus, R. W. (1992). *Behavior assessment system for children.* Circle Pines, MN: American Guidance Service.

Search Institute. (2002). *The asset approach.* Minneapolis, MN: Author.

Shapiro, E., & Cole, C. (1994). *Behavior change in the classroom: Self management interventions.* New York: Guilford.

Singer, M., Miller, D., Guo, S., Flannery, D., Frierson, T., & Slovak, K. (1999). Contributors to violent behavior among elementary and middle school children. *Pediatrics, 104,* 878–884.

Tracy, E. M., & Whittaker, J. K. (1990). The Social Network Map: Assessing social support in clinical social work practice. *Families in Society, 71*(8), 461–470.

10 CHAPTER | School Social Work and Crisis Intervention

DONNA SECOR, M.S.W.
Forest Hill Schools, Grand Rapids, Michigan

CHAPTER OUTLINE

CHAPTER OVERVIEW

School social workers have skills that enable them to be leaders of crisis intervention teams. This chapter (1) outlines methods of intervention at the scene of a trauma, (2) identifies survivors who could experience the most intense impact, (3) describes methods of intervening at the small group and classroom level, and (4) identifies best and promising practices.

INTRODUCTION

The school social worker is a key member of any school crisis or trauma response team, often functioning as chair of the team or as a leader in the intervention process. School social workers with skills in crisis intervention techniques, group process, staff consultation, and linking with families are ideally suited to assist school communities facing crisis situations.

School crises may involve the death or serious injury of a student or staff member or a national trauma, such as the attacks of September 11, 2001. The nature of the trauma and how it is handled determine the degree of impact on the school community and will dictate many aspects of the response. For example, the death of a popular high school football player often has a very widespread impact on a school since that player may have been known to most of the staff and student body and is likely to have 40 or 50 teammates and a half dozen coaches who may need support. The school crisis team should consist of "representatives from every component of the school," who work full-time in the school or are easily available when a crisis occurs (Fanolis, 2003, p. 219). The crisis team needs to anticipate the extent of the impact of the event on the school community and prepare an appropriate level and type of response.

Virtually all schools have some kind of crisis response plan; however, they should be reviewed or updated on a regular basis. For example, the attacks of September 11, 2001, and the anthrax scare now dictate that crisis plans address potential acts of terrorism (Poland, 1994).

The school social worker can provide leadership and consultation in developing and updating these plans. An effective plan should address the areas of safety and security; dissemination of accurate information to team members, school staff, students, parents, and the community (including the media); and meet the emotional and psychological needs of all parties (Schonfeld & Newgass, 2003). Crisis plans should also be evaluated after each traumatic event as part of an operational debriefing to assess what worked well and where there is room for improvement (Steele, 1998).

SCENE OF THE TRAUMA

Occasionally, the school social worker may be called to the scene of a trauma, such as the hospital where accident victims are taken. If possible, school staff should avoid significant involvement outside of school in the immediate aftermath of a tragedy. For example, in one situation a school social worker was called to the hospital where the student victim of a fatal accident was taken. The waiting room of the emergency room was filled with other students, parents, and relatives of the victim who were all actively grieving. Extensive involvement in this scenario led to some traumatization of the school social worker that impaired her ability to plan and respond in the school building the next morning. Hospitals generally have their own personnel on staff or on call to assist students or parents who need help in that setting. The school social worker can alert hospital social workers to the basic details of the trauma to better prepare them to address student and family needs.

Sample Crisis Response Plan

Purpose
The purpose of a crisis plan is to be able to respond immediately to a traumatic event, such as the death of a student, staff member, or an immediate family member or a disaster, or other event.

Crisis Team Members
Members should include building administrators, school social workers, counselors, school psychologists, and other members (as designated by the building), such as secretaries, special education staff, a peer listening coordinator, and building security.

Crisis Team Responsibilities
- Determine the course of events surrounding the crisis or traumatic event.
- Share relevant information and facts to control rumors.
- Assess the potential impact on the school community and provide for the safety of students.
- Determine how best to communicate relevant information to staff, students, and parents.
- Conduct activities in response to staff, student, and parent needs.
- Determine needed involvement of outside resources, including mental health staff.
- Convene building crisis team in September every year.
- Review team membership and crisis plan.
- Review building preparedness.
- Update phone lists and e-mail.
- Review crisis plan at staff meeting.

If Crisis Occurs Outside of School
- Notify principal.
- Principal should contact superintendent and building mental health staff (school social worker, counselor, and school psychologist).
- Principal should call authorities or family to get facts.
- Principal should notify and convene crisis team as soon as possible.
- Focus on school-based interventions rather than the accident scene or hospital.

If Crisis Occurs at School
- Call main office or 911 in life-threatening situation—give school name and address.
- Obtain staff or student's emergency card.
- Contact central office.
- Utilize "code red" plan as needed to secure building and protect students.
- Proceed with normal day as much as possible.
- Notify and convene crisis team immediately.

Crisis Team Actions
- Meets as soon as possible (within hours)
- Shares information
- Assesses impact on school community
- Plans for needed district staff and reporting places
  - Contacts student services to request needed mental health staff
  - Contacts central office to request needed teaching staff assistance
- Selects designee to contact family
  - Offers support
  - Obtains information; clarifies family's wishes and funeral arrangements
- Decides how/when to notify staff
- Decides how/when to notify students—writes script
- Decides how/when to communicate with parents
  - Phone contacts: assigns callers and writes script
  - Letters home to parents
- Identifies "primary survivors" within the school and district
- Makes recommendation to central office about notification of other building and district staff; consider districtwide e-mail
- Plans for the school day
- Plans for staff meeting before or after school, depending on timing
- Shares as much accurate information as possible
- Provides appropriate handouts to assist staff
- Plans for mental health staff
  - Areas for individual/group counseling
  - Hallways
  - Teacher's lounge
- Plans for classrooms
  - Provides coverage for student's classes
  - Assesses which classrooms may need extra support
  - Plans after-school staff meeting to share information and debrief
- Crisis team reconvenes to plan for coming days
  - Reviews classes to cover
  - Identifies and plans for at-risk students
  - Plans mental health staff availability: staff and students
  - Plans for visitation and funeral coverage
  - Plans for student's personal possessions, locker clean-out
  - Removal of student from school database
  - Considers appropriate memorials, moment of silence, memory books, cards

Additional Concerns
- Media contact channeled through central office; no media access to students or staff
- Special considerations for suicide: discourage memorials at school, additional supports to primary survivors and other at-risk students
- Designee to provide for ongoing support and communication with family
- Debriefing for crisis team and building staff

INITIAL INTERVENTIONS

In the initial 24 hours following a crisis, school social work interventions should focus on meeting the basic needs of grieving students. Steps should be taken to address their immediate safety needs, including providing protection from the media and from further trauma. The roles of each of the crisis team members should be identified in the school's crisis plan. Students are often offered a safe area within the school building to gather in the hours immediately following a trauma or loss. Led by the school social worker or a school mental health staff member, with support from other available adults (parents, teachers, and teachers' aides), supervision should be provided and the mental health staff should be available to address any student questions or concerns. The availability of food and beverages offers a concrete form of nurturance and can be helpful for grieving students who may have had little or nothing to eat since the traumatic event. All these details should be addressed in the school's crisis plan.

Use of a technique known as "defusing" is recommended in the first few hours of the response (Steele, 1998). The basics of defusing include providing survivor support and nurturance as well as providing the opportunity to ventilate, tell their stories, and validate the normalcy of their feelings and responses. The "tell the story" technique is useful for school social workers in many forms of grief and trauma work. The student is invited to relate everything he or she can remember about the traumatic event, including sensory impressions, in as much detail as he or she likes, and to name the associated feelings. Multiple opportunities to tell the story help facilitate a sense of mastery of the trauma (Steele, 1998).

MOST IMPACTED OR PRIMARY SURVIVORS

In addition to a number of building-wide interventions that are appropriate in helping a school community respond to a crisis, best practice requires a plan for individual or group interventions with those students or staff who are most closely involved in the trauma (Zenere, 1998). The process of identifying those who were closest or most involved in the trauma should begin at the initial crisis team meeting. Close friends, students from the neighborhood, and brothers, sisters, or cousins in the school are likely to be substantially affected. If the student was involved with an athletic team, the school band, choir, or other club or activity, members of that group should be considered for intervention.

As noted previously, the process of identification begins with the crisis team and also involves interviewing other students and staff to obtain additional names for a list that can be used to plan both initial interventions and later follow-up. Sometimes, students will "self-refer" by approaching crisis team members or other staff to reveal their relationship to the traumatic event. Students or staff who may not have been close to the victim of the immediate trauma but who have experienced a recent loss or trauma, such as the death of a family member, are at increased risk as well and should be considered for inclusion on the list.

SMALL GROUP INTERVENTIONS

Beginning approximately 24–72 hours after the traumatic event, structured small group interventions may be used with students who are the most impacted. These interventions are appropriate with children and adolescents 7–14 days following an incident (Steele, 1998). Debriefings are generally utilized with students 12 years of age or older or with staff members, whereas defusing techniques are appropriate for use in a small group format with elementary-aged students (Mitchell & Everly, 1993).

The activity-oriented defusing process helps younger students express an experience for which they may not have words. After presenting appropriate details about the trauma and correcting rumors, an opportunity is provided for the students to share their experiences. The school social worker may model discussion of feelings or use a feelings chart. Students may be asked to draw a picture about the event and tell a story about it. Drawing has been demonstrated to be a valuable technique in trauma response with children (Steele, 2001). Other art projects, such as creating cards and banners, were utilized in many schools after the September 11, 2001, attacks. In the defusing process, children will learn that they are not alone with their fears and their reactions. The session can end with some positive reflections, snacks, or a fun activity.

The debriefing technique known as Critical Incident Stress Debriefing (CISD) was developed by Mitchell and Everly (1993) and is frequently used within and outside the school setting. To be effective, the debriefing format should be followed as closely as possible. Debriefing in groups involves a maximum of approximately 15 students and two facilitators. Time frames of 45 minutes to 1½ hours are recommended for middle school students and from 1 to 2 hours for high school students and adults (Johnson, 1993).

Participants are asked to remain in the group for the entire session, respect confidentiality, not interrupt others, and not engage in any blaming. In general, school social workers with group and crisis experience and familiarity with the CISD material should be able to conduct debriefing groups; however, some formal training in CISD is desirable. The "cofacilitator" should also have some group experience. Drinks or other refreshments may be provided. CISD is distinct from a "therapy" group in that the facilitators maintain focus on specific steps in the process and completing them within the recommended time frame.

Specific questions are used, some of which are posed to the entire group in a "go around" in which one person gets to share thoughts and feelings and then the next persons does the same until everyone in the group has had a chance to speak. Other questions are addressed to the group for anyone to answer. As part of the process, facilitators observe the participants to determine who might need additional assistance or other follow-up.

CLASSROOM PRESENTATIONS

Another group that is always part of response planning comprises the current classmates and teachers of the student, or the current students of a teacher who dies unexpectedly. Best practice in this situation dictates that the school social worker or other school mental health professional intervenes directly with this group (Steele, 1998). In an elementary "self-contained" classroom situation, one or more crisis team members should be present in the classroom as the school day begins and make a presentation to the class about the loss. A crisis team member may remain in the room for the remainder of the day to provide assistance as needed. At the secondary level, a team member(s) should follow the student's schedule through the day, making a presentation to each class.

The presentation may be as short as 10–15 minutes or as long as an entire class period. Most teachers are grateful for this form of support since they are often struggling with their own response to the event or may feel uncomfortable engaging in this kind of discussion with their class. The school social worker should be prepared for student responses ranging from silence (which may be most common) to lengthy discussion and questioning. Particularly when the students are not making overt responses, the school social worker may do some modeling by expressing some of his or her personal reactions. The following are suggested elements of a classroom presentation (Brohl, Brohl, & Steele, 2002):

 ## Suggested Elements of Classroom Crisis Presentation

Review the facts: Begin with a description of the facts of the tragedy, as they are known, in as much detail as seems appropriate for the age of the students. The school social worker might ask, "Have any of you heard anything different about the accident?" Other questions about the event are invited in an effort to provide accurate information and dispel rumors that commonly begin to circulate during a school crisis. These rumors can be destructive and create additional anxiety or trauma. Students can be asked if they have suffered a recent loss, if they had recent interactions with the victim, and what upsets them most about the death.

Normalize: Let the students know that their feelings and behaviors, such as numbness, disbelief, anger, sadness, difficulty concentrating, changes in eating and sleeping patterns, anxiety or nervousness, nightmares, fear of being alone, giddiness, or silliness, are common. Let them know that these responses may be occurring now or they may experience them in the future.

Help them anticipate coming events: Discuss events related to the crisis that will occur in the immediate future (i.e., hospital visits, funeral services, or other memorials). It is

SERVING AS A RESOURCE FOR STAFF

In addition to classroom presentations, the school social worker may make a presentation and/or provide written resource materials at the staff meeting that is held during the initial response. Teachers are grateful for specific suggestions about how to discuss the incident with their students and how to answer questions.

Teachers should be encouraged to provide simple, straightforward information and age-appropriate answers to questions. They can be encouraged to listen to the students' "stories" in a neutral way and assure their students of the normalcy of a wide range of grief or trauma reactions. Handouts for teachers should be tailored to the level of the students and the nature of the trauma. School social workers should have sample materials readily available for use in a variety of crisis situations. For example, on September 11, 2001, many school social workers throughout the country assisted in preparing letters and other communications to staff and parents about how to help children. Resources were essential in the highly emotionally charged atmosphere of that day, when everyone, including school social workers, was experiencing a reaction to the trauma.

Another helpful staff intervention is for the school social worker to spend time in the "teacher's lounge" during breaks and at lunch. Teachers can be questioned about how their day is going, how their students are responding, how they are feeling, and whether they need any assistance. This technique serves a dual

important to be sensitive to cultural differences in the way grieving and parting ceremonies are conducted. Students can be questioned about prior experience with funeral home visitations or other types of parting ceremonies. The school social worker can briefly describe what to expect, how they might feel, and what they can do if they become upset.

Discuss healthy coping strategies: To initiate this discussion, students may be asked about what they have done in the past to cope with problems. Student responses or suggestions from the facilitator may include talking to parents or peers, drawing, writing, listening to music, exercising, and taking time for play or other fun activities, depending on the age of the students. The goal is to help students regain a sense of control and a belief that no matter how impossible circumstances may seem, there are things they can do to improve their situation. Another option for this part of the presentation, depending on the nature of the crisis, would be to have students discuss possible ways to prevent a similar tragedy in the future, as another means of helping students regain a sense of control (Brock, 2002).

Conclusion: The closing may include some additional discussion, such as a plan for creating or sending cards to the family. Final questions are invited, and students are informed about how and where they can receive individual assistance for themselves or a friend.

purpose of providing support to teachers and assisting in the school social worker's assessment of the overall response to the crisis. Periodic "check-ins" with the classrooms of substantially impacted staff members, including teachers, coaches, band directors, and other school personnel, may provide needed support and are often greatly appreciated by staff. School social workers can assist students and school personnel in planning memorial activities (Schonfeld & Newgass, 2003).

SERVING AS A RESOURCE FOR PARENTS

Various forms of communication with parents are part of any school crisis response. "Scripts" for school secretaries to read to parents who need to be contacted in the course of a school day or letters sent home at the end of a school day not only provide information about the crisis but also usually include guidance to parents in assisting their children through the trauma.

Information for parents might include a brief list of the kinds of reactions they could see in their children, a brief list of helping strategies, and suggestions for where they can obtain further information, such as Internet websites or local mental health agencies.

The school social worker may serve as the crisis team's liaison with the victim's family. This role may include obtaining information, providing support, and clarifying the family's wishes with reference to funerals and memorials. The school social worker may also field telephone calls from parents who contact the school with concerns and work with parents of the most severely exposed or at-risk students.

FOLLOW-UP

In the course of their involvement in the crisis, the school social worker and other members of the crisis team are likely to identify individuals who should be followed during the weeks and months after the event. The school social worker may consider forming a support group for survivors that may meet with gradually decreasing frequency over the following months. A number of structured formats are available for grief and trauma work with small groups.

The school social worker may also work individually with students who continue to struggle with their recovery. Use of drawings and techniques such as the series of 24 "trauma questions" recommended by the Institute for Trauma and Loss in Children can provide an effective focus for the intervention (Steele, 2001). These include questions such as

- What was happening when you found out?
- What were you doing?
- What made you most afraid?
- What scares you now?
- What is your biggest worry?

Debriefing, which may be referred to as "operational debriefing," of the crisis team members provides an opportunity for them to share their reactions

Summary of School Social Work Tasks in Crisis Intervention

- Serve as a key member in the crisis response process
- Assist with identifying the "most impacted" survivors
- Serve as a resource and support to teachers and administrators
- Make presentation(s) at staff meetings
- Make classroom presentations
- Provide individual and small group interventions
- Provide assistance/consultation/presentations to parents
- Make referrals or request assistance from outside resources
- Consider need for support for students at visitations or funerals
- Follow-up with individuals or groups
- Arrange or conduct debriefings for staff and crisis team members

to the trauma, evaluate and share new information, plan additional interventions, and address ways for them to care for themselves (Steele, 1998).

Finally, the anniversaries of traumatic events are often difficult times for students, staff, and others. The school social worker may consider keeping a record of these events in the form of a calendar to help staff and administrators anticipate and plan for possible responses.

SUMMARY

Crisis intervention literature has documented the significant negative impact on survivors or witnesses of traumatic events, as well as the increasing empirical evidence that crisis response techniques that facilitate ventilation, social support, and adaptive coping are effective tools for prevention and intervention (Flannery & Everly, 2000). School social workers possess the expertise to utilize these techniques to assist in addressing the mental health needs of children and adolescents in traumatic situations. Their ability to plan and implement appropriate responses to crises greatly enhances the value of school social workers within their school communities.

School Social Work Companion Website

Please be sure to check out our companion website at www.thomsonedu.com/social_work/bye, where you will find relevant materials for each chapter, including flashcards, online practice quizzes, and PowerPoint slides.

References

Brock, S. (2002). Group crisis intervention. In S. Brock, P. Lazarus, & S. Jimerson (Eds.), *Best practices in school crisis prevention and intervention* (pp. 385–402). Bethesda, MD: National Association of School Psychologists.

Brohl, N., Brohl, P., & Steele, W. (2002). *Schools response to terrorism: A handbook of protocols*. Grosse Pointe Woods, MI: Institute for Trauma and Loss in Children.

Fanolis, V. (2003). The use of crisis teams in response to violent or critical incidents in schools. In J. Miller, I. Martin, & G. Schamess (Eds.), *School violence and children in crisis: Community and school interventions for social workers and counselors* (pp. 217–223). Denver, CO: Love Publishing.

Flannery, R. B., & Everly, G. S. (2000). Crisis intervention: A review. *International Journal of Emergency Mental Health, 2*(2), 119–125.

Johnson, K. (1993). *School crisis management: A hands on guide to training crisis response teams.* Alameda, CA: Hunter House.

Mitchell, J., & Everly, G. (1993). *Critical incident stress debriefing: An operational manual for CISD, defusing and other group crisis interventions.* Ellicott City, MD: Chevron.

Poland, S. (1994). The role of school crisis intervention teams to prevent and reduce school violence and trauma. *School Psychology Review, 23,* 175–189.

Schonfeld, D., & Newgass, S. (2003, September). *School crisis response initiative.* U.S. Department of Justice, Office for Victims of Crime Bulletin.

Steele, W. (1998). *Trauma debriefing for schools and agencies.* Grosse Pointe Woods, MI: Institute for Trauma and Loss in Children.

Steele, W. (2001). *Kids on the outside looking in after loss.* Grosse Pointe Woods, MI: Institute for Trauma and Loss in Children.

Zenere, F. (1998). *NASP/NEAT community crisis response.* Bethesda, MD: National Association of School Psychologists.

Consultation in School Social Work

CHAPTER **11**

JOSEPH R. GIANESIN, Ph.D.
Springfield College, Springfield, Massachusetts

CHAPTER OVERVIEW

After reading this chapter, readers will (1) become familiar with what is meant by consultation; (2) learn how consultation done by social workers has evolved; (3) develop an understanding of the necessary skills and knowledge base necessary for effective consultants; (4) understand the special skills and knowledge that social workers use while consulting; (5) gain an understanding of consultative roles and the consultation process; (6) become familiar with different consultative approaches for the three main recipients of social work consultation in schools—parents, teachers, and administrators; and (7) understand the challenges and shortcoming of consultation in schools.

INTRODUCTION

Public education has undergone significant changes in the past 20 years. Teachers are required to handle larger classes and children have more complex needs than ever before. It is not possible for teachers or school administrators to answer every child's need based on their own training and expertise. In addition, professional pupil support personnel, such as school social workers, are charged with the responsibility of aiding educators in meeting these complex needs. School social workers are faced with multiple tasks that include large caseloads of students that require them to perform psychosocial assessments, direct service to individuals and groups, family liaison work, ongoing contacts with agency and community staff, and staff development activities. School social workers are finding it necessary to develop alternative strategies to accomplish and meet the multiple demands of schools. Consultation is a necessary skill for school social workers; it allows them to properly assess and implement individual educational plans to help students be successful in school.

Why Consultation?

A major component of a school social worker's role is consultation with parents, teachers, administrators, and outside referral sources. Consultation offers a powerful tool for changing the classroom and the school environment. Time constraints and the demand for more services require school social workers to use efficient and cost-effective methods. Working with one teacher in a consulting capacity can change the classroom environment and improve the lives of all students in the classroom. Providing direct service to individual students or a small group of students is time intensive; school consultants can intervene with a greater number of students and institute change for longer periods of time.

Consultation has also been an effective way to encourage the use of primary prevention strategies such as affective education programs. Many behavioral problems stem from the interactions of individuals in the classroom. By improving those interactions, school social workers can often change the climate in the classroom and relieve stress and negative responses.

Historical Perspective and Definition

Consultation in social work settings has been around since the beginning of the profession and yet articles were not published under the term "consultation" until after World War II. Since then, numerous articles have distinguished social work consultation from other types, such as mental health consultation. Kadushin (1977) defined social work **consultation** as "a problem-solving process in which help, purely advisory in nature, is offered by the social work consultant to a **consultee** (individual, group, organization, community) faced with a job-related problem" (p. 37). Kurpius and Fuqua (1993) noted that the definition of consultation and the role of the consultant have evolved throughout the years from that of one-on-one content expert to process helper and collaborative consultation. The ecological and person-in-environment perspectives provide social workers with a unique consultative framework.

School Social Work Consultation

School social work consultation can be challenging because it takes place in a host setting. In many other fields of social work, the consultation process is much simpler because there is a common professional language understood by both the consultant and the consultee. In public education, the primary function of schools is to educate students. Social workers operating in schools are required to navigate a system that often is unaware of the ethical and central principles of the social work profession. For example, issues such as confidentiality, advocacy, client self-determination, and some ethical mental health principles are not common for educators. To be an effective school consultant, social workers must familiarize themselves with how schools are organized with respect to the roles and responsibilities of teachers and administrators. In addition, they need to develop an educational vocabulary familiar to teachers and other school staff. Basic teaching and learning strategies combined with effective behavioral techniques are an essential for school consultants.

School social workers are in a position to become effective consultants because of their holistic perspective, their specialized knowledge, and their ability to transfer skills across disparate settings. According to Dane and Simon (1991), social workers in host settings such as schools are often viewed by staff as possessing special expertise in the areas of human services, community resources, community organization, and assistance in obtaining financial benefits. Social work has always been a profession noted for its advocacy and prevention efforts. School social workers have the opportunity to be effective consultants because they have the skills to manage the tension and value differences that often occur between parents and school personnel. Social work education is unique because of the emphasis placed on issues of diversity and the strength's perspective.

EFFECTIVE CONSULTANT SKILLS AND KNOWLEDGE

School social work consultation requires expertise in the following:

1. Sensitivity and respect regarding cultural diversity
2. Effective communication skills
3. Consultation theory and process
4. Behavioral techniques
5. Childhood developmental theory and theories of human behavior
6. The *Diagnostic and Statistical Manual of Mental Disorders*, 4th edition (*DSM-IV*)
7. Staff development and community resources

Multicultural Perspective

The school social work consultant must have a multicultural perspective and skills working with diverse groups. The demographics of schools have changed drastically during the past decade. Teachers and other school staff are dealing with multiple cultures in schools. Many teachers and staff have little knowledge of cultural norms and often become frustrated when they try to communicate with parents and guardians who are from different social, economic, or cultural backgrounds.

School consultants should have a working knowledge of the cultural groups represented in their schools. Demographics often change in schools, and that requires school staff to become proficient and knowledgeable about the new cultural and ethnic groups. For example, in a district in Massachusetts, there has been a substantial increase in an immigrant population from Russia and Bosnia. School social workers employed in that school district took continuing education courses to gain insight into that particular culture.

Effective Communicators

Communicating effectively with people is extremely important in any professional role. For the school consultant, communication is the avenue upon which all interactions are based. This includes the ability to relate to a number of constituents in a variety of roles. Consultants often have to navigate the gap between professional dialog and the common language of parents and others who may not have formal educational backgrounds and knowledge of the complex educational system. Effective social work consultants use effective communication skills in their consultative role. Knowledge of group process, decision making, active listening, and conflict mediation skills are essential tools for the school consultant. According to Gutkin and Bossard, (1984), consultation is a collaborative effort between consultant and consultee, a process in which "success is going to hinge largely on communication and relationship skills" (p. 822). Thus, establishing rapport and collaborative relationships through effective communication between teachers, parents, and administrators is important to the success of the consultation (Gianesin, 2004).

Consultation Theory

Knowledge of consultation theory and process is essential to the school-based consultant. Generally, there are three models of consultation theory that are utilized in school settings: behavioral consultation, mental health consultation, and problem-focused consultation (Early, 1992). Students are rarely directly involved during consulting sessions. For school social workers, the consultation process is triadic in nature, involving the school social worker; the parent, teacher, or administrator; and the student. Consultation is directed at helping the student gain the most from the school environment. As Drisko (1993) stated, "Social work consultation can increase teachers' sensitivity to the unique needs of students, improving the quality of the students' day-to-day experience, and generally improving their learning" (p. 20). The complexity of developing relationships among the participants and the value in maintaining trust and rapport while giving advice and sharing expertise can determine the success or failure of the consultative process.

Behavioral Techniques

An effective consultant is proficient in effective school behavior management programs and behavioral interventions. To reduce their budget, many school districts are creating self-contained classrooms to educate students who previously were sent out of the district to specialized day treatment or residential programs. Many social workers are being called to consult with teachers and staff on programmatic issues, program development, and program structure. These classrooms may be staffed by teachers who have limited knowledge about token economies, behavioral interventions, discipline with emotionally charged students, etc. Social workers are in a key position to advocate for services that best serve children and to initiate programs that have empirical evidence to document effectiveness. This includes deescalation techniques, crisis intervention, management strategies, and disciplinary policies.

Developmental Knowledge

In addition to a working knowledge base of behavioral interventions, a school social work consultant must have in-depth knowledge of childhood development. The literature on the importance of early childhood development is vast. The school social work consultant is called upon to describe the differences between abnormal and normal behavior patterns to parents and teachers. Often, this can be done effectively by utilizing a developmental model in the areas of physical, social–emotional, psychological, and cognitive functions. Maintaining an updated knowledge base is extremely important. There is research on gender differences in development between boys and girls. Gurian (2001) offered insights on how boys and girls learn differently and described how gender can make a difference in areas such as deductive and inductive reasoning, abstract and concrete reasoning, and the use of language. Having this type knowledge enables the social work consultant to help teachers and parents develop effective teaching and behavioral strategies.

Working Knowledge of *DSM-IV*

School social work consultants are often called upon by school personnel and parents to explain a mental health diagnosis. This includes an explanation of symptoms, corresponding behaviors, and possible treatment interventions that include common pharmacological treatments. Because social workers may be the only mental health experts in schools, school personnel often rely heavily on their opinions and consultation. School social workers are asked to interpret reports by outside mental health professionals, such as psychiatrists, psychologists, and clinical social workers. A working knowledge of the *DSM-IV* is extremely important for the school social work consultant. Their broad perspective of both the medical and the ecological models of mental health treatment can offer a balanced perspective on the child. Great care must be taken to balance the pathological symptoms with the strengths perspective when consulting with parents and school personnel. Caution must be taken to alleviate the tendency for people to seek simple solutions when a diagnosis is given.

Staff Development and Community Resource Knowledge

One of the most important skills that an effective school social work consultant should possess is the ability to conduct staff development workshops and presentations to school personnel, parents, and interested community members.

Often, the expertise the consultant acquires is valued by administrators who know they have problems in their school. Consultants are often viewed as specialists whose knowledge may benefit a larger constituency. For example, in one school district in which a rash of suicides and suicidal attempts occurred, the school-based consultant conducted several staff development sessions with school personnel and parents with regard to recognizing warning signs of depression and self-abusive behaviors. Additionally, knowledge of community resources, networking contacts with human service providers, and links to outside agencies and individuals, such as the probation department, psychotherapists, and other providers, are essential for a competent consultant.

CONSULTANT ROLES

The objective observer and reflector role entails the ability to observe and analyze the environment and interactions and, based on the observations, assist the consultee to develop interventions. In practice, a consultant takes the time to observe the student in a number of settings. These may include structured settings that have clear and consistent boundaries and behavioral expectations, such as the classroom. It might also include observing the child in unstructured environments such as the playground, where the child is able to interact without the

Noteworthy roles that school-based consultants perform

1. Objective observer/reflector
2. Fact finder
3. Process counselor
4. Alternative identifier and linkage resource person
5. Trainer/educator
6. Informational expert
7. Advocate

| Case | **Case Example** |

John, the teacher, was concerned about Fred's inability to sit still in the classroom. John reported that the child was often out of his seat without permission. The school social worker observed in the classroom and found that the child appeared to become anxious, vying for but not getting the teacher's attention immediately. When Fred got out of his seat without permission, he was able to garner the undivided attention of the teacher and the negative behavior was reinforced.

constraints of intense adult supervision. Additionally, the objective observer and reflector role enables the consultant to gather behavioral information on students, noting the antecedents, frequency, and duration of particular targeted problem behaviors. Observing and gathering data can help lead to an effective intervention.

Consultants can inquire and ask important questions. Adults may be so frustrated with a child's problems that they see the child as all bad. Social workers can gain an understanding of adults' perceptions and expectations of a child by having them describe the child's behavior in detail. Often, the consultant can bring about change in perception of the consultee by reviewing their concerns. This process contributes to discussing the consultee's observations, including listing the frequency of the problem behavior demonstrated by the child, the time of day that it occurred, and the triggers and responses.

As indicated in the previous example, the role of the consultant is to be a fact finder. This enables the consultant to gather the data regarding important variables. Data gathering involves not only observation techniques but also interviewing all of the concerned parties, reviewing records, and examining the context in which the interactions take place. For many consultants, these fact-finding efforts can be the most time-consuming task, but they are necessary for a full assessment of the situation.

The consultant must act as a process counselor. In this regard, the consultant spends time communicating effectively with the consultee, initially establishing trust and confidence but also helping that person gain a fuller understanding and different view of the child. Teachers and parents alike often feel like failures when really they have the capacity to be successful in the management of the child. Utilizing many consulting models, the process counselor can devise interventions that are acceptable to the consultee.

The consultant must have a good working knowledge of resources in the community. For many consultants, the use of a community human service directory listing the multiple services and contacts for referrals is essential to the consultation process. In addition, an effective consultant should have a working knowledge of resource contacts within agencies that are utilized often. For example, departments of social services, probation departments, and crisis intervention services require knowledge of the application procedures and contact person, general eligibility guidelines, and operating hours.

As previously stated, the consultant needs to have skills conducting training and staff development. This trainer/educator role, along with that of informational expert, gives the consultant opportunities to disseminate valuable information to larger groups of people. Staff development training also exposes more personnel to the consultant's expertise and increases the likelihood of making changes in the school and classroom environments.

THE CONSULTATION PROCESS

Many school social work consultants agree that no matter what model of consultation one utilizes, the process generally involves one or more of the models indicated but all use the following six stages: (1) developing and strengthening relationships, (2) establishing a contract, (3) identifying a problem, (4) exploring alternatives, (5) formulating a plan for intervention and outcome goals, and (6) evaluating the plan/intervention.

The relationship between the school consultant and the consultee is essential to the success of consultation (White & Mullis, 1998). Consultations fail due to poor interactions between the consultant and the consultee. It is imperative that the consultant establish rapport and trust with the consultee. This means that the consultee is informed about why and how the consultation referral was initiated. The consultant takes great care in establishing communication and confidentiality guidelines. Bostic and Rauch (1999) believe that the consultant should cultivate respect for everyone in the system. This assists the consultant in strengthening all the relationships between the major stakeholders and promotes collaboration and cooperation. In addition, the consultant should involve those members who are outside the system that may contribute resources or have important linkages to the child.

Often, a **contract** is agreed upon in either written or verbal form and describes the purposes, objectives, ground rules, expectations, resources, and time lines for the consultation. Formulating a plan for intervention and goal setting is a natural progression from exploring the alternatives. For many consultants, contracting with the consultee with regard to intervention plans includes the time the plan will start and end along with goals that will be achieved. During the development process, the consultant must remain student oriented, tapping into individual, familial, community, and organizational strengths and resources to meet the needs of the consultee. As the consultation process progresses into future stages, goals and objectives are consistently revisited and revised, allowing the consultant to obtain commitments to specific solutions. Reviewing each intervention and the length of time that the consultee will commit to the interventions is important because follow-up regarding the recommendations is evaluated and intervention strategies are modified if necessary.

The third step in the consultative process is problem identification. Many encourage consultants to spend enough time gathering reliable data, both qualitative and quantitative. Accurate data are important for defining the problem.

Utilizing a solution-focused technique, consultants would ask specific questions about what the student said or did. They would inquire how the teacher or parent responded to the situation and clarify the goal of misbehavior. To help the consultee move beyond a set pattern of thinking, the consultant challenges assumptions that the consultee may have regarding the situation.

Problem confirmation and exploring alternatives comprise the fourth stage of the consultation process. This is an extremely important stage as the consultant and consultee formulate a list of alternatives to deal with the problem. Often, a good consultant will explore all the interventions tried to date and help the consultee create new options or modify previous plans.

Many consultants try to explore alternatives to the current situation. When consulting, school social workers need to break down problems into manageable parts by working on one problem at a time. Initially, choosing a concrete problem is best. It is wise to help the consultee understand that things will likely get worse before showing improvement. Competent consultants avoid direct suggestions and ask questions such as "Have you thought about . . .?" "What would happen if you . . .?" and "Would you be willing to consider . . .?" This kind of questioning helps the consultees gain trust in their own judgment and take ownership of the interventions.

Lastly, a key component to a successful intervention plan is the evaluation process. Many consultants establish a baseline of behaviors or a good description of the problem at the beginning. They often use scaling questions with the consultee, asking him or her to evaluate the severity of the problems on a scale from 1 to 10. This measurement can serve as a means for evaluating the consultation. Other consultants use a satisfaction questionnaire.

CONSULTING WITH TEACHERS, PARENTS, AND ADMINISTRATORS

A consultant needs to know how to work effectively with individuals and groups. Often, the consultant must enter the relationship without a predetermined, fixed plan of operation and must apply an integrated, multidimensional approach to consultation (Parsons & Kahn, 2005). The consultant is required to be flexible and responsive to both the demands and the opportunities of the situation, shifting the consultation from the parent to the teacher and, possibly, the administrator.

With so many points of focus, one might become overwhelmed with the role of consultant. The process of selecting which consultee depends on the nature of the problem, the goal, the needs of the school, and the expertise and style of the consultant. In the following case of Eduardo, the consultant applies the consultation process to the teacher, the parent, and the administrator. The case illustrates how the consultation process is implemented with these three separate consultees but with one goal in mind—to assist the student (Eduardo) in getting the most out of his academic experience.

In the case of Eduardo, Mrs. Gonzales is experiencing an immediate need for intervention. Conceptualizing the consultation from only the teacher's perspective

Case | # Case Example

The Case of Edwardo R.

Eduardo was referred to the school social worker's office by his teacher, Mrs. Gonzales. Eduardo is in sixth grade. He lives at home with his mother (physically disabled due to a car accident) and two young siblings, a sister (8 years old) and a brother (3 years old).

Mrs. Gonzales sent Eduardo to the social worker's office with a note that read as follows:

> Eduardo needs your help! He is out of control in my classroom. He is inattentive in class and is constantly bothering other children around him. He is always fidgeting in his seat, making loud noises, and touching the property of the other students. He never completes any of his school work.
>
> I have tried everything with him, including keeping him in for recess, keeping him after school, and isolating his seat in the back of the room. I have tried to get his mother to cooperate with no success. When I do get to talk with her on the phone, she complains about her physical limitations and how overwhelmed she is at home with the younger siblings. The last time I talked with her, she hung up on me because I suggested he might benefit from an evaluation for hyperactivity. Please help this kid get his act together; otherwise he is not welcome in my room.

About the Consultee

Mrs. Gonzales has been a teacher for the past 18 years. She has taught grades K–3 for most of her career. The school recently had to reduce the number of third-grade classrooms and she was placed in the only opening left in the school at the sixth-grade level. Mrs. Gonzales states, "I just loved the younger children; they were much more compliant and they listened to me. These older kids are a handful." Mrs. Gonazales expressed concern over the fact that the principal feels she does not have very good classroom management skills. She indicated she was being evaluated this year and that she is a bit uneasy about not having taught sixth grade.

---

would limit the consultant's ability to see all aspects of this case. However, the teacher is the logical place to start because she has made the initial referral and is asking for assistance. If the consultant follows the consultative process, the first task is to develop a relationship with the teacher and establish trust.

Consulting With Teachers

Consulting with teachers is increasingly recommended as a strategy for delivering intervention services to students with academic difficulties (Green & Shinn, 1990). School social workers who intervene with teachers as a consultant can help bring positive change for both the teacher and the student in the classroom. Teachers frequently want advice and information regarding student misbehavior in the classroom, parent problems, or classroom management and discipline. The consultant assists teachers to feel competent in making changes to help

Observations

In meeting Eduardo, the social worker notes that he is distractible, disheveled, and moves constantly around the room. He gives the social worker very little eye contact and is not sure why he had to come to see the social worker. He complains that his teacher is always yelling at him to sit down and be quiet. He relates that she is really boring and has it in for him.

In describing his home life, Eduardo explains that he lives in a two-bedroom apartment with his mother and two siblings. He shares a room with his younger brother, who is constantly wetting the bed and wants to sleep with Eduardo. His mother stays at home most of the time. She has no car and depends on a neighbor to get her to doctor appointments and the grocery store. They have a TV at home that Eduardo plays video games on when he comes home from school. He is responsible for baby-sitting his younger brother and sister (whom he fights with constantly) while his mother gets a break to go to a friend's apartment in the same building. According to Eduardo, "My mom needs a break so she hangs out and drinks a few beers with her friend. She doesn't feel so good since the accident and has to take lots of pills. Sometimes I worry about her drinking so much but I know she needs time away from us."

About the School

The school contains grades K–6, with a student population of 340 students. The school has 15 classroom teachers, 2 special education teachers, a part-time school nurse, and an itinerate school social worker who is there 3 days a week. This is the first year the school social worker is assigned to this elementary school. Within the past 5 years, there has been a slow reduction of children at the school due to plant closings and unemployment. Many of the parents in the surrounding community work in blue-collar jobs. Housing is fairly cheap and there has been a recent influx of Puerto Rican families into the community, which was primarily Polish.

The goal of the school is to foster "academic excellence in all our children." There has been a great deal of pressure put on the school to raise test scores. Teacher evaluations are now being conducted with test scores of each classroom in mind. There is uneasiness in the climate of the school.

---

students be more successful at school. Generally, three models of consultation are used with teachers: behavioral, collaborative, and mental/health consultation.

Behavioral consultation is well suited for schools because it offers the consultee alternatives in dealing with students who have developmental disabilities and disruptive behavior disorders. According to Sabatino (2002), a behavioral model formulates the problem in terms of dysfunctional behavior. The goal is to reduce or eliminate undesirable behaviors and replace or increase the frequency of desired behavior. A behavioral model also helps implement the mandates of the Individuals with Disabilities Education Act (1997) because it addresses behavior that interferes with the student's instruction or the learning opportunities of peers. Many behavioral consultations concentrate on the academic and social problems of individual students. However, some behavioral consultation services have expanded to include districtwide, schoolwide, and specific program consultation.

The second model of consultation is **collaborative decision making**. This model implies shared ownership of problems and solutions. The process includes sharing of skills and working together to achieve a common goal by pooling knowledge, skills, and resources. School social workers use this model frequently because, in theory, the consultant and consultee are on equal grounds. This model values teamwork and collaboration with multiple professionals. It is designed to enhance professional capabilities and to successfully bridge differences between all the interdisciplinary fields. According to Early (1992), the consulting relationship of the social worker with the teacher is that of colleague rather than outside expert, with both having parallel status.

The **mental health model** helps teachers understand the dynamics, symptoms, and manifestations of mental health disorders with individual children. The need is for an expert diagnosis and a recommendation regarding diagnosis or dysfunction. The consultant's goal is to provide diagnosis, prescription, and treatment alternatives. It is assumed that the teacher does not have expertise in this area that the consultant can provide. For school social workers, mental health consultation is an opportunity to apply ecological theory by helping the consultee analyze and observe the environment and the interactions among the participants to develop interventions that are sensitive to these observations.

Successful consulting with teachers requires a blameless intervention. It is important to cultivate positive relationships among teachers and staff using a collaborative approach. Availability and predictability in appointments with teachers build confidence in the reliability of the consultant. Confidentiality is essential in this process and requires that the consultant state boundaries and limits of the consultative relationship from the very beginning. An essential step in consulting is to learn the teacher's beliefs, educational philosophy, forms of classroom discipline, and his or her most memorable experiences with parents or students.

An effective school social work consultation can increase the teachers' sensitivity to the unique needs of students and help the teachers respond in a proactive way. Care must be given to establishing trust, conveying support, and establishing a working relationship with teachers. The consultant should make the meetings meaningful, and the outcome should aid teachers in understanding their students while improving their skills and developing successful intervention strategies.

Questions for a Behavioral Consultation With a Teacher

- What did the student do? (Identify target behavior.)
- How did the teacher respond to the behavior?
- How did the teacher feel when the misbehavior was occurring?
- How did the student respond to the teacher's corrective action?
- What could the teacher have done differently?

Case	**Case Example Continued**

Case Application With the Teacher and Eduardo

In reviewing the case of Eduardo, it may appear obvious that the focus of the referral could be narrowed and restricted to working directly with Eduardo or it could be working with Mrs. Gonzales and her entire sixth-grade class. The intervention for either of these options may be limited to modifying Eduardo's inattentive behaviors or increasing Mrs. Gonzales's classroom management skills. Goals and interventions could be expanded to include helping Mrs. Gonzales understand the developmental needs of students in sixth grade compared to their third-grade counterparts. Additionally, besides the age of the students, Mrs. Gonzales is dealing with changes in curriculum and insecurity about how the principal might perceive her ability to manage a classroom. Lastly, if the focus is only on Eduardo, then an intervention that helps the teacher understand his family background and possible psychosocial stressors could lead to more empathy and tolerance regarding his behavior on the part of the teacher.

In the case of Eduardo, the consultant chose to focus the intervention on Eduardo. The consultant concluded that he needed to gain the trust and confidence of the teacher, and possibly the best avenue to accomplish that was to focus on modifying Eduardo's behaviors. He surmised that the teacher was feeling insecure and to approach her with classroom management as an initial objective would be too threatening. The consultant decided that the collaborative model seemed to be best suited in dealing with Mrs. Gonzales. Knowing that the initial contact with Mrs. Gonzales was crucial to any future work, the school social worker began the initial consultation meeting by affirming some of the teacher's perceptions regarding Eduardo:

> Mrs. Gonzales, I can see why you have so many concerns about Eduardo. In the short time he was in my office, I was able to observe the inattentiveness and fidgety behaviors you described in your referral note. I am sure you could add some important information that would help me understand him better. Before we begin to talk about this, I would like to let you know that our discussion about Eduardo and your interactions with him and the rest of the class are confidential unless it falls under the mandated reporting clause. My role here is to assist you any way that I can. Hopefully, we can do this as a collaborative, problem-solving team. [Mrs. Gonzales seemed to relax and feel much more at ease.] I suspect that it must be hard to change classrooms and grades. It must put some extra pressure on you to have to learn a whole new curriculum. With all of that, to have a student who is not responding to all your extra planning and work has to be frustrating. Now what more can you share about Eduardo that can help us modify his behaviors?

Mrs. Gonzales began to share all the information she knew about Eduardo. In classroom observations and subsequent meetings, the consultant was able to set goals and objectives that not only dealt with Eduardo's behavior but also assisted the teacher in gaining an empathetic response regarding the home issues Eduardo was encountering. In addition, the teacher asked for assistance with her classroom management skills and gaining a better understanding of the developmental needs of students in her sixth-grade class.

| Case | **Case Example Continued** |

Consultation With the Principal

In the consultation process with Mrs. Gonzales, it became apparent to the consultant that there were some individual and system issues that he needed to address with the principal. Since this was his first year at this school, the school social worker had been conscientious about keeping the principal informed about his activities and job responsibilities. He had replaced a social worker who had been in the school for 15 years and had established herself as an influential force with staff and the administration. The new social worker was working diligently to forge his own identity within the school. During his weekly feedback sessions with the principal, the social worker listened carefully to the principal's concerns about how his school was progressing on the standardized tests that were now required by the state and federal government. He was worried that the test scores would be lowered by teachers such as Mrs. Gonzales, whose classroom management skills were suspect, and the fact that there seemed to be an increase in the number of kids with behavior and social–emotional problems.

Principal and Administrator Consultation

Consultation for school administrators, such as special education directors and principals, can be an effective means for making change from the practice to policy levels. Program consultation and the district's philosophical underpinning can be influenced positively by a social work consultant who is accepted and respected by administrative staff.

Principals are the leaders of schools and the most crucial individuals in regard to the adaptation of innovative practices (Sarason, 1971). They have tremendous impact on the school culture and climate. Because the attitudes of principals toward consultative services may influence teachers and other building staff, one of the first steps in the consultative process is to obtain support from the school administrator. Anything the consultant does is dependent on the principal giving permission and support. Without the principal's support, most consultations will fail. It is imperative to establish a line of communication with the principal to keep him or her informed of your efforts and how you perceive different problems. The successful school social worker can observe the trends within the school and begin to address systemic issues. It is critical to keep the principal informed of the efforts made to remedy a problem by sharing your observations and thoughts without breaking the confidentiality boundaries. Successful consultants share their philosophy even if it differs from that of the consultees. Most principals like to hear a unique perspective that they have not heard or considered. School social workers bring an ecological and strengths perspective that is dissimilar from an administrator's training.

This vignette of Eduardo exemplifies how the consultant can be effective at many levels. Despite the good intentions of many consultants, there are instances when the consultee is resistant to any intervention.

After listening carefully to these remarks, the school social work consultant asked the principal whether he had considered that Mrs. Gonzales might be feeling vulnerable and insecure because she had moved from teaching third grade to teaching sixth grade. The principal replied, "She's lucky she didn't get transferred to another school. It was the only opening in the building but I can see how that change might play into her not doing so well with sixth graders." The consultant saw this as an opportunity to address the climate of uneasiness in the school. He proceeded to inquire, "I wonder if all of the teachers are feeling a little vulnerable with so much pressure being put on the standardized tests. Maybe we need to have a discussion with the faculty so that they can express themselves a little and put the standardized tests into the proper perspective." The principal was not quite sure about that but told him he would think about it. Additionally, the consultant shared his perceptions about how a schoolwide behavior management system had been successful in another elementary school in which he had worked: "Sometimes teachers can change grades but the change is lessened by the fact that the same classroom management techniques can be used at all grade levels. Even the kids like that because the same language and procedures are used. It sure can cut down on the disciplinary hours that school principals spend on dealing with problem kids." That seemed to get the attention of the principal.

CONSULTING WITH PARENTS AND FAMILY MEMBERS

Consulting with parents can be productive and positive. The initial engagement of the parent is the most important task for the social work consultant. Successful school consultants know that when there is a discussion about a child with the parent, the child is an extension of the parent's ego. In short, when you talk about the behavior of the child, the parent is going to take that as a reflection of himself or herself. This is why it is so important to be positive from the beginning of the encounter. Talk about the good things you see in the child. Show that you are interested and want to help. From a family therapy perspective, the concept of "joining with the parent" to alleviate the problem speaks to establishing a trusting relationship. Effective consultants stress the idea that you need to work together and to let the parent know his or her help is important.

Many social work consultants find that asking the parents about their own past experiences in school can give them insight as to how they view the school system and their child. Chavkin (1974), Dinkmeyer and Carlson (2001) and Gianesin (2004) contributed to the following list of recommendations for working with parents regarding school-related issues:

- Focus on how you can help the child become successful in school.
- Be positive and let the parents know you genuinely care about their child.
- Tell parents how important they are to the consulting process.
- Talk to parents on their own level at a mutually convenient time and place. Do present your ideas first. Seek their opinions and develop plans together.
- Notice body language as well as what the parents say and do not say.
- Do not interrupt; be attentive and listen with interest.
- Ask questions that require more than a "yes" or "no" answer.

| Case | **Case Example Continued** |

The Parent as the Consultee

After having met with the teacher, Mrs. Gonzales, for several sessions, the consultant suggested a meeting with Eduardo's mother. After the mother, Mrs. Rodriguez, failed to attend two scheduled meetings due to transportation problems, the consultant arranged for transportation to the school for her. After arriving at the appointment, Mrs. Rodriguez presented herself as overwhelmed and overburdened. She constantly complained of back pain and asked to sit in three different chairs before she felt comfortable. Her affect was sad and depressed, as evidenced by her disheveled appearance and body language. The consultant decided to meet with the mother individually and then bring the teacher in to discuss Eduardo's classroom behaviors. The social worker started the meeting by stating, "Mrs. Rodriguez, I am so glad to have the opportunity to meet with you regarding Eduardo. The school is concerned that he may not be getting the most from his education and we need your help to understand him better. We believe you know him better than anyone else so we are counting on you to give us a better understanding about him." At that point in the interview, Mrs. Rodriguez broke down in tears stating, "This is the first time anyone has asked my opinion. Usually the school calls to tell me how bad Eduardo is behaving. They always call me and say he needs drugs to keep him from acting that way. I don't want to put him on drugs because I know what they can do to a person. That is why I was a little reluctant to come here before." The consultant took the time to listen carefully and solicited an in-depth education and social history of Eduardo. It became very evident that Eduardo had moved around a great deal. His school experience was filled with suspensions and isolation based on his inattentiveness, lack of concentration, and high activity in the classroom. He had never received any counseling services because his mother did not have the funds to pay for it. She had recently been placed on Supplemental Security Income benefits due to her disability so that made him eligible for mental health services through the local community mental health center.

- Recognize it takes time to develop trust and rapport.
- Summarize the meeting and your understanding.
- Follow through with any promises you have made.
- Keep the parents informed of the success or failure of your action plan.

Parent consultation can be very challenging, especially if there has been significant conflict between the school and the parent. Often, consultants can get caught in the middle because they feel obligated to advocate for parents and children who are unwelcome in school settings. It is important to focus on the needs of the child and to advocate and secure learning environments that are healthy and safe for students.

DEALING WITH RESISTANCE

Teachers often resist consultation when they did not request it (Early, 1992). In practice, most school consultation referrals are based on problems identified by administrators rather than teachers (Drisko, 1993). These types of referrals exacerbate concerns over teacher inadequacy and raise concerns over evaluation by

Meeting With the Consultant and Teacher

Mrs. Gonzales joined the social worker and the parent following the initial interview with Mrs. Rodriguez. The consultant explained to the teacher that Mrs. Rodriguez had been very helpful in giving him a history and background of Eduardo. He summarized the material that helped bring the teacher up to date and also gave the message to the parent about how much he had listened to her story. He reiterated that the reason they were all there was to help Eduardo get the most from his school experience. Mrs. Gonzales had been prepped ahead of time by the consultant as to how to approach the mother and the kind of information that would be helpful in the meeting. Mrs. Gonzales described the behaviors she was seeing in Eduardo and how she had modified her classroom practices to accommodate and change some of his behaviors. Mrs. Rodriguez related to the teacher and consultant that "Eduardo seems a little happier lately and actually says he likes school now. That's a big change because he usually hates school." Both the consultant and the teacher stated they were glad that things had gotten better but that he still needed a great deal more help and that they were worried about him because he was going to be in middle school the following year. Mrs. Rodriguez broke down again and indicated she was worried about Eduardo too: "He really takes care of me and the other kids and I know he has a problem. I just don't know what to do." After reassuring Mrs. Rodriguez, the consultant and teacher came up with several strategies that would take some pressure off the family and Eduardo. These included a referral for an after-school program for Eduardo and his younger sister and a referral for preschool services for the 3-year-old brother. Additionally, they were able to set up an appointment for Eduardo at the mental health center to have him evaluated by a child psychiatrist. Eventually, Eduardo was diagnosed with attention deficit hyperactivity disorder and was prescribed medication that assisted him in maintaining his attention span in school. Mrs. Rodriguez was extremely satisfied with the outcome because she was able to begin a rehabilitation and job training program.

others. Confidentiality, trust, and loyalty of the consultant are important issues to consider when resistance is apparent.

Social workers and other helping professionals tend to label behaviors that oppose the direction in which the social worker wishes to proceed as resistance (Hepworth, Rooney, & Larsen, 2002). **Resistance** has been defined by some as "holding back, disengaging, or in some way subverting change efforts whether knowingly or not without discussion" (Nelson, 1975, p. 587). When resistance is evident, many authors voice their recommendation to side with the defenses. For example, when school staff or parents resist viewing the student as others do, or they have unrealistic or inappropriate expectations of students, the consultant must empathize with their point of view and ask them to explain their rationale for taking a particular position. Another strategy for dealing with resistance is to anticipate the resistance before it starts. Many consultants engage the consultee in a discussion about their apprehension and reluctance regarding the nature of the consultation. The best way to avoid resistance is to clarify the roles of the participants and permit free choice as to whether or not to proceed. Building trust and rapport is one of the most important steps in the consultative process.

| Case | **Case Example** |

Identifying the Cause of Consultee Resistance
Each of the following demonstrates an intervention in which a consultant attempted to deal with consultee resistance.

Situation 1: Passive Aggressive—Too Busy and Forgetful

> **Consultant:** The last two times you and I met, you indicated an interest in trying out some of the new techniques we talked about. I can appreciate and can sympathize that you are busy and have a number of tasks you are responsible for as a classroom teacher. You have been very apologetic about not implementing any of the suggestions. As you were telling me why you were not able to implement our strategies, I noticed that you appear to be upset about something. Could we talk a little more about how you have been feeling about working together on this problem?

Situation 2: The Principal Made Me Do It

> **Consultant:** I know the last time we talked, you seemed a bit upset about the principal making the initial referral about Johnny. I wonder whether you are upset that the principal thinks you need outside help when you believe you could handle this on your own or that the situation is hopeless. I think I could be of help to you but only if we can both agree that you want and need the additional input. I certainly don't have all the answers but I might be able to approach the problem with Johnny from a different perspective that might help you understand his behavior. Are you interested in learning more about that?

Situation 3: The "Yes but" Form of Resistance

> **Consultant:** I guess I am a little confused right now. Throughout the last few minutes, I have been giving a number of suggestions that you seem to agree with initially. When we begin to talk about how to put them into place and ways to implement them, you seem to have a "but" as to why it won't work. Is there something here that I am missing? I want to be of assistance so help me understand how I can do this.

SUMMARY

For many school social workers, consulting has become useful for helping individuals such as teachers, parents, and principals maximize their effectiveness with children. In addition, consulting can provide a tool that impacts larger systemic issues and helps teachers positively influence their classrooms. Consultation is always a triadic relationship because the school social worker (consultant) works with a second person or persons (consultee) for the purpose of benefiting a third person or persons (client) (Parsons & Kahn, 2005).

In summary, a consultant's role requires the completion of four critical phases to provide the most optimal student-centered environment. The first phase is the preconsultation, in which the consultant must study any available diagnostic materials that pertain to the student, the classroom, the school, or the community with regard to the problem. The consultant should investigate the resources of the school system and understand the organizational leadership and structure of the system, the demands and resources of the school, and how these impact on the problem or student in question.

The second phase of the consultation process is establishing rapport with all parties involved. This phase is crucial to the efficacy of the plan's implementation. The consultant must work to establish a feeling of mutual respect and teamwork. The likelihood of collaborative success increases if the consultant remains sensitive to the participant's efforts with the student and has a thorough understanding of each member's role and responsibility in the process.

The third phase of the consultative process is two pronged: plan development and plan implementation. During the development process, a consultant must remain student oriented, tapping into individual, familial, community, and organizational strengths and resources to meet the needs of the student. He or she needs to be passionate and compassionate when conveying information and recommendations during the planning process. The implementation of the plan requires that the consultant be available and remain supportive of both the school and the parent.

Lastly, a key component to a successful consultation plan is the evaluation process. Follow-up and evaluation are essential to understand the effectiveness of the consultation. Successful consultants meet with the consultee to evaluate whether the goals they mutually agreed upon were met.

Another step crucial to the efficacy of the consultant is related to the skill of the consultant and not the consultation process. The development of competency in communication skills, *DSM-IV* expertise, and other skill sets mentioned previously enable the consultant to deliver the best possible services to the school and the child. Knowledge of local, state, and federal mandates helps the consultant navigate through hearings and challenges that often occur when conflicts do arise.

School Social Work Companion Website

Please be sure to check out our companion website at www.thomsonedu.com/social_work/bye, where you will find relevant materials for each chapter, including flashcards, online practice quizzes, and PowerPoint slides.

References

Bostic, J., & Rauch, P. (1999). The 3 R's of school consultation. *Journal of the American Academy of Child and Adolescent Psychiatry, 38*, 339–343.

Chavkin, N. (1974). *Talking with parents.* Champaign, IL: University of Illinois, Colonel Wolf School, Institute for Research on Exceptional Children.

Dane, B., & Simon, B. (1991). Resident guests: Social workers in host settings. *Social Work, 36*(3), 207–214.

Dinkmeyer, D., & Carlson, J. (2001). *Consultation: Creating school-based interventions* (2nd ed.). Philadelphia: Brunner–Routledge.

Drisko, J. W. (1993). Special education teacher consultation: A student-focused, skill-defining approach. *Social Work in Education, 15*(1), 19–28.

Early, B. (1992). An ecological-exchange model of social work consultation within the work group of the school. *Social Work in Education, 14*(4), 207–214.

Gianesin, J. (2004). The art of school social work and advanced generalist practice. In A. Roy & F. Vecchiolla (Eds.), *Thoughts on an advanced generalist education* (p. 205). Peosta, IA: Eddie Bowers.

Green, S., & Shinn, M. (1990). Curriculum-based measurement: Facilitating dynamic, outcomes-based consultation. *Journal of Educational and Psychological Consultation, 11*(4), 321–341.

Gurian, M. (2001). *Boys and girls learn differently! A guide for teachers and parents.* San Francisco: Jossey-Bass.

Gutkin, T., & Bossard, M. D. (1984). The impact of consultant, consultee, and organizational variables on teacher attitudes toward consultation services. *Journal of School Psychology, 22*, 251–258.

Hepworth, D., Rooney, R., & Larsen, J. (2002). *Direct social work practice* (6th ed.). Pacific Grove, CA: Brooks/Cole.

Kadushin, A. (1977). *Consultation in social work.* New York: Columbia University Press.

Kurpius, D., & Fuqua, D. (1993). Fundamental issues in defining consultation. *Journal of Counseling and Development, 7*, 598–600.

Nelson, J. (1975). Dealing with resistance in social work practice. *Social Casework, 56*, 587–592.

Parsons, R., & Kahn, W. (2005). *The school counselor as consultant.* Belmont, CA: Thompson–Brookes/Cole.

Sabatino, C. (2002). School social work consultation and collaboration: Integration of services across professional boundaries. In R. Constable, S. McDonald, & J. Flynn (Eds.), *School social work: Practice, policy, and research perspectives* (5th ed., pp. 208–229). Chicago: Lyceum.

Sarason, S. (1971). *The culture of the school and the problem of change.* Boston: Allyn & Bacon.

White, J., & Mullis, F. (1998). A systems approach to school counselor consultation. *Education, 119*(2), 242.

School Social Work: Key Issues and Considerations for Practice

12 CHAPTER | Confidentiality in the Schools

SANDRA KOPELS, M.S.W., J.D.
University of Illinois at Urbana-Champaign
School of Social Work

CHAPTER OVERVIEW

This chapter discusses (1) the importance of confidentiality to social work values and ethics; (2) the difficulties that school social workers have in trying to maintain confidentiality in the school setting; (3) the importance of confidentiality as a core social work value; (4) ethical and legal requirements to observe confidentiality at both the federal and the state level; (5) situations that may impact the ability to maintain confidentiality, including situations of mandated disclosures such as child abuse reporting or risk of a student's harm to self or others; and (6) best practice factors to consider in the decision to maintain or disclose student information.

INTRODUCTION

As mentioned in previous chapters, there are very real role challenges for school social workers who work in a host educational environment. Confidentiality is one of the core social work values. Although best practice suggests that confidentiality must be adhered to, this can be problematic for social workers who practice within the educational setting. Maintaining confidentiality in the school environment is further complicated by a confusing and conflicting myriad of state and federal laws.

TERMS RELATED TO CONFIDENTIALITY

The differences between the terms privacy, confidentiality, and privilege are discussed here. **Privacy** is a concept that is deeply ingrained within the psyche of the American people individually and within our society. It is the belief that individuals have the right to be left alone and should be able to exercise control over their own information (Shattuck, 1977). Although the U.S. Constitution does not expressly mention the right to privacy, recognition that individuals have a right to personal privacy has been implied from numerous court decisions. The right to privacy is not absolute; individual interests to be left alone or to control their own information may be pitted against governmental interests in protection of the general public or the legitimate need to know information about its citizens for the daily functioning of society.

Most people understand the everyday notion of confidentiality. If an individual agrees to keep a friend's confidence, then the individual will not reveal the confidence unless the friend agrees. In this situation, the ideal of confidentiality is based on trust and the moral obligation to maintain the secret. Because the disclosure of information occurs outside of a professional relationship, generally this type of confidentiality is not legally enforceable (Dickson, 1998).

Confidentiality in the professional arena is much more complicated. Confidentiality is the ethical principle that all social workers adhere to through their commitment to the core principles of the social work profession. Throughout the course of their social work education, social work students learn that they are to respect the confidentiality and privacy of information they obtain in working with clients (National Association of Social Workers [NASW], 1999). When clients disclose information, it may be very personal and private to them. Disclosing this information has the potential of being highly embarrassing to them; however, it may be necessary for successful diagnosis or achievement of treatment goals. Social workers who do not respect their ethical obligations to their clients may find themselves subject to lawsuits for monetary compensation or sanctioned by their licensing boards and/or professional associations.

Confidentiality is not an absolute concept. Within the NASW *Code of Ethics* (1999), social workers are told that they should protect the confidentiality of all information obtained in the course of professional service. However, this information may be disclosed for compelling professional reasons (*Code of*

Ethics 1.07). This chapter discusses situations in which school social workers may have compelling professional reasons to disclose confidential information.

Privilege, or **privileged communications,** is the idea that certain client information that is obtained within a professional or protected relationship cannot be revealed in court proceedings. The legal system in the United States is based on the adversarial process and the notion that truth can only be reached with the full disclosure of all relevant information. Accordingly, in court proceedings, all admissible evidence should be introduced to assist the fact finder in making his or her decision. Testimonial privileges go against that concept because even though the privileged information might be highly useful to decide important issues in the case, other policy considerations counter its admissibility.

Privilege laws are complicated and vary by profession, the type of information that is communicated, whether the legal proceeding is in state versus federal court, and many other factors. Even if a communication is privileged, the client or a person on behalf of the client may waive (give up) the privilege. However, when communications are deemed privileged, the information will not be introduced into the court proceedings. Although client communications to a professional may be made with the expectation that the professional will maintain the confidentiality of the information, unless a communication is privileged, its confidentiality may not be honored (Dickson, 1998). The U.S. Supreme Court has recognized that communications between a licensed psychotherapist (including social workers) and his or her client made in the course of diagnosis and treatment are protected from compelled disclosure in court proceedings (*Jaffee v. Redmond*, 1996). Therefore, in certain situations social workers may be able to offer privilege to their clients.

WHY WE DISCUSS CONFIDENTIALITY IN THE SCHOOLS

As discussed later, social workers have an ethical obligation and often a legal obligation to maintain the confidentiality and privacy of the information they gather about their clients. This obligation is applicable in the course of providing social work services in any setting in which they work. However, within the schools the maintenance of confidentiality is complicated by a number of factors that are unique to the school setting. There are competing demands for information that often conflict with the ethical obligations of social workers to maintain confidentiality.

The values of the social work profession instruct social workers to have respect for and maintain confidences on behalf of the people for whom they work. Other than social workers, psychologists and guidance counselors may be the only professionals within schools who are cognizant of and share an ethical or legal obligation to maintain confidentiality. Other school personnel, including administrators, teachers, aides, and clerical staff, are not bound by such values or duty, nor do they share the ethical viewpoint on maintaining confidentiality. Their focus is on the educational needs of children, not their overall emotional well-being.

Generally, other school personnel who desire information about students do so based on their legitimate concerns for the students' educational achievement and the school climate. However, if a social worker does not discuss specifics of a child with them, this may cause misunderstandings and frustrations on the part of those with whom the school social worker collaborates. Because the others do not subscribe to the same ethical obligations, they may not understand why the social worker will not share information with them.

In addition to school personnel, other people may be interested stakeholders in obtaining information regarding a child, including parents, neighbors, other service providers, law enforcement, and community members. Parents generally do not understand why social workers may not want to disclose information to them about their minor children. Parents believe that because they are the parents, and because their children are underage, they are entitled to know everything their children share. However, their interest in knowing what information their children share is different than their rights to know such information and from the obligations on the part of the social worker to maintain the confidentiality of the information. It must be remembered that not all parents seek information to improve the welfare of their children. Some parents are in conflict with their children. In those cases, parental knowledge of the contents of the social work relationship may only serve to exacerbate parent–child differences and jeopardize the physical or mental health of the children (Croxton, Churchill, & Fellin, 1988).

Finally, social workers should consider why people request information about a child. As mentioned previously, people are often motivated by genuine interest and concern for a child's well-being. Other people (e.g., school administrators) may have a stake in obtaining information for the maintenance of a safe school. Others, such as the police or community members, may want information about a child who has committed crimes or is endangering the broader community environment. Still other people are motivated by gossip or nosiness and have no positive motivation for requesting the information.

ETHICAL COMPLICATIONS IN MAINTAINING CONFIDENTIALITY

Social work values and ethics require that social workers observe the confidentiality of information of the people with whom they work. Typically, social workers look to the NASW's *Code of Ethics* (1999) as a starting point for understanding their ethical duties to maintain confidentiality. Generally, sections 1.07 and 1.08 of the *Code of Ethics* caution social workers to use due care in protecting the information of people with whom they work, to discuss the limits of confidentiality with their clients, and to only disclose information if there are compelling reasons to do so. School social workers share the same ethical duties as social workers in other settings. However, the unique complexities of maintaining confidentiality in the school environment have resulted in the National Association of Social Workers (NASW) and other professional organizations issuing position statements on the maintenance of confidentiality in schools.

In 1991, the NASW Commission on Education issued the first position statement unique to the school social worker and confidentiality. Its purpose was to offer general principles to guide conduct involving the school social worker and confidentiality and to assist social workers with difficult decision making. It discussed ethical issues, legal issues, the convergence of ethics and law, and provided confidentiality guidelines for specific situations. The position statement asserted that the school social worker has ethical obligations to more than one client in any given situation, including the student, parents, school personnel, and the community as clients of the school social worker. The position statement also stated that the responsibility of the school social worker to maintain student confidentiality needed to be balanced with the social worker's responsibility to parents and school administrators.

In response to the NASW Commission on Education's (1991) statement, Kopels (1992) argues that viewing multiple parties as clients complicates decision making about confidentiality because it makes all these individuals equally important. She contends that although parents, school personnel, and community members may have legitimate reasons to want information about a child, they should not be regarded as clients who are equally entitled to access. Instead, she posits that looking at the student as the only client to whom the school social worker owes a duty of confidentiality simplifies decision making. Rather than treating these other entities as clients and juggling their competing interests with those of the student, the school social worker needs to decide whether compelling professional reasons exist to disclose the student's information.

Kardon (1993) agrees with Kopels' position that labeling all school personnel and the community as clients of the school social worker is overly expansive. However, he takes issue with Kopels' adherence to the ethical values of confidentiality in the school setting. Kardon believes that confidentiality has little bearing on the promotion of healthier relationships between the student and the school; because social work referrals come from concerned teachers, parents, and administrators, information sharing is required between these individuals.

School social workers are often asked to consult with parents and school personnel to improve a child's functioning in the school. In Chapter 11, Gianesin discusses the various consultative roles that school social workers assume in their work. Regardless of their consultation roles, Gianesin acknowledges the importance of school social workers to maintain confidentiality and for consultants to discuss confidentiality boundaries and limitations at the outset of the consultation relationship. Although school social workers may need to share certain information about students and their family situations with the people with whom they consult, they should provide only the minimum information necessary to accomplish the consultation purpose. Not all information the school social worker learns about a student needs to be shared.

The Illinois Association of School Social Workers (IASSW) adopted its own position statement on the school social worker and confidentiality (*School Social Worker and Confidentiality*, 1993). IASSW notes that a major conflict exists between the duty of the school social worker to keep certain disclosures confidential and the responsibility of the school personnel to divulge information.

IASSW believes that decision making in actions related to confidentiality versus disclosure should be guided by ethical considerations, the determination of the "need to know," professional judgment of the social worker, the nature of the problem, applicable laws, and the best interest of the client.

The School Social Work Association of America (SSWAA) adopted a position statement on confidentiality in the schools in March 2001. SSWAA believes that the best interests of the student should serve as a guide in decisions regarding preserving the confidentiality of information versus sharing it. Moreover, school social workers must weigh the consequences of sharing information and assume responsibility for their decisions.

All three positions statements note that the laws governing information disclosure are complicated and often conflicting; however, social workers should be familiar with federal, state, and local laws that clarify responsibilities related to confidentiality in specific situations.

LEGAL REQUIREMENTS REGARDING CONFIDENTIALITY

There is no single legal requirement regarding school social workers and confidentiality in the schools. Instead, school social workers need to be familiar with a patchwork of federal laws that impact information disclosure in the schools. Some of the major laws, and what they address, are presented here. Best practices require that school social workers understand the details of the laws and how those details affect their practice. Additionally, school social workers must be aware of any laws, unique to their state, that apply to their practice in their schools.

Education Records

Perhaps the most important federal law governing school student records is the Family Educational Rights and Privacy Act of 1974 (FERPA). This law was enacted to combat existing practices and give parents certain rights in relationship to their children's educational records. Under FERPA, at a minimum, schools that receive federal financial assistance are required to have policies and practices that inform parents about the specific types of educational records that exist and procedures to access them; the right to access their children's education records within 45 days; the right to request changes to the records, challenge inaccuracies, and provide their own statement, if necessary; the right to provide written informed consent for most disclosures; and to see the school's records of disclosure (Fischer & Sorenson, 1991; Kopels, 2004). It is important to note that FERPA provides these rights to parents; students do not have independent rights of their own until they reach the age of 18 years. At age 18, FERPA rights transfer to the student and the student controls information access and disclosure, not the parents. Unfortunately, parents have little remedy if school districts do not follow the provisions of FERPA because courts have routinely ruled that parents have no right to sue schools under FERPA.

Special Education Records

As discussed in other chapters, as part of the multidisciplinary team, school social workers play a vital role in the special educational process. Within IDEA regulations, there is a clear relationship that derives from and is parallel to the confidentiality requirements under FERPA. States must detail the policies and procedures that they have undertaken to ensure protection of the confidentiality of any personally identifiable information collected, used, or maintained under IDEA. Personally identifiable information includes (1) the child's name or name of the child's parent or other family member; (2) the address of the child; (3) a personal identifier, such as the child's social security number or student number; or (iv) other information that would make it possible to identify the child with reasonable certainty [34 C.F.R. §300.500(b) (3)].

IDEA regulations provide that parents must be informed when personally identifiable information is no longer needed to provide educational services to the child. This notice normally would be given after a child graduates from or otherwise leaves the school. The purpose of the notice is to give parents an option to destroy records that are no longer needed for the child's education that may concern a child's performance, abilities, and behavior. Parents may choose to request the destruction of records because destruction provides the best protection against improper and unauthorized disclosure of sensitive personal information. However, parents may desire to keep the records because they may be needed in the future to support applications for the child's receipt of social security benefits, insurance, or for other purposes.

HIPAA

Among other aims, the federal Health Insurance Portability and Accountability Act of 1996 (HIPAA) was enacted to improve portability and continuity of health insurance; to combat waste, fraud, and abuse in health insurance and health care delivery; to improve access to long-term care services and coverage; and to simplify the administration of health insurance. As part of HIPAA, national standards were created to protect the privacy of personal health information (Standards for Privacy, 2003). The "privacy rule" requires covered entities (health plans, health care clearinghouses, and health care providers who conduct certain health care transactions electronically) to implement standards to protect and guard against the misuse of individually identifiable health information. The provisions of the privacy rule went into effect in April 2003.

According to HIPAA regulations, "individually identifiable health information" is a subset of health information and includes

> information, including demographic data, that relates to the individual's past, present, or future physical or mental health or condition, the provision of health care to the individual, or the past, present, or future payment for the provision of health care to the individual, and that identifies the individual or for which there is a reasonable basis to believe can be used to identify the individual. (45 C.F.R. § 160.103)

In its definition of protected health information, the privacy rule excludes education and certain other records subject to or defined in FERPA.

Because the definition of protected health information does not include educational records under FERPA, it might appear that HIPAA does not apply to the school setting. Certainly, it seems to be Congress' intent that educational records are not subject to the privacy provisions of HIPAA. However, two caveats are necessary. First, HIPAA contains a provision that if state law is more stringent than HIPAA, then state law must be followed. Therefore, if a state's law defines individually identifiable health information to include educational records, then the other provisions of HIPAA will apply.

Second, the type of information that is contained within school records does not only pertain to students' educational needs. Depending on the nature of their physical or mental health problems, students may require a variety of services that are provided both within and outside of the school setting. For example, a student who has severe psychological problems may be hospitalized in a psychiatric inpatient setting. A student who has chronic health problems, such as kidney disease, may need hospitalization for his or her illness. It is not uncommon for the records of the psychiatric or medical hospitalization to be sent to the school and included in the student's records in an effort to coordinate services and understand the student's unique needs. Therefore, although HIPAA may not include education records per se, the other records within the school student record may fall under the provisions of HIPAA. Since compliance with the privacy provisions of HIPAA has only been required recently, much about its implementation remains unknown. School social workers would be wise to follow the development of this law.

State Law

Some states pass laws that are derived from the previously mentioned federal laws and are consistent with and/or expand upon the minimum requirements of federal law. For example, consistent with FERPA, Illinois has a school student records act that governs access to records of schoolchildren in Illinois. Within this law, parents who request access to their children's school records must be provided it within 15 days of their request, rather than the 45 days allowed by federal law (Illinois School Student Records Act, 2003).

Additionally, some states pass laws that impact on confidentiality in a given setting (e.g., alcohol treatment and mental health centers), by profession (e.g., social work licensing laws and mental health counselors), by type of problem (e.g., mental health, AIDS, child abuse, and sexual disease transmission), or by the age of the child (e.g., emancipation laws and special consent laws). To illustrate this point, in a presentation to school social workers about confidentiality in Illinois schools, the presenter noted that the sources of state law for her presentation came from Illinois' Abused and Neglected Child Reporting Act, AIDS Confidentiality Act, Clinical Social Work and Social Work Practice Act, Consent by Minors to Medical Treatment Act, Emancipation of Minors Act, Mental Health and Developmental Disabilities Confidentiality Act, School Student Records Act, and the Juvenile Court Act (Kopels, 2003). Accordingly, in many states the sources of laws on confidentiality may be vast and difficult to assess. Clearly, social workers must be aware of the state laws on confidentiality that impact their practice.

SITUATIONS THAT COMPLICATE MAINTAINING CONFIDENTIALITY

The previous discussion relates to ethics and laws that require social workers to maintain confidentiality of certain records and communications. Other situations may obligate social workers to reveal information they have about clients. The NASW code of ethics allows social workers to disclose confidential information for compelling professional reasons. There is no definitive statement on reasons viewed as compelling enough. However, the preamble to the code states that the general expectation that social workers will keep information confidential "does not apply when disclosure is necessary to prevent serious, foreseeable, and imminent harm to a client or other identifiable person" (NASW, 1999). It is widely accepted that the prevention of harm to clients or others encompasses situations of child abuse and the "duty to warn."

Child Abuse and Neglect Reporting

Social workers, regardless of their practice setting, are considered to be mandated reporters of child abuse. Accordingly, in the course of their professional responsibilities, if social workers discover that children with whom they are working are abused or neglected children according to that state's legal definition, the law mandates that they report their beliefs to a designated agency responsible for the investigation of these reports. Social workers do not have to be certain that abuse or neglect actually occurred. Typically, the law only requires that they act in good faith and report when they know, learn, or have reasonable suspicions or beliefs that abuse or neglect may have occurred (Kopels, 2006). With child abuse and neglect reporting, the law generally does not recognize confidentiality or privilege. Recognition of a mandated reporter's duty to report child abuse and neglect is often written into the law as an exception to confidentiality. In fact, social workers who fail to report known or suspected abuse or neglect can find themselves subject to criminal penalties, such as jail or fines, as well as civil penalties, such as licensure actions, professional sanctions, or monetary judgments.

School social workers often encounter situations of child abuse or neglect. In the course of providing counseling, students may admit to the social worker that their parents are abusing them. A social worker may observe cuts and bruises on a child and suspect that the child is being abused. A teacher may refer a student who is having attention problems to the school social worker. The social worker may learn that the student is tired because he or she has nowhere to sleep at night because the family is homeless. School social workers are mandated reporters who are crucial to the effort to combat child abuse and neglect. In Illinois in fiscal year 2002, of the 12,273 child abuse and neglect reports made by school personnel, 3,715 were made by school social workers (*Child Abuse and Neglect Statistics Annual Report*, 2002).

The Duty to Warn

Another compelling professional reason for social workers to disclose client information is in a **duty to warn** situation. The concept of duty to warn is generally misunderstood by social work and other mental health professionals (Kopels & Kagle 1993). Generally, when a client discloses information to a therapist that indicates to the therapist that the client poses a risk of harm to third parties, the therapist is allowed to violate the duty to maintain confidentiality and disclose information to protect the third parties.

The landmark duty to warn case is *Tarasoff v. Regents of University of California* (1974). In *Tarasoff*, a graduate student, Prosenjit Poddar, told his psychologist that he intended to kill an unnamed but readily identifiable woman, Tatiana Tarasoff. The psychologist consulted with his supervisor and others and also asked the campus police to detain Poddar. Poddar later killed Tatiana. Tatiana's parents then sued the psychologist and others for their failure to warn them of the harm posed to Tatiana by Poddar. The California Supreme Court ruled that

> when a doctor or a psychotherapist, in the exercise of his professional skill and knowledge, determines, or should determine, that a warning is essential to avert danger arising from the medical or psychological condition of his patient, he incurs a legal obligation to give that warning. (*Tarasoff* at 555)

The California Supreme Court later amended its own ruling and broadened the duty to warn to a duty to protect. In the second *Tarasoff* case (1976), the court stated,

> When a therapist determines, or pursuant to the standards of his profession should determine, that his patient presents a serious danger of violence to another, he incurs an obligation to use reasonable care to protect the intended victim against such danger. (*Tarasoff II* at 347)

The court stated that the discharge of the duty can occur in a variety of ways, depending on the nature of the case, including warning the intended victim or others likely to apprise the victim of the danger, notifying the police, or taking whatever other steps are reasonably necessary under the circumstances.

The *Tarasoff* case was a California case and is a precedent in California courts. Other states have had their own duty to warn cases that follow or disagree with the *Tarasoff* rulings. However, the impact of the *Tarasoff* decision is demonstrated through the general acceptance of the duty to warn or protect in ethical codes, legal statutes that limit therapist liability, and amendments to confidentiality laws that allow therapists to disclose information to warn or protect third parties. Within the helping professions, it is also agreed that professionals can disclose information that would protect clients from harming themselves.

How does the duty to warn or protect apply in the school setting? The principles of the *Tarasoff* case, other court decisions, and exceptions to confidentiality laws allow a school social worker to disclose information that would otherwise be confidential to protect students and others from situations in which students may be harmful to third parties or themselves. However, these disclosures usually are not mandatory; instead, they are based on the discretion of the social worker. Unlike situations involving the abuse and neglect of children, which social workers are required by law to report, the duty to warn or protect relies on the clinical judgment of the social worker to assess the degree of danger or harm to the individual or others and to take action, if warranted.

Harm to Others

Clearly, the maintenance of safety in public schools is one of the highest priorities for the schools. The school shooting tragedy in Littleton, Colorado, at Columbine High School illustrates the importance of breaking confidentiality to warn others of impending actions of students that may harm others. In that case, Dylan Klebold and Eric Harris brought guns to school and killed 13 students and a teacher, and they injured many others before they, in turn, were killed. Harris had a diary in which he discussed wanting to kill at least 500 students, making bombs, interest in the Goth subculture, computer games, being bullied, etc. (Disaster Center, 2004). If a social worker had been involved with Harris and he had discussed the contents of his diary or thoughts to the social worker, then the social worker could have disclosed this information to the proper authorities to avoid the disaster. The proper authorities might be the police, the school principal, the parents, or whoever else would have the ability to prevent such a tragedy.

In the course of their job duties, social workers may learn about all types of behaviors that can cause harm to the student or others, including overt behaviors such as bringing guns or other weapons to school, engaging in fights, or selling drugs to other students. These behaviors may also include threats or plans that may harm others, such as bomb threats, violence against other students, and property damage. Social workers may learn of these incidents through discussion with the perpetrators of the harm or from parents or other students who are troubled by information they have gathered. The school social worker is required to use his or her clinical judgment to assess the risk of harm to the student or others. Generally, the more serious the social worker considers the incident to be, the more likely the social worker would disclose the information. For example, if a student tells the social worker that he or she brought a gun to school, shows the gun to the social worker, and states that he or she plans to ambush another student after school, the social worker would assess the threat as serious and immediate and disclose the information to avert harm to the other student. However, if the student tells the social worker that he or she is thinking about spray painting a building next month to protest a cause, the social worker would probably assess the seriousness and immediacy of this action as minimal. Instead of disclosing the information, the social worker could use his or her therapeutic skills to provide an effective intervention for the student.

Is bullying the type of behavior that is included in harm to others? If a social worker is told that another child is bullying a student, can the social worker disclose this information to protect the student?

Case | Case Example

In a recent court decision (*Albers v. Breen*, 2004), a seventh-grade student, Shea, told his mother that three male students bullied him (the court complaint does not describe the bullying behavior). Shea's mother told the school principal that her child was being bullied but did not tell him the names of the bullies. Because the bullying made Shea reluctant to go to school, the mother called the school, seeking the assistance of a social worker to counsel her son. The social worker contacted the mother and made arrangements to counsel Shea. The mother told the social worker that the principal wanted to know the names of the bullies but that Shea did not wish to reveal them. The social worker told the mother that she would not share the names with the principal, and because of that promise the mother told the social worker the boys' names. Later that day, the social worker met with Shea and promised him that nobody would find out that Shea had revealed the names of the boys. Without the mother's or Shea's consent, the social worker told the principal the boys' names. The principal informed one of the boys that Shea had complained about him. Because of these disclosures by the social worker and the principal, the mother sued the school. She sought monetary compensation because Shea suffered emotional distress, received private counseling, and was forced to attend a different school the following year.

In the court case, the mother argued that the school social worker improperly revealed confidential communications made by her and Shea when the social worker disclosed the names of the bullies to the principal. The court ruled that the social worker was justified in revealing this information under an exception to the state's mental health confidentiality laws. The laws require confidentiality except when a therapist, in his or her sole discretion, determines that disclosure is necessary to protect the person or others against a clear, imminent risk of serious physical or mental injury, disease, or death. The court found that the state statute left to the therapist's sole discretion the decision of whether disclosing otherwise protected information was necessary to protect the child from harm. The social worker argued that Shea had told her that he was being "shoved and kicked" by the other boys and, as a result, she believed he was at risk of further harm. Because the social worker was acting within her discretion, the court ruled against the mother's complaints that the social worker revealed confidential information without justification.

It should be noted that the court only dealt with the issue of whether the school social worker was legally justified when she revealed Shea's information to the principal despite her promise to Shea and his mother that she would keep this information confidential. Although the social worker may have acted legally, she did not act in a fully ethical manner. The NASW *Code of Ethics* (1999, 1.01, 1.07e) also instructs social workers to inform their clients about the limits of confidentiality, especially when the social worker learns that the client or others may be at risk of harm from their own actions or the actions of others. If the social worker would have discussed these ethical responsibilities with Shea and his mother before they disclosed the names of the bullies, they would have had the choice of disclosing the information. Had they been so informed, they may not have felt as betrayed when the social worker broke her promise of maintaining their confidentiality.

Harm to Self

There are many situations in which school social workers learn that children are behaving in ways that may be harmful to them. Because of this, school social workers may be required to reveal confidential information to protect the student from harm. Examples of behaviors that may be viewed as harmful to self include suicide attempts, self-mutilation, alcohol or drug use, eating disorders, and sexual activity. Regarding sexual activity, additional issues include the use of birth control, having unprotected sex, pregnancy, abortion, and HIV/AIDS.

In some of these circumstances, the severity of the degree of harm to the child varies; in more severe situations, it may be much less difficult for social workers to decide whether they are required to reveal the confidences. For example, a student who expresses suicidal ideation and contemplates committing suicide demonstrates a very serious risk of harm to himself or herself. Social workers who believe that a student may be suicidal would definitely choose to disclose information to keep the child from dying. In fact, court cases have discussed school personnel's duty to disclose information to avert teen suicide (*Eisel v. Board of Education of Montgomery County*, 1991). On the other hand, if a student discloses that he or she is romantically involved with another student of whom her or his parents disapprove, the social worker may be less likely to disclose the information. In the social worker's professional judgment, the degree of harm to the student is minimal, and the social worker chooses to maintain the student's confidence and trust.

Other situations are complicated by the age of the student. In some circumstances, a school social worker may be more concerned about a younger child who engages in the same activity as does an older child. For example, a 17-year-old senior may tell the school social worker that she is having sexual intercourse with her 18-year-old boyfriend, whom she plans on marrying immediately after she graduates from high school. Other than cautioning her about having unprotected sex, the school social worker may choose not to disclose that information, viewing it as confidential. However, if an 11-year-old sixth grader discloses to the school social worker that she is having sexual intercourse with her 18-year-old boyfriend, whom she plans on marrying when she graduates from high school in 7 years, the social worker would probably assess the level of harm to the 11-year-old much differently. Although the activity is the same—sexual intercourse—the school social worker may assess the consequences of that behavior much differently for the younger child. To protect the child from the consequences of a sexual relationship with a much older person who most probably is taking advantage of her, the social worker may choose to disclose the information.

Certain behaviors may be problematic for the social worker only because the student's status is that of a minor. For example, a student may reveal that he or she is regularly drinking alcohol. If an adult told his or her social worker that he or she was drinking, there would be no duty to report the drinking to the adult's parents or spouse because there is nothing illegal about the activity. However, because under the law minors are not allowed to drink, a student's disclosure of his or her drinking may be more complicated for the social worker to handle.

In other situations, the behavior may be troubling for the social worker because of the social worker's own personal values. For example, a student may engage in sexual activity and disclose to the social worker that she is pregnant and does not want her parents to find out. Does the social worker reveal the pregnancy to the parents? Pregnancy in and of itself may not be viewed as harmful. However, the pregnancy of a minor who may not seek medical care can be harmful to both the minor and the fetus. If the student wants information about an abortion, which is legal, and the social worker does not believe in abortion, can the social worker disclose the information to the parents under the guise of preventing harm to the fetus?

BEST PRACTICES IN MAINTAINING OR DISCLOSING STUDENT INFORMATION

Obviously, the maintenance of confidentiality within the schools is a very complicated matter. Therefore, we should examine what are the best practices that govern the social workers' decisions about when they must maintain the confidentiality of the information communicated to them and when they must, should, or may disclose information confided to them.

Best practices require that school social workers become familiar with the NASW *Code of Ethics* (1999) as well as the position statements on confidentiality advanced by NASW, SSWAA, and any state association of school social work in their practice state. These ethical codes and guidelines reflect the best practice principles as determined by school social work practitioners. Moreover, school social workers must be familiar with federal laws and the laws in their states that govern mandatory and permissive disclosures of client information. Best practices require that social workers practice in accordance with the law.

Therefore, once familiar with ethical and legal requirements, social workers should start with the premise that all information gained by them in the course of their employment is confidential. Against this backdrop, the school social worker should consider whether there are compelling professional reasons that this information be disclosed. These compelling reasons may be because social workers have a duty to disclose in certain circumstances, such as with child abuse reporting, or because they have the discretion to disclose the information to prevent individuals from harming themselves or others.

If a school social worker believes that a situation may warrant disclosure of information, certain best practice principles should direct the decision to disclose. Social workers should consider the following factors:

- Does the law require or allow this information to be disclosed (e.g., information about a child at a case study evaluation)?
- What will the information disclosure accomplish? If it is likely to prevent serious harm to a student or others, the information should be disclosed. If it is requested because it is interesting or may fuel gossip, then the information should not be disclosed.

- Has the social worker conducted a careful and thorough assessment of the realities of the dangerousness of a situation? A child with mental retardation may make a bomb threat for attention and not have the ability to carry out the threat.
- Has the social worker documented all decisions and actions related to the disclosure? This should include documenting the reasons certain actions were not taken as well as why certain actions were taken. If the school social worker discusses the matter with a supervisor or consultant, the advice from the consultation should also be documented.
- Is the social worker revealing only the minimum information necessary for the purpose? When the social worker informs the school principal that another child is bullying a student, the name of the man with whom the student's mother is having an affair is unnecessary information, whereas the bully's name is necessary.
- Is the social worker balancing the interests of others to the information disclosure against the student's rights not to have the information disclosed? It must be remembered that just because individuals want information, they may not be entitled to it.

SUMMARY

Maintaining confidentiality is vital to the values and ethics of the social work profession and of utmost importance in preserving the trust of social work clients. However, the maintenance of confidentiality is not an absolute. School social workers should use best practices to ensure that they practice legally and ethically and to govern their decisions to maintain or disclose confidential information.

School Social Work Companion Website

Please be sure to check out our companion website at www.thomsonedu.com/social_work/bye, where you will find relevant materials for each chapter, including flashcards, online practice quizzes, and PowerPoint slides.

References

Albers v. Breen, 2004 Ill. App. LEXIS 362 (1st Dist., 2004).

Child abuse and neglect statistics annual report. (2002). Table 9. Retrieved May 11, 2004, from www.state.il.us/dcfs/docs/cants2002table9.shtml

Croxton, T. A., Churchill, S. R., & Fellin, P. (1988). Counseling minors without parental consent. *Child Welfare, 67*(1), 3–13.

Dickson, D. T. (1998). *Confidentiality and privacy in social work: A guide to the law for practitioners and students.* New York: Free Press.

Disaster Center. (2004). Retrieved May 22, 2004, from www.disastercenter.com/killers.html

Eisel v. Board of Education of Montgomery County, 324 Md. 376, 597 A.2d 447 (1991).

Family Educational Rights and Privacy Act of 1974. 20 U.S.C. §1232(g).

Fischer, L., & Sorenson, G. P. (1991). *School law for counselors, psychologists, and social workers* (2nd ed.). New York: Longman.

Health Insurance Portability and Accountability Act of 1996. P.L. 104–191.

Illinois Association of School Social Workers. (1993). *School social worker & confidentiality*. Retrieved May 19, 2004, from www.iassw.org/pp-confidentiality.htm

Illinois School Student Records Act. (2003). 105 Illinois Compiled Statutes §110(5)(c).

Jaffee v. Redmond, 518 U.S. 1 (1996).

Kardon, S. (1993). Confidentiality: A different perspective. *Social Work in Education*, 15(4), 247–250.

Kopels, S. (1992). Confidentiality and the school social worker. *Social Work in Education*, 14(4), 203–205.

Kopels, S. (2003). *Confidentiality in the school setting: Is it possible?* Paper presented at the 33rd annual fall conference of the Illinois Association of School Social Workers, Arlington Heights, IL.

Kopels, S. (2004). Student rights and control of behavior. In P. A. Meares (Ed.), *Social WORK services in schools* (4th ed., pp. 119–148). Boston: Pearson, Allyn & Bacon.

Kopels, S. (2006). Laws and procedures for reporting child abuse: An overview. In C. Franklin, M. B. Harris, & P. Allen-Meares (Eds.), *The School Services Sourcebook* (pp. 369–375). New York: Oxford University Press.

Kopels, S. & Kagle, J. D. (1993). Do social workers have a duty to warn? *Social Service Review*, 67(1), 101–126.

National Association of Social Workers. (1991). *The school social worker and confidentiality*. Silver Spring, MD: Author.

National Association of Social Workers. (1999). *Code of ethics*. Washington, DC: Author.

School Social Work Association of America. (2001). *School social workers and confidentiality*. Retrieved June 25, 2001, from www.sswaa.org/about/publications/confidentiality.html

Shattuck, J. H. F. (1977). *Rights of privacy*. Skokie, IL: National Textbook.

Standards for Privacy of Individually Identifiable Health Information; Final Rule. 45 C.F.R. Parts 160 and 164 (August 2003).

Tarasoff v. Regents of University of California, 529 P. 2d 553 (1974).

Tarasoff v. Regents of University of California, 551 P. 2d 334 (1976).

13 CHAPTER | Incorporating Best Practices

DAVID R. DUPPER, Ph.D.
University of Tennessee–Knoxville

CHAPTER OVERVIEW

After reading this chapter, readers will (1) become familiar with what is meant by "best practices;" (2) learn several essential components of best practices with clients and client systems, including best practice guidelines with culturally diverse populations; (3) be able to discuss the relationship between best practices and social work values and ethics; (4) be able to discuss the relationship between best practices and ecological/prevention approaches; (5) become familiar with several examples of best practice guidelines for student- and system-focused interventions; and (6) gain an understanding of the challenges of implementing best practice interventions and programs in the unique organizational setting of the school.

INTRODUCTION: WHAT ARE "BEST PRACTICES"?

In this age of increasing public scrutiny and accountability, social workers and other mental health providers are required to control costs and provide statistical evidence that their interventions are effective. Best practices are increasingly important to justify the expenditure of public tax dollars on school social work services as well as to stave off possible cutbacks during times of retrenchment.

Best practices are those interventions and programs that

1. "possess scientifically credible evidence of effectiveness" (Thyer, 2002, p. 739);
2. take into account social work values and the expectations of clients (Gibbs & Gambrill, 1999); and
3. lead to the best outcomes at the least cost for individual students, small groups of students, families, schools, and communities.

STEPS IN EVIDENCED-BASED PRACTICES

A number of steps have been identified in the implementation of evidenced-based practice (Cournoyer & Powers, 2002; Gibbs & Gambrill, 1999).

Step 1: Become Motivated to Apply Evidenced-Based Practice

Although many social work educators emphasize the importance of selecting interventions that are evidenced based, most school social workers, faced with large caseloads and excessive paperwork, do not take the time to seek out the professional literature. Instead, they rely on practice wisdom, appeals to authority, or intuition to guide their practice decisions (Gambrill, 1999). In this age of increasing accountability and scrutiny, it is important to make practice decisions based on the best available scientific evidence rather than good intentions. It is possible to be an empathic, warm-hearted practitioner who also uses analytical and scientific skills in making practice decisions (Gibbs & Gambrill, 1999).

 Case Example

In an effort to reduce the high number of suspensions at a middle school she served, Anna, a school social worker, implemented a "state-of-the-art" school-based prevention program designed to reduce student suspensions based on the guidelines and principles discussed in this chapter.

Step 2: Formulate a Searchable Practice Question

The second step involves developing an answerable question that is specific and involves a description of the client or client system, intervention method, and desired outcome(s). It can involve a remedial intervention or a prevention program.

| **Case** | **Case Example Continued** |

Anna, the middle school social worker, formulated a searchable practice research question: What intervention(s)/program will work best as a nonpunitive alternative to student suspensions?

Step 3: Conduct a Comprehensive and Efficient Practice Effectiveness Search of Reputable Resources

| **Case** | **Case Example Continued** |

Anna conducted an Internet-based search of the professional literature to locate the most current studies on prevention programs that reduced the number of suspensions. Second, she conducted a comprehensive and efficient search of databases and reputable online resources. To locate evidenced-based research articles, she used the following search terms with wild card characters: "research*," "evidence*," and "intervene*" in conjunction with "alternative to suspension," "school-based," and "prevention." She searched the following databases: ERIC, Social Sciences Citation Index, Social Work Abstracts, Dissertation Abstracts, PsycINFO, and Web of Science. She also searched the following websites to locate current (no more than 5-years old) scientific reports and best practice guidelines on alternatives to suspension: National Association of Social Workers (www.naswdc.org), School Social Work Association of America (www.sswaa.org), U.S. Department of Education (www.ed.gov), Education Week on the Web (www.edweek.org), and the Office of Juvenile Justice and Delinquency Prevention (www.ojjdp.ncjrs.org).

In conjunction with the more specific terms in the question, this step involves the use of key words such as "research," "study," "effectiveness," "efficacy," "outcome," "evaluation," "model," "intervention," and "prevention" (Cournoyer & Powers, 2002). In this example, a combination of the preceding terms was used in conjunction with the more specific key terms in the question (e.g., "bullying"). We use this combination of terms to search databases. Fortunately, an increasing number of databases are available online and can be accessed from home computers or laptops connected to the Internet. One useful search tip is to use the root word with the wildcard character (*). This step will search all articles that include words such as "researched" or "researching." Another useful search tip is to use "and" between search terms to narrow your search or use "or" between search terms to broaden your search. Important databases for school social workers that can be accessed online include those mentioned in the case example. These databases contain abstracts of refereed journal articles and books. In addition, a number of websites contain scientific reports that focus on current research and best practice guidelines for problems facing school-aged children and youth. These websites include those mentioned in the case example.

Step 4: Critically Analyze the Practice Effectiveness Research Literature in Terms of Validity, Reliability, and Usefulness

The next step involves a critical evaluation of a particular study or a meta-analysis. It involves an analysis of the methodology used in a particular study in relation to internal and external validity, the validity and reliability of the measures used to assess change, and its usefulness in answering the research question posed. Gibbs and Gambrill (1999) developed a very helpful exercise (Exercise 12, pp. 161–170) and Quality of Study Rating Form that can be used to evaluate the quality of a particular study. Summarize what you have learned from your search and critical analysis. What is the evidence that a particular intervention or program is effective for a particular client or client system? Is there a lack of evidence to sufficiently answer your practice question?

| Case | **Case Example Continued** |

Anna critically analyzed each study for validity, reliability, and usefulness by asking the following questions: Does the methodology used in each study control for threats to internal and external validity? And, What measures were used to assess change in each study and are these measures valid and reliable? She also examined each program to ensure that it contained both individual-change strategies that focused on the development of social competence and school-change strategies that aimed at changing the culture of the school. In addition, she focused on only those programs that were designed for middle school youth and consisted of multiple years of intervention (e.g., "booster sessions") using a well-tested, standardized intervention with detailed lesson plans and student materials.

Step 5: Obtain Informed Consent and Apply the Evidenced-Based Intervention

If you have found an empirically supported treatment/intervention for your particular practice question, you will next pursue the mutually agreed upon goals through the implementation of this empirically supported treatment/intervention. An essential aspect of implementation is close attention and monitoring of intervention integrity. It is important that the practitioner seeks the client's informed consent to participate in the specific intervention/treatment. In the case of minor children, the parent or legal guardian must provide this informed consent and the minor child should give his or her assent orally or in writing. This informed consent should include an assessment of the risks and potential benefits of participating in the intervention/treatment.

Case	Case Example Continued

In an effort to reduce the high number of suspensions at a middle school she served, Anna selected one of the interventions she learned about in her literature review. After obtaining permission from the school administrator, Anna obtained informed consent from the parents of students who had high rates of school suspensions. Once consent was obtained, she implemented a state-of-the-art school-based prevention program designed to reduce student suspensions with close attention to intervention integrity (e.g., ensuring that each component of the intervention is carried out as planned).

Step 6: Evaluate the Outcome of the Intervention Against Performance Criteria

This step involves the formulation of goals that are specific and relevant to the client's presenting problem. It is important to measure change in the desired direction by comparing preintervention (or baseline) data with data collected during the intervention phase. For an in-depth discussion of single-system methodology designed for practitioners, see *Evaluating Practice: Guidelines for the Accountable Professional* by Bloom, Fischer, and Orme (1999).

Case	Case Example Continued

Anna assessed the effectiveness of her intervention by comparing the rates of school suspensions after the intervention with rates of suspension before the intervention was implemented. She then reported her findings to her supervisor, and they developed a feasibility plan to expand the implementation of the program.

Step 7: Teach Others to Do Evidenced-Based Practice

Once it has been shown that a particular intervention or program is effective, it is essential that this information be shared with your colleagues at work and at professional conferences. It is also important to advocate for the utilization of these steps with your supervisor and professional colleagues.

There is little evidence to suggest that social workers currently use research findings to support their practice decisions (Cournoyer & Powers, 2002). Most school social work practitioners "are unlikely to have the time, inclination, support, or resources to either read research or integrate it into their day-to-day practice" (Holosko & Leslie, 1998, pp. 436–437, as cited in Cournoyer & Powers, 2002, p. 798). To develop and nurture an evidenced-based professional culture that focuses on the implementation of best practices, it has been suggested that a "research coordinator" or a team of professionals identify and disseminate research-supported best practices to individual practitioners in schools (Cournoyer & Powers, 2002). Moreover, social work educators need to move from "authority-based" teaching to "evidenced-based" teaching (Gambrill,

Case	Case Example Continued

Anna was pleased that the prevention program she implemented was successful and the number of student suspensions in the middle school decreased by 70%. She decided to share information about her results with other school social workers at a state conference in a formal presentation.

1999), and professional social work associations (e.g., School Social Work Association of America) need to develop and disseminate school social work best practice guidelines based on effectiveness research.

CULTURAL DIVERSITY AND BEST PRACTICE

There is a growing mismatch between linguistically, culturally, economically, and racially diverse children entering monolingual, white, Anglo, middle-class schools. Consequently, it is imperative that school social workers become sensitive to cultural differences and learn specific competencies that will increase the likelihood of interacting effectively with diverse children and their families.

Ortiz and Flanagan (2002) state that "cultural competence is not a discreet skill or set of facts [but rather] represents the integration of a wide variety of knowledge bases and specific competencies" (p. 347). For school social workers, cultural competence begins at a personal level. School social workers must appreciate the extent to which one's own culture influences interactions with individuals from a different culture. For example, they might ask the following:

- What are my attitudes about and expectations toward culturally diverse students and their families?
- What are my attitudes toward parents who live in poverty?
- To what extent do my white, middle-class values of individualism, interpersonal competition, punctuality, and materialism impact my practice with culturally diverse students and families who may hold very different values?
- Do I view differences in terms of right versus wrong, good versus bad, rational versus irrational, or do I view them as "differences among people"?

If an individual school social worker does not directly confront these issues in an honest and candid manner, it is easy to see how his or her interactions with culturally diverse students and families will suffer due to conflict, miscommunication, and misunderstanding.

To truly understand student misbehavior from a culturally competent perspective, school social workers must recognize and appreciate the cultural context of the school and the role that the school plays in determining the success of certain groups of students. Since schools teach the deeply held values of the mainstream white middle-class culture and inculcate these deeply held values in each and every student in attendance, students whose cultural background and values "are not consonant with the values taught in school, may respond in ways that run counter to the typical educational expectations" (Ortiz & Flanagan, 2002, p. 344). For many students whose cultural background and values run contrary to the values of the school culture, school can be a hostile environment and their misbehavior may result from a number of cultural collisions. Rather than focusing their efforts on searching for individual pathology, culturally competent school social workers must first examine the extent to which these cultural collisions may help to explain the learning and/or behavioral difficulties of culturally diverse students.

Best practice guidelines for practice with culturally diverse students and families include the following:

• Although members of various cultural groups will most likely share certain tendencies, individuals of the same cultural background will not necessarily behave in the same manner (Ortiz & Flanagan, 2002).

• Social class has a profound impact on essentially every variable that influences an individual's physical and psychological growth and development (Huang & Gibbs, 1992).

• The level of acculturation is an essential aspect of intervention planning. It is essential that the school social worker assess and evaluate acculturation levels carefully prior to engaging in any form of service delivery. For more detailed information on factors and levels of acculturation, see Sattler (1998) and Atkinson, Morten, and Sue (1989).

• Relationships with extended family members are extremely important in African American and Latino families and should be an integral part of the assessment and intervention planning (Ortiz & Flanagan, 2002).

• Becoming proficient in a small number of skills that show deference and respect, such as greeting a person or family in a culturally sensitive manner, can go a long way in building rapport (Ortiz & Flanagan, 2002). For example, getting right to business with a Hispanic family could cause discomfort because it is important within this culture to first spend time in small talk and to allow the conversation to naturally move to the issue of concern (Ortiz & Flanagan, 2002).

• Prolonged eye contact between Latinos is considered disrespectful, including any eye contact between a child and an adult (Ortiz & Flanagan, 2002).

• Rapport can be more easily established with parents who are not fluent in English when they are given the opportunity to express themselves in their native language. This opportunity is afforded to these parents through the services of an interpreter/translator (Helms & Cook, 1999).

• More than anything else that might be said or done, culturally competent practice demands that practitioners genuinely respect the native values, beliefs, and attitudes of other cultures (Ortiz & Flanagan, 2002).

BEST PRACTICES AND SOCIAL WORK VALUES AND ETHICS

An essential component of best practices in school social work is adherence to the values and ethics of the social work profession. The National Association of Social Workers' (NASW) *Code of Ethics* (1999) incorporates several important elements of best practices: (1) the promotion of social justice and social change (Preamble), (2) sensitivity to cultural and ethnic diversity (Preamble), (3) professional competence (sections 1.04, 2.10, 4.01), and (4) evaluation and research (section 5.02). In fact, section 4.01 (b) of the code focuses directly on several essential components of best practices, stating

> social workers should strive to become and remain proficient in professional practice and the performance of professional functions. Social workers should critically examine, and keep current with, emerging knowledge relevant to social work. Social workers should routinely review professional literature and participate in continuing education relevant to social work practice and social work ethics.

Furthermore, section 4.01 (c) states that "social workers should base practice on recognized knowledge, including empirically based knowledge, relevant to social work and social work ethics."

NASW's *Standards for School Social Work Services* (2002) requires school social workers to "remain current by continuously scrutinizing and improving theory, policy, and practice" (Standard 1); "make use of technology systems . . . to demonstrate accountability" (Standard 2); maintain accurate data that are relevant to planning, management, and evaluation of SSW services (Standard 11); "select and apply empirically validated or promising prevention and intervention methods" (Standard 23); "evaluate their practice and disseminate findings" (Standard 24); and remain knowledgeable of best practice models, participate in professional conferences, and contribute to and promote professional publications (Standard 27).

BEST PRACTICES IN PREVENTION APPROACHES

Several decades of prevention research has greatly expanded our knowledge base of "what works" in school-based programs (Sloboda & David, 1997). We are ready to spend $20,000–$30,000 a year on a prison cell but, unfortunately, we do not see the value in addressing problems involving our youth before they get out of control. Rather than waiting for problems to become serious and intervening in largely ineffective ways (i.e., "too little, too late"), best practices demand that we advocate for the development and implementation of evidenced-based prevention programs in schools.

Although there is little schools can do about an at-risk student's family or neighborhood or innate ability, there are many factors within the school environment that can be changed. It is important to conceptualize school-related problems through an "ecological lens." Many student misbehaviors result from a complex interaction of factors rather than isolated acts resulting from personal inadequacies and pathology. Although there is considerable controversy regarding the extent to which schools provoke or ameliorate student aggression and violence (Goldstein, Harootunian, & Conoley, 1994), researchers have uncovered a number of school risk factors that provoke, exacerbate, or maintain disruptive student behavior.

 ## School Risk Factors

- Suspension and corporal punishment (DeRidder, 1990; Hyman, 1990)
- Punitive or inadequate attendance policies (First, Kellog, Almeida, & Gray, 1991)
- Grade retention (Bracey, 1992)
- Negative teacher expectations and attitudes (Gandara, 1989; Pollard, 1989)
- Absence of a stimulating and innovative curriculum (Hahn, 1987; Wehlage & Rutter, 1986)
- Large school size (Bryk & Thum, 1989)

Fortunately, researchers have also uncovered several protective factors that can promote the successful development of at-risk children and buffer against school risk factors that might otherwise compromise development and school success.

 ## School Protective Factors

- Attachment relationships with emotionally significant adults
- Appropriate degree of environmental structure and control
- A developmental approach in curriculum that supports coping and self-esteem

Garbarino, Dubrow, Kostelny, and Pardo (1992)

Based on these findings, school social workers should explore ways of reducing the impact of school risk factors and ways to implement various school protective factors as part of their overall program design. For example, programs that support the establishment of strong relationships between students and adults outside the immediate family, such as relationships with teachers, serve as an important protective factor for students in times of deprivation or stress.

BEST PRACTICE GUIDELINES FOR INTERVENTIONS

Research has yielded several essential components of successful school-based prevention programs. A listing of best practice guidelines that should be followed in developing and implementing student-focused interventions is presented here

(Elliott, 1998; Henggeler, Schoenwald, Borduin, Rowland, & Cunningham, 1998; Kendall, 1993). For more detailed discussions of best practice guidelines, proven and promising programs and interventions, and contact information for a variety of student- and system-focused interventions, see Dupper (2002). The following are best practice guidelines in developing and implementing student-focused interventions in school settings:

• Cognitive–behavioral interventions have been shown to be particularly effective in minimizing behavioral problems in school settings compared to psychotherapy and intensive casework approaches. Cognitive–behavioral interventions consider the influence of significant others in the student's environment on his or her thoughts, feelings, and behaviors.

• Effective cognitive–behavioral strategies include modeling, role-play exercises, behavioral contingencies, self-monitoring and self-instruction, and problem-solving training.

The following are best practice guidelines in developing and implementing school-based prevention programs and school-change programs (Bosworth, 1997; DeJong, 1994; Gottfredson, 1997; Sloboda & David, 1997):

• Successful school-based prevention programs do more than reach the individual child; they seek to change the entire school environment.

• Individual-change strategies attempt to develop social competence by changing students' knowledge, skills, attitudes, beliefs, or behaviors using interactive teaching techniques (e.g., role plays with peers) rather than lectures.

• School-change strategies include programs aimed at changing the culture of the school and clarifying and communicating behavioral norms (e.g., "the use of alcohol and drugs is not the norm for teenagers").

• Prevention programs should focus on youth during the critical middle/junior high years and should consist of multiple years of intervention (e.g., "booster sessions") using a well-tested, standardized intervention with detailed lesson plans and student materials.

• Prevention programs that have been found to be effective are aimed at clarifying and communicating norms about behaviors and include comprehensive instructional programs that focus on social competency skills that are delivered over extended periods of time and continually reinforced in the school environment.

CHALLENGES IMPLEMENTING BEST PRACTICES IN SCHOOLS

The implementation of best practices on both the micro and the macro levels entails fundamental change. Current individualistic approaches must give way to approaches that target both individuals and conditions within the school environment. In answering "who is my client?" school social workers must include students, parents, teachers, administrators, school policies and practices, school board members, neighborhoods, and the larger community. In framing their practice in these broad terms, school social workers must be careful not to underestimate the resistance they will face. They must be aware that "man's desire to change is more than matched by his ingenuity in avoiding change, even when the desire to change is powered by strong pain, anxiety, and grief" (Sarason, 1971, p. 121).

One of the major barriers to change is the search for individual pathology that "dominates eligibility evaluations and confers an overall, often implicit, obsession with deficits that deflects attention away from effective treatment" (Reschly & Ysseldyke, 2002, p. 7). Despite the fact that evidenced-based interventions take into account the influence of significant others in students' environments, there is strong resistance by most adults in schools to examine the ways in which their attitudes and behaviors may be contributing to student problems in schools, much less change their behaviors. This adult resistance serves to perpetuate the preoccupation with individual pathology in students in seeking to address learning and behavioral problems. It is difficult work for school social workers to change these entrenched adult attitudes but a move toward best practices demands that this occur.

SUMMARY

The challenge of working in a host setting in which education is valued, rather than social work, cannot be overemphasized. School social workers must be able to "join" the school so that they can be effective and, simultaneously, maintain their unique professional identity as social workers. This is difficult work since there is a tremendous "pull of the system" to "fit in" and to not "rock the boat." Sometimes, this "pull" can be very subtle. To implement best practices, school social workers must learn how to challenge the status quo and facilitate systemic change on behalf of vulnerable groups of students without becoming marginalized.

School Social Work Companion Website

Please be sure to check out our companion website at www.thomsonedu .com/social_work/bye, where you will find relevant materials for each chapter, including flashcards, online practice quizzes, and PowerPoint slides.

References

Atkinson, D. R., Morten, G., & Sue, D. W. (Eds.). (1989). *Counseling American minorities*. Dubuque, IA: Brown.

Bloom, M., Fisher, J., & Orme, J. (1999). *Evaluating practice: Guidelines for the accountable professional* (2nd ed.). Boston: Allyn & Bacon.

Bosworth, K. (1997). *Drug abuse prevention: School-based strategies that work*. Washington, DC: ERIC Clearinghouse on Teaching and Teacher Education.

Bracey, G. W. (1992). Technology, falling SAT scores, and the transformation of consciousness. *Technos, 1*, 8–11.

Bryk, A. S., & Thum, Y. M. (1989). The effects of high school organization on dropping out: An exploratory investigation. *American Educational Research Journal, 26*, 353–383.

Cournoyer, B. R., & Powers, G. T. (2002). Evidenced-based social work. In A. R. Roberts & G. J. Greene (Eds.), *Social workers' desk reference* (pp. 798–807). New York: Oxford University Press.

DeJong, W. (1994, Spring). School-based violence prevention: From the peaceable school to the peaceable neighborhood. *Forum, 25.*

DeRidder, L. M. (1990). How suspension and expulsion contribute to dropping out. *Education Digest, 56,* 44–47.

Dupper, D. R. (2002). *School social work: Skills and interventions for effective practice.* Hoboken, NJ: John Wiley.

Elliott, D. S. (1998). *Prevention programs that work for youth.* Boulder: University of Colorado, Center for the Study and Prevention of Violence.

First, J. M., Kellog, J. B., Almeida, C. A., & Gray, R. (1991). *The good common school: Making the vision work for all children.* Boston: National Coalition of Advocates for Students.

Gambrill, E. (1999). Evidenced-based practice: An alternative to authority-based practice. *Families in Society, 80,* 341–350.

Gandara, P. (1989). Those children are ours: Moving toward community. *Equity and Choice, 5,* 5–12.

Garbarino, J., Dubrow, N., Kostelny, K., & Pardo, C. (1992). *Children in danger: Coping with the consequences of community violence.* San Francisco: Jossey-Bass.

Gibbs, L., & Gambrill, E. (1999). *Critical thinking for social workers: Exercises for the helping profession* (Rev. ed.). Thousand Oaks, CA: Pine Forge Press.

Goldstein, A. P., Harootunian, B., & Conoley, J. C. (1994). *Student aggression: Prevention, management, and replacement training.* New York: Guilford.

Gottfredson, D. C. (1997). School-based crime prevention. In L. W. Sherman, D. Gottfredson, D. MacKenzie, J. Ech, P. Reuter, & S. Bushway (Eds.), *Preventing crime: What works, what doesn't, what's promising* (pp. 125–182). A report to the U.S. Congress prepared for the National Institute of Justice by the Department of Criminology and Criminal Justice, University of Maryland.

Hahn, A. (1987). Reaching out to America's dropouts: What to do? *Phi Delta Kappan, 69,* 256–263.

Helms, J. E., & Cook, D. A. (1999). *Using race and culture in counseling and psychotherapy.* Boston: Allyn & Bacon.

Henggeler, S. W., Schoenwald, S. K., Borduin, C. M., Rowland, M. D., & Cunningham, P. B. (1998). *Multisystemic treatment of antisocial behavior in children and adolescents.* New York: Guilford.

Holosko, M., & Leslie, D. (1998). Obstacles to conducting empirically based practice. In J. S. Wodarski & B. A. Thyer (Eds.), *Handbook of empirical social work* (vol. 2., pp. 433–451). Thousand Oaks, CA: Sage.

Huang, L. N., & Gibbs, J. T. (1992). Partners or adversaries: Home-school collaboration across culture, race, and ethnicity. In S. L. Christenson & J. C. Connoley (Eds.), *Home-school collaboration: Enhancing children's academic and social competance* (pp. 81–110). Silver Spring, MD: National Association of School Psychologists.

Hyman, I. A. (1990). *Reading, writing, and the hickory stick: The appalling story of physical and psychological abuse in America's schools.* Lexington, MA: Lexington Books.

Kendall, P. C. (1993). Cognitive–behavioral therapies with youth: Guiding theory, current status, and emerging developments. *Journal of Consulting and Clinical Psychology, 61,* 235–247.

National Association of Social Workers. (1999). *Code of ethics*. Washington, DC: Author.

National Association of Social Workers. (2002). *Standards for school social work services*. Washington, DC: Author.

Ortiz, S. O., & Flanagan, D. P. (2002). Best practices in working with culturally diverse children and families. In A. Thomas & J. Grimes (Eds.), *Best practices in school psychology IV* (Vol. 1, pp. 337–351). Bethesda, MD: National Association of School Psychologists.

Pollard, D. S. (1989). Reducing the impact of racism on students. *Educational Leadership, 47*, 73–75.

Reschly, D. J., & Ysseldyke, J. E. (2002). Paradigm shift: The past is not the future. In A. Thomas & J. Grimes (Eds.), *Best practices in school psychology IV* (Vol. 1, pp. 3–20). Bethesda, MD: National Association of School Psychologists.

Sarason, S. B. (1971). *The culture of the school and the problem of change*. Boston: Allyn & Bacon.

Sattler, J. (1998). Clinical and forensic interviewing of children and families. In *Guidelines for the mental health, education, pediatric, and child maltreatment fields* (pp. 264–265). San Diego: Author.

Sloboda, Z., & David, S. L. (1997). *Preventing drug use among children and adolescents: A research-based guide*. Washington, DC: National Institutes of Health, National Institute on Drug Abuse.

Thyer, B. A. (2002). Principles of evidence-based practice and treatment development. In A. R. Roberts & G. J. Greene (Eds.), *Social workers' DESK reference* (pp. 739–742). New York: Oxford University Press.

Wehlage, G. G., & Rutter, R. A. (1986). Dropping out: How much do schools contribute to the problem? *Teachers College Record, 87*, 374–392.

Research and Evaluation of School Social Work Practice

CHAPTER 14

MELISSA JONSON-REID, M.S.W., Ph.D.
GWB School of Social Work, Washington University, St. Louis, Missouri

CHAPTER OUTLINE

CHAPTER OVERVIEW

Although most practitioners will not become academic researchers, there are many reasons why they need to be good consumers of existing research and users of basic research skills. This chapter takes a practical, down-to-earth approach to introducing major research methods and resources for use by the school social work practitioner. Readers will gain an understanding of (1) the importance of research to best practice, (2) the application of research, (3) common approaches to research in the field, and (4) special issues that impact the use of research.

INTRODUCTION: WHY IS RESEARCH PART OF BEST PRACTICE?

As David Dupper stated in Chapter 13, you must become motivated to apply an evidence-based "best practice" perspective. This means you must both stay informed about research and apply research principles to evaluation of your own practice. Why? Research is fundamentally linked to best practice issues such as ethics, accountability, visibility, and expanding services.

Ethics   Being aware of what the research offers about the best practices for various issues is a critical part of ethical social work practice (National Association of Social Workers [NASW], 1999, sections 4.01, 5.01–5.02; 2002). It is our responsibility to the students, families, and educational staff we serve to use the most effective and efficient means of helping students overcome academic and socioemotional barriers to participation in school. This means keeping current on existing research and evaluating our own practice.

Accountability   Research is also mandated by many educational funding sources. The No Child Left Behind Act made clear that schools are expected to demonstrate achievement of objective criteria or risk loss of federal funds and other sanctions (U.S. Department of Education, 2003). In difficult fiscal times, the emphasis on accountability tends to increase as policymakers and program managers seek areas to cut back (Jayaratne, 2004). Because school social workers are not mandated members of the public school staff like teachers, we must be aware of our extra burden to demonstrate how we contribute to the lives of students and to the broader goals of the educational institution (Dibble, 1998). Furthermore, most grants require data to demonstrate the need for programs and a complete evaluation of the results.

Visibility   School social workers must be "visible" (Goren, 2002). One form of visibility is literally finding ways to increase face-to-face contact with colleagues (being present at special events, eating in the teachers' lounge, participating in meetings, etc.). Another form of visibility is letting people know what you are accomplishing. Making a call to a teacher for an update on a student's behavior after you have been working with him or her not only helps you evaluate the efficacy of your intervention but also reminds the teacher of your efforts. Presenting data to the school board on improvements in attendance of students you served shows them you are helping improve the district's performance and are a valuable member of the educational team.

Expand Services   A good reason to engage in research is to provide information that supports expanded services (Sohng & Weatherley, 2002). It is easier to advocate for additional social work staff or to write a grant to provide funds for new programs if you can offer objective data to demonstrate needs and potential gains. Although anecdotes and case examples put a human face on pleas for expansion of services, they are not sufficient in today's fiscal environment.

THE ECOLOGICAL PERSPECTIVE AND SCHOOL SOCIAL WORK RESEARCH

As Kendra Garrett presented in Chapter 3, the ecological perspective is a key aspect of school social work practice; it is also important to research conducted in the school setting. Multilevel factors (also known as **confounding factors**) can influence the results as well as the implementation of an intervention. For example, in the mental health field there is increasing recognition that confounding factors such as organizational structure and policy influence the implementation and success of interventions, even when they have been shown to be effective in other settings (Burns, 2002). This means that (1) you must consider the multilevel factors that are present in your practice setting and how they impact the intervention, and (2) you must keep data on these factors to try to tease out what role they played after you measure your outcome.

For example, school bullying is a major concern in the United States as well as in many other countries (Nansel et al., 2001; Wei, 2004). A variety of programs with at least some research exist (Northwest Regional Educational Laboratory, 2001; Samples & Aber, 1998). Imagine you identify the Olweus Bully/Victim program (Samples & Aber, 1998) as an evidence-based practice that you hope to use. What factors might impact your ability to apply this intervention? At the school system level, the school budget may influence your ability to deliver the intervention as suggested. Student cultural groups at your school may differ from those where the program was implemented previously. This can result in a mismatch between the program design and the target population (see Chapter 13). At the teacher level, the number of years in the classroom may impact the way in which the material is delivered. At the individual student level, a child's family functioning may impact the ability to benefit from the program. In this example, you would need to assess whether there were sufficient funds to deliver the entire program, how students at your school might differ from those in prior studies, the average number of years in the classroom for teachers at your school, and a measure of the participating children's family functioning.

CULTURALLY COMPETENT ASSESSMENT AND RESEARCH

Cultural competence is also key to research in school social work practice. **Culture** (i.e., language, religion, social norms, socioeconomic status, and other factors related to group membership) influences the application as well as the process of research (Boynton, Wood, & Greenhalgh, 2004; Rubin & Babbie, 2005).

Conducting culturally competent research means that you consider these influences at all phases in the research process. Some general points are illustrated here to encourage the reader to think critically in this area.

Many intervention studies have been limited to white, English-speaking participants (Royse, Thyer, Padgett, & Logan, 2001). As a consumer of research, it will be up to you to consider whether or not existing knowledge can be directly applied to your situation given what you know about the student or student group. How do you assess this?

- Ask a leader from the community of interest to help you understand how this particular group may view a problem or form of intervention (Boynton et al., 2004).
- Contact the author(s) of the study or program and ask if he or she has done work with your population that is not yet published.
- Do your own needs assessment survey of students from this group and compare the results with what is offered in the program.

Another key aspect of culturally competent research is related to data collection. Many tests have not been normed across cultural groups (Malgady, 1996). Perhaps you intend to use a scale to collect information or are using data already collected by the school, such as an IQ test. You will want to ask yourself the following questions about the instrument:

- Has it been used with your population before (Malgady, 1996)?
- Was it or can it be effectively translated into the person's native language (Pan, 2003)?
- Does your population of interest use the same words to describe the issue measured by the scale (Ortega & Richey, 1998; Pan, 2003)?

If you answer "no" to one of these questions, changes will have to be made if you want the data collected to be useful. For instance, you may need to have someone translate the instrument into a different language. If so, you must also ask a different person to back-translate (i.e., retranslate it back into English) the scale to make sure that the translation of ideas stayed true to the original intent (Morales, 2001).

Finally, interactions with people while conducting research are best approached with the same considerations as interactions in a practice context (Rubin & Babbie, 2005). A school social worker should apply the same principles learned for culturally competent direct practice (see book Introduction) whenever contact is made with individuals for the purpose of research.

CONSUMING RESEARCH

We have discussed the importance of research to school social work and how concepts from social work practice, such as the ecological perspective and cultural competence, are key to the research process. Now, we begin to explore specific topics related to how we use research.

As Dupper noted in Chapter 13, the particular program or treatment to be used with a client or client system should be based on scientific evidence that it works. This is one way in which you are a consumer of research. The book titled *Evaluating Research Articles* by Girden (1996) may be helpful. Consuming research is also a critical part of evaluating your own practice. Reading articles about similar programs can provide ideas or a template for how to evaluate your program (Jayaratne, 2004). Furthermore, in order to build knowledge and help other practitioners take advantage of what you learned, you need to be able to understand how your results fit with or differ from existing knowledge. This is important when you communicate your results to others. Consuming research means finding applicable and reputable sources of information.

Researching Need and Data

Prior to developing your program, you will identify and assess the extent of the need for the program. This is discussed in greater detail later.

- There are national education data from sources such as *Indicators of School Crime and Safety* (National Center for Education Statistics, 2002) or the Department of Education (www.ed.gov).
- State-by-state trends can be found in reports by the Children's Defense Fund (www.childrendefense.org) or Kids Count (www.aecf.org). Most state departments of education have websites that provide district- and sometimes school-level data for test scores, attendance, graduation, and other student characteristics.
- You may use existing data kept by the school, such as disciplinary reports or grades.

Building on Similar Evaluation Methods

Although your program or approach might be "new," it is likely that others have either conducted similar programs or at least attempted to address similar problems (Jayaratne, 2004). To compare your intervention to other approaches, it would be best if you measured the outcomes the same way other studies do. These studies can be found in journals such as *Children & Schools, School Social Work Journal, Research on Social Work Practice, Social Work, Journal of School Health, Journal of Emotional and Behavioral Disorders,* and *Evaluation and Program Planning.*

You can locate journals electronically by using key words such as "bullying and intervention" to search for articles. There are many databases to search, but the most useful are PsychINFO, ERIC, and Social Work Abstracts. You can also find explanations of methods in grant reports or program reports online at sites such as www.ed.gov (education programming), www.acf.hhs.gov (child welfare, Head Start, and others), and www.cdc.gov (violence prevention and intervention).

Placing Your Results in Context   Prior research can help place your findings in context when you disseminate the information. If this was a new approach, how do your results compare to the outcomes of other types of approaches? If this was the first time an intervention with prior research was tried with a new population, were the outcomes the same? If not, your evaluation may help others understand that this program has limitations with certain populations.

CONDUCTING RESEARCH

Defining Real-World, Measurable Outcomes

Any service provided to a student or student group should be done with a set goal (or outcome) in mind. In order to communicate whether or not that goal was reached, you need a measurable outcome. This should be specific and relevant to the client's presenting problem. Ideally, the measured outcome will also be of interest to other stakeholders in the school setting (Dibble, 1998). As Goren (2002) noted, school social workers must be seen as having "value" and this is largely demonstrated by communicating the outcomes achieved. The last thing you want to hear at the end of your project when you proudly report your findings is "So what?"

Real-world practice is also messy. This is one reason why it is sometimes difficult to translate findings from highly controlled studies of interventions to the field (Burns, 2002). For example, we may want to provide services for six months but only have the funds for three months. Our outcomes must be of import but they must also be realistic given the population, issue, resources, and setting (Rossi, Freeman, & Lipsey, 1999). Before you think about how to deal with data, you want to answer the "who," "what," "how," and "where" of your situation so that the measured outcomes make sense.

Who?   Of course, you know who needs your services, right? We do not, however, always take the time to critically assess who is getting our services and how that might impact outcomes. For example, let's say you wish to run a social skills group for shy students. Students who are very shy and isolated will probably make greater gains. Why? Well, there is something researchers call **regression to the mean**. This means that if someone is on the extreme end of shyness before the intervention, his or her next measure will tend to be less extreme (Posavac & Carey, 1997). If all your group members are extremely shy, then it may be more difficult to determine if your program worked or if they would have improved that much anyway. This is one example of why evaluation texts advise you to have a control or comparison group. It is also one reason we need to measure these initial characteristics (also known as baseline) of the target clients.

If you plan to do a research study and you want to be able to say that this program "works for all fifth graders," you have to have a representative sample of all fifth graders. This means that the students in the study must be "typical" of fifth graders throughout the country. If you take a random sample by putting all fifth-grade students in a hat and then selecting 100 of them without looking, this group should be representative. Researchers then say their results are generalizable to the full target population. As a practitioner, however, it is often not possible to randomly select whom you will serve. It is therefore very important that you clearly describe your sample so that when you present your results later, others can assess how similar or different their students are compared to yours. This description should, at a minimum, include demographic characteristics (age, gender, race, etc.) and baseline measures.

What? You must be clear about what issue you are addressing (Jayaratne, 2004). Researchers like to call this **operationalizing**, but this simply means that the outcome is so clear that it can be accurately measured. Terms such as "improving adjustment" are vague. What kind of adjustment? Adjustment to what? Decreasing student absences by 25%, on the other hand, is clear and measurable. What if it is clear but you cannot measure it? For example, you could implement a dropout prevention program that ends in the sophomore year before you can measure graduation. Then you need to think about what can be measured, such as credits completed or intentions to graduate (Davis, Johnson, Miller-Cribbs, & Saunders, 2002), that is most clearly associated with staying in school. As stated previously, this "what" should also be realistic given the limitations of the program and the target population.

How? Will you provide individual, small group, or schoolwide services? Are you delivering all the services or are there other staff involved? You should record all the elements and the process of intervention carefully, as if you were writing down a recipe for cookies for someone who wants them to turn out just like yours. This is also called a "process evaluation" or "monitoring evaluation" or part of assessing "treatment fidelity" (Jayaratne, 2004; Posavac & Carey, 1997; Rossi et al., 1999). Sometimes, the "how" requires alteration to "what" you choose as your outcome measure. Why? Well, let's say a program manual states that the outcomes are based on an 8-week program delivered 3 hours a week. You can run the program for 8 weeks, but you only have one hour per week. It is reasonable to anticipate that the student improvements may be smaller than reported in studies of the full program.

You must also consider the "how" of the evaluation. The ideal standard for measuring an intervention is to randomly assign who gets treatment and then compare the treated client(s) to the untreated clients. This is called a **"true experimental design"** (Rubin & Babbie, 2005). This is difficult to accomplish in the real world. It may be possible, however, to have a comparison student (for one-on-one services) or students (programs and groups). These students do not get the intervention but they are not randomly assigned (Rubin & Babbie, 2005). A comparison group might be composed of similar students who attend a different school and are not participating in the program or perhaps from a waiting list. It is important to consider this before you implement the intervention so you can think about ways to construct a comparison group.

Where? You are charged with creating a program to reduce disruptive classroom behaviors. You do a thorough job of reviewing research on evidence-based methods. You discover an approach verified in an experimental design study that was done in a carefully controlled environment. You sigh . . . your quest for the perfect solution has ended, right? Well, maybe, but your school setting is not a controlled environment. What works outstandingly well in a laboratory-like setting may not always generalize to the field (Burns, 2002). You need to critically assess differences between the setting where you work and the setting described in the research. The closer your situation is to the situation described in the study, the more optimistic you can be about its use at your school.

Objectives   Often, your goal may be complex or long term. For example, if a child has a serious behavior problem, it is not realistic to expect that the issue will be resolved immediately. You must therefore include **objectives,** or intermediary steps, that can be used as benchmarks to determine if the service appears to be having the desired effect (Jonson-Reid, 2000). Measuring interim objectives will allow you to make course corrections during services if needed. The measurement of intermediary steps will also help you to describe your work should a program get "cut" midstream or a student move prior to the conclusion of services. These objectives should be logically related to both the service and the later outcome.

A chart such as the following can help you organize your thoughts:

Prior research	Who am I serving?	What is my target issue or goal?	How is the intervention delivered?	Where is the service being delivered?	List of objectives
What has been done already? Can I use the same approach?	Demographic characteristics and baseline assessment: How similar or different is my client system compared to the prior work?	What exactly do I reasonably expect to impact?	What is the duration and content of the intervention? Is this similar or different to prior research on this intervention?	What aspects of the school environment are relevant to the program?	What can I measure that will help me understand if I impacted my target issue?

Who Is the Audience for My Research?

There is one more consideration prior to specifying the method for collecting data to evaluate your work. Although we do research on practice for the benefit of the students, families, and educational systems, the audience for the final results can influence what one measures or at least how findings are presented (Hendricks, 1994; Patton, 1997). Ideally, you want the information to get used, so you should tailor how you report your findings to the desired audience. As Hendricks stated, "what good is speaking truth to power if no one is listening?"

The research audience may be you, the referring party, program funders, school or district administration, or even other practitioners and academia.

- *Yourself.* Sometimes you are just gathering information to improve your own practice. Clearly, you will want to know if your students' problems are improving, but you will also want to gather enough information so that you can identify necessary course corrections. You will not worry, however, about constructing a final report for presentation.
- *Referring party.* Sometimes school social work is so busy that it is easy to forget the need to give feedback to the referring party. This need not be a breach of confidentiality. The communication may be limited to the fact that you are providing services and asking about changes in behavior relative to the reason the student was referred to you. Such feedback may be as informal as a conversation or as formal as a letter.
- *Grant funders.* If your audience is a grant funder, you may already have a format for designing the evaluation and reporting the results. Always refer back to the funding application and follow evaluation guidelines provided. Why? You are likely to want money from this funder again. So, you will want to make sure that you are including the components the funder expects to see. This allows the funder to assess whether or not you are a good investment in the future.
- *Educators/organization.* It is critical to show how your services tie into goals that are meaningful not only for the individual student but also for the school. For example, attendance is tied to educational funding. If you are doing something that is likely to improve your clients' attendance, then this is a great outcome to measure. Reports of results for your school are more likely to be acknowledged if you can make them brief and, when possible, include graphs to emphasize your point.
- *Other practitioners and academics.* Practitioners and academics need to stay informed. Do not overlook opportunities such as conferences and journals to disseminate your results. If you intend to do this, you will need to be more concerned with rigor and statistical findings than you might if you were just communicating information within your school. It need not, however, be a complicated or perfect study.

The Data   Now you have your background information, your outcomes, and an understanding of your audience. You will next select a method for measuring your results. Part of this process is to select the data source. Jayaratne (2004) divides data types into hard data (objective reports), standardized tests, observations, rating scales, questionnaires, simulations, graphics, interviews, and self-reports. A full discussion of this issue is beyond the scope of this chapter, but several good research methods texts exist that provide detailed explanations of the pros and cons and steps involved in various approaches to collecting data.

Overview of Advantages and Disadvantages of Data Types   Primary data collection means that you get information from subjects rather than use archival records or other preexisting data. Discussions of the advantages and disadvantages of different data sources can be found in most research texts (Rossi et al., 1999; Royse et al., 2001; Rubin & Babbie, 2005).

- Previously constructed scales or surveys decrease your prep time and may have good research behind them to indicate how they are best used. Of course, there may also be a fee for acquiring them.
- Surveys (in person or by mail or phone) may be used to examine changes (see Miller, 1994, for a guide to survey use). Generally, in-person surveys (done at school) will provide you with a better return rate than will surveys sent home. A very low return rate will cast doubts on whether or not your intervention worked. For example, if your results are positive but only 30% of the students responded, how do you know if the students for whom it did not work were part of the 70% who did not respond?
- Interviews can be used but they are more time-consuming/expensive and can be more intimidating for the person being interviewed (Rubin & Babbie, 2005).
- Focus groups can also be used, but these are best thought of as providing information about general impressions of the intervention, the meaning of various concepts, and suggestions for change. Focus groups should not be used as a way of measuring individual gains (see Dean, 1994, on using focus groups).
- You might collect data on subjects based on someone else's observations. For example, a simple checklist could be developed to ask a referring party to rate improvement on a scale from "none" to "total." This is less invasive than collecting data from subjects, but you need confidence in the observer's accuracy.
- You might also use secondary data, either archival records from computer systems or preexisting information such as census data. Such data sources are noninvasive for the subject and are often less expensive and labor-intensive than primary data collection methods. Of course, you must rely on the accuracy of how data were entered and cannot usually customize the questions asked.

CONFIDENTIALITY AND HUMAN SUBJECTS

School social workers are often intervening with sensitive issues, and confidentiality is complicated in a school setting (see Chapter 12). Although it is natural to have concerns about maintaining confidentiality when keeping records, without keeping records we cannot evaluate what we do and be sure we are providing best practice. Therefore, spend some time identifying a process and location for the safekeeping of records. Passwords can be used to protect computer files, locks can be used on file cabinets, etc. If possible, avoid carrying around information or reusing the same computer disk at different sites. Such practices increase the likelihood that data will get lost and that there will be an accidental breach in confidentiality. If you must transport information from location to location, try to replace names and identifying information with a case number.

Also, have a list of case numbers that is linked to the identifying information in a locked location at your main office.

Whenever you do research, you must follow the proper procedures regarding the treatment of human subjects, including "informed consent" (Posavac & Carey, 1997).

- You fully explain the intervention as well as data kept on the intervention and any limits to confidentiality with clients (and, in the case of minors, their parents).
- Subjects must know that they can freely withdraw without penalty and great care should be taken that the intervention will pose no risk to the client system (another good reason to use research to find best practices).
- They need to know if the information will be collected anonymously (cannot be linked to subjects) or will be kept confidential (only you will be able to link information to individuals).

Related to this is the need to make sure you are clear with referring parties about the type of feedback you will be able to provide regarding progress.

CONDUCTING AN EVALUATION

Now that we have reviewed some general concepts, we are ready to discuss some of the primary forms of research you might conduct. The better your method, the more confidence you can have in your results. Your method or approach to collecting and analyzing data is known as your **research design**. This includes how you get your sample, how you monitor the service, how you measure the outcome(s), and how you analyze the outcome. A brief section on how to approach statistics is offered to help provide guidance in this area, but a full discussion is beyond the scope of this chapter. The following discussion focuses on issues associated with **quantitative data** collection (i.e., things you can count) rather than **qualitative data** collection (i.e., data interpreted for meaning). This is both a function of the limits of a single chapter and because in most instances school social workers are seeking empirical data to select and/or justify services.

What Is a Needs Assessment?

A critical part of best practice is to understand the nature of the problem and what assets and barriers exist so that you can appropriately target your services; this is a **needs assessment**. As Rossi and colleagues (1999) explain, you need to understand the "size, distribution, and density of the problem" (p. 126). This should be an ongoing process. For example, maybe next year a new population of refugees will resettle in your district's attendance area. You need to know what the needs of this new population are, how big the needs are, and how many schools it will impact.

You need to identify the problem(s) and how big the problem is currently (**prevalence**) and whether or not the rate of new cases is increasing or decreasing during a given time period (**incidence**). This helps you gauge whether or not the service needs are likely to remain the same, increase, or decline. Bleyer and Joiner (2002) suggest using a table in which you list the various kinds of information you want, prioritize the importance of that information, and identify sources.

Stakeholders   It is important to involve a variety of stakeholders in the assessment process (Bleyer & Joiner, 2002). Parents and guardians play a critical role in supporting school success and your interventions (Epstein, 2001). Asking them what needs they perceive provides another perspective and involves them as team members with you focused on the success of their children. Depending on the resources available to you, you might send home a yearly survey to all parents or distribute it at a parent organization meeting, or you might ask teachers if you can randomly pick a sample of parent/teacher conferences and survey those parents.

Educators, staff, and administrators must also stay in the loop. By regularly tracking what they view as major issues and thinking about how your services help meet those needs, you will increase the likelihood that they will work with you to support the needs of at-risk students. This can be done formally through surveys in educators' boxes or at staff/faculty meetings or informally in the teacher's lounge, in regular meetings with the principal, or even in hallway discussions. Do not overlook staff in this process. Your best sources of information may be the receptionist, who sees the children and families each morning as they arrive; the bus driver, who sees them as they leave; or the custodian, who knows the children who "hang around" after school.

Finally, there are community members and other agencies that you interact with and rely on to promote events or provide services outside the school setting. An ongoing process of assessing needs from their perspective builds these partnerships and increases communication about how to improve, expand, or provide new services. You might use phone calls, a survey, or even e-mail to stay in touch.

Organizational Needs   In addition to examining the needs of individual students, families, educators, and other stakeholders, it is also important to examine the organization (school or district) as a unit. It is important to recognize what formal processes must be used in order to effect change in your particular setting (Pawlak & Cousins, 2002). It is also important to identify organizational issues that can impact the success of your services. Researchers often talk about this as an organization's culture or climate.

School culture, or the norms and expectations held by the various stakeholders (Dupper, 2003), can heavily influence both how students are treated and how easy it may be to introduce changes (Pawlak & Cousins, 2002). For example, in recent years many schools have adopted a "zero tolerance" policy that in some cases dramatically altered how disciplinary infractions were handled (The Civil Rights Project, 2000). Such norms may be the target of change or at least must be clearly understood by the social worker in order to advocate for the programs and services children need. **School climate** is the feeling students, educators, and staff have about the school (Dupper, 2003). Different aspects of school climate, such as low teacher morale, might impact the energy they are able to give to working with you to help a student. Measuring organizational culture and climate related to social service intervention is a relatively new area, but Glisson and colleagues have developed and are validating scales in this area (see Glisson & Hemmelgarn, 1998). There are also several measures available to assess various aspects of the culture and climate in the school environment (Baraily & Huber, 2002).

The case example below details how Jane, a school social worker, approaches her needs assessment.

Translating Needs to Services   After you identify the needs of the population you serve and assess the various factors that influence those needs, you must connect the needs to the appropriate intervention. You return to existing research, texts, and other resources to identify the best individual, group, or programmatic approaches to addressing this need. You consider the "who," "what," "how," and "where" and real-world outcomes mentioned previously. It is also important to report your findings to the stakeholders and obtain their ideas for program needs.

How Do I Assess Individual and Group Treatment Outcomes?

If your approach includes individual or small group treatment, it is likely that you will be using a single-subject research design. Perhaps the most common form of **single-subject research** involves collecting baseline information (e.g., the status

---

Case	Case Example

Jane is concerned about substance abuse at her high school because she has recently had several students referred to her for this reason. She needs to know how prevalent this problem is. Thus, she needs to collect data. Jane first turns to the research and finds national yearly surveys of substance abuse among youth (Johnston, O'Malley, & Bachman, 2003). She decides to use a survey with very similar questions so that her school can gather the information for internal use and compare its situation to that of other schools. She presents her plan to gain administrative approval. She will construct her survey drawing on the national survey and perhaps add a few questions of her own to capture specific aspects of the local school. She will carefully consider what specific substances the school wants information about and whether or not the school will ask separate questions about "one time," "recent," or "regular" use. She will consider the cultural and linguistic composition of the students. After the necessary modifications and translation, she will then pilot test the survey with a few students to check for understanding of the questions. Although she is planning to conduct an anonymous survey (no names), she will likely need parent consent. She will need teacher buy-in to help deliver the surveys in the most appropriate class. Then, she will have to tabulate the results and report to the stakeholders. Obviously, Jane will need to build in plenty of time to take on this effort, and the school will need to invest some resources in the production and copying of the survey.

of the problem before intervention), measuring progress throughout the intervention, and then measuring the outcome sometime after the intervention has ended—also known as an **A-B-A design** (Dupper, 2003; Rubin & Babbie, 1997). The amount of change in the baseline (the first A stage) tells you whether or not the intervention had an immediate effect (the B stage) and whether or not that effect lasted (the second A stage). This latter stage is also known as examining maintenance of effect. Ideally, the measure of the goal will improve significantly over the initial baseline measure. Such significance can be measured by score changes in behavioral scales for individuals or even in reported observations from the referring party. For example, a student is referred for withdrawn behavior that registers in the clinically significant range on the Child Behavior Checklist (time A1). After intervention, the score is reduced below the significant range (time B). The actual change may be difficult to assess with statistics for a single child, but the fact that the condition was clinically significant before intervention and is no longer in the clinically significant range after the intervention is very important. If the student's behavior either continues to improve or remains at the new level (time A2), then you can say that you have maintenance of effect or longer term success.

Measures of Baseline Problems   Whether you are assessing an individual client or a group, the first step is determining the best means of measuring the initial problem and later change. Standardized measures or scales that have good empirical support are the preferable means of assessing externalizing (e.g., aggression and delinquency) and internalizing (e.g., depression and withdrawal) behaviors. These types of measures are well documented and help you compare your results with those of other studies. You can locate good measurement instruments in a variety of ways:

- An abbreviated list of measures can be found in Dupper (2003), although it omits the Child Behavior Checklist, which is a commonly used tool in schools (Achenbach, 2000).
- Compendiums exist such as *Conducting School-Based Assessments of Child and Adolescent Behavior* (Shapiro & Kratochwill, 2000).
- Scales for specific issues can also be found online through organizations such as the Centers for Disease Control and Prevention (Dahlberg, Toal, & Behrens, 1998) or university projects (Baraily & Huber, 2002).

Of course, it is important to approach measurement selection from a culturally competent viewpoint to assess whether or not it will be of use with your students. To obtain copies of these scales, you can contact your local university, or a reputable psychologist in the area who does testing work, or perhaps your own district special education department can assist you with commonly used assessment instruments. You can also contact the publisher of the scale and order copies.

Other measures you can use in assessment include archived information such as school attendance or disciplinary records and nonstandardized teacher observations. Your own classroom observations, in which you record the frequency, duration, and severity of specific behaviors, can also be used.

Group Designs   Group designs also require baseline measures. Due to space constraints, all the variations of group designs are not reviewed here. These can be found in any research text or a summary can be found in Jayaratne (2004). Most important, if possible, have a control or comparison group rather than just measure the outcomes of the client system. Why? People are complex and live in complex environments, so it can be difficult to tease out program or treatment effects from other possible causes. For example, let's say you implement a bullying prevention program at an elementary school, but at the same time a community-wide violence prevention campaign is in full force. If bullying at your school declines, how will you know if it was due to your program or the community information? Comparing the results of the intervention group to those of another group (or school or individual) that does not get the intervention helps you answer this question.

Experimental Designs   If you can randomly assign students who need a service to either getting a service (treatment) or not (control), then you can control for the other factors (called confounding factors) that might be influencing the outcome. Random assignment to intervention is different than the random selection discussed previously. Random selection of students from a school allows you to generalize back to the school population. Random assignment of some of these students to treatment and some of them to either "regular services" or a wait list helps you control for confounding factors.

Quasi-experimental Designs   It may be impossible or unethical to randomly select children to participate in an intervention. We can, however, have a comparison group that is not exposed to the intervention but was not randomly assigned. The comparison group should be as similar as possible (e.g., gender, race, age, culture, socioeconomic status, and developmental capacity) to the group receiving services and cannot receive the service during the same period of time (Rubin & Babbie, 2005). A comparison group is not as strong a design as a randomly assigned control group (there may still be unmeasured factors that are influencing your results), but it is a stronger design than just following the intervention group alone.

How Do I Evaluate Programs or Services?

School social workers may develop and implement large-scale service approaches such as conflict resolution programs or schoolwide reform efforts (Dupper, 2003). On the other hand, social workers in schools may focus on case management and crisis intervention with large numbers of students rather than providing individual or group counseling or programs (Jonson-Reid, Kontak, Citerman, Essma, & Fezzi, 2004). Furthermore, services may be implemented at a single school or provided at multiple schools.

Some of the approaches to evaluation are similar to those discussed previously for single-system design or group design. You still want a baseline measure of the problem(s). You also want a clear description of the "who," "what," "how," and "where." You may even have a control group or comparison group, if possible. However, there are some special circumstances to consider.

What If I Serve Multiple Schools?   If you serve multiple schools, you may feel overwhelmed by the day-to-day process of keeping up with crises, student needs, and program demands (Jonson-Reid et al., 2004). It is particularly important that you design a system that can capture similar information across sites and is not unwieldy to implement. Computerization, even if the initial thought seems frightening to you, is likely to be a major help in the long run. You will want participants, interns, and other program staff to use the same forms or input screens at each site to collect information (Jonson-Reid, Kontak, & Mueller, 2001). A standard form and means of tracking what happened will help you be able to compile the information later without having to painstakingly read through notes in 300 case files at the end of the year.

Also, before you try to combine information into a single report, do not forget to note any major differences in the school sites. You may need to evaluate results by site rather than overall if these differences are significant. For example, a program may operate differently at an elementary school compared to a high school. Even if you are serving a single grade level, there may be one school that is an alternative school or a school that has a specialized program that sets it apart.

Interns   If you supervise student interns, make sure that the importance of evaluating interventions is built in to your initial training with them. It is highly likely that this is an expectation of the graduate MSW program as well (Torres & Patton, 2000). Make record keeping a standard part of their workload, and remember to check in during supervision to make sure this is happening. Also be aware that a possible advantage of having interns is that they may have to do an evaluation or research project for a class. If so, this is a great resource that you should incorporate into your evaluation plan for the year.

PROCESS INFORMATION AND INTERPRETING RESULTS

One of the keys to interpreting results—particularly in a nonrandom design—is process information. **Process information** includes how the intervention was implemented and other factors, such as attendance at sessions and whether or not students were also getting other services (Rossi et al., 1999). Process information may also include organizational factors such as problems scheduling group meetings because of class time. This information is used in conjunction with the outcome results provided by scores on scales or other data. Let's look at an example.

Limitations   No research endeavor is perfect. If possible, we consider how to reduce the number of limitations prior to doing research. However, there are

| Case | Case Example |

John was referred by his teacher to the school social worker, Tim, for disruptive class-room behavior. Tim did some research and decided that a cognitive behavioral approach to treatment had the best empirical support. He used the Child Behavior Checklist, Teacher Form to provide a baseline for John's behavior. The plan was to meet with John individually for 3 months. At the end of 3 months, his post-test scores and classroom observation by the teacher revealed no change. Tim may interpret this as evidence that the chosen approach to treatment did not work. Tim remembered to document the process, however, and due to frequent absences John only attended half of the sessions. Furthermore, although his parents consented to the intervention, there appeared to be little structure or support for the effort from home. With this information, it seems less likely that the intervention approach was flawed.

an infinite number of things that can go wrong with the intervention or the research process that impact the interpretation of the results. For example, a subject does not fill out a survey correctly, or half the students in a group leave.

Problems such as these do not mean that you throw up your hands and throw out the data. However, these are limitations that need to be considered when thinking about what happened. It is a good idea to spend some time listing all the limitations that you can think of prior to writing up or talking about your final results. Then consider the seriousness of each limitation (not all limitations are major problems) and how you can address questions about the limitations. For example, let's say you conduct a needs assessment survey of 500 students. Five students fail to answer the survey properly and the data must be thrown out. On the one hand, this is a limitation. On the other hand, it is a very small proportion of the students surveyed. It is unlikely that such a small amount of missing information will seriously bias your results.

SPECIAL ISSUES

Prevention   In general, intervention is easier to measure than prevention because if you are preventing something, you are hoping that it will not happen for a group of students who are not yet engaged in that behavior. For example, in a smoking prevention program with first graders at an elementary school, you are trying to make sure that students do not smoke. However, the high-risk period for beginning to smoke is likely much later—approximately age 11 (Johnston et al., 2003). If your program only lasts 1 year, you cannot just use rates of smoking in older students as baseline information, although you will still measure this just in case you can follow the group until high school. In most cases like this, the outcome of interest takes much longer to develop than your program evaluation funding will allow. Therefore, you will also want to measure risk factors associated with smoking. These are like the interim objectives presented previously (Jonson-Reid, 2000). The idea is that if you impact a risk factor such as attitude toward smoking, then hopefully that will decrease the likelihood of smoking later.

Measuring Preexisting Trends   Sometimes we are seeking to intervene in problems that are already on the decline. This is another reason to capture baseline rates for the problem of interest over time (incidence), if possible. For example, if smoking rates are on the decline prior to your prevention program, then after the program you hope to show a greatly accelerated decline. If smoking rates decline at the same rate or level off, then perhaps the decline would have happened naturally.

Ongoing Services   Sometimes you may provide students with services for a long time. Perhaps a student has school social work services written into an Individual Education Plan for special education and it is unlikely, given the disability, that short-term services will be all that is needed. In such cases, you will want a system for continually monitoring improvement and perhaps meeting some goals and then setting new ones. You are no longer interested in a pre- and post-test case but rather incremental changes over time that are measurable and lead to needed adjustments in intervention and services. Goal attainment scaling (Royse & colleagues, 2001) may be a helpful approach in such instances.

Developing and Using a Management Information System   The larger your caseload, the more likely your evaluation will require some automation to make it manageable. A management information system is a computerized means of tracking your caseload characteristics, services, and even outcomes. Hopefully, you already have an intake system in place in which you record certain information about referred students, referral reasons, referral source, etc. You can add a systematic way of recording services to students such as cataloging the type and frequency of services over time. Finally, you can record some measure or measures of the results of the services. You can enter such information into a computer database without being a high-tech computer genius or buying a new expensive system (Jonson-Reid et al., 2001). Once the information is entered, reports can be generated about how many students you serve, the types of referrals, and various outcomes without time-consuming rummaging through stacks of case files. Programs such as Microsoft Access or other Windows-based data programs are probably already available in the district. Of course, the old adage "garbage in, garbage out" applies here. If you start such a system, you must spend the time to correctly enter your data.

Statistics   Let's say you need some statistical work done so that you can demonstrate whether or not your results were statistically significant for your grant. Statistics may not be an area in which you have training. Fortunately, there are some fairly user-friendly resources to help guide you (Weinbach & Grinnell, 1997). Also, you may want to build partnerships with district research staff. If you do not have such resources, look outward to nearby universities and colleges. If you have sufficient money, you can even pay a professional evaluator.

The goal of statistical analysis is generally the search for a statistically significant improvement. This means that your results were unlikely to occur by chance alone. The greater the significance (measured by a p value of 0.05 or less), the smaller the p value (generally $0.0001 < p < 0.05$), the less likely you obtained the result by chance. You must keep in mind that statistics are sensitive to the number of students you serve. For example, obtaining a statistically significant result may not be possible if you are serving a very small number of students. It is always a good idea to look for practical significance, a meaningful change that may or may not also be statistically significant. If you only serve five students in a conflict management group and all of them improve their behavior so that it is no longer a problem, this is practically significant even if the group is too small for statistical significance.

What If the Service Does Not Work?   One of the major fears in evaluation is that we will find that nothing happened. It is natural to fear that such a result could jeopardize funding or even one's job. On the other hand, continuing to provide services without checking to determine if you are producing something worthwhile is just as likely to place you at risk. Arguably, continuing to provide an ineffective service is also unethical. It is important to view your evaluation as part of the overall district efforts toward improving education. Work with your supervisor to caste the evaluation process in terms of providing ongoing feedback to developing the highest quality service rather than an all-or-nothing test (Patton, 1997). Also, continual monitoring of your practice allows you to make alterations as needed and is less likely to result in a negative outcome than a single attempt to measure what happened at the end of a program.

Partnerships   One of the functions identified as a part of school social work practice is the liaison between home, school, and community (Allen-Meares, 1994). We are used to creating partnerships, but sometimes school social workers neglect to consider research partnerships. Sometimes the idea of evaluation can seem overwhelming, and even if you do most of it, you still may need help with analyzing data. Research partnerships with university students or professors or even research centers can provide assistance to school social workers in the field (Austin et al., 1999; Jonson-Reid et al., 2001; Lawson, 1998). Researchers at academic institutions may be willing to provide services for free in return for joint publication of results or even as a community service.

Dissemination   Evaluation without communication of your results is unlikely to produce any of the benefits of evaluation mentioned at the beginning of the chapter, with the exception of your own self-improvement. It is hoped that you will not stop at reporting to local stakeholders. There is a great need in the area of school social work to increase our knowledge about what school social workers are doing and what methods are effective in what settings (Franklin, 1999). There are regional conferences and national conferences sponsored by various school social work associations such as the School Social Work Association of America. Such associations are eager to have sessions run by practitioners who have done some research on an intervention or service. Newsletters such as that by the National Association of Social Work, School Social Work Section are another venue for practitioners to disseminate results to an audience that is largely composed of practitioners. Finally, do not overlook journals just because you are not an academic researcher. For example, *Children & Schools* has a Practice Highlights section designed especially to attract short articles from the field.

SUMMARY

School social workers cannot work in silence and hope to be either recognized for their worth or quietly ignored during budget cuts. Evaluation of treatment and services is critical to ethical practice, building awareness of the value of school social work services, building our understanding of what works, and expanding services. It is hoped that this chapter has provided some tools and resources to encourage you to include research in your application of "best practice."

School Social Work Companion Website

Please be sure to check out our companion website at www.thomsonedu.com/social_work/bye, where you will find relevant materials for each chapter, including flashcards, online practice quizzes, and PowerPoint slides.

References

Achenbach, T. M. (2000). Child Behavior Checklists (CBCL/2-3 and CBCL/4-18), Teacher Report Form (TRF), and Youth Self Report (YSR). In A. J. Rush, Jr., et al. (Eds.), *Handbook of psychiatric measures* (pp. 310–314). Washington, DC: American Psychiatric Association.

Allen-Meares, P. (1994). Social work services in schools. A national study of entry-level tasks. *Social Work, 39,* 560–565.

Austin, M. J., Martin, M., Carnochan, S., Goldberg, S., Berrick, J. D., Weiss, B., & Kelley, J. (1999). Building a comprehensive agency–university partnership: A case study of the Bay Area Social Services Consortium. *Journal of Community Practice,* 6(3), 89–106.

Baraily, S., & Huber, M. (2002). *Comparative table of school climate assessment instruments for middle school and high school students.* Retrieved January 31, 2005, from www.emc.cmich.edu/CharacterEd/assessments.htm

Bleyer, L., & Joiner, K. (2002). Conducting a needs assessment in a school setting. In R. Constable, S. McDonald, & J. Flynn (Eds.), *School social work. Practice, policy and research perspectives* (5th ed., pp. 194–207). Chicago: Lyceum.

Boynton, P., Wood, G., & Greenhalgh, T. (2004). Reaching beyond the white middle classes. Hands on guide to questionnaire design. *British Medical Journal, 328,* 1433–1436.

Burns, B. (2002). Reasons for hope for children and families: A perspective and overview. In B. Burns & K. Hoagwood (Eds.), *Community treatment for youth. Evidence-based interventions for severe emotional and behavioral disorder* (pp. 1–15). New York: Oxford University Press.

Civil Rights Project. (2000, June). *Opportunities suspended: The devastating consequences of zero tolerance and school discipline polices.* Retrieved November 30, 2003, from www.mti-sys.com/issd/news/zt_report2.html

Dahlberg, L., Toal, S., & Behrens, C. (1998). *Measuring violence-related attitudes, beliefs and behaviors among youths. A compendium of assessment tools.* Atlanta, GA: Centers for Disease Control and Prevention.

Davis, L., Johnson, S., Miller-Cirbbs, J., & Saunders, J. (2002). A brief report: Factors influencing African American youth decisions to stay in school. *Journal of Adolescent Research, 17,* 223–234.

Dean, D. (1994). How to use focus groups. In J. Wholey, H. Hatry, & K. Newcomer (Eds.), *Handbook of practical program evaluation* (pp. 338–350). San Francisco: Jossey-Bass.

Dibble, N. (1998). Outcome evaluation and school social work services. *Section Connection, 4*(2), 1–5, 9.

Dupper, D. (2003). *School social work: Skills and interventions for effective practice.* Hoboken, NJ: John Wiley.

Epstein, J. (2001). *School, family, and community partnerships.* Oxford: Westview.

Franklin, C. (1999). Research on practice. Better than you think? *Social Work in Education, 21,* 3–10.

Girden, E. (1996). *Evaluating research articles from start to finish.* Thousand Oaks, CA: Sage.

Glisson, C., & Hemmelgarn, A. (1998). The effects of organizational climate and interorganizational coordination on the quality and outcomes of children's service systems. *Child Abuse & Neglect, 22,* 401–421.

Goren, S. (2002). The wonderland of social work in the schools or how Alice learned to cope. In R. Constable, S. McDonald, & J. Flynn (Eds.), *School social work. Practice, policy and research perspectives* (5th ed., pp. 53–60). Chicago: Lyceum.

Hendricks, M. (1994). Making a splash: Reporting evaluation results effectively. In J. Wholey, H. H., & K. Newcomer (Eds.), *Handbook of practical program evaluation* (pp. 549–575). San Francisco: Jossey-Bass.

Jayaratne, S. (2004). Evaluating practice and programs. In P. Allen-Meares (Ed.), *Social work services in schools* (4th ed., pp. 327–358). Boston: Allyn & Bacon.

Johnston, L. D., O'Malley, P. M., & Bachman, J. G. (2003). *Monitoring the future national survey results on drug use, 1975–2002. Volume I: Secondary school students* (NIH Publication No. 03-5375). Bethesda, MD: National Institute on Drug Abuse. Retrieved February 1, 2005, from monitoringthefuture.org/pubs/monographs/vol1_2002.pdf

Jonson-Reid, M. (2000). Evaluating empowerment in a community-based child abuse prevention program: Lessons learned. *Journal of Community Practice, 7,* 57–76.

Jonson-Reid, M., Kontak, D., Citerman, B., Essma, A., & Fezzi, N. (2004). School social work caseload dynamics and outcomes: Year one results from a longitudinal study. *Children & Schools, 26*(1), 5–22.

Jonson-Reid, M., Kontak, D., & Mueller, S. (2001). Creating a management information system for school social workers: A field–university partnership. *Children & Schools, 23*(4), 198–211.

Lawson, H. (1998). Academically based community scholarship, consultation as collaborative problem-solving, and a collective responsibility model for the helping fields. *Journal of Educational and Psychological Consultation, 9,* 195–232.

Malgady, R. (1996). The question of cultural bias in assessment and diagnosis of ethnic minority clients: Lets reject the null hypothesis. *Professional Psychology, Research and Practice, 27,* 73–77.

Miller, T. (1994). Designing and conducting surveys. In J. Wholey, H. Hatry, & K. Newcomer (Eds.), *Handbook of practical program evaluation* (pp. 271–292). San Francisco: Jossey-Bass.

Morales, L. (2001). Cross-cultural adaptation of survey instruments: The CAHPS experience. In *Assessing patient experiences with assessing healthcare in multicultural settings.* Santa Monica, CA: RAND. Retrieved January 20, 2005, from www.rand.org/publications/RGSD/RGSD157

Nansel, T. R., Overpeck, M., Pilla, R., Ruan, W., Simons-Morton, B., & Scheidt, P. (2001). Bullying behaviors among U.S. youth: Prevalence and association with psychological adjustment. *Journal of the American Medical Association, 285,* 2094–2100.

National Association of Social Workers. (1999). *Code of ethics.* Washington, DC: Author. Retrieved December 20, 2003, from www.socialworkers.org/pubs/code/code.asp

National Association of Social Workers. (2002). *Standards of practice.* Washington, DC: Author.

National Center for Education Statistics. (2002). *Indicators of school crime and safety: 2001.* Retrieved November 6, 2003, from http://nces.ed.gov/pubsearch/pubsinfo. asp?pubid=2002113

Northwest Regional Educational Laboratory. (2001). *Schoolwide prevention of bullying.* Retrieved January 31, 2005, from www.nwrel.org/request/dec01

Ortega, D., & Richey, C. (1998). Methodological issues in social work research with depressed women of color. In M. Potocky & A. Rogers-Farmer (Eds.), *Social work research with minority and oppressed populations* (pp. 44–70). New York: Haworth.

Pan, Y. (2003). *The role of sociolinguistics in the development and conduct of federal surveys.* Washington, DC: U.S. Census Bureau. Retrieved January 20, 2005, from www.fcsm.gov/03papers/Panfinal.pdf

Patton, M. Q. (1997). *Utilization-focused evaluation. The new century text* (3rd ed.). Thousand Oaks, CA: Sage.

Pawlak, E., & Cousins, L. (2002). School social work: Organizational perspectives. In R. Constable, S. McDonald, & J. Flynn (Eds.), *School social work practice, policy and research perspectives* (5th ed., pp. 314–327). Chicago: Lyceum.

Posavac, E., & Carey, R. (1997). *Program evaluation: Methods and case studies.* Saddle River, NJ: Prentice-Hall.

Rossi, P., Freeman, H., & Lipsey, M. (1999). *Evaluation. A systematic approach* (6th ed.). Thousand Oaks, CA: Sage.

Royse, D., Thyer, B., Padgett, D., & Logan, T. (2001). *Program evaluation. An introduction.* Belmont, CA: Brooks/Cole.

Rubin, A., & Babbie, E. (2005). *Research methods for social work* (5th ed.). Pacific Grove, CA: Brooks/Cole.

Samples, F., & Aber, L. (1998). Evaluations of school-based violence prevention programs. In D. Elliot, B. Hamburg, & K. Williams (Eds.), *Violence in American schools* (pp. 217–252). New York: Cambridge University Press.

Shapiro, E., & Kratochwill, T. (2000). *Conducting school-based assessments of child and adolescent behavior.* New York: Guilford.

Sohng, S., & Weatherley, R. (2002). Practical approaches to conducting and using research in the schools. In R. Constable, S. McDonald, & J. Flynn (Eds.), *School social work. Practice, policy and research perspectives* (5th ed., pp. 298–313). Chicago: Lyceum.

Torres, S., Jr., & Patton, R. (Eds.). (2000). *Teaching school social work: Model course outlines and resources*. Arlington, VA: Council on Social Work Education.

U.S. Department of Education. (2003). *No child left behind*. Retrieved November 6, 2003, from www.ed.gov/nclb/landing.jhtml

Wei, H. (2004). *Bullying behaviors among Taiwanese 7th graders: Differential risk factors and psychosocial maladjustment of bullies and victims*. Unpublished doctoral dissertation, Washington University, St. Louis, MO.

Weinbach, R., & Grinnell, R., Jr. (1997). *Statistics for social workers* (4th ed.). New York: Longman.

15 CHAPTER | Legal Issues in School Social Work

GAYLON J. NETTLES, M.S.W., J.D.
Indiana Department of Education

CHAPTER OUTLINE

Disclaimer: This chapter is furnished with the understanding that the author is not engaged in providing legal or other professional advice. Any opinions are those of the author and not of the Indiana Department of Education. Hypothetical cases are composites of actual cases resulting in intervention by the author. No information is used that could identify a child or the parents. Best practice responses are the author's legal opinion.

CHAPTER OVERVIEW

After reading this chapter, readers will be able to (1) define the terms law, rule, policy, and ethical code; (2) describe the access and due process issues for children who are compelled to be in school, who are homeless, and who have special needs; (3) identify the issues, rights, and limitations of the "gatekeepers" of referrals in schools; (4) identify what laws apply to privacy of personal clinical and educational records; (5) identify under what circumstances the practitioner may be required to breach privileged or confidential communications; and (6) identify the school social worker obligation to provide service under state and federal law.

INTRODUCTION

A fundamental philosophy of the U.S. constitutional form of representative government is that government is the servant of the people and not their master. All persons are entitled to full and complete information regarding the affairs of government and the official acts of those who represent them as public officials and employees. Providing persons with the information is an essential function of a representative government and an integral part of the routine duties of public officials and employees, whose duty it is to provide the information (Indiana Code 5-14-3-1). School social workers embrace, as a matter of ethics, this fundamental American concept—that we are servants of the people.

LAW, RULE, POLICY, AND ETHICAL CODES DEFINING PRACTICE

Education is the only practice area, besides health, in which every practitioner and every student has been both a participant and a consumer of the service. It is the only practice area in which the people are compelled by law to participate from approximately age 7 to approximately age 18. Laws, rules, policies, and ethical codes not only dictate the requirements to educate and be educated but also, in some cases, dictate the quality of service required. School social workers work with children of all socioeconomic levels and all levels of intellectual capability as well as their parents and the administration. Knowledge of laws, rules, or policies is essential in the assessment and referral process of practice. Advocacy for the client without knowledge of the applicable laws or rules will be limited in scope at best and possibly harmful to the best interests of the client.

Avoid referring to laws as "Public Law number...." **Public laws** are acts of Congress or your local state legislature that have been signed into law. Each year, the legislature passes bills and chief executives sign them into laws and each law is given a public law number. A public law may have sections that change several different statutes. For example, the first bill signed into law each year will be called Public Law 1 (or other terms depending on the state). Each year there will be a Public Law 1. That public law may have hundreds of pages and change dozens of statutes that are not relevant to each other. School personnel get into the habit of referring to important educational legislation as "public law xyz" and forgetting that each year there will be a different public law xyz with different contents. If you must refer to a public law by number, use the year following the public law number, such as Public Law 221–2004. That will distinguish it from other years. Otherwise, refer to the statute affected by the public law change.

Law, Code, and Statutes

The process of law making is not discussed in this chapter. That is better left to books on government. Laws used in the context of this chapter are statutes of both the state and the federal government. Federal laws are laws of Congress and, as such, are the supreme law of the land (the U.S. Constitution). What this means to social workers is that in a conflict between a federal law and state law, the federal law controls unless the federal law gives precedence to the state law. State laws will generally control over local policies or rules. You will sometimes hear the term **common law**, which is "the law derived from judicial decisions rather than a statute or constitution" (*Black's Law Dictionary*). Federal laws, sometimes also called "code," are found in the *United States Code* (USC). The USC or *United States Code Annotated* (USCA) is a series of volumes of books that include all of the federal laws. If you want to see commentary on past cases, including definition of terms and sometimes a brief history, you should use the USCA.

Laws or statutes are usually found in a series of volumes of books (or online). Washburn University has a very good general search engine found at www.washlaw.edu, and each volume addresses a different topic. Statutes are created by a state legislature or the U.S. Congress. Code describes different types of statutes from federal and state to municipal. Municipal codes, or local ordinances passed by city or county governing bodies, usually define the rules for building standards, environmental management, zoning limitations, water, sewage, and other local (and very important) limitations and guidelines for our everyday quality of life. Knowledge of the law, or how to find the laws and rules, is an essential tool of school social work practice. The simplest and most efficient way to access information is through the following websites:

- Lawcrawler at http://lawcrawler.findlaw.com/index.html
- Hieros Gamos at www.hg.org/index.html
- Legal Information Institute at www.law.cornell.edu/topics/topic1.html

Rules

Rules may be federal, state, local, or school district. Laws are usually created to impose a duty, solve a problem, or provide for a right or remedy. **Rules** are administrative procedures put in writing to carry out laws. Both can be enforced, and both may carry sanctions. Laws may or may not be explicit as to how they will actually be put into practice. For example, a law requiring student services in schools will not mean much without rules defining what those student services will be and how they will work in the school system. State boards of education do that.

Rules are usually carefully crafted to clarify what the intent of the law may be. Rules are also called "regulations" and "administrative law." Agencies of government responsible for certain areas of jurisdiction (e.g., education) are given power to create rules to govern or carry out the requirements of the enabling federal or state law. Federal rules are found in the *Code of Federal Regulation* (CFR). Notice of rules is through the *Federal Register*. States will have some mechanism to give notice of state rule change. You will frequently see references to Title I or Title IX. "Titles" are used in regulations of the CFR and sometimes in state code.

Policy

Policies may be federal, state, or local. **Policies** are usually internal rules of an agency. Paradoxically, a policy at the local level may have a more profound impact than a policy at the highest level of state or federal government. The reason is that statutes are usually a structure (see the discussion on laws) and provide for a requirement but without detail for carrying out the requirement. In education, policies are usually left to the local school districts to ensure the educational function of the school services. Legislatures, state and federal, are not going to define what time the buses run, for example. Policies affecting social work practice include the following and may be defined locally in the school district (the list is not complete): tardiness, truancy, process for referring to special education, process for referring for discipline, alternatives to suspension/expulsion, process for handling suicidal students, policies for handling school safety issues, and status of the social worker as a certified or uncertified employee.

Ethical Codes

Ethics are rules of practice accepted by the profession of social work. They are codified benchmarks that provide you with the best advice and experience of generations of social workers and leaders of the profession. A practitioner who knowingly violates the ethical code does so at his or her peril. Although ethical codes are not state imposed laws or rules, they are strictly adhered to by the profession and violations of the ethical codes can have far-reaching professional and practice implications. See the following links for information on social work ethical standards:

- National Association of Social Workers (NASW): www.socialworkers.org/pubs/code/code.asp
- NASW School Social Work Standards: www.socialworkers.org/sections/credentials/school_social.asp

ACCESS ISSUES FOR STUDENTS AND SCHOOL SOCIAL WORK PRACTICE

Access issues include artificial or physical impediments, barriers, policies, practices, or administrative failures that have the practical or constructive effect of preventing or impairing access to educational services. Access issues differ with different populations.

Compulsory School Attendance

Three entities have responsibilities or duties under compulsory school attendance laws: the student, the parent, and the school. The student, when he or she is able to make cognitive decisions, is responsible for being in school. Failure to do this is called **truancy**. When a parent fails to ensure a child attends school, it is considered **educational neglect**. When a school fails to ensure a child attends school, it is **institutional neglect of a duty**. Sanctions for failing to carry out these duties vary from school district to district throughout the country and are based on state law. Generally, a truant child may be incarcerated for a "status offense," or an offense based on the child's status as a juvenile and the violation of a law. In contrast, an adult cannot be incarcerated for not going to school. Parents may be considered to have committed neglect of a dependent if they fail or refuse to ensure their child attends school as required. Attendance may not be in a public school and the state law may be satisfied by private school attendance. Depending on state law, school district administrators may be held responsible for failing to ensure a child under their authority attends school.

Student Due Process

Removing a student from school requires due process of law. **Due process** is not just a phrase. It is a state and federal constitutional right that provides for certain protections and procedures before a student can be denied statutory or common law privileges and benefits of an education in public schools. Removing students from school requires certain procedures to protect them. School social workers should carefully analyze the record of any student to ensure that discipline is in accordance with local policy and state and federal law (U.S. Supreme Court: *Goss v. Lopez*).

 | **Case Example**

A student has a long history of acting out behavior. An incident of insubordination with a teacher is the final act that causes him to be considered for suspension or even expulsion. The principal is fed up and brings the student into the office. The student is told to clear out his locker and not come back until he is told to come back. You see the student in the mall a month later. He has never been contacted and has been told not to come on school grounds again by the principal.

Best Practice
1.   Verify that he is suspended or expelled. If there has been no hearing or meeting, go to step 2.
2.   Find out if he is pending expulsion. Expulsion would have required some sort of notice be sent to the family (Supreme Court of the United States). He may have been sent the notice. Suspensions have a limit under your state law, but they may be extended to the expulsion hearing date.
3.   If none of this has happened, check with your principal. It could be a mistake. If it is not a mistake, find out why the student is still not in school. Compulsory school attendance laws require children to be in school.

Homeless Children and Youth

The McKinney–Vento Homeless Assistance Act (USC 11431 et seq. Go to the U.S. Department of Education homepage at www.ed.gov and search for "homeless") is a federal law that protects homeless children from the burdens of legal settlement or right to attend school issues due to their frequent moves.

The term **homeless children and youths** is defined by the McKinney–Vento Homeless Assistance Act as individuals who lack a fixed, regular, and adequate nighttime residence and includes children and youths who are sharing the housing of other persons due to loss of housing, economic hardship, or a similar reason; are living in motels, hotels, trailer parks, or camping grounds due to the lack of alternative adequate accommodations; are living in emergency or transitional shelters; are abandoned in hospitals or are awaiting foster care placement; children and youths who have a primary nighttime residence that is a public or private place not designed for or ordinarily used as a regular sleeping accommodation for human beings; children and youths who are living in cars, parks, public spaces, abandoned buildings, substandard housing, bus or train stations, or similar settings; and migratory children who qualify due to their living circumstances (2 USC 11434a.).

Children do not have the right to go to school wherever the parent wants. Even payment of taxes does not ensure the right to attend in a specific district.

Case	**Case Example**

A social worker has a new student in school and the record on the student shows frequent moves without an obvious reason such as parental reassignment. The file may also contain letters of concern from administrators or teachers due to absences, immunization problems, indications of learning problems but no Individualized Education Plan (note that schools have 60 days to develop a plan), and no telephone point of contact. Families may not consider themselves homeless but may meet the federal definition. The social worker reviews the parameters of the McKinney Act and determines that there is a likelihood that the student is homeless. This information is passed on to the homeless liaison (required by federal law) and the principal. The administration is made aware of the protections afforded the child. Key among them is the right to stay at the "school of origin" even though the family may move around the county, city, or neighborhood and out of the district. Children removed from their homes in the school district are placed in a shelter outside of the district pending placement in foster homes. The social worker receives reports that the children are not receiving an education.

Best Practice

School social workers should always do an assessment when there is a reasonable suspicion of homelessness by federal definition. A homeless child does not have to be destitute and without shelter. Children in shelters are not considered to be in permanent placement and should be provided transportation to school by their school of origin. Federal law on the homeless overrides state or local policy concerning the right to attend school. A homeless child and the child's family may need intervention by the school social worker in and out of school to ensure that education is being provided to the child. A child removed from the district may still be eligible for services from that district.

The residence of the parents will probably be the legal issue. Homeless children are not necessarily lacking a place to reside or living on the streets. They may be doubled up with another family, living in a shelter, or living in a motel. The residence of the parent or custodian may be changing monthly or weekly, and a normal residence may not be possible. This federal law can supercede any state law or local policy because of the supremacy clause.

Migrant Children, Children With Limited English Proficiency, and Children of Immigrant Families

The Migrant Education Even Start Family Literacy program grants are intended to help break the cycle of poverty and illiteracy of migratory families by improving the educational opportunities of these families through the integration of early childhood education, adult literacy or adult basic education, and parenting education into a unified family literacy program. Indiana Code 5-14-3-1 states,

> This program is implemented through cooperative activities that: build on high-quality existing community resources to create a new range of educational services for most-in-need migratory families; promote the academic achievement of migratory children and adults; assist migratory children and adults from low-income families to achieve by challenging state content standards and challenging state student performance standards; and use instructional programs based on scientifically based research on preventing and overcoming reading difficulties for children and adults.

Go to the U.S. Department of Education homepage at www.ed.gov and search for "migrant."

School social workers will be among the first to become aware of language needs of students or cultural or racial concerns of the parents. These programs

---

Case | **Case Example**

Jose is a migrant student whose family has "settled out," or established a permanent local address. Jose does not have a Social Security Number and his parents have been identified as undocumented aliens.

Question: Can Jose expect to be admitted to school?
Answer: Yes. The immigration status of a student will not prevent a student's attendance in school (Legal Information Institute webpage, U.S. Supreme Court, found at http://supct.law.cornell.edu/supct/cases/name.htm).

Practice Points
Migrant and limited English proficiency issues will probably be the function of the office responsible for Title I (34 CFR Part 200). Each state will have a point of contact at the state level for migrant affairs through the Title I office. If you serve a migrant population, they have special and unique practice issues. They are educationally at risk, and the cultural differences make social workers an important educational resource for community support as well as intervention for medical, legal, familial, and quality-of-life issues. Keep in mind that in many countries people who call themselves social workers are government workers who may not be benevolent.

providing services for migrant children, and children who are neglected, delinquent, or at risk of dropping out, are found in Title I (34 CFR Part 200 (Title I), Subpart B (200.80), Subpart C (200.81), and Subpart D(200.90)). Grants for the assistance of children with limited English proficiency are available at English Language Acquisition, Language Enhancement, and Academic Achievement Act. 20 USCA 6811, et seq. Also go to the U.S. Department of Education website for grants (www.ed.gov/fund/landing.jhtml?src=rt). School social workers should familiarize themselves with these statutes and rules.

Exceptional Children

Children with special needs are sometimes stereotyped as disabled, handicapped, or even gifted. With the caveat that all children are exceptional, the issues of disabled children have statutory implications for school social workers. The Individuals with Disabilities Education Act (IDEA) and Section 504 of the Rehabilitation Act of 1973 (Section 504 Citation) provide for an appropriate education for children who qualify for services. Other chapters in this book provide an in-depth analysis of IDEA (see Chapter 16) and school social work practice within special education as well as confidentiality (see Chapter 12). This chapter discusses access issues related to disability law. Who are the gatekeepers for entry into services in the schools, and what is the nexus with school social workers?

GATEKEEPERS FOR REFERRALS: IMPLICATIONS IN LAW

Health Care Professionals

Disabilities in the general practice of social work are not necessarily disabilities in school law. Also, what is considered a disability in school law may not be considered a disability by a physician or other health care provider. For example, a child with asthma may not be considered disabled by a physician who can treat

Case | **Case Example**

A student has had an exceptional number of absences due to a variety of symptoms. In discussing the student with her physician, the social worker discovers that the student has allergies so severe that they may affect her attendance in school. Although significant to the physician, it is not a problem that the physician would normally associate with a school-related problem except to write orders that the student should stay home during episodes of distress. To the school, it is significant and could result in the student missing 20, 30, 40, or more days of school. The social worker should seek a meeting with the school administration and the parents under Section 504 of the Rehabilitation Act of 1973. It requires an evaluation of impairment of a major life function (compared to IDEA's 60-day window for a final decision) and if the symptoms are severe enough the services can be bumped up to the local division for exceptional children and assessed for IDEA. Critical for Section 504 is that the student is considered to be protected when the student is "regarded as impaired." For a discussion of Section 504 in a question/answer format, see the Office of Civil Rights' (OCR) website at www.ed.gov/about/offices/list/ocr/504faq.html.

the condition. The same child may be considered disabled by a school if the child misses an unusual number of days due to the illness. The caveat is that it may be a disability if it impairs a major life function and prevents the student from receiving an appropriate education.

Law Enforcement

Students may go through their entire school experience with an impairment and never be evaluated. Some impairment may emotionally or mentally incapacitate a student and cause behaviors that create legal problems before any evaluation of a disability occurs. (For a discussion of this issue, see Bartlett, 2004.) Police involvement with any student should raise alarms for social workers. Obviously, every student with a legal problem is not necessarily disabled, but social workers cannot afford to stereotype any student based on the student's behavior. Where others see a "bad kid," social workers see a disturbed young person. Impairments come in many forms and some do not rise to the level of a "disability" requiring special services as defined by federal law.

Case | **Case Example**

A student is arrested for possession of a controlled substance downtown during the summer break. She admits to being addicted. A student who is addicted and not in recovery is not considered disabled and is not protected by IDEA or Section 504 for the use of illegal drugs. Services for alcohol problems may be allowed. For a discussion of Section 504, see the OCR website. Although schools may not be required to serve a child disabled by addiction, the social worker will need to assess the student's needs and provide services without regard to the administrative definitions of disability.

Teachers

Teachers are an obvious gatekeeper. Anyone who refers a student to you will want, reasonably, to know what is going on with the student. You cannot disclose specifics of your treatment to a teacher and, depending on your state, you may be explicitly prevented from discussing a client by privilege or confidentiality laws. Even without laws of privilege the Family Educational Rights and Privacy Act (FERPA) (34 CFR Part 99) will prevent disclosure except for health and safety reasons. Teachers may know changes in the student's habits and perhaps personal information (e.g., family crises). They may not be thinking in terms of a disability, but they may be able to give information that is reliable and will assist in an assessment of a disabling condition. Teachers may also be a first point of contact for information concerning school safety issues.

One frequent question concerns the degree of disclosure allowed by law to teaching staff. The answer is that it depends on state law. FERPA allows disclosure to anyone with a "legitimate educational interest." This would reasonably

Practice Points Regarding Disclosure of Information

1. Everyone may be looking at the same student and seeing different things. The principal may see a malingerer who is using the illness to "get over." The teacher may see the student as another bit of extra work because of the accommodation that is necessary. The parents may see a sick child who is not being served appropriately. The student may not have ever been different and may not consider himself or herself impaired.
2. Depression may also be impairment.
3. Age is irrelevant. A student may be discovered impaired in the last semester of his or her senior year after 12 years of attendance problems (a true case). Federal protections, such as Section 504 and IDEA, will follow a student into college and the workplace.
4. A long history of absenteeism due to a variety of medical problems may point to a single problem that has never been discovered. Medical professionals may never have detected the problem. Trust your judgment and seek consultation with other clinical social workers.
5. Social workers are professionals in their own right. You should pursue your instincts and your best practices in assessment to ensure a student is appropriately served. The fact that another professional states that a student is not impaired is important but not necessarily relevant to your assessment.
6. These are not just practice points. Students' rights to be accommodated are protected by federal and state law. School social workers are an integral part of their treatment and play an important role in protecting these rights.

include teachers. Some states provide for privileged communication of social workers with their clients. This is a stricter standard than that of FERPA. In these states, school social workers would not be able to disclose any information concerning the client (student) without the student's informed consent. Your state law would govern the exceptions, which are usually child abuse information, suicidal ideation, or homicidal ideation. If a student is disabled, the Individualized Education Plan (part of the federal IDEA) would govern disclosures as part of an evaluation and assessment.

Parents

As a school social worker, parents are your greatest asset. Unfortunately, in education parents may sometimes be perceived as a threat or intrusive. In any other setting, the parent of a child would be considered a critical source of information. Social workers recognize the systemic nature of any problem and recognize the parent as a critical element in a child's life as part of the assessment. Parental involvement is a requirement of IDEA and Section 504. Special services cannot be provided without parental consent. For some parents, a social worker may be their only access to the system. The following website provides information on special education law: www.reedmartin.com. A state department of education website for special education law is http://doe.state.in.us/exceptional/ speced/welcome.html.

Laws, rules, and policies provide a structure for service. They are only as effective as the practitioner's knowledge of them. These statutes on disability law are complex and have decades of case law and administrative opinion. On any question of interpretation of statutes, seek the counsel of clinical practitioners who have knowledge of the practice area and seek out attorneys who know school law. All attorneys and practitioners are not qualified to opine on these matters.

RECORDS PRIVACY

FERPA is the statute governing records in public schools. Records of school social workers are not subject to review by anyone if they are kept in the sole possession of the maker of the records. Any records that are shared with at least one other person are considered education records and as such are subject to review by the parent or eligible student (a student older than age 18). The Family Policy Compliance Office of the U.S. Department of Education is responsible for record-related questions and issues. At its website (www.ed.gov/policy/gen/guid/fpco/index.html), you will also find the regulations governing records and resources for parents and student. State laws may also provide protection from disclosure. If your state has licensure or certification of social workers, the state statute should address the question.

A federal law titled the Health Insurance Portability and Accountability Act (HIPAA) has affected the privacy of records of what is called "covered entities"(45 CFR Parts 160 and 164. HIPAA Privacy, Security and Enforcement). For the rules and law on HIPAA, go to www.hhs.gov/ocr/hippa. This privacy law often affects the services of clinical social workers working in schools on a contracted basis. However, school records are protected by FERPA, not HIPAA. In certain circumstances, schools may have obligations under HIPAA. For a discussion of the

 Practice Points Regarding FERPA and HIPAA

1. School social workers have ethical codes that prevent sharing information without informed consent. However, FERPA governs how we share and when we may share information in public schools.
2. Check your state laws to find out if you have any additional state protections (or burdens) relative to disclosure. In cases in which a state privilege exists, a social worker cannot disclose any information without informed consent of the client unless there is a threat of child abuse, suicide, or homicide.
3. If you are not a school employee (i.e., you are an independent contractor), you may be subject to HIPAA.
4. Records containing student personally identifiable information and not kept in your sole possession are educational records and parents (and eligible students) have a right to access them.

difference between FERPA and HIPAA, go to http://doe.state.in.us/exceptional/
speced/pdf/hipaa-ferpa.pdf.

REPORTING OF CHILD ABUSE AND NEGLECT

Reporting requirements and parameters of responsibility for reporting are controlled by state law. As a general rule, suspicion of neglect or abuse must be
reported. Failure to report may also be an offense. School social workers will
encounter abuse and neglect of children. The best interest of the child must
always be served, but the reporting of the abuse and neglect in schools may have
certain parameters required by law or rule. For example, in Indiana a person
in the schools may be identified to receive reports. The reporter is still responsible for ensuring that the report was made and, if not, to make the report.

The National Association of Counsel for Children is a nonprofit child advocacy association that offers substantive legal analysis of child maltreatment and
reporting requirements (http://nacchildlaw.org/childrenlaw/childmaltreat-
ment.html). The best source of local information is your local child protection
services office. If in doubt, report it. Do not take the investigation upon yourself. Turn the issue over to the authorities responsible for the investigation under
your state laws.

Case	Case Example

1. Susie has unexplained bruising and discloses that she is being disciplined by her
   mother's boyfriend. Report it.
2. John reports repeated unwanted touching by a member of the school staff. Note:
   As a social worker it is appropriate to ask questions and elicit information that
   other nonclinical professionals might not be prepared to assess. In this case, depending on your personal opinion, you may want to ask what kind of touching.
   If a staff person is patting the student on the head and the student finds that of-
   fensive, that may be a simple matter to remedy. If the student is being touched on
   more intimate parts of the body, that may determine your next step. Social workers, as well as other student service professionals, sometimes are put in the position of warning other staff as to state and federal laws and rules regarding sexual
   harassment or abuse. In the final analysis, if you believe abuse or neglect has occurred, even by mistake, you must report it. No person is immune to these laws
   based on their position.

Practice Points
1. Know your state laws on reporting. Know your school policy.
2. If you believe abuse or neglect has occurred, report it.
3. If you need to consult, keep in mind that it is your suspicion that is important, not
   the suspicion of other third parties.
4. Failing to report suspected abuse or neglect may be prosecuted just as the crime itself may be prosecuted.

SUMMARY

Knowledge of laws, rules, and policies that affect children in schools, and their parents, is as essential to advocacy in school social work as knowledge of psychology. Change, when it occurs, is often dramatic and may affect constitutional or civil rights. Laws, rules, and policies often change annually or even daily and affect every population within the educational system. Access issues frequently affect the most disenfranchised and powerless in our society. Understanding how to find legal information, assess it, and use it appropriately can be a powerful tool for the school social worker and his or her client.

School Social Work Companion Website

Please be sure to check out our companion website at www.thomsonedu.com/social_work/bye, where you will find relevant materials for each chapter, including flashcards, online practice quizzes, and PowerPoint slides.

References

Bartlett, L. D. (2004, April 8). Special education students and the police: Many questions unanswered. *Education Law Reporter, 185*(1), 1.

Garnett, S. C. (2002). *Updated guidance for homeless children in the school nutrition programs.* Washington, DC: U.S. Department of Agriculture, Child Nutrition Division, Food and Nutrition Service.

Indiana Department of Education, Division of Exceptional Learners. (2005). Retrieved March 13, 2005, from www.doe.state.in.us/exceptional/speced/welcome.html

Indiana Department of Education, Office of Student Services. (2005). Retrieved March 13, 2005, from www.doe.state.in.us/sservices/welcome.html

Indiana Department of Education. (2005). School social work homepage. Retrieved March 13, 2005, from www.doe.state.in.us/sservices/socwork.htm

Lake, S. E. (Ed.). (1998). *School law handbook.* Horsham, PA: LRP.

Levin, M. I. (Ed.). (2003). *United States school laws and rules.* St. Paul, MN: West Group.

Russo, C. J. (2004). *Reutter's the law of public education.* New York: Foundation Press.

West's Education Law Reporter. (2004). St. Paul, MN: West Group.

School Social Work Practice With Students With Disabilities

CHAPTER 16

JAMES P. CLARK, M.S.W.
School Social Work Services, Heartland Area
Education Agency 11, Iowa

CHARLENE THIEDE, M.S.W.
School Social Work Services, Iowa Department
of Education

CHAPTER OUTLINE

CHAPTER OVERVIEW

After completing this chapter, readers will be able to describe and give examples of the following (1) best and promising practices in special education; (2) key provisions of Public Law (P.L.) 94-142, the Education of All Handicapped Children Act, and the impact of special education mandates on school social work practice; (3) school social work assessment in special education; (4) the importance of being knowledgeable about cultural and linguistic differences; (5) conducting functional behavioral assessments; and (6) developing behavioral interventions.

Case | ## Case Example: Timmy's Story

Timmy Nelson, a third grader, was in trouble with his teacher again! His math assignment was not finished and he was sent in from recess for starting a fight during a dodge ball game. His teacher knew that his father recently left his mother alone with three little boys. Timmy was the oldest. She sympathized with Timmy and she had tried everything she knew how to do to help him keep up with his class, but he kept falling further behind. She decided to talk to the social worker on the special education team in her building. Timmy needed more help than she could give him.

Timmy sat with his shoulders slumped on a chair in the principal's outer office. Brown hair was matted around a sweaty face. His faded t-shirt and jeans were dirty. As Terry Hart, the school social worker, entered the room, a pair of frightened blue eyes looked up at him.

"Knock knock" Mr. Hart began. Timmy looked surprised and it took him a minute to respond, "Who's there?" . . . "Dwayne" . . . "Dwayne who?" . . . "Dwayne the bathtub I'm drowning!"

Mr. Hart responded by grabbing his nose and pretending to gasp for air. As he sat down beside him, Timmy began to smile.

Many children such as Timmy have problems that exhaust the capacity of the general education classroom. However, the decision to provide special education requires a comprehensive individual assessment. The evaluation team must determine that the student is eligible by showing that a disability described in the law is present. The team must demonstrate need by showing that because of the disability the student requires special education in order to receive a "free and appropriate public education" (FAPE). Evaluation teams may document need by showing that interventions implemented in the general education program failed.

Mr. Hart worked with Timmy, his teacher, and his mother to identify and implement interventions that would enable him to succeed in his regular classroom. Their work together would help the school staff and his mother decide whether he needed special education services.

Special education is the specially designed instruction and related services that are needed by students with disabilities in order to receive benefit from their schooling. After reading this chapter, you will be able to describe how school social workers participate in multidisciplinary special education teams to conduct evaluations, to develop individual education plans, and to deliver services to students with disabilities and their families. You will be able to list special education laws and describe how they shaped social work practice in schools. You will also see how the selection of best practices described in Chapter 13 can be used to identify and implement best practices for students with disabilities.

INTRODUCTION: BEST AND PROMISING PRACTICES IN SPECIAL EDUCATION

Chapter 13 describes the steps practitioners follow to identify and implement evidence-based practices. Dupper maintains that these practices are evidence based, consistent with social work values, and meet clients' needs efficiently. Professional organizations such as the National Association of Social Workers (NASW) and the School Social Work Association of America (SSWAA), together with regional and state school social work associations, bring research and practice experience together to build a consensus about what constitutes best practice.

NASW developed the first professional standards for school social work in 1978. The standards were revised in 1992 and updated in 2002 (NASW, 2002). Position papers issued by NASW, SSWAA, and regional and state associations provide evidence of this consensus. Practitioners draw upon the latest research to select best practices.

The No Child Left Behind Act (NCLB) of 2002 and the reauthorization of the Individuals with Disabilities Education Act (IDEA) in 2004 raised the bar used to evaluate research used to design interventions and strategies for students with disabilities. School social workers in special education must ensure that they select evidence-based strategies with a high probability of achieving successful outcomes when they participate in designing a student's Individual Education Program (IEP).

IEP teams make high-stakes decisions about special education eligibility and planning. Special education is an entitlement. Federal and state laws and regulations protect the rights of students and their families in the evaluation and planning process. Only special education laws provide an entitlement. Other general education programs provide services and have requirements, but these are not entitlement programs.

Social workers in special education must understand special education laws and regulations to provide effective services to students with disabilities and their families. Knowledge is power. School social workers use their knowledge of the law to advocate for and to empower students and their families. However, understanding special education legislation also helps practitioners understand the evolution of social work practice in schools.

EQUAL EDUCATIONAL OPPORTUNITY FOR STUDENTS WITH DISABILITIES

It is remarkable to consider that it was not until 1975 that the United States took the national educational policy position that local schools have the obligation to educate children with disabilities. Prior to this time, public schools could legally refuse to educate children with disabilities. These children attained equal educational opportunity only after a long and difficult struggle, similar to the civil rights movement. The legal rights of students with disabilities can be considered in two important eras. The first era was the struggle to gain access to a free and appropriate public education. In the second era, a new struggle began, which has focused on the outcomes resulting from this access to public education.

The First Step: Federal Support

The first significant initiative in the development of a national legislative mandate for educating students with disabilities began in 1965 with the enactment of P.L. 9-10, the Elementary and Secondary Education Act of 1965 (ESEA). For the first time, limited federal grant money was available to states for special education instructional programs, including the hiring of special education teachers. When ESEA was amended in 1969, provisions for funding services such as social work, counseling, and school psychology were added to the law. As a result, new school social work positions were established to address the needs of students with disabilities.

The Courts Support the Struggle for Equal Access

Two landmark court cases at this time further affirmed the right of students with disabilities to an appropriate education. In 1971, the *Pennsylvania Association for Retarded Citizens (PARC) v. Commonwealth of Pennsylvania* decision established the responsibility of local schools to provide full access to a free public education and established an expectation for students to be educated in "the least restrictive setting." In 1972, in a class action suit the *Mills v. Board of Education of the District of Columbia* decision further affirmed the responsibility of local schools to provide education to students with disabilities. It prohibited schools facing funding problems from limiting programs to students with disabilities that were not limited in programs for students without disabilities. This decision granted students with disabilities full procedural safeguards in decisions regarding changes in their educational program. This meant that students and their families would have the right to legally challenge educational decisions.

Civil Rights Legislation for Individuals With Disabilities Impacts Schools

Although not education legislation, the enactment of P.L. 93-112, the Rehabilitation Act of 1973, specifically Section 504, provided significant support for the development of federal policy defining the obligation of local schools to educate students with disabilities. The provisions of Section 504 were very broad and continue to apply to all agencies that receive federal funds, including public schools. The purpose of Section 504 is to ensure that agencies receiving federal funds make their programs accessible to all individuals with disabilities. For schools, this includes students and adults, whether they are school employees or members of the public who wish to access school programs. The Act states,

> No qualified individual with disabilities shall, solely by reason of her or his disability, be excluded from the participation in, be denied the benefits of, or be subjected to discrimination under any program or activity receiving federal financial assistance. [29 U.S.C. § 794(a)]

Section 504 defines an individual with a disability as someone who has a mental or physical impairment that substantially limits one or more major life activities, including providing self care, performing manual tasks, walking, seeing, hearing, speaking, breathing, learning, and working. Examples of conditions that may be considered a disability include cancer, asthma, attention deficit disorder, arthritis, hearing impairment, and visual impairment.

Several provisions of Section 504 have particular relevance to schools. Students with disabilities must be provided "reasonable accommodations" that are needed to obtain a FAPE. The concept of "appropriate" is a key provision of this law. For a student with a disability, being in a general education classroom may not necessarily mean that he or she has access to a public education if the student's disability prohibits him or her from actually benefiting from the instruction. Students with disabilities may need accommodations such as Braille text, preferential seating, textbooks with large print, or access to computers for writing and other tasks. Some students with disabilities may also need "specialized instruction" in order to benefit from the general education program.

Section 504 requires that schools notify parents of all students that these protections are available. In addition, each school must establish a written policy stating that the school does not discriminate on the basis of disability. The policy must include a description of the process used to identify students who may have a disability and may be in need of reasonable accommodations in order to receive a FAPE. To ensure full implementation, schools are required to designate an employee, known as the 504 coordinator, who is responsible for coordinating activities needed to comply with Section 504 requirements and for facilitating the development of individual plans (commonly referred to as "504 plans") that outline the specific accommodations needed by students with disabilities.

FAPE Mandated for Students With Disabilities in 1975

In 1975, primarily as a result of persistent advocacy by parents of children with disabilities, Congress enacted P.L. 94-142, the Education of All Handicapped Children Act. Congress passed this legislation on behalf of the 1 million children with disabilities who had been excluded entirely from public education or had been provided only limited access to public school programs. P.L. 94-142 established unprecedented assurances for children with disabilities to be educated in public schools. It has proven to be the most significant piece of special education legislation in the history of U.S. public education. The purpose of the law was to ensure access to a free appropriate public education for all handicapped children that includes individually designed special education and related services, protections for the rights of handicapped children and their parents, assistance to states and localities for the education of all handicapped children, and assessment to ensure the effectiveness of these efforts to educate all handicapped children (Title 34 CFR § 300.1). The law defined handicapped children as "those children evaluated . . . as being mentally retarded, hard of hearing, deaf, speech impaired, visually handicapped, seriously emotionally disturbed, orthopedically impaired, other health impaired, deaf-blind, multi-handicapped, or as having specific learning disabilities" (Title 34 CFR § 300.7).

With initial federal funding, states were mandated to begin a "child find" process to identify children with these handicapping conditions who needed, and were entitled to, special education and related services.

KEY PROVISIONS OF P.L. 94-142, THE EDUCATION OF ALL HANDICAPPED CHILDREN ACT

Free and Appropriate Public Education

FAPE became the cornerstone provision of the Act. It was defined as the special education and related services that a student with a disability needs in order to benefit from public education. These special education and related services were to be

- provided at public expense, under public supervision and direction, and without cost to the student's family;
- in line with the standards of the state educational agency;
- applied to all public preschool, elementary, or secondary schools in the state; and
- provided in conformity with an IEP (Title 34 CFR § 300.13).

Least Restrictive Environment

Every handicapped child must be provided a free appropriate public education in the least restrictive environment. This provision was designed to ensure that handicapped children have the opportunity to be educated with children who are not handicapped. The provision stated, "That to the maximum extent appropriate, handicapped children, including children in public or private institutions or other care facilities, are educated with children who are not handicapped" [Title 34 CFR § 300.550(b)(1)]. An even stronger expectation is evident in the following regulation:

That special classes, separate schooling or other removal of handicapped children from the regular educational environment occurs only when the nature or severity of the handicap is such that education in regular classes with the use of supplementary aids and services cannot be achieved satisfactorily. [Title 34 CFR § 300.550(b) (2)]

Thus, the least restrictive environment requirement starts with the assumption that handicapped children will be educated in general education classrooms with nonhandicapped peers except in cases in which this may not be appropriate or when supplementary aids and services cannot be satisfactorily provided in general education classes.

Individualized Education Program

The IEP documents decisions made by the IEP team. IEP teams must include the child's parents or guardians, a general education teacher, a special education teacher or other special education service provider, an individual who can interpret evaluation results, and a school representative who is qualified to provide or supervise special education and is knowledgeable about and can commit the school's resources that may be needed. Others, at the family's invitation or with their permission, may also participate. The document or IEP developed by this team is considered to be a contract between parents and the school that specifies what services will be provided to the child in order for the child to receive FAPE.

Parent Participation in Decision Making

A host of procedural safeguards designed to ensure the participation of parents in the development of appropriate educational programs were included in the law. Parents were defined as required members of the IEP team. Schools were required to invite parents to meetings and to provide them with adequate notice of actions the school proposed to take in implementing the student's special education program. Parents were ensured access to due process procedures, including the right to request a hearing to challenge educational decisions when disagreements with their child's school could not be resolved in a less formal manner.

The Right to Special Education and Related Services

Handicapped children were ensured access to "specially designed instruction, at no cost to the parent, to meet the unique needs of a handicapped child, including classroom instruction, instruction in physical education, home instruction, and instruction in hospitals and institutions" [Title 34 CFR § 300.26(a)]. Congress clearly intended handicapped children to receive an appropriate individualized education that could be provided in a variety of settings.

Handicapped children were also guaranteed the provision of related services, such as "transportation and such developmental, corrective, and other supportive services as are required to assist a handicapped child to benefit from special education" (Title 34 CFR § 300.24). Congress recognized that many handicapped children need a variety of specialized supports to ensure that they can participate in, and benefit from, instruction. Related services are of particular interest for school social workers because they represent services they may provide. For example, students with emotional disturbance might exhibit behavior that is so disruptive that they cannot consistently attend class or engage in specially designed instruction when they are present. These students might need intensive social and emotional support provided by direct counseling or consultation with the teacher to develop behavioral interventions.

The Rights of Young Children to Special Education and Early Intervention

When Congress enacted P.L. 99-457, the Education of the Handicapped Amendments of 1986, it extended the mandate of P.L. 94-142, Part B, to children from ages 3 to 21 (the original provisions required states to serve handicapped children from ages 5 to 21), and it added a new Part H that provided a discretionary grant to serve children from birth to age 3. Key provisions of Part H were important to social work practice. It required an Individualized Family Service Plan (IFSP) to be developed for children who were determined eligible for services. A service coordinator (case manager) was required for each eligible child and his or her family to coordinate evaluations and services included in the IFSP. Social work services were specifically identified as an early intervention service.

Rights of Students With Disabilities Extended in a New IDEA

In 1990, Congress enacted P.L. 101-476, the Individuals with Disabilities Act. For the first time, social work services were referenced in the Act (not just in the regulations). Also, Congress adopted "people first language," changing the term "handicapped children" to "children with disabilities" throughout the Act and its regulations. This new IDEA established an emphasis on teaching children with disabilities in the general curriculum of the school (i.e., the curriculum provided to all students). Separate special education curricula had been criticized for lowering expectations for students with disabilities.

Special Education Laws and Regulations Call for and Define Social Work Services

Although school social work was not specifically identified as a related service in P.L. 94-142, NASW advocated successfully for a definition of "social work services in schools" to be included in the implementing regulations. This was important because it legitimized the social work role in ensuring that handicapped children received an appropriate public education, and it authorized the use of federal special education funding for social work services in schools as a related service.

The implementing regulations defined social work services in schools as

- preparing a social or developmental history on a handicapped child;
- group and individual counseling with the child and family;
- working with those problems in a child's living situation (home, school, and community) that affect the child's adjustment in school; and
- mobilizing school and community resources to enable the child to receive maximum benefit from his or her educational program. [Title 34 CFR § 300.24(b) (13)]

Three essential social work functions are evident in this definition—assessment, intervention, and case management. The definition did not limit social workers to these three functions. Rather, these functions were intended to illustrate the nature and type of services that could be provided to ensure the handicapped child is able to benefit from special education.

Social work services appeared in the legislation that expanded access to young children in early intervention services. The implementing regulations for this law expanded the specifically mentioned activities beyond those mentioned in the regulations for P.L. 94-142. Table 16.1 summarizes the social work functions mentioned in special education regulations and laws.

SPECIAL EDUCATION MANDATES IMPACT SCHOOL SOCIAL WORK PRACTICE

Schools hired more social workers in response to the passage of the ESEA of 1965 and the 1969 amendments. However, the numbers of school social workers being hired mushroomed in 1975 when social work was specifically mentioned in the implementing regulations of the Education of All Handicapped Children Act (P.L. 94-142). These legislative mandates increased the number of social workers hired by schools, and they changed the types of services social workers delivered (Alderson, 1977).

Since the days when charity organization societies provided casework and settlement houses led the demand for social reform, there has been tension between social workers who favor services to individuals to enhance their functioning and those who advocate social action to change society. In schools, the pendulum between individual and environmental change has swung back and forth in response to the legislation that funds services.

Social workers hired after the passage of ESEA tended to emphasize both school and student change. This approach was consistent with the ecological approach described in Chapter 3. Ecology is the study of relationships among organisms and their environment. By drawing upon the ecological perspective, social workers were able to resolve the individual versus environmental change

Table 16.1 | Social Work Services Described in Federal Laws and Regulations

Social Work Service	Function	Law/Regulation
Preparing a social or developmental history	Assessment	P.L. 94-142 and regulations
Making home visits to evaluate a child's living conditions and patterns of parent-child interaction	Assessment	P.L. 99-457 and regulations
Preparing a psychosocial developmental assessment of the child within the context of the family	Assessment	P.L. 99-457 and regulations
Group and individual counseling with the child and family	Intervention	P.L. 94-142 and regulations
Providing individual and family-group counseling with parents and other family members, and appropriate social skill-building activities with the child and parents	Intervention	P.L. 99-457 and regulations
Working with those problems in a child's living situation (home, school, and community) that affect the child's adjustment in school	Intervention	P.L. 94-142 and regulations
Working with those problems in a child's and family's living situation (home, community, and any center where early intervention services are provided) that affect the child's maximum utilization of early intervention services	Intervention	P.L. 99-457 and regulations
Assisting in developing positive behavioral intervention strategies	Intervention	P.L. 105-17 and regulations
Mobilizing school and community resources to enable the child to receive maximum benefit from his or her educational programs	Intervention	P.L. 105-17 and regulations
Identifying, mobilizing, and coordinating community resources and services to enable the child and family to receive maximum benefit from early intervention services	Case management/ service coordination	P.L. 94-142 and regulations

debate by focusing practitioners on the interaction between the two. According to Germain (1982), the defining characteristic of social work practice is that it focuses on the interface between an individual's coping skills and the demands of his or her environment. Social workers address this interaction between the individual and his or her environment by seeking a better match between the two. This may mean increasing the coping skills of the individual or making changes in the demands of the environment. An ecological approach encourages school social workers to help students and their families improve their coping skills while also targeting changes in schools and communities to provide an environment that better meets student needs. This approach builds on individual or family strengths and pays less attention to their deficits.

Special education legislation initially led social workers in the opposite direction. The initial interpretation of the legal requirements led to an "illness orientation" with school professionals "diagnosing" disabilities and proposing treatment plans. School social workers became members of multidisciplinary teams charged with the responsibility for "child find"—the identification process that determined which students met the criteria for special education entitlement. This emphasis on "gatekeeping" encouraged social workers to focus on the identification and remediation of individual deficits. As early as 1978, researchers concluded that special education legislation had resulted in a new role for social workers in schools. Timberlake, Sabatino, and Hooper (1982) stated,

> The tasks of the school social worker . . . appear to be moving in the direction of diagnosing handicapping conditions, giving the system feedback about the data collected in diagnosis, and collaborating with community agencies to provide services for these children when the school system is unable to provide for their needs. (p. 71)

For many years, special education policy and legislation moved school practitioners away from the ecological and strengths-based models preferred by the social work profession. At the same time, this legislation and policy increased the numbers of social workers in schools. This increase in numbers led to an increase in the amount of collaboration between social workers and their colleagues in education. Social workers used this opportunity to influence schools more broadly. They helped schools increase parent involvement, create a caring school environment, and develop community partnerships. Research has shown these practices to be effective in increasing achievement for students (Barr & Parrett, 2003).

SCHOOL SOCIAL WORKER ASSESSMENTS IN SPECIAL EDUCATION

Students must be evaluated in order to determine if they are entitled to special education services and these evaluations filled most of the social workers' time. Initially, prevailing practices utilized a "battery approach" in which a predetermined set of assessment procedures were focused primarily on entitlement decision making. The purpose of administering an assessment battery is "to examine and describe the characteristics of the student and compare them to preestablished criteria for specific disability categories" (Clark, 2002, p. 4). In other words, in a system concerned with child find, the primary purpose of assessment was to identify which children met the established eligibility criteria and should therefore receive services.

The federal regulations initially described the social history as one of a social worker's functions. As a result, the social history became the cornerstone of a social worker's contribution to the special education evaluation. However, this social history was not the same as the history conducted in mental health or social service settings. School social workers conducted "developmental" or "education" social histories that gathered information needed to determine whether the student was eligible for special education services.

Social workers interviewed the student and the student's family to collect information for the education social history. They usually gathered data that either supported or refuted the eligibility criteria for a particular disability. For example, the criteria for mental retardation include the presence of developmental delays across all domains. Therefore, if a child's adaptive behavior skills at home and in the community are within normal limits, the child does not meet this disability criterion for mental retardation.

The developmental delays exhibited by a child with mental retardation must have been evident throughout the child's development. These delays must not be related to a lack of opportunity to learn that could be the result of social or economic conditions or cultural differences. Judging the impact of environmental conditions and cultural factors became an important part of the social worker's contribution in a special education evaluation.

CULTURAL AND LINGUISTIC DIFFERENCES AND DISABILITY

Culturally competent professional practices are critical for social workers conducting special education evaluations. Economic, social, and cultural variables can result in students being inappropriately placed in special education. **Disproportionality** refers to the over- or underrepresentation of students from diverse racial or linguistic groups in special education. Reschly (1996) called the disproportionate representation of minority students in special education programs the "quintessential special education dilemma."

For more than three decades, disproportionality for diverse racial, ethnic, and linguistic groups has been a concern in special education (Jefferson-Jenkins, 2003; Reschly, 1996). Experts identify multiple causes. It is rooted in racial, ethnic, and linguistic differences, school factors such as teacher effectiveness, biased perceptions about students from diverse groups, inadequate and inappropriate referral and evaluation procedures, and biased tests (Jefferson-Jenkins, 2003).

Disproportionate representation of minority students in special education may also be related to the unequal distribution of educational resources in schools and to the unequal levels of achievement among subgroups of students that it causes. Scores on the National Assessment of Educational Progress from 1992 to 1998 documented that by the end of 4th grade African American, Latino, and students from lower socioeconomic backgrounds were 2 years behind their peers. By 8th grade, the gap had grown to 3 years, and by 12th grade the gap had widened to 4 years (Haycock, Jerald, & Huang, 2001).

Educators believe that social workers have expertise and knowledge about the impact of social, cultural, and environmental factors on children's development and learning. Therefore, social workers play an important role in assessing these factors when students are being considered for special education. Social workers must understand normal child development and the impact of health, environmental, and cultural variables on a child's development and learning. School social workers need strong communication skills to help educators to recognize the impact of those variables on individual student performance. This is sometimes difficult when influential educators within a building are determined to see a child removed from the regular program.

Of course, conducting a multidisciplinary assessment battery is costly. Such assessments are rarely cost-efficient because many of the students who are referred do not qualify for services. Even before the 1997 reauthorization of IDEA changed the focus of special education evaluations, schools began to establish "pre-referral" processes to ensure that students referred for evaluation had first received appropriate interventions and accommodations to address problems in the general education class. Social workers such as Mr. Hart, described in the overview of this chapter, played an important role in developing interventions for students that often resulted in resolving student problems in general education and preventing the students from needing special education.

Social Work Assessment Activities Engage Families

Early on, practitioners realized that social work evaluations were doing more than generating data for decision making. The family interview afforded the social worker a unique opportunity to use his or her professional skills to engage the family in a relationship. As a result, the social worker was able to serve as a liaison or a mediator between the school and the family. The social worker synthesized data about the child for the school and communicated information from the school in a way that enhanced family support for school policies and decisions. Social workers supported and empowered families to ensure that family information about a child's strengths and special needs was included in the school's decision-making process. The social history became a vehicle for involving families as partners with school staff in developing appropriate education plans (Henry, DeChristopher, Dowling, & Lapham, 1981).

An informal study by practitioners in Hawaii supported this claim (Sheridan, 1984). Assessments that included a social history interview with the family produced more significant data for school teams than social work assessments based on other data only. Follow-up interviews with families who participated in an interview with the school social worker indicated that this experience enhanced their understanding of their child's problems at school more than any other information they received from the child's school before. Several respondents indicated that the interview caused them to view the school more positively than they had before. These outcomes were so positive that the practitioners who conducted the study decided to continue to require the social history in social work special education evaluations. As new special education legislation changed the focus of special education assessments, the importance of the connection between social workers and families remained strong. Recent research in education confirms what social workers always knew: The most potent force in improving student achievement in education is the involvement and participation of the family (Fan & Chen, 2001; Henderson & Mapp, 2002).

THE NEW ERA OF RESULTS

Special education entered a new era with the enactment of P.L. 105-17, the Individuals with Disabilities Education Act of 1997, commonly referred to as IDEA '97. Since the enactment of P.L. 94-142 in 1975, the primary emphasis of federal policy had been on ensuring that students with disabilities were identified and provided access to a free appropriate public education (i.e., child find). Viewing the mission of child find as essentially having been successfully accomplished, Congress now turned its policy attention to the matter of outcomes or results. IDEA '97 renewed the emphasis on children with disabilities participating in the general curriculum of the school and added emphasis on the need to ensure that these children were actually progressing in this curriculum. Provisions were added requiring students with disabilities to participate in general assessments of the achievement levels and progress of all students. They are also required to report the progress of students with disabilities to parents.

Of interest to school social workers was the addition of "parent counseling and training" to the list of related services, which was defined as "assisting parents in understanding the special needs of their child, and helping parents to acquire the necessary skills that will allow them to support the implementation of their child's IEP or IFSP" [Title 34 CFR § 300.24(b) (7)]. Also, the new regulations focused on the behavioral needs of students with disabilities in the development, review, and revision of their IEPs. This provision states that "the IEP team also shall in the case of a child whose behavior impedes his or her learning or that of others, consider if appropriate, strategies, including positive behavioral interventions strategies, and supports to address that behavior" [34 CFR § 300.346(a) (2) (I)].

Students With Disabilities and School Discipline Policies

Of special interest to school social workers were the new provisions in IDEA '97 related to disciplining students with disabilities who exhibit behavior that violates school rules and codes of conduct. In response to concerns about the exclusion of students with disabilities from school for behavioral reasons, and with the interest of balancing the imperative to provide students with disabilities a free appropriate public education (with the interest in ensuring safe school environments for adults and students), Congress included a complex set of procedures to be followed when school personnel disciplined students with disabilities. Included in these procedures were requirements for conducting functional behavioral assessments and implementation of behavioral intervention plans when schools propose to discipline students with disabilities by removing them from school for significant amounts of time.

In recognition of the knowledge and skills that social workers bring to bear on addressing the behavioral needs of students with disabilities, particularly in the school disciplinary process, the statement "assisting in developing positive behavioral intervention strategies" was added to the definition of social work in schools as a related service in IDEA '97 [34 CFR § 300.24 (b) (13) (v)].

Implications for Best Practices in Assessment and Intervention

The shift from process to outcomes has required changes in the assessment and intervention practices of school social workers. The primary purpose of school social work assessment has changed from entitlement decision making to intervention planning and problem solving. Clark (2002) suggested that this requires a shift from an "assessment battery" or "student eligibility" approach to a "functional approach" to assessment and intervention. Clark identified a number of problems with assessment battery approaches:

> First, assessments that focus on characteristics of the student often fail to examine variables in the environment that may be exacerbating or even causing and maintaining problem behavior. Second, since these data are mostly descriptive, there is usually little if any information generated that is helpful in designing interventions. Third, while these assessment data may establish the existence of a disability they do not adequately establish whether the student needs special education, a requirement of federal law. Fourth, a battery approach is an inefficient and sometimes inappropriate process for using precious professional resources. Too much time is spent administering assessment instruments that could be spent in designing, implementing, and testing the effectiveness of interventions. Also, because assessments are not individually tailored and based on the nature of the presenting problem, professionals are often involved who may not need to be. Fifth, because the battery approach predetermines the assessments that will be conducted and which professionals will conduct them, professional judgment and decision making are not duly respected. Finally, an assessment battery approach delays significantly the helping efforts of professionals. Intervention efforts must wait until eligibility has been determined. (p. 4)

A functional approach to assessment examines the reasons for and effects of behaviors, which is helpful in the IEP process (Clark, 1998). IDEA '97 federal regulations contained strong policy support for shifting to functional approaches to assessment and intervention. For example, in the requirements addressing evaluation procedures for determining eligibility, the regulations required that "a variety of assessment tools and strategies are used to gather relevant functional and developmental information about the child" [Title 34 CFR § 300.532(b)]. The regulations also required that "tests and other evaluation materials include those tailored to assess specific areas of educational need" [Title 34 CFR § 300.532(d)] and that "the public agency uses assessment tools and strategies that provide relevant information that directly assists persons in determining the educational needs of the child" [Title 34 CFR § 300.532(j)].

These requirements state clearly the need for assessment approaches to be individually tailored, functional in nature in order to generate information that is useful in designing and implementing effective interventions, and directed at examining the particular needs of each child.

In July 2002, a report titled *A New Era: Revitalizing Special Education for Children and Their Families* was issued by the President's Commission on Excellence in Special Education. The report cited significant concern regarding practices used in the assessment and identification of students with disabilities, charging that the system waits for children to fail before intervening rather than using a more preventative approach. A major recommendation of the commission report proposed the use of "response to intervention," a functional problem-solving approach to assessment and intervention development in which interventions are developed early in response to concerns about student performance. Progress monitoring data are then used to determine the effectiveness of interventions and to make decisions regarding which students need special education services.

Many of the recommendations of the commission were included in the most recent reauthorization of the IDEA when the Individuals with Disabilities Education Improvement Act (IDEA-IA) was signed into law on December 3, 2004. IDEA-IA 2004 included provisions for greater alignment with NCLB; changes in procedures for initial evaluations and reevaluations; changes in discipline procedures for students with disabilities; changes in procedures and content for IEPs; and increased requirements for states to collect data and monitor the disproportionate representation of students from culturally, ethnically, racially, and linguistically diverse backgrounds in special education. Perhaps most significantly was the inclusion of response to intervention as an approach that may be used in determining special education eligibility [§ 614 (a) (6) (B)]. To ensure that resources can be used in a manner to support these practices, the Act includes a provision to allow states to use up to 15% of their annual federal IDEA grant for "early intervening services" [§ 613 (f)].

The primary purpose of assessment and intervention practices in a system now concerned with results is problem solving. In order to address this purpose, school social work assessment and intervention practices must now take a functional approach to assessment. Although child find is a continuing obligation of schools and cannot be neglected, assessment and intervention practices must now place greater emphasis on the efficient collection of assessment data that lead to the development and implementation of effective interventions and on the use of professional judgments and data-based decision making (Clark, 1998). Decisions about whether students with disabilities need special education must now rely heavily on these functional assessment data; on the impact of cultural, racial, ethnic, and linguistic diversity; and on data collected about the effectiveness of interventions.

FUNCTIONAL BEHAVIORAL ASSESSMENTS AND BEHAVIOR INTERVENTION PLANS

Research in education and the behavioral sciences has demonstrated enhanced effectiveness for behavior intervention plans that are based on data from a functional behavioral assessment (FBA). Depending on the hypotheses resulting from the FBA, the intervention plan might include making changes in the environment to reduce the efficiency of the inappropriate behavior, teaching alternative forms of appropriate behavior that achieve the same outcome or goal as the inappropriate behavior, or reinforcing appropriate behavior that interferes with the occurrence of the inappropriate behavior (Flannery, O'Neill, & Horner, 1995). School social workers initially were reluctant to adopt a model that came from behavioral theory and practice. However, they quickly began to see similarities between this approach and traditional social work practice. The functional assessments and behavior intervention plans developed by social workers were distinguished by their inclusion of perspectives and strategies from ecological and strengths-based social work practice.

Consistent with new research and shifts in educational policy, NASW's 2002 *Standards for School Social Work Services* promote "a functional approach to assessment" using an "ecological perspective" (Standard 12). Social workers brought this ecological perspective (see Chapter 3) and their set of professional skills to the process of conducting functional assessments and developing intervention plans for students in general and special education. School social workers continue to interview students and their families, but the social history is no longer the cornerstone of a social worker's special education assessment (see Raines, 2002; Clark, 1998). Now social workers use multiple strategies to collect data from multiple sources in order to develop effective interventions for students that can also be used to support entitlement decision making when appropriate.

Discussion of Case Example

During the home visit with Miss Good, Jason's mother, Wilma Smith, nervously admitted that she was not completely honest with the school when she enrolled Jason in August. She did not tell the school that he had been treated by a psychiatrist and was taking psychiatric medications before they moved to Happy Creek. She hoped that he would not need these medications in his new school.

Mrs. Smith expected Miss Good to be upset and she was surprised when she did not criticize or blame her for not telling the school about Jason's mental illness. Instead, Miss Good calmly continued to ask questions about how the

Case | **Case Example**

Jason, a new fourth-grade student at Happy Creek Elementary School, was referred to the building child study team by his teacher. She reported that he hit and kicked other students, refused to follow directions, and destroyed assignments in anger. He was already entitled to special education and was receiving 40 minutes of specially designed instruction in a special education classroom.

Miss Good, the social worker on the building child study team, began to gather data in order to help the school develop a program to meet Jason's needs in the least restrictive setting.

She reviewed his school record and discovered that Jason had been in a special education class for most of the day in his previous school. At the end of third grade, the IEP team changed his program to increase the time he spent in the general education classroom because he was doing very well. Members of that team had no idea that Jason would be in a completely different school environment when the new program began.

During the home visit, Miss Good established a relationship with Jason's mother. Her interview enabled her to understand the context surrounding Jason's angry behavior at school. She also became aware of his strengths.

Despite mental illness and an abusive home situation, he had a good year in third grade. Culture is an environmental variable that complicates and challenges the coping and adaptive skills of individuals (see Chapter 3). Jason developed the skills needed to succeed in Megalopolis. He had learned to act tough in order to avoid fights on the rough and tumble playground of that school. His skills in math were at grade level, and they were almost at grade level in reading.

Unfortunately, the behaviors that enabled Jason to succeed in Megalopolis were not adaptive in a small rural school. Acting tough frightened his peers in Happy Creek. His academic skills were above average in his Megalopolis classroom, but in Happy Creek most students were at least at grade level.

When Miss Good returned to school, she shared only the information about Jason that was needed for the school staff to address Jason's needs. The school nurse helped Mrs. Smith get an emergency appointment for Jason with the psychiatrist at the local mental health center. Jason's behavior improved with the return to medication, but he continued to have incidents of aggressive and defiant behavior on the playground, in the halls, and in his general education classroom.

Miss Good was motivated to implement evidenced-based practices (see Chapter 13). She read professional journals in social work and special education and attended workshops offered by her employer and by professional organizations. She understood the most recent special education legislation. She knew that the U.S. Congress included an empirically validated approach to managing problem behavior in IDEA '97 in order to change practice in the field (Telzrow & Tankersley, 2000). IDEA '97 required practitioners to conduct a FBA when a student with a disability faced a disciplinary action that could result in a change of program. Jason's behavior was causing the school to consider removing him from the regular class completely. Miss Good knew that a behavior plan based on a FBA was more likely to be effective than a plan that was developed without one.

school could help him. Mrs. Smith began to relax and trust Miss Good to help her son succeed in school.

Because of the trust that had been established, Mrs. Smith tearfully told Miss Good that she did not know who Jason's biological father was. She lied to her son, saying that her live-in boyfriend was his real father. Unfortunately, this boyfriend was abusive. Last summer, the 10-year relationship came to an end because she met a kind, older man from Happy Creek. He invited her and her sons to live with him. Since the move, Jason waited for a phone call from his "father" in Megalopolis, but she knew that this call would never come.

Social workers bring their unique perspective to the task of conducting a FBA (Clark, 1998). Behavior is assessed ecologically by evaluating a student's interaction with his or her environment across school settings, the home, and the community. School social workers consider a broad range of possible functions or goals of student behavior (Raines, 2002).

Using the Preliminary Functional Assessment Survey/Teacher Version (O'Neill, Horner, Albin, Storey, & Sprague, 1990), Miss Good interviewed Jason's teachers. His teachers identified aggressive behavior and failure to follow teacher directions as the most important problem behaviors. However, these behaviors were not occurring evenly across school settings.

His teachers kept track of his behavior and reported that he averaged 1.4 incidents of inappropriate behavior per hour during a 5-day period. Most of these incidents happened during reading and language arts or during unstructured times such as recess. Jason's behavior was appropriate during math and when he was working alone with an adult. These data became the baseline from which future interventions could be measured.

Miss Good adapted the questions on the Preliminary Functional Assessment Survey/Teacher Version to apply to behavior outside of school. She wanted information about behavior at home to engage his mother's support for the intervention and perhaps her willingness to implement the same strategies at home. She knew that consistent expectations and outcomes across settings increased the chances that the new behaviors would become permanent.

Jason behaved appropriately when he was alone with his mother doing something he liked, such as going to garage sales. However, if she asked him to do homework or chores, or if she was busy interacting with his brother, Jason began to behave inappropriately. Jason's problem behaviors had increased since their move to Happy Creek. He used to like going to school, she said, but now he came home each day looking sad and angry.

Miss Good used the Student-Assisted Functional Assessment Interview (Kerns, Dunlap, Clarke, & Childs, 1994) with Jason. Jason described the work assigned by his teachers as "too easy." He denied needing help from his teachers because he already knew how to do his work. He said that he worked better alone because his classmates "messed with him." Jason said that he could beat up all the kids at his old school, and he would beat the kids up here too if they kept messing with him.

Jason's A-B-C Chart

A = Antecedent	B = Behavior	C = Consequences or Outcome
The teacher asks Jason to read silently and do a worksheet.	Jason gets angry, tears up his paper, slams his desk, and kicks a peer.	Jason is sent out of the classroom. Jason avoids the task. (Escape)
The teacher asks Jason to do a math time test.	Jason is the first in the class to finish the test.	The teacher and peers notice and praise Jason. (Attention)
Jason goes to garage sales alone with his mother.	Jason is cooperative and pleasant.	His mother gives him money to spend and praises him. (Attention)
Mrs. Smith helps his brother with homework while Jason watches television.	Jason acts irritable, making noises and turning up the sound on the television.	Jason's mother stops working with his brother and tries to get Jason to turn down the television. (Attention)
Jason and Miss Good are talking together.	Jason tells Miss Good fantastic stories about how strong he is.	Jason gets Miss Good's attention. (Attention–grandiosity)

Miss Good, together with his mother and the members of the child study team, used an A-B-C chart to summarize the data (Raines, 2002).

Their hypothesis was that the function of Jason's behavior was to gain positive attention or to avoid a frustrating task that might detract from his self-esteem. Raines (2002) suggests that self-esteem is a significant motivator for students with a fragile sense of self. These students may be threatened by tasks that seem either too easy or too difficult and may avoid them in order to preserve their self-esteem. This hypothesis seemed to fit the data from Jason's FBA.

The team used the functional assessment data and a planning template developed by Lohrmann-O'Rourke, Knoster, and Llewellyn (1999) to develop a behavior intervention plan for Jason. The team brainstormed interventions in each of the following five categories:

Jason's Behavior Intervention Plan

Antecedent/setting event (Environmental changes that make the problem behavior less likely)

- Jason will be in the special education room during times when problem behaviors are most likely.

Alternative skills (teaching new behaviors to replace the inappropriate ones)

- Jason will learn appropriate ways to enter a classroom, to greet others, to ask for help, and to ask to join others.
- Jason will learn to identify inappropriate behaviors.

Instructional consequence (ways to cue and reinforce appropriate behavior)

- The regular and special class teachers will respond to positive behavior used to gain attention immediately.
- Jason will be able to select a reward when his behavior meets a specific goal for the day.

Reduction procedure (logical and natural consequences to reduce the problem behaviors)

- When Jason is sent out of the regular class he will go to his special class, where he will be given time to calm down and to develop a plan to return.
- When Jason returns to his regular class he will complete the task he was doing when he was asked to leave.

Long-term plan (strategies to improve the quality of life in the long term for the client)

- Jason will identify nonverbal expressions of basic emotions in himself and others.
- Jason will recognize his own internal emotional states and use coping skills to manage them.

Jason's special education teacher would teach Jason appropriate ways to get attention from adults and peers in his special education class. To get Jason to accept responsibility for his behavior, Miss Good designed a special rating chart for Jason and his teacher. After each period of the day, they would each rate Jason's behavior independently. A rating of 1 indicated that Jason was sent out of the class, a rating of 2 indicated the need for many reminders to behave appropriately, a rating of 3 indicated only a few reminders were needed, and a rating of 4 indicated good behavior without adult reminders. At the end of the day, Jason and his teacher compared their ratings. Jason won rewards based on the amount of agreement between his rating and that of his teacher. The purpose was not to reward good behaviors but to create a shared understanding of what was, and what was not, appropriate behavior.

This plan proved to be very effective. Within a few weeks, Jason and his teacher were almost always in agreement in their ratings. The teacher began to ask Jason what a 4 (the highest rating) would look like on the bus during a field trip or what he could do to increase the likelihood of a 4 during recess. Therefore, in addition to agreeing with his teacher about the ratings, the ratings became higher.

Behavior Intervention Plans May Include Direct Social Work Services to Students

One of the needs identified in the functional assessment was to increase Jason's ability to manage his emotions. Using the process for implementing best practices described in Chapter 1, Miss Good formulated a researchable question: What intervention would help Jason manage his emotions? Using EBSCO-Host, she reviewed the literature on emotional development. In a review of scientific

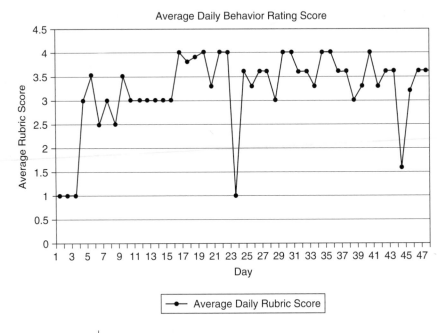

Figure 16.1 | Jason's Average Daily Behavior Rating Score

data from studies using new brain imaging technologies (Goleman, 1995), she learned about how emotional intelligence is developed. She realized that Jason would only be able to manage his emotions when he became aware of his own feelings and could recognize the feelings of others. Nowicki and Duke (1992) suggested using pictures of faces to teach students to recognize nonverbal cues.

Jason liked competition, so Miss Good engaged him in a matching game using card-sized pictures of human faces. She put the pictures down in sets of two and asked Jason to choose the pairs of pictures that matched. She encouraged him to look at the parts of each face to determine if they looked the same or different. When Jason became skilled at matching the pictures, they began to connect each set of expressions with the feeling it represented. One day, Miss Good took a photo of Jason in the hall. When she asked him to match his picture to one of the pictures in the game, he accurately placed it by a face that looked "scared." For the first time, Jason began to talk about the things that scared him at school.

Jason was a child with a serious mental illness who needed special education services to succeed in school. The first three scores represent the baseline when Jason was sent out of the classroom every day. During the next 47 days, Jason frequently achieved scores of 3 or 4. However, despite these gains, he still had two very bad days.

Case | Case Example

Terry Hart whistled as he washed his late model sedan. A school social work salary rarely provides the resources for fancy cars, he thought. Putting two sons through college does not help either! An unfamiliar car pulled into the driveway beside him. Terry looked up into the bright blue eyes of the young man at the wheel.

"You don't remember me do you Mr. Hart?" he asked with a smile. Terry thought he saw something familiar in those blue eyes. "Timmy Nelson, you are Timmy Nelson!" "I go by Tim Nelson now" the young man said. "I saw you there and I just wanted to stop to say thanks." "Thanks?" "You may not realize it, but you made a difference for me. I'm going to be a dad myself in a month or so and I want to be a good one. I remember how hard it was for me when my dad took off. But then you came along. You believed in me and I guess it made me believe in myself." "Thanks," Terry said, his voice getting a little husky, "Congratulations on that new baby. I know you will be a good dad!"

SUMMARY

The case examples used in this chapter are based on real cases with altered names and locations to ensure confidentiality. School social workers in special education serve many students like Timmy and Jason. Sometimes these students do come back, like Timmy did, to thank the social worker who made a difference in their lives.

With the right kind of help, many of the children and youth who face barriers to learning can overcome those barriers without special education, as Timmy did. Other students, such as Jason, need special instruction and related services to become successful learners. Although the best practices in assessment and intervention presented in this chapter have particular applications in special education, these practices can and should be applied to all students.

School Social Work Companion Website

Please be sure to check out our companion website at www.thomsonedu.com/social_work/bye, where you will find relevant materials for each chapter, including flashcards, online practice quizzes, and PowerPoint slides.

References

Alderson, J. (1977). A perspective on the many faces of school social work. *School Social Work Journal, 2*(1), 15–25.

Barr, R., & Parrett, W. (2003). *Saving our students saving our schools: 50 proven strategies for revitalizing at-risk students and low performing schools.* Glenview, IL: Skylight Professional Development.

Clark, J. (1998). *Functional behavioral assessment and behavioral intervention plan: Implementing the student discipline provisions of idea '97—A technical assistance guide for school social workers.* Northlake, IL/Washington, DC: School Social Work Association of America/National Association of Social Workers School Social Work Section.

Clark, J. (2002). School social work assessment: Battery versus functional approaches. *Section Connection, 8*(1), 4–5.

Fan, X., & Chen, M. (2001). Parental involvement and students' academic achievement: A meta-analysis. *Educational Psychology Review, 13,* 1–22.

Flannery, K., O'Neill, R., & Horner, R. (1995). Including predictability in functional assessment and individual program development. *Education and Treatment of Children, 18,* 499–509.

Germain, C. (1982). An ecological perspective on social work in the schools. In R. Constable & J. Flynn (Eds.), *School social work: Practice and research perspectives* (pp. 25–35). Homewood, IL: Dorsey.

Goleman, D. (1995). *Emotional intelligence: Why it can matter more than IQ.* New York: Bantam.

Haycock, K., Jerald, C., & Huang, S. (2001). Closing the gap: Done in a decade. *Thinking K-16, The Education Trust, 5*(2), 3–20.

Henderson, A. T., & Mapp, K. (2002). *A new wave of evidence: The impact of school, family and community connections on student achievement.* Austin, TX: National Center for Family and Community Connections with Schools, Southwest Educational Development Laboratory.

Henry, D., DeChristopher, J., Dowling, P., & Lapham, E. (1981, April). Using the social history to assess handicapping conditions. *Social Work in Education, 3*(3), 7–19.

Jefferson-Jenkins, C. (2003, October). *Disporportionality: What is it? And why do we care?* Presentation at the National Center for Culturally Responsive Educational Systems Forum on Disproportionality, Denver, CO.

Kerns, L., Dunlap, G., Clarke, S., & Childs, K. (1994). Student-assisted functional assessment interview. *Diagnostique, 19*(2–3), 29–40.

Lohrmann-O'Rourke, S., Knoster, T., & Llewellyn, G. (1999). Screening for understanding: An initial line of inquiry for school-based settings. *Journal of Positive Behavior Interventions, 1*(1), 35–42.

Mills v. Board of Education of the District of Columbia, 458G. Supp. 866(DDC, 1972).

National Association of Social Workers. (2002). *NASW standards for school social work services.* Washington, DC: Author.

Nowicki, S., & Duke, M. (1992). *Helping the child who doesn't fit in.* Atlanta, GA: Peachtree.

O'Neill, R., Horner, R., Albin, R., Storey, K., & Sprague, J. (1990). *Functional analysis of problem behavior: A practical assessment guide.* Sycamore, IL: Sycamore.

Pennsylvania Association of Retarded Children (PARC) v. Commonwealth of Pennsylvania, 334 F. Supp. 1257 (E.D. Pa. 1971).

President's Commission on Excellence in Special Education. (2002). *A new era: Revitalizing special education for children and their families.* Washington, DC: U.S. Department of Education, Office of Special Education and Rehabilitative Services.

Raines, J. (2002). Brainstorming hypotheses for functional behavioral assessment: The link to effective behavioral intervention plans. *School Social Work Journal, 26*(2), 430–445.

Reschly, D. (1996). *Disproportionate minority representation in general and special education programs: Patterns, issues and alternatives.* Des Moines: Iowa Department of Education and the Mountain Plains Regional Resource Center.

Sheridan, M. (1984). Evaluating students' special education needs. *Social Work in Education, 6*(2), 93–105.

Telzrow, C., & Tankersley, M. (Eds.). (2000). *IDEA amendments of 1997: Practice guidelines for school-based teams.* Bethesda, MD: National Association of School Psychologists.

Timberlake, E., Sabatino, C., & Hooper, S. (1982). School social work practice and P.L. 94-142. In R. Constable & J. Flynn (Eds.), *School social work: Practice and research perspectives* (pp. 49–72). Homewood, IL: Dorsey.

School Social Work: Emerging Trends and Looking Ahead to the Future

17 CHAPTER | Technology and School Social Work

BRENDA COBLE LINDSEY, M.A., M.S.W.
University of Illinois at Urbana–Champaign,
School of Social Work

MARGARET KING WHITE, M.S.W.
University of Illinois at Urbana–Champaign

CHAPTER OUTLINE

Chapter Overview

Introduction

Best and Promising Practices

Technology Uses in Assessment and Data Collection

Application of Strengths-Based Practice and Technology

Summary

CHAPTER OVERVIEW

This chapter discusses (1) how to integrate technology into what you already do on a daily basis as a school social worker, and (2) ways in which you can adapt current interventions and practices to make them more engaging and effective through technology. This chapter relates to other chapters in the book by introducing an approach that encourages you to creatively adapt the best and promising school social work practices by integrating technology in new and interesting ways.

INTRODUCTION

Computer technology is a part of everyday life. It provides opportunities for enhanced communication, learning, and information sharing (Van Horn & Myrick, 2001). Technology use in education has experienced rapid growth, as evidenced by the fact that schools with access to the Internet increased from 35% to 95% between 1994 and 1999 (National Center for Educational Statistics, 2000). The youth of today have been referred to as the **e-generation** because three in five children younger than the age of 18 years and more than 78% of children between the ages of 12 and 17 years spend time online (Levin & Arafeh, 2002). In fact, the use of computers among children ages 6–17 years closely mirrors the amount of time spent watching television (Corporation for Public Broadcasting, 2002). On average, children spend 3.1 hours per day watching television and 2.9 hours per day using digital media, including the Internet, software programs, and video games. Computer technology offers enhanced opportunities for learning by providing an entertaining way to discover new information and communicate with others.

School social workers can make use of software, websites, and other forms of technology as a way to enhance their practice. Rather than viewing technology as a new and different type of approach, this chapter highlights creative uses of technology into school social work practices. Integrating technology into the type of activities currently conducted by school social workers provides a way to easily engage others in the therapeutic process while serving as an excellent method of case documentation.

BEST AND PROMISING PRACTICES

Animated Cartoon Character Software and Narrative Therapy

School social workers can utilize interactive software programs as a tool to facilitate greater understanding of a child's thoughts, feelings, and behaviors (Petrucci, Kirk, & Reid, 2004). These programs are able to keep a child's attention while encouraging communication about difficult problems. Children are able to select characters, background settings, and problem situations to explore various behaviors that might bring about different endings to the story. Several programs that school social workers might find helpful are Bruce's Multimedia Story for pre-K to grade 3 (Information PLUS 3, 1998), Kids Works for pre-K to grade 4 (Knowledge Adventures, 1997), and Hollywood High for grades 6–12 (Grolier Interactive, 1996). These programs are relatively inexpensive and may already be available within the school and used by teachers or the school librarian for literary instruction.

Storytelling and narrative therapy techniques can be one framework to use with animated cartoon character software. Narrative therapy is a powerful technique that can be tailored to teach problem-solving and coping skills for almost any type of issue, age, grade, or phase of therapeutic intervention.

Narrative therapy allows children and adolescents to separate themselves from their problem by creating scenarios that reflect characteristics of their situation but allows opportunities to explore different responses that might bring about resolution of the issue in different ways (Winslade & Monk, 1999). This approach is nonthreatening and useful in addressing troublesome issues. The story can be developed as a stand-alone technique or updated continuously throughout the intervention process (Davis, 1990).

An initial strengths-based assessment of the child or adolescent should be completed in order to develop a comprehensive understanding of issues (Saleebey, 2002). Based on information gathered during the assessment, school social workers will be better able to determine whether it is more appropriate to help the child create a direct or indirect story (Davis, 1990). Direct stories are personalized by using the child's actual name and situation. Indirect stories are written in an unobtrusive way by using storybook characters, animals, and dream scenarios as a way to mirror the child's situation. Decisions regarding the type of story to use should be based on the length, breadth, and depth of the child's issues (Winslade & Monk, 1999).

Davis (1990) provided the following suggestions for creating therapeutic stories:

- Use language the child will understand. This means simple language for children and more complex language for adolescents.
- Reflect the child's situation at the beginning of the story. Characters should include important people in the child's life and be created in such a way so as to reflect their unique qualities. In the case of an indirect story, the gender of the main character and family constellation should mirror that of the child.
- Use metaphors to illustrate problem-solving skills or highlight an aspect of the child's situation that deserves stronger emphasis.
- Embed messages or directives within the story that convey hope that the child is able to successfully resolve his or her problem situation.

Narrative stories are a creative way to help children develop new skills and insights into their problem situation.

Social Stories and Interactive Children's Software

Social stories are a variation of narrative therapy. Originally developed as a technique for teaching autistic children how to play games, social stories have been expanded to teach social cues and appropriate behaviors to children with mild to moderate autism as well as those with Asperger's syndrome (Barry & Burlew, 2004). Task analysis is used to break down desired behaviors into step-by-step actions. Specific skills are introduced and connected to complex behaviors. Social stories offer the experience of practicing the desired behavior through repetition and corrective feedback. These stories are presented on an ongoing basis and children are prompted to display appropriate behaviors in social situations (Barry & Burlew, 2004). The language of social stories is directive and includes descriptions of visual and verbal cues that help the child identify when and how to respond in certain social situations (Gray, 1995).

In addition, social stories include a description of how others might react when the child displays desirable or undesirable behaviors. Traditionally, social stories have been created through the use of toys in guided play, tape-recorded stories, and crayons and paper (Barry & Burlew, 2004). Interactive software for children is another technique that could be utilized and is a way of integrating technology into school social work practice. Software programs that may be used for this purpose include Kidspiration 2 (CCV Software, 2004), Hyperstudio 4 (Sunburst Technology, 2004), Easybook Deluxe (Sunburst Technology, 2004), and Amazing Writing Machine (The Learning Company, 1996).

Card Maker Software Programs

Computerized card maker programs can be used as a simple method of teaching social skills and the pillars of Character Counts, which include kindness, empathy, compassion, and caring. School social workers can help students create cards that may be sent to others for birthdays, as thank-you notes, apologies, and for other special occasions. In addition, cards can be a way for students to communicate with noncustodial parents or with those who are ill. Some sample programs that can be used include Hallmark Card Studio (Vivendi, 2004), Print Shop (Riverdeep, 2002), and Disney Classic Print Studio (Walt Disney Company, 2001).

Video and Digital Cameras

Video can be used as a method of feedback to show clients how they appear to others by showing videotape of their client's behaviors and responses (Barker, 2003). For the school social worker, videotape can be a powerful tool. It can be used to record behavior in the classroom, playground, cafeteria, and bus. This can be a practical source of information for teaching and reinforcing social skills, guiding development of scripts for social stories, and providing reinforcing behavioral feedback for parents. In the classroom setting, video can be a method of obtaining behavioral observations of individual students, teacher and student interactions, and classroom management techniques and for practicing social skills lessons. School social workers interested in utilizing videotape in this way should take care to ensure their school or district has a policy regarding the use of video in the student handbook. Parent consent for videotaping and disseminating results is advised.

Video Clubs for Professional Development

Video clubs for school staff can be an effective professional development tool (Sherin & Han, 2002). Organized small groups of staff members agree to tape themselves teaching. Members meet on a regular basis to review and discuss the videotapes, which encourages thoughtful reflection of teaching methods. Video clubs can also be utilized as a supervision tool for school social workers to encourage critical analysis of practice.

Digital Cameras

Digital cameras can be integrated with some of the programs mentioned previously. For example, school social workers can utilize Adobe Premiere (Adobe Systems, 2004) to morph, or change, digital photographs in an attempt to define themselves in a creative manner. Digital photographs can also be used to design "photo journaling" entries that detail student success or positive behaviors at school. The digital journal can be burned or saved on DVD-R for home viewing.

Microsoft PowerPoint Presentations

PowerPoint (Microsoft, 2003) is an ideal tool for presentations to students, parents, faculty, the board of education, and the community. School social workers can design in-service training programs based on evidence-based practices for addressing problem behaviors, effective parenting techniques, methods that promote positive learning environments, as well as availability of community resources. Other possibilities for integrating PowerPoint into school social work practice include creating classroom presentations on appropriate social skills. These presentations could also provide step-by-step instructions that show how to (1) organize desks, lockers, and assignments; (2) teach effective study skills; (3) make new friends; and (4) mediate conflict. Often, English teachers can be persuaded to give students extra credit for these presentations, so they can serve a dual purpose.

Instant Messaging

Instant messaging (IM) refers to simultaneous conversations that take place through the Internet. Students can communicate with others worldwide without leaving the comfort of their homes. IM has replaced the phone call of past generations (Hird, 2000). Students chatter to discuss school events, get "online" advice, gossip, or simply socialize. While away from their computer, students can leave "away messages" informing others of their activities. School social workers should be aware that their students may communicate with each other through IM, and issues that arise as a result of these conversations may spill over into the school setting.

TECHNOLOGY USES IN ASSESSMENT AND DATA COLLECTION

Adaptive Behavior

Computer technology continues to improve and offers enhanced opportunities for integration into direct practice (Petrucci et al., 2004). For school social workers, programs related to assessment and data collection have become widely used and readily accepted. Many companies that publish psychological testing materials, including adaptive behavior assessments and other clinical tools, offer software programs designed to reduce practitioner error by increasing accuracy and efficiency of scoring and interpretation. Examples of widely used assessment tools that offer an accompanying software scoring and interpretation program include Vineland Scales of Adaptive Behavior Scales Scoring Program (Sparrows, Balla, & Ciochetti, 2000), Scales of Independent Behavior-Revised (Bruninks, Woodcock, Weatherman, & Hill, 1997), and Behavior Assessment Scales for Children 2 (Reynolds & Kamphaus, 2004). These programs allow users to enter data and receive a detailed report that compares individual responses to national norms for reliability and validity. Potential clinical symptoms and problematic behaviors can be quickly identified and facilitate responsive interventions.

Functional Behavior Assessment

The use of functional behavior assessment and behavior intervention plans have become an essential part of planning for students with disabilities whose behavior interferes with their learning or that of others. This requirement has brought about an increased focus on applied behavior analysis and development of positive behavior interventions (Sugai et al., 2000). Examples of interactive software that provide training in these areas include Functional Behavioral Assessment (Liaupsin, Scott, & Nelson, 2001) and Behavior Intervention Planning (Scott, Liaupsin, & Nelson, 2001). These programs offer step-by-step instructions on how to determine the purpose behind problematic student behavior as well as ways to utilize data to develop an individualized intervention plan. Materials can be adapted for use as an individual training module or as part of a presentation to a large group. The suggested amount of time required to complete the respective programs is 3 or 4 hours for the Functional Behavioral Assessment program and 1.5 to 2 hours for Behavior Intervention Planning.

Single-Case Research

Single-case research is one of the most effective ways to evaluate practice (Bloom, Fischer, & Orme, 1999). This evidence-based practice approach encourages school social workers to evaluate the effectiveness of interventions through ongoing data collection efforts (see Chapter 14). Computer technology provides an easy way to collect and analyze data in a timely manner (Petrucci et al., 2004). Although there are a number of data management programs, Excel (Microsoft, 2003) and Lotus 1-2-3 (IBM, 2000) are commonly used. If more sophisticated data analysis is required, SPSS (SPSS, 2004) can facilitate the process. These types of software programs can simplify data collection and analysis, thereby contributing to practice evaluation efforts. Excel can also be utilized as a data source for keeping track of student and parent contacts.

Policy Advocacy

Impacting public policy is an integral part of the social work profession. The World Wide Web offers limitless opportunities to school social workers and others interested in advocating on behalf of disadvantaged and vulnerable target populations. Karger and Stoesz (1998) detailed an organized collection of policy issues and problems as well as various organizations and their websites that target change in specific areas. These types of websites frequently offer opportunities to join a listserv or receive electronic updates about current issues. The School Social Work Association of America website (www.sswaa.org) contains a number of links that enable school social workers to keep abreast of issues related to the profession.

Acceptable Use Policy

Safety procedures need to be implemented before students are permitted to use the Internet or e-mail as part of school-sponsored activities (Candau et al., 2001). It is essential that students be protected from accessing websites with inappropriate material as well as restricting access from those who might harm children. One way to ensure student safety in this area is to establish and implement an **acceptable use policy** (AUP) at school. An AUP is a written agreement signed by students, parents, and teachers that describes types of acceptable uses and consequences for violating the agreement. The AUP should contain guidelines for publishing student names, pictures, and audio clips. The following websites contain helpful information about online student safety issues: Child Safety on the Information Highway at www.safekids.com/child_safety.htm; Teen Safety on the Information Highway at www.safekids.com/safeteens/safeteens.htm; and the National Center for Missing and Exploited Children website at www.netsmartz.org, which explains the dangers found on the Internet.

Cultural Competence and Technology

It is essential for school social workers to keep in mind ethnicity, age, religion, and disability issues when selecting appropriate types of software programs and websites to use in their practice. Care should be taken to ensure that the information, program, and technology contain characters, backgrounds, and settings that reflect the child's age, culture, and developmental ability. A related issue is the disparity in the number of schools with high populations of minority and disadvantaged student populations that have access to the Internet (Corporation for Public Broadcasting, 2002). Despite critical gains in recent years, less than one third of low-income, African American, and Hispanic children have access to the Internet at school. The crisis-level budget shortfalls faced by schools make it difficult to keep pace with current technology. School social workers need to remain aware of resources and actively seek resources to expand access to technology use at school.

APPLICATION OF STRENGTHS-BASED PRACTICE AND TECHNOLOGY

The concept of integrating technology into school social work practice is intended to capitalize on the types of activities that school social workers are currently providing to students. A hallmark of the social work profession is the use of a strengths-based approach to practice. Technology offers opportunities to increase effectiveness and efficiency of the strengths-based approach in a fun and interesting way. Computer technology holds the promise of providing students and social workers alike the chance to experience success in ways they never dreamed possible.

Case	**Case Example 1**

Hunt and Robson (1999) highlighted how video can be used to improve the home–school connection with early childhood students and their parents. Under the direction of school staff, inner-city parents filmed their children and produced a video illustrating early childhood life in the school. The project, When I'm 100, Will I Reach the Sky? was associated with increased self-esteem of parents, facilitated a greater understanding of preschool curriculum activities, and encouraged them to become a strong partner in their children's education. Unexpected outcomes of the study included highlighting ways to encourage parental participation and using video to facilitate training of student teachers.

Case	**Case Example 2**

A school social worker worked with a student whose father was dying of cancer. The main focus of interventions was related to grief and loss issues. One of the therapeutic techniques employed in this case was to use Hallmark Card Studio (Vivendi, 2004) to help the child create a card for her dying father. The card was a way for the child to begin to say goodbye to her dad while conveying a sense of appreciation to him for the role he played in her life:

Dear Dad,

I liked the time when you baked with me. We made muffins. They tasted scrumptiously good. Did you know I took a Jacuzzi at Mrs. Jones' house the third time you went into the hospital? I looked all bubbly and the bubbles went up to my neck. And I made myself look like Mickey Mouse with bubbles. I bet if you saw me you would stick your hand in the bubbles and you would laugh. I remember white water rafting with you in a yellow raft. And remember when your friend said, when you are in a yellow raft you are a chicken. And then our leader said yellow rafts are the toughest rafts. I think we were the chickens. I remember the time I tried to dive off your shoulders and that was fun. I enjoy playing with you.

XXXXXXXOOOOOOOOOOXXXXXXXXOOOOOOOOO. This is a love letter.

Love, A

| Case | **Case Example 3** |

A school social worker used Kids Works Deluxe (Knowledge Adventure, 1997) with the following script as a framework for child interviews required as part of evaluations to determine eligibility for special education:

> Once upon a time there was a girl or boy named_____. She or he lives with _____. (Include all adults, children and ages, and pets in the home. In divorce situation, list other parent, location, others in the home, and how often the student visits or lives there.) Her or his best friends are _____.   For   fun,   _____   likes   to _____. At school, _____ her or his favorite things are _____. At recess, _____ likes to _____. One thing _____ does not like about school is _____. The easiest thing for _____ at school is _____. The hardest thing for _____at school is _____. If _____ could have three wishes they would be _____.

SUMMARY

Technology is a promising way to enhance school social work practice. By creatively integrating technology into the types of activities currently provided, interventions can become more stimulating as well as entertaining. Technology also holds many possibilities for facilitating evaluation of practice as well as utilizing the World Wide Web for policy advocacy efforts. Care should be taken to ensure student safety by developing school policies regarding acceptable use of the Internet.

School Social Work Companion Website

Please be sure to check out our companion website at www.thomsonedu.com/social_work/bye, where you will find relevant materials for each chapter, including flashcards, online practice quizzes, and PowerPoint slides.

References

Barker, R. (2003). *The social work dictionary* (5th ed.). Washington, DC: National Association of Social Workers.

Barry, L., & Burlew, S. (2004). Using social stories to teach choice and play skills to children with autism. *Focus on Autism and Other Developmental Disabilities, 19*(1), 45–51.

Bloom, M., Fischer, J., & Orme, J. (1999). *Evaluating practice* (3rd ed.). New York: Free Press.

Bruninks, R., Woodcock, R., Weatherman, R., & Hill, B. (1997). *Scales of Independent Behavior-Revised Scoring Program*. Itasca, IL: Riverside.

Candau, D., Doherty, J., Hannafin, R., Judge, J., Yost, J., & Kuni, P. (2001). *Intel: Teach to the Future*. Santa Clara, CA: Intel.

Corporation for Public Broadcasting. (2002). *Connected to the future: A report on children's internet use*. Retrieved March 13, 2005, from www.cpb.org/ed/resources/connected

Davis, N. (1990). *Once upon a time. . . .Therapeutic stories to heal abused children*. Oxon Hill, PA: Psychological Associates of Oxen Hill.

Gray, C. (1995). Teaching children with autism to "read" social situations. In K. A. Quill (Ed.), *Teaching children with autism: Strategies to enhance communication and socialization* (pp. 219–241). Albany, NY: Delmar.

Hird, A. (2000). *Learning from cyber savvy students: How Internet-age kids impact classroom teaching*. Sterling, VA: Stylus.

Hunt, K., & Robson, M. (1999). Empowering parents of pre-school children. *International Journal for the Advancement of Counseling, 21*, 43–54.

Karger, H., & Stoesz, D. (1998). *The Internet and social welfare policy. A supplement to American social welfare policy: A pluralist approach*. Boston: Addison-Wesley.

Levin, D., & Arafeh, S. (2002). The digital disconnect: The widening gap between Internet-savvy students and their schools. *Education at a Distance, 16*(2), 1–4.

Liaupsin, C., Scott, T., & Nelson, C. (2001). *Functional behavioral assessment: An interactive training module* [Computer software]. Longmont, CO: Sopris West.

National Center for Educational Statistics. (2000). *Internet access in U.S. public schools and classrooms: 1994–99* (NCES 2000-086). Washington, DC: U.S. Department of Education, Office of Educational Research and Improvement.

Petrucci, C., Kirk, S., & Reid, W. (2004). Computer technology and social work. In A. Roberts & K. Yaeger (Eds.), *Evidence-based practice manual: Research and outcome measures in health and human services* (pp. 89–94). New York: Oxford University Press.

Reynolds, C., & Kamphaus, R. (2004). *Behavior assessment scales for children* (2nd ed.); Scoring Program [Computer software]. Minneapolis, MN: American Guidance Service.

Saleebey, D. (2002). *The strengths perspective in social work practice* (3rd ed.). Boston: Allyn & Bacon.

Scott, T., Liaupsin, C., & Nelson, C. (2001). Behavior Intervention Planning [Computer software]. Longmont, CO: Sopris West.

Sherin, M., & Han, S. (2002). Teacher learning in the context of a video club. *Teacher and Teacher Education, 20*, 163–183.

Sparrows, S., Balla, D., & Ciochetti, D. (2000). Vineland Adaptive Behavior Scales Scoring Program [Computer software]. Minneapolis, MN: American Guidance Service.

Sugai, G., Horner, R., Dunlap, G., Hieneman, M., Lewis, T., Nelson, C., Scott, T., Liaupsin, C., Sailor, W., Turnbull, A., Turnbull, H., Wickham, D., Reuff, M., & Wilcox, B. (2000). Applying positive behavioral support and functional behavioral assessment in schools. *Journal of Positive Behavioral Interventions and Support, 2*, 131–143.

Van Horn, S., & Myrick, R. (2001). Computer technology and the 21st century school counselor. *Professional School Counseling, 5*(2), 124–130.

Winslade, J., & Monk, G. (1999). *Narrative counseling in schools: Powerful and brief*. Thousand Oaks, CA: Corwin Press.

18 CHAPTER | The Transition from Student to School Social Worker

MICHELLE ALVAREZ,
M.S.W., Ed.D.
University of Southern Indiana

CHAPTER OUTLINE

CHAPTER OVERVIEW

After reading this chapter, readers will be able to (1) describe school social work licensing from a state perspective, (2) create a job search plan specific to school social work, (3) identify the contributions that professional organizations can make to their career and ongoing professional development, (4) develop strategies for staying apprised of best practices in the field of school social work, and (5) be knowledgeable about advanced practice certification at the national level. In order to keep up to date on information covered in previous chapters, it is essential to connect with professional organizations and read professional journals. Professional resources are highlighted in this chapter.

INTRODUCTION

Case	Case Example: Debbie's Story

Debbie graduated approximately 5 years ago with her MSW and Pupil Personnel Services Credential (required in California) and wanted to work as a school social worker. She could only land an hourly job with a mental behavioral health provider that hires a variety of therapists. She was placed 25 hours per week in an elementary school and worked several months. The teachers participated in the governance of the school and together with the principal found money and offered her a full-time job. They didn't want to lose her. This obviously would not have happened if Debbie had not accepted the hourly position and then displayed a high level of competence, energy, and professional practice. They were impressed with her school social work background.

Steve Manos, San Diego Region School Social Work Coordinator and Board Member, California Association of School Social Workers (personal communication, April 26, 2004; reprinted with permission from Debbie Boerbaitz, MSW, PPS Social Worker, Chula Vista Elementary School District)

In the fall of the final academic year, school social work students begin to think about finding a job. In many states, there are few job openings. Therefore, the importance of developing a job search plan is essential. To begin the process of seeking employment, there are some basic questions that school social work students need answered: (1) What type of certification or licensure do I need to practice in the state in which I would like to be employed? (2) How do I find school social work positions? and, once employed, (3) How do I keep up to date on issues in the field of school social work? This chapter answers all of these important questions and leaves the reader with practical ideas for finding a position.

STATE SCHOOL SOCIAL WORK LICENSURE/CERTIFICATION

The issue of state-level school social work licensure can be very confusing. In this section of the chapter, licensure is used synonymously with certification because the latter term differs by state. Each state defines the requirements for licensure. Although some states have very detailed requirements for obtaining school social work licensure, many have few or no separate licensure requirements. To add to the confusion, some states require licensure by the state department of education, some require general social work licensure, and some require both licenses (dual licensure). **Dual licensure** in the field of school social work means that two licenses are needed to practice school social work: one is a state-level social work license, such as Licensed Social Worker (LSW), and is awarded by a state agency that licenses professions; the other is also a state-level school social work license but this one is awarded by the state's department of education. According to a National Association of Social Workers' (NASW; 1996) report, states that require dual licensure to work in a public or state department of education accredited private school include Delaware, District of Columbia, Idaho, Indiana, Louisiana, Minnesota, Nevada, New Hampshire, New Mexico, Rhode Island, and Utah.

State school social work licenses can require coursework, a specified number of hours in a school-based field placement, and/or an exam. Johnson-Reid and Wood (1999) updated the NASW (1996) list of department of education requirements for school social work licensing in all 50 states and the District of Columbia. Johnson-Reid and Wood's survey addressed coursework needed for licensure, and they found that "in some states no reference to specific courses are made but exam or competencies listed suggest the need for specialized training. Social work students should be aware of such requirements and try to meet them during their professional education" (p. 2). To find this information, the School Social Work Association of America (SSWAA) maintains a web page that lists state departments of education and information about the school social work licensing requirements for each state (www.sswaa.org/links/statedoe.html).

In the 1990s, as states began passing educational reform legislation they included the development of standards and outcomes for training teachers. Additionally, with the passing of the No Child Left Behind Act in 2002, further emphasis was placed on "highly qualified" teachers. As a result, teacher licensing requirements have undergone changes in format and structure at the state level. With these changes came revisions in school social work licensing requirements and in some states the implementation of new school social work licensing. Several states (i.e., California, Idaho, Illinois, Indiana, and Washington) have written or are in the process of writing entry-level school social work standards. These standards provide the basis for assessing applicants for the first level of school social work licensing in that state. It is important to know and understand the licensing requirements.

NATIONAL CERTIFICATION

Voluntary advanced national certification is available for teachers, counselors, and other school personnel through the National Board for Professional Teaching Standards (NBPTS). National certification is obtained through a performance-based assessment process that includes a written exam, submission of videotapes, and essays reflecting on skills and knowledge. Shaffer (1996) understood the implications of advanced practice national certification when he wrote about the formation of NBPTS as one of the "high-profile initiatives to radically alter teacher status, education, and effectiveness" (p. 195). In this same article,

Shaffer predicted that "educational reform and concomitant changes in teacher preparation and licensure statutes will no doubt cause us to reexamine the regulation of school social work practitioners" (p. 195). In return for obtaining NBPTS national certification, teachers are rewarded with substantial salary increases (up to $10,000 for the 10-year life of the national certification), pay scale changes, increased professional development support, and reclassification to the highest level of teacher licensing available in that state. The rewards vary by state, but more information can be found at www.nbpts.org/about/state.cfm.

Potential incentives and rewards provided to teachers for advanced practice national certification could also be made available to school social workers. However, there are no plans for NBPTS to develop a school social work certification (NBPTS, personal communication, February 2004). NASW (2004) offers a Certified School Social Work Specialist (C-SSWS) credential, which although not as rigorous as the performance-based assessment completed for NBPTS certification, holds the potential to be considered equivalent to NBPTS certification. Information on the C-SSWS can be obtained at www.socialwork ers.org/credentials/specialty/c-ssws.asp. Georgia and Louisiana have been lobbying for the C-SSWS to be recognized as equivalent to NBPTS. This is an evolving issue that should be watched closely.

FINDING EMPLOYMENT

> One recommendation I would give is that they learn the language of education just as they learned the language of social work.
>
> *Gail Beaton, School Social Worker, Kokomo, Indiana (personal communication, April 12, 2004)*
>
> It is important for students to learn whom they should send a resume to—not always the superintendent or the director of special education—all districts do it a bit differently. Sometimes you need to send more than one letter to different persons in the same district.
>
> *Beverly Baronic-Yeglic, Past President of the Michigan Association of School Social Workers; Southgate Community School Social Worker; and Adjunct Professor at Wayne State University and the University of Michigan (personal communication, April 18, 2004)*

Resume Writing

The search for employment as a school social worker necessitates the development of a resume that reflects experience and highlights skills that are attractive to a school administrator. A publication titled *Job Search Handbook for Educators* is updated yearly by the American Association for Employment in Education (www.aaee.org) and has tips for resume development, conducting a job search in the field of education, and the projected rate of supply and demand by field. The handbook is often available from the career offices on campuses.

When seeking school social work positions, you should use your resume to emphasize experience in general education, special education, and alternative

Examples of Significant Accomplishments

1. Planned, developed, and implemented Wyoming's first school district program on personal safety with regard to sexual assault, which is now part of the school's health curriculum. Achieved the following level of success:
    a. A 98% participation rate of students in first through third grades the first year the course was taught.
    b. Showed a statistically significant improvement in students' knowledge of self-protective behaviors at the end of the curriculum.
    c. Received less than 2% negative feedback on the program through the follow-up surveys with the parents at the end of the instructional unit.
2. Successfully returned five students who had been in out-of-district placements. This allowed them to live at home and reduced the high cost of their education. Also planned and developed the programming within the district to accommodate these and future students with services equal to and higher than provided at institutions.

Bill Lee, School Social Worker, Fremont County School District, Wyoming (personal communication, December 15, 2003)

education as well as preschool, elementary, middle school/junior high, and high school. It is important to utilize terms that reflect your knowledge of both the social work and the education fields. Emphasis on accountability in education can be addressed by describing student outcomes from your school-based field experience, linking services to school improvement plans and school "report cards." The above example, taken from the resume of a school social worker with 30 years of experience, demonstrates how student outcomes from their field experience can be incorporated into a resume.

On your resume, list all association memberships, school social work-specific courses, school-based field placements, and anticipated eligibility for school social work and social work licensure. Resume writing is a skill taught on many campuses through the career development department. Take advantage of resources made available to students.

Professional Portfolio

Some students will be required to submit a professional portfolio when interviewing for a school-based field placement. Student teachers are often required to create a portfolio and school administrators are familiar with this method of reviewing the qualifications of a job applicant. The creation of a professional portfolio can be advantageous for a school social work applicant. A portfolio is a "three-dimensional resume, or a visual representation of one's teaching experiences and accomplishments . . . an ongoing record of their career, to provide any viewer with evidence of their expertise" (www.professionalteacher.com/home/index.cfm?s=723.b0406762y.0131306n80, paragraph 1). The portfolio is a well-organized notebook containing a resume, letters of recommendation, licensure, and samples of work and other items that demonstrate the applicant's skills and knowledge. Do not place too many items in a portfolio, which would overwhelm an administrator; rather, highlight your greatest accomplishments. Some students have begun to create online portfolios or place it on a CD-ROM and provide either a copy of the CD-ROM or a link to the portfolio with the resume at the interview.

Networking

Networking is the key to finding a job in school social work. Interestingly, Mau and Kopischke (2001) found that

> although most literature indicated that the most effective job search method for white-collar workers is informal contact through networking, the present study showed that the formal approach through the use of resumes and want ads seemed to be the most common job search method. (p. 4)

Networking is often overlooked as an effective job search tool. Networking includes meeting school social workers in the area in which you want to work; attending state, regional, and national conferences; and joining electronic mailing lists.

One final option is to learn about grant writing and write a grant for a local school district to employ a school social worker. Grant funding is available at the local level (e.g., foundations, businesses, town/city government departments, and Rotary and other membership groups), state level (e.g., state department of education and health), and federal level (e.g., U.S. Department of Education Office of Juvenile Justice and Delinquency Prevention, and the Substance Abuse and Mental Health Services Administration). Network to find out where funding is available to support and employ school social workers. One federal grant, the Elementary and Secondary School Counseling Programs grant, awards funding "to local educational agencies to enable such agencies to establish or expand elementary school and secondary school counseling programs" (U.S. Department of Education, 2004, p. 30). Funding notices for this grant are available at the beginning of the calendar year and can be found at www.grants.gov. Other federal grant opportunities exist with the Department of Housing and Urban Development, Department of Justice, and Department of Health and Human Services.

> I highly recommend informational interviewing or shadowing for a day—I would welcome the opportunity to help a new graduate in that manner.
>
> *Laura Olesko, School Social Worker, Michigan (personal communication, December 12, 2003)*

Create a plan for meeting school social workers and potential employers. Begin with your university professors. Interview them about tips for finding jobs in your area or making contacts with school social workers in the area where you want to work. Next, set up appointments for phone and in-person interviews, or job shadow school social workers. Learn about their role and their school/district. Find out the starting salary, the length of the contract, the position titles for which school social workers are hired in the district, and who supervises school social workers. Ask for a copy of a job description and ask school social workers if they have any tips for becoming employed in their school district. Often, school social work organizations list job openings on their websites. Mau and Kopischke (2001) found "a significant correlation between the number of job search methods used and the number of interviews" (p. 4). Therefore, multiple methods of job hunting will increase the likelihood of finding a school social work position.

Professional Organizations

> Professional membership is valuable. Educators have a strong leaning toward their professional organizations. Once they found I also had a strong involvement in my professional organization it seemed to increase their respect for the profession.
>
> *Gail Beaton, School Social Worker, Kokomo, Indiana (personal communication, April 12, 2004)*

Professional organizations regulate the field, provide representation to legislative bodies at state and federal levels, develop practice standards and position statements, provide opportunities for professional development, help develop leaders in the profession, and promote individual growth in knowledge and skills as a student and as a professional. For students, professional organizations provide a place to meet other social workers and network for jobs. They also provide discipline-specific information. In your job search, it is important to keep up to date on issues that impact the field of school social work. Professional organizations in the field of school social work are active at the state, regional, and national levels.

State-Level Professional Organizations

> I cannot underestimate the value of joining a social work organization way before graduation; at meetings you meet school social workers on hiring committees, who know of job openings before jobs are posted. In my district we drew on members for substitute positions and hired two elementary social workers.
>
> *Beverly Baroni-Yeglic, Past President of the Michigan Association of School Social Workers; Southgate Community School Social Worker; and Adjunct Professor at Wayne State University and the University of Michigan (personal communication, April 18, 2004)*
>
> I found involvement in the state professional groups helpful to try to learn the insiders' view of just what it is that the school social worker does. Sometimes I still have some difficulty articulating it, but was glad to have some ideas and feel for it through my contact with working professionals, conference planning, and attendance. It gave me an edge in learning where there were going to be job openings as people anticipated retirement. I also had a nice network of colleagues with whom I could consult and share resources and ideas
>
> *Charlie Karl, LSW, School Social Worker/Home and School Visitor, Abington School District; member of the Pennsylvania Association of School Social Work and the Pennsylvania State Educational Association (personal communication, April 12, 2004)*

There are three types of school social work organizations at the state level. These school social work organizations are affiliated with SSWAA, NASW, or both national organizations. A list of all state organizations affiliated with SSWAA can be found at www.sswaa.org/links/regions.html. State chapters of NASW, a number of which have school social work committees, can be found at www.socialworkers.org/chapters/default.asp. Some of these state organizations have websites that list school social work positions (e.g., www.iassw.org/jobs.htm and www.njassw.org/jobs.html) that students can monitor throughout their final semesters to search for positions of interest.

Regional-Level Professional Organizations

The Midwest School Social Work Council (www.midwest-ssw.org) was the first regional organization formed. Development of the Midwest Council began as a method of cultivating leadership in the field of school social work and has culminated in "one of the largest school social work organizations in the United States and serves as a model for other regions" (SSWAM, 2004, p. 3). The Midwest Council is composed of eleven state school social work organizations (IL, IN, IA, KS, KY, MI, MN, MO, NE, OH, and WI). The council hosts a regional conference each fall and provides state school social work organization members with a forum for discussing current state and national issues related to the field.

The three other regions are the Northeast Coalition of School Social Work Associations, which represents six states (CT, PA, MA, NH, NJ, and NY); the Southern Council of School Social Workers, which encompasses school social work associations in seven states (FL, GA, MS, NC, SC, VA, and TN); and the Western Alliance of School Social Work Organizations, which represents nine states (AZ, CA, CO, ID, MT, NM, UT, WA, and WY). Although the Western Alliance disbanded in 2005, there is hope that the region will remain strong in the area of school social work and that these states will remain active at the national and state levels. Contact information for the regional school social work associations is available at www.sswaa.org/links/ regions.html.

National-Level Professional Organizations

The field of school social work has enjoyed continuous growth and expansion since the early 1900s. As the number of school social workers increases, so does the need for leadership, advocacy, and research in the field. Franklin (2001) states that "for a practice-based profession to have a strong infrastructure, it must have strong national associations that help form united membership, and leadership who can respond to legislative priorities, policy formulation, and training needs of the profession" (p. 1). Franklin also points out that "national school social work associations . . . help us keep important data on services and increase networking, communication, and affiliation among members" (p. 1). There are two national organizations that school social workers (and students) should consider joining. As a student, you are given information about the NASW (NASW, 2004). NASW offers a reduced rate for membership for students. NASW is a professional organization for all social workers regardless of their specialty area; NASW has created specialty sections, including one for school social workers. The Specialty Practice Section is described as follows on the NASW web page:

> The NASW Specialty Practice Sections (SPS) are an essential resource for social workers whose interests and practice needs vary. The NASW SPS are designed to provide content expertise and inform members about current trends and policy issues that impact social work practice and service delivery. The sections will link you to key information and resources to help you stay at the forefront of your specialty. As an NASW SPS member you receive:
>
> - Practice-specific newsletters, updates, and web-based advocacy alerts that focus on program, policy, practice, and legislative issues relevant to the section
> - The InterSection, an annual bulletin that provides a broad overview of trends in the social work profession
> - Members-only web page
> - Networking opportunities with colleagues through the members-only online forum
> - Professional advancement opportunities (http://naswdc.org/sections)
> - A free joblink web page (http://joblink.socialworkers.org/search.cfm)

The NASW School Social Work Section offers members an online discussion board that is a good place to post questions for school social workers throughout the nation about their roles, job openings, and current issues in the field. A NASW journal dedicated to school social work, *Children & Schools*, is available at many university libraries and by subscription. Finally, NASW convened a group of experienced school social workers to write (1978) and then update (1992 and 2002) *NASW Standards for School Social Work Services*. For many school systems, these standards will reinforce current practices. For others, they will provide a challenge and goals to be achieved. For school social workers, these standards validate the uniqueness and diversity of school social work as a specialty practice area and affirm the value of school social work in enabling students to achieve maximum benefits from their educational experiences (National Association of Social Workers, 2002).

School Social Work Association of America

> I work as the only school social worker in a rural district. The only way I stay in touch is through organizations like SSWAA, which I just found out about and recently joined. I came back from the conference feeling connected and energized because of the networking made possible through the organization.
>
> *Monica Strambi, School Social Worker, Kings Canyon Unified School District, California (personal communication, April 19, 2004)*

SSWAA is the only national professional organization dedicated solely to the field of school social work. SSWAA's mission is as follows: "The School Social Work Association of America is dedicated to promoting the profession of school social work and the professional development of school social workers in order to enhance the educational experience of students and their families" (SSWAA, 2004). SSWAA hosts a national conference each year that provides workshops and keynote speakers on cutting-edge topics related to school social work. Information on the yearly conference is posted on the SSWAA web page at www.sswaa.org. Also available on the website are resolutions regarding ratios of school social workers to students and information on school social work training programs, bullying, psychotropic medications, promoting school attendance, and mental health in schools. The resolution statements and position papers are developed each year by the board and members of SSWAA. Publications available from SSWAA include a description of school social work as a career, information on confidentiality in schools, special education-related topics, and a brochure on positive school-home communication.

SSWAA members receive the *SSWAA Bell*, a newsletter mailed to members on a quarterly basis, and the *SSWAA E-Bell*, a weekly electronic newsletter with links to up-to-date research and information. SSWAA employs a lobbyist who represents the membership at meetings and hearings of the U.S. Department of Education; Congress and Committees (House and Senate and National Department of Education); Committee for Education Funding, National Association of Pupil Service Organizations; Juvenile Justice Roundtable; and Coalition of Citizens with Disabilities. The lobbyist keeps the SSWAA board members and state/regional leadership current on legislation that impacts the field (SSWAA, 2004).

CULTURAL COMPETENCE

It is essential that students demonstrate entry-level competence in this area. Skills related to cultural competence can be highlighted in resumes and addressed in cover letters. Through networking with local school social workers, culture and diversity within the school district can be explored and examples of cultural competence discussed. In addition to getting involved in diverse communities, attendance at professional conferences and reading organizational newsletters and journals serve to expand school social workers' competence in this area.

APPLICATION OF THEORY TO PRACTICE AFTER GRADUATION

The application of theory to practice is covered in previous chapters and is incorporated into the curriculum of undergraduate and graduate social work programs. However, once students graduate it is important to continue learning about the application of theory. Application of ecological, strengths-based, and resiliency theories is addressed in conference workshops, newsletters, and journal articles provided by state, regional, and national professional organizations. Maintaining this link to current information contributes to school social workers' competency in this area.

SUMMARY

The goal of this chapter was to give readers information about school social work licensing/certification in the 50 states and the District of Columbia, offer ideas for creating a job search plan specific to school social work, provide some basic information on professional organizations and the resources they offer school social workers, and share with the reader information about national certification as an evolving issue in the field. It is hoped that school social work students will utilize some of these strategies to pursue a school social work position. Creativity, persistence, resources provided by professional organizations, and a network of school social workers in the field can lead to successful employment as a school social worker.

School Social Work Companion Website

Please be sure to check out our companion website at www.thomsonedu.com/social_work/bye, where you will find relevant materials for each chapter, including flashcards, online practice quizzes, and PowerPoint slides.

References

Franklin, C. (2001). Now is the time for building the infrastructure of school social work practice. *Children & Schools, 2*(2), 67–71.

Johnson-Reid, M., & Wood, A. (1999). *School social work in 50 states: Entry level certification update 1999.* Washington, DC: National Association of Social Workers.

Mau, W. C., & Kopischke, A. (2001). Job search methods, job search outcomes, and job satisfaction of college graduates: A comparison of race and sex. *Journal of Employment Counseling, 38*(3), 141–149.

National Association of Social Workers. (1992). *NASW standards for school social work services.* Washington, DC: Author.

National Association of Social Workers. (1996). *School social work certification requirements from state departments of education: What you need to know to apply for a school social work position.* Washington, DC: Author.

National Association of Social Workers. (2002) *NASW standards for school social work services.* Retrieved May 2, 2004, from www.socialworkers.org/sections/credentials/school_social.asp

National Association of Social Workers. (2004). *School social work section.* Retrieved April 28, 2004, from www.naswdc.org/sections/default.asp

Professional Teacher.com. (2004). *The teaching portfolio.* Retrieved May 15, 2004, from www.professionalteacher.com/home/career_center_the_portfolio.cfm?s=320.j0708442m.035v019o60#what_is_it

School Social Work Association of America. (2004). *Mission.* Retrieved March 27, 2004, from www.sswaa.org

School Social Work Association of Minnesota. (2004). Retrieved May 20, 2004, from www.sswam.org/SSWAM/History/midwest_council.htm

Shaffer, G. L. (1996). School social work certification in a climate of educational reform. *Social Work in Education, 18*(4), 195–199.

Substance Abuse and Mental Health Services Administration. (2004). *Developing competitive SAMHSA grants, glossary of terms.* Retrieved May 22, 2004, from www.samhsa.gov/grants/TAManual/GlossaryMasterFinal.htm

U.S. Department of Education, Office of Safe and Drug-Free Schools. (2004). *Elementary and secondary school counseling programs (CF 84.215E) application packet.* Retrieved March 15, 2004, from www.ed.gov/fund/grant/apply/appforms.html ?exp=0

19 CHAPTER | International School Social Work

MARION HUXTABLE, M.S.W.
International Network for School Social Work

CHAPTER OVERVIEW

After reading this chapter, readers will be able to (1) describe the primary mission of school social work throughout the world, (2) explain how school social workers help students access and benefit from education, (3) contrast the way school social work services are provided and the roles school social workers play in different countries, (4) identify reasons pilot programs are effective in developing new school social work services, (5) describe the importance of outcome research for international school social work, and (6) know how to connect with other school social workers throughout the world.

INTRODUCTION

The primary mission of school social work throughout the world since it began more than a century ago has been to help every child enroll and complete school successfully. This chapter describes how school social workers in a growing number of countries are working to include all children in schools that meet their needs and prepare them to fulfill their potential.

- The chapter begins with a brief history of the origins, growth, and current worldwide status of school social work, referring to programs in 31 countries in Europe, the Americas, Asia, Australasia, and Africa.
- It provides information about the approximate extent of school social work in several countries where it is well established and recent growth in new areas.
- The chapter also summarizes common worldwide problems affecting the education of children, including personal, family, and educational problems, in order to illustrate the need for professional social work services in schools.
- The international commonalities in the role and activities of school social workers are described, together with national differences, including the aegis under which the service is provided, the title used, and the role of practitioners.
- The chapter raises common issues that affect the profession of school social work throughout the world, such as the need for research, publications, training, certification, and funding. The issue of acceptance of school social work in the educational establishment of different cultures and how this affects the role is also discussed.
- The chapter concludes with a summary of the growth of international contacts between school social workers and international activities in school social work, and it provides resources available for obtaining more information. Potential opportunities for future collaboration between school social workers in different countries are covered.

SOCIAL WORKERS MEET THE NEEDS OF SCHOOLCHILDREN

Social workers are increasingly working in schools throughout the world. By bringing services to the child in school, social workers can more easily locate those needing assistance and provide services that help them to benefit from their education. At the same time, school social workers can develop prevention programs that benefit the entire school. In many countries, social workers view schools as an ideal setting in which to fulfill social work's mission of improving the lives of children by providing direct services and advocacy to individuals while at the same time promoting change in the school's environment to improve the well-being of all children.

While social workers are becoming more aware of how they can work effectively with children in schools, schools are discovering obstacles that must be addressed if they are to be successful in their mission of educating children. These obstacles relate to complex human factors not easily resolved by teaching methods alone. When a country establishes the goal of universal education, schools need help enrolling children who previously were excluded or unable to attend because of poverty, handicaps, or other social problems. In developing countries, helping children to attend school and remain to complete their education is still the main focus.

Once universal education has been achieved, school systems everywhere face the challenge of ensuring that the education provided is appropriate for all children, including children with disabilities, children from ethnic or linguistic minority groups, and children from low-income families, while keeping all these groups in mainstream schools and learning at a high level. Schools must address the complex social, emotional, cultural, and health factors that combine to interfere with learning. The problems typically manifest themselves in poor attendance, low achievement, behavioral problems, or dropping out of school (Caldas, 1993). These are the common problems faced by school systems everywhere.

Schools in many countries are increasingly charged not just with helping the individual child to overcome these problems but also with developing preventive programs to address social problems that affect children, such as child abuse, bullying, drug abuse, teenage pregnancy, and discrimination of all kinds. Schools throughout the world are attempting to develop programs to promote mental health, not only to improve children's ability to benefit from school but also as a public health measure to reduce the impact of mental illness on communities. To understand the international interest in addressing mental health issues in schools, see the International Alliance for Child and Adolescent Mental Health and Schools website at www.intercamhs.org.

Schools need school social workers, together with other specialized support personnel such as school nurses, school psychologists, and special education teachers, to address this range of complex issues and to help children overcome obstacles that prevent them from succeeding in school. Social workers contribute their knowledge of family issues, community resources, and problem solving to the multidisciplinary teams. The traditional social work perspective of the systems approach is also a valued concept that can guide the multidisciplinary team to focus on improving the school environment, developing prevention programs, and avoiding stigmatizing individual students who are experiencing problems in school.

HISTORY, GROWTH, AND CURRENT STATUS OF SCHOOL SOCIAL WORK IN THE WORLD

The following sketch of the history of school social work in more than 30 countries cannot do justice to the complex history of the profession, especially in countries that have a rich tradition of school social work and extensive literature on the topic. More information on the particulars of the professional role and how it developed in various countries can be found in *School Social Work Worldwide* (Huxtable & Blyth, 2002). The present synopsis, rather than attempting to replicate this existing work, devotes special attention to the spread of school social work to some countries where its establishment has not previously been documented in social work literature in the West, including Mongolia, Sri Lanka, Saudi Arabia, and the United Arab Emirates.

When universal compulsory education was first introduced in the United Kingdom, Canada, and the United States, schools began to use nonteaching personnel to visit homes to promote enrollment and investigate why children were not attending school. These attendance officers and visiting teachers were the pioneers of school social work at the end of the 19th century and beginning of the 20th century (Blyth & Cooper, 2002; Costin, 1969).

There were many social obstacles in the way of children attending school. Child labor was common, and many children were unable to take advantage of their new right to attend school. Families needed children to work to supplement family income and often did not understand the benefits of education. Schools needed officials to enforce attendance and families needed help to make it possible to send their children to school. In the late 19th century, the forerunners of education welfare officers in the United Kingdom were attendance officers employed by school boards to enforce school attendance. More than 100 years later, there are approximately 3,000 education welfare officers in the United Kingdom, still focusing mainly on attendance work (Blyth & Cooper, 2002). In some places, however, education welfare is known as education social work and provides a wider range of social work services.

In the United States, workers called visiting teachers, placed in schools by community agencies (starting in 1906 and 1907 in Boston, Hartford, Chicago, Connecticut, and New York City) and a few years later employed by boards of education, worked to increase the enrollment and retention of children in school (Commonwealth Fund, 1927). The role of the visiting teacher developed a true social work approach early on and has evolved to include a variety of roles and services during the past 100 years. The title of school social worker was adopted in the 1930s (Costin, 1969). By 2003, there were at least 16,000 school social workers in the United States (www.ideadata.org/tables25th/ar_ac3.htm), including practitioners in every state. Canadian school social work, rooted in the work of attendance officers from the earlier part of the 20th century, incorporated knowledge from the mental hygiene movement and now offers a wide range of social work services in about half of the provinces (Loughborough, Shera &Wilhelm, 2002).

The Nordic countries (Sweden, Finland, Norway, Denmark, and Iceland) introduced school social work between the 1940s and 1970s. The role in these countries is very similar and includes both social work and guidance/counseling with a strong emphasis on prevention (Anderson, Pösö, Väisänen, & Wallin, 2002). There are approximately 300 school social workers in Finland (S.-L. Makkonen, personal communication, October 14, 2003) and between 1,500 and 2,000 in Sweden (E. Lauritzen, personal communication, August 19, 2003). The Netherlands also introduced school social work in the 1940s.

Social welfare personnel in Ghana were assigned to work with schools in the 1950s, and in the 1960s the Ghana Education Service started its own school welfare service to ensure that children attend school and that their needs are met so that they can benefit from their education (Sossou & Daniels, 2002). Professionally qualified teachers were given further professional training to provide welfare services to the schools. Work on supporting the goal of universal education continues, but a wide range of social work services are also offered, employing approximately 250 workers in 2003 (E. Mahama, personal communication, November 7, 2003).

In the 1960s, Argentina started to provide school social work services (Tonon, 2002), followed by Australia, Germany, Poland, Singapore, the United Arab Emirates, and Hong Kong in the 1970s. School social work is a new development in Austria, Korea, New Zealand, Switzerland, Saudi Arabia, Sri Lanka, Macedonia, Mongolia, Taiwan, and several Eastern European countries, including Russia, Latvia, Hungary, and Estonia, and has been demonstrated only as a small pilot program in Japan.

School social workers who have introduced the program in their country within the past 30 years are typically still defining the role, explaining it to the educational establishment, and attempting to institutionalize it in their country. Often, the numbers of school social workers are small, or the program only exists in certain areas or as a demonstration project, whereas in a few countries the service has been implemented rapidly and effectively. The following examples show the variation in the way the program has been developing in recent years.

In Sri Lanka, a pilot project was started in 2001 by SERVE, a social agency that is sponsored by Save the Children Norway. It employs 14 social workers and a handful of social work students in 22 schools in Colombo, Gampaha, Kalutara, and Putalam, providing a wide range of social work services (S. de Mel, SERVE, Sri Lanka, personal communication, July 30, 2003). In a country of nearly 20 million people that has seen two decades of ethnic conflict, it is clear that much could be done if the program were fully implemented in Sri Lankan schools to help the children, not only with the usual tasks of growing up but also with the stress of growing up in a country in which peace is still not certain.

In Korea, social workers based in community welfare centers are starting to provide services to schools. Since teachers in Korea view students' concerns as their own responsibility, gaining acceptance for the role of school social worker is one of the first obstacles to overcome in implementing a program effectively. As in several other countries, including the United States, school counseling, limited to those with a teacher's license, is established in the schools. Since there is some overlap of roles, the challenge for school social workers is to define their role and demonstrate why they are needed in addition to school counselors.

The Korean Ministry of Education selected four schools throughout the country in which to determine if school social work could solve problems of students considered "trouble-making," such as those who "cut classes, violate dress codes, smoke and drink, or disobey teachers" (Han & Kim, 2002, p. 39). The pilot programs were considered to be effective and school social work is seen as a growing trend; however, school social workers are still hired on soft money and there is no legal mandate (Han & Kim, 2002).

The fledgling program, although still limited to approximately 60 practitioners, has a good base for future development. Preparation has included visits by social workers to study school social work programs in the United States and Sweden, and the establishment of the Korea Association of School Social Work Practitioners as well as the Korea Society of School Social Work. The Society publishes the *Korean Journal of School Social Work* and a newsletter; two textbooks have been published and school social work is an elective course in schools of social work.

In Mongolia, there has been rapid progress in placing social workers in schools in a short period. Mongolia reports a literacy rate of 99.2% (comparable to high-income Western countries) with no significant difference between males and females (www.odci.gov/cia/publications/factbook/geos/mg.html# People and stats.uis.unesco.org/eng/TableViewer/wdsview/dispviewp.asp). However, there was concern about a rapid increase in the early 1990s in the number of young people dropping out before completing their secondary education. Needs assessments were done in 1995 and 1998 to determine the need for social workers in schools. A model project started in 1997 at two schools focused on working with needy children and preventing them from dropping out.

The dropout prevention project was then implemented in 13 schools in urban and rural areas, and by the late 1990s school social work positions were created in the compulsory schools. The Ministry of Education supports this program, and legal sanction for the employment of school social workers has been created in the amended Education Law of Mongolia. Social workers (using the title "school social worker") are employed by the school system in more than 600 schools (including all secondary schools) throughout the country.

To help students experience success in school, Mongolian school social workers address special education needs and problems with attendance, learning, emotional functioning, behavior, families, and child abuse. School attendance had been the main focus. Services include assessment, casework, counseling, group work, prevention work, and protecting children's rights.

Training a large number of specialists in such a short period of time has been a challenge. Tailor-made programs of in-service training, orientation, and short-term courses in social work have substituted for formal college training. For the past several years, more than 200 social workers have been trained through the financial support rendered by Save the Children, UK and Save the Children, Norway. Although there is no specialized college training for school social workers, some universities, such as the Social Work Department at the

State Pedagogical University, retrain teachers in a short period as school social workers. The publication of *School Social Work Practice*, a quarterly journal published by the School Social Work Administration, and the establishment of a professional association, the School Social Work Association of Mongolia, "Oyunii gegee," have also helped the rapid preparation of staff (B. Tumurbaatar, State Pedagogical University of Mongolia, Ulaanbaatar, Mongolia, personal communication, September 5, 2003; and K. Ulziitungalag, State Pedagogical University of Mongolia, Ulaanbaatar, Mongolia, personal communication, September 24, 2003).

The United Arab Emirates is another country that has implemented a comprehensive program of social work in schools within a relatively short period. Interestingly, school counselors are not employed and school psychologists must each serve several schools. To be placed in a school setting, social workers must have a university degree in social work with 4 years of experience in an educational field (M. I. El Walily, personal communication, July 7, 2003). It appears that social work is the preferred support service in schools, and that schools have a better coverage as measured by social workers per school than in any other country.

Schools in Saudi Arabia have extensive counseling services. The title of the position can be either school counselor or social specialist, and a bachelor's degree in social work, sociology, or psychology is required. The Act of Establishing the Administration of School Counseling and Guidance initiated the program in 1981 in order to provide professional counseling in schools (Al-Garni, 2002). Counseling was defined as a "constructive process aiming to help the student to understand himself, his personality, and his experiences; to identify his problems and develop his capacities; and to reach his goals in congruence with Islamic foundations" (Al-Garni, 2002, p. 48). This definition shows that the intervention is focused on students' behavior, a growing concern in a country in which almost half the population is younger than age 16 (*World Factbook*, 2003). Deviant behavior by young people, including "truancy, academic failure, and verbal and physical deviant acts," are some of the behaviors that have increased along with social change (Al-Garni, 2002, p. 48). Although the role appears to combine social work and counseling, it does not yet include aspects of social work that go beyond individual deviance to understand the causes of deviance and advocate for changes in the system that could reduce its incidence. How the role of social workers in schools has been influenced by educational philosophies, which in turn reflect political, social, and family structures, is discussed in the following sections.

THE ROLE OF THE SCHOOL SOCIAL WORKER AND ITS VARIATIONS

Analysis of the role of school social work in the countries mentioned in the previous section would require more detailed information than is available. It would constitute a rich study revealing how a professional role develops in the context of national politics, culture, educational philosophies, and the expectations of the social work profession. Although formal comparative research has not been conducted, some ideas are offered here regarding the values and goals of school social work, the titles used by practitioners and the meaning and implications of these titles, and the aegis under which the work is carried out.

The following are common values, goals, and principles in school social work that transcend cultural and historical differences and unite the profession:

• The rights of children (especially the right to appropriate education and equal opportunity) and the goal of helping all children reach their potential are the guiding principles for all school social workers.

• School social workers worldwide intervene in some common problems that prevent students from reaching their full potential as learners. Their clients are frequently students who tend to be marginalized in the school system as a result of poverty, minority status, disabilities, or academic and behavioral problems or students who are stressed due to school, personal, or family problems.

• School social workers in different countries have much in common regarding the methods used, despite the great variation in culture between these countries. Home–school communication, direct counseling for students, consultation with teachers, advocacy for students, and collaboration with community agencies have been the main functions of school social work.

Although school social workers espouse these common goals, the extent to which advocacy and systems change is attempted depends on how much is allowed by the system in which they work. For example, regarding the expectations of schools in Korea, Kim (2002) notes, "Because of the high value placed on college entrance, most teachers and schools are not concerned about the individual potential of students and ignore the special needs of students with disabilities" (p. 208). He states that "by being an education reformer, the school social worker can be a policymaker, which is urgently needed for the full implementation of school social work in Korea" (p. 213).

Although school social work programs have much in common, there are some significant differences between countries, and even within countries. These differences, however, are less important than the common values, goals, and principles that unite the profession. Some of the major differences relate to the professional titles used, the significance of these titles, and the aegis under which school social work programs operate.

PROFESSIONAL TITLES

Differing approaches to school social work in different countries are revealed by the professional titles used. Titles and the meaning they carry for the individuals holding the titles are important to the identity of a profession. It is also important to have a stable, clear title that has a positive meaning not only for the clients who use the service but also to foster an established role for school social work in the international community of professions. The following summary of the titles currently used is important to the discussion of professional identity and image.

Many countries have adopted the title school social worker, including Australia, Canada, Estonia, Germany, Hong Kong, Japan, Korea, Singapore, Sri Lanka, Taiwan, and the United States, although individual workers sometimes work under differing titles when performing a specific role in a school. For example, in Canada many social workers hold the dual title school social worker/attendance counselor. Some countries adopted the term school social work and translated it into their own language (e.g., Schulsozialarbeit in Germany), whereas in Japan the English words school social work are used.

In the United Kingdom, two titles are used—education welfare officer and, less frequently, education social worker. The term **welfare** means "well-being;" however, it also carries the sense of government intervention, especially when paired with the word "officer." Although the term welfare in the United Kingdom did not previously have negative connotations, there has been an ideological shift since the 1980s away from the social contract, in which welfare is seen as a right, toward individual initiative and the market economy, resulting in new perceptions of the term welfare. The two titles currently in use (education welfare officer and education social worker) point to questions of divergent training, philosophy, and roles that continue to trouble education social work in the United Kingdom. Most practitioners use the title education welfare officer, and the main role performed under this name continues to be attendance enforcement, with less emphasis on the broader activities of advocacy, mental health work, and prevention, which are the signature of social work.

Malta uses the term education welfare and Ghana has used both education welfare and school welfare, reflecting these two countries' historical connections with Britain, whereas Hong Kong, Australia, and Canada use the title school social worker. In both Malta and Ghana, work on attendance continues to be a major focus. In Ghana, where the role is also very broad, practitioners attempted to change the title to school social worker to align their work with wider international standards. However, "the title welfare officer is so deeply imbedded in the minds of teachers, education personnel, and parents that the change is hard to be made" (E. Mahama, School Social Workers Association of Ghana, personal communication, November 17, 2003).

In the Nordic countries, the title of school curator (from the Latin root *cura* meaning care) shows concern for the development of individuals and groups. The role of the school social worker in these countries encompasses a broad range of prevention, intervention, and advocacy.

In Argentina, the recent change of title from school social worker to social assistant, and the accompanying reduction in professional requirements for holding the positions, represents a significant downgrading of the profession (Tonon, 2002). This example illustrates the significance of professional titles and the importance of establishing a stable identity for the profession both within nations and internationally.

THE AEGIS OF SCHOOL SOCIAL WORK

School social work has been sponsored by school systems, local government, private social service agencies (with or without government funding), and even international aid organizations. This variety is illustrated by the following examples.

In Hong Kong, the service has typically been provided by nongovernmental agencies using government funding. In Singapore, the service may be provided either by an agency or by the school. In Korea, the pilot program has placed school social workers in schools with funding from the Ministry of Education. In Ghana, the Ministry of Education provides the service but has located it in a separate department, the Welfare Unit, rather than under the Learning and Teaching Department. School social workers in the United Arab Emirates are employed by the Ministry of Education & Youth. In Germany, school social work is the result of collaboration between youth welfare agencies and the school system. In Canada, the employing agent depends on the province; in Ontario, Alberta, Saskatchewan, and Manitoba, the school board hires school social workers, and in other provinces a social agency does the hiring. In the Nordic countries, the school social worker is an integral part of the school; however, there are also some social workers placed in schools by social services. The newly developed school social work program in Mongolia has legal sanction through education law and social workers are employed by the school system.

In the United States, most school social workers are committed to maintaining their long tradition of employment by the school system, believing that this allows them more influence in educational decisions and opportunities to work with the entire school population. There are advantages and disadvantages to working within the school system. In some countries, school social workers believe that working outside the system makes them better able to advocate for students without being unduly influenced by the school as the employer. On the other hand, working within the school enables the school social worker to develop working relationships with all the staff of the school, including administrators, teachers, and others, and to work with this network of adults to provide support for students and improve the school culture.

It may be that the ideal situation is for school social workers to be employed directly by the school system for the traditional goal of supporting children's education, but to develop additional services through social agencies to meet other needs. For example, in recent years, there has been a movement toward school-linked services in the United States, in which social work services are provided by a separate agency in collaboration with the school. Many communities throughout the country have established formal relationships between schools and social and health services, locating those services close to schools or in schools in order to be readily available to families. These services are usually provided in addition to school social work services, and ideally there is a close working relationship between the school social worker and school-linked services staff (Aguirre, 1995; Briar-Lawson, Lawson, Collier, & Joseph, 1997; Corrigan & Bishop, 1997; Cousins, Jackson, & Till, 1997; Tapper, Kleinman, & Nakashian, 1997).

ISSUES FOR SCHOOL SOCIAL WORK AS AN INTERNATIONAL PROFESSION

School social work is a profession that is growing and changing. Several countries have started school social work services, and in countries such as the United States and The Netherlands the profession is becoming stronger. More than 27,000 school social workers are known to be active throughout the world (Huxtable, 2003). Large numbers of school social workers are employed in the United States, United Kingdom, Sweden, Germany, Saudi Arabia, and the United Arab Emirates. Hungary, Macedonia, Japan, Sri Lanka, and Taiwan have fledgling programs of school social work with less than 50 practitioners. Other countries, such as Australia, have school social workers but in such small numbers that the service is restricted to a few basic functions such as crisis intervention. Schoolchildren in Japan still do not have the support of a school social worker despite many efforts to introduce the program. Although there is much stress among schoolchildren in Japan, the school system has been slow to change to meet students' needs and to provide support programs such as school social work (Yamashita, 2002).

In several countries, school social work is a young profession that is still in the process of defining its role, establishing its position in the educational establishment, and providing professional preparation for workers. In countries where it is well established, such as the United States and the Nordic countries, the profession still faces these same issues as it seeks to improve its standing, enhance its performance, and organize its members. If it is to define itself as an international profession, it is even more necessary to address these issues systematically.

ARTICULATING THE UNIQUE ROLE OF SCHOOL SOCIAL WORK

The paramount concern is to articulate why the profession is needed and why it should be funded. This is crucial where the service does not yet exist and social workers are attempting to introduce it, such as in Pakistan (Haseeb-ur-Rahman, Community Development Concern, Sialkot, Pakistan, personal communication, July 17, 2003). Equally important is to introduce school social work in a way that the national educational establishment will accept it. Although it is easily accepted in the United States, where school social workers have a long tradition of working closely with teachers, it may be difficult in some cultures to introduce a new profession into an arena that teachers believe is theirs. In Japan and Korea, it is traditional for teachers to take care of the students' problems (Kim, 2002; Yamashita, 2002). In Slovakia, where teachers, specialized teachers (educators), educational advisors, psychologists, and child guidance centers all play a role, it is a challenge to articulate the distinct role of school social work (Labath & Siroky, 2002).

Although school social work has its unique goals and perspective, there are countries where it merges with another profession. In several European countries, for example, there is a blending of the school social work role with **social pedagogy**, a similar profession that works with individuals, groups, communities, and social organizations using human relations skills to assist in the human development of client groups in various settings, including schools. In Germany there is some blending of the roles of the school social worker and the social pedagog, whereas in some Eastern European countries the school social worker is not seen as distinct from the social pedagog. In fact, the terms used for school social workers are **pedagog skolny** in Poland and **socialais pedagogs** in Latvia (M. Bochenska-Seweryn and K. Kluz, Jagiellonian University, Krakow, Poland, personal communication, 1999; L. Smirnova and O. Denisov, Latvia Association of Social Workers, Riga, Latvia, personal communication, 1999). Blurring of roles in these countries shows the complexity of articulating a unique role for school social work.

Demonstrating the uniqueness of school social work's contribution in the education of children is the key to interpreting the school social work role. The systems approach of social work, which focuses attention on all aspects of the child (physical, emotional, and intellectual) and the child's environment, distinguishes it from other disciplines that care for a more limited aspect of the student's development and are less involved with the relationship of the child to the whole community. It is important, therefore, to be able to demonstrate the value of the social work approach (Kim, 2002; Yamashita, 2002).

Social work's traditional emphasis on strengths rather than on diagnosing problems, as in the medical model, should also be emphasized. Social work should lay claim to this paradigm and embrace methods that use it, such as those that flow from the resiliency research of recent years (Werner & Smith, 1989). This approach distinguishes school social work from the role that school psychologists are often asked to play. For example, in Slovakia, "problem students are sent to the psychologist. He, too, regards social workers as competitors" (Labath & Siroky, 2002, p. 16). Labath and Siroky stress the importance of distinguishing between the role of the psychologist and that of the social worker. Perhaps the combination of the systems approach and emphasis on using the child's strengths, rather than diagnosing problems, is the answer to this question.

The traditional roles of school social work in improving attendance and providing a liaison with the student's family are also a unique contribution to school systems. School social workers should never neglect attendance work because schools in every country need professional help in handling this complex problem, and traditional social work skills using the systems approach are well suited to the work.

In developing countries, attendance work is especially needed to ensure that children are enrolled and have the means to continue to attend school. Similarly, schools usually welcome school social workers' efforts to reach out to families with home visits. The connection that school social work offers between the school and the wider community is also of increasing importance because school personnel recognize that they are not working in a self-contained environment that functions in isolation. School social workers' knowledge of community agencies positions them for establishing and maintaining school-linked services of various kinds.

A central concern among school social workers in most countries is how to provide sufficient service to meet students' needs in the face of inadequate funding, particularly government funding. The profession must compete for funds, and to do this it must be able to document that it can produce results that are valued in the educational establishment and also effectively use these results to promote school social work services. Improved funding depends on convincing legislators and policymakers of the need for school social work services. Professional school social work associations can organize their members to educate the public about the value of the profession, lobby for improved funding, and provide documentation of the effectiveness of their work.

The largest national groups of school social workers (in the United States, the Nordic countries, and the United Kingdom) do have specialized school social work professional associations, and political activity is a priority for these groups. Yet, in most countries, there is neither adequate research nor a professional association for effective lobbying on behalf of school social work. When a new school social work association is formed, as in Ghana and Mongolia, practitioners discover that they have an effective vehicle for interpreting their role to policymakers (E. Mahama, School Social Workers Association of Ghana, personal communication, November 17, 2003; B. Tumurbaatar, State Pedagogical University of Mongolia, Ulaanbaatar, Mongolia, personal communication, 2003).

Professionalizing School Social Work

Conducting research, publishing professional journals and textbooks, and organizing a national professional association are key aspects of professionalizing any field of work. In the case of school social work, there is still much to be done. The United Kingdom, United States, Mongolia, Korea, Sweden, Finland, Ghana, Japan, and Saudi Arabia have national school social work associations. Journals on school social work have been published in the United States, Korea, and Mongolia, and textbooks have been published in the United States (Allen-Meares, 2003; Dupper, 2002; Constable, Flynn, & McDonald, 1999), Austria (Vyslouzil & Weissensteiner, 2001), and Korea (Han, Hong, Kim, & Kim, 1997), whereas in other countries there are only occasional journal articles, government reports, and unpublished articles.

It is not necessarily the countries with the longest history of school social work that have indicators of an advanced profession. For example, Mongolia, where school social work was started as recently as the late 1990s, has a professional association and a quarterly journal. It is no coincidence that school social work has become rapidly institutionalized in Mongolia. In Korea, although school social work is only a few years old, there are specialized courses in school social work, masters and doctoral-level research theses, a journal, textbooks, and a professional school social work association. This careful preparation has enabled school social work to make a strong beginning in a conservative educational establishment, where schools are "disinclined to open doors to outside experts or institutions for help" (Han & Kim, 2002, p. 35).

BEST AND PROMISING PRACTICES

The value of the school social work role can often be demonstrated to the educational establishment and policymakers using evidence of its effectiveness. School social workers are involved with some of the most urgent and recalcitrant problems that schools face, such as school violence, high dropout rates, poor attendance, and behavioral problems. Studies that show a statistically significant benefit from social work intervention are needed in order to demonstrate to schools how school social workers can help them reduce these risks.

Many countries, such as the United States, are currently focusing on improving academic outcomes, so school social workers must be able to not only demonstrate reduction in dropout rates and high-risk behaviors but also demonstrate how social work services contribute to students' academic success in school. Internationally, the school social work profession needs demonstration projects that show novel approaches to specific problems, such as school violence, high dropout rates, poor attendance, and poor academic outcomes, together with measurable results and the ability to replicate the work. Since many practitioners are not equipped to carry out their own research, they need partnerships with universities, professional associations, and government organizations in order to produce valid documentation of their work.

INTERNATIONAL ACTION IN SCHOOL SOCIAL WORK: CULTURAL COMPETENCE

During the past decade, the social work profession has become more aware of the potential of international activities to strengthen the profession and to extend its influence. Books that highlight social work in different countries and international affairs in social work (Hokenstad, Khinduka, & Midgely, 1992; Hokenstad & Midgely, 1997) attest to this increasing interest. International social work organizations, such as the International Federation of Social Workers, the International Association of Schools of Social Work, and the International Council on Social Welfare, help provide social work with a global presence.

Schools of social work are starting to include international content in their curricula. For example, the accrediting body for schools of social work in the United States, the Council on Social Work Education, includes references to international policies in the *Proposed Educational Policy and Accreditation Standards* (2001). Erasmus, the European Community Action Scheme for the Mobility of University Students, was introduced in 1987 to facilitate mobility of students and teachers within the European Union (Socrates-Erasmus, 2000). These programs will make it easier for the profession of social work to influence social policy nationally and internationally.

Most social workers, including school social workers, focus exclusively on local problems. The focus must be expanded to respond to the increasing globalization that not only permeates economic and social life in the 21st century but also has a profound impact on social work practice. For example, many school social workers deal directly with international problems when they work with immigrant children, especially refugee children who have been traumatized by wars or dislocation (Kelen, 2003). A global perspective helps social workers understand their own practice and also advances transformation of school social work into a global profession with unified goals and activities. A broader perspective could possibly influence the educational establishment by expanding the knowledge base and cultural competence of educational institutions.

School social workers have started to realize the potential of international activities as a result of several developments since 1990, including the following:

- The formation of an international network, International Network for School Social Work (internationalnetwork-schoolsocialwork.htmlplanet .com), organized in 1990.
- Two international conferences held in Chicago in 1999 and Stockholm, Sweden, in 2003. (The third international conference will be held in Pusan, Korea, in 2006.)
- The publication of the book, *School Social Work Worldwide* (Huxtable & Blyth, 2002), with chapters on school social work in 12 countries.
- An international edition of the *Journal of School Social Work* published in spring 2002 with articles from seven countries.

The advent of the Internet and electronic communications makes it possible for school social workers to link up with colleagues and become internationally active. Social workers in countries where school social work is a new field can now quickly find information and make contacts throughout the world.

TECHNOLOGY AND INTERNATIONAL SCHOOL SOCIAL WORK

School social workers have much to gain from increasing their international contacts. Sharing information to help provide the best service to clients is one of the most obvious areas in which international activity can help school social workers. Technology has made it possible for school social workers to communicate directly with peers in other countries using the International Network for School Social Work. This network, which contains links to the websites of school social work associations from several countries, is a first step in linking school social work associations throughout the world. The recently formed International Alliance for Child and Adolescent Mental Health and Schools (www.intercamhs.org), e-mail, electronic newsletters, and list-serves make it possible to exchange ideas, research, programs, and training. Information is also readily available throughout the world through the ERIC database, which includes vast numbers of documents relevant to school social work (www2 .uncg.edu/~ericcas2/index.html). Medscape provides research on children's health and disabilities (http://pediatrics.medscape.com).

The electronic newsletter of the School Social Work Association of America is frequently used by social workers overseas requesting information from school social workers in the United States. This is starting to be an effective means of giving support, materials, and training opportunities to school social workers overseas, as occurred when a U.S. school social worker provided training in Ghana (Shanedling, 2003).

Social workers in countries where school social work is just being developed, such as Sri Lanka, or where social workers are trying to start a program, such as Pakistan, are seeking assistance with training personnel. An international network of schools of social work that offers specialty coursework in school social work could provide a global resource for social work training and extend training in school social work to areas that have no specialized courses. The expense of travel for personnel usually prohibits sending workers overseas for training. Universities that have developed distance learning through online courses in social work could offer university courses to students where school social work courses have not been developed. Such an effort would require a commitment to international work in order to adapt courses to differing cultures and needs.

A promising arena for international activity is advocacy for children's rights. Although the Convention on the Rights of the Child, including the right to education and other economic, social, civil, and cultural rights, has been ratified by all countries except the United States and Somalia (United Nations Children's Fund, 2000), school social workers are aware of the need for vigilance in protecting children. The ease of international contact makes it possible for school social workers to extend their influence to advocate for children and their education on a worldwide basis. It is an opportunity that has been little used thus far.

Opportunities to advocate for children internationally can be fruitful. For example, a subgroup (Education, Media and Literacy) of the Non-Governmental Organization Group for the Convention on the Rights of the Child has a major focus on preventing violence against children in schools. School social workers throughout the world were invited by the International Network for School Social Work to submit examples of proven violence reduction interventions to the International Federation of Social Workers to be shared with the Non-Governmental Organization Group. Currently, the International Federation of Social Workers is one of the few international social work organizations active in advocating for human rights and contributing social work knowledge to international social movements. The lack of an international organization representing school social workers impedes involvement in such advocacy. The first step toward an international school social work association is to strengthen national professional organizations, and the second step is to join the national groups together to form an international association.

SUMMARY

Educating the world's children is a challenge in the 21st century. The Millennium Report of the Secretary-General of the United Nations stated that "education is the key to the new global economy" and urged the Millennium Summit to "endorse the objectives of demonstratably narrowing the gender gap in primary and secondary education by 2005 and of ensuring that, by 2015, all children complete a full course of primary education" (Annan, 2000, p. 5). Children bear the brunt of global problems, such as poverty, war, and environmental degradation, and their education is threatened by these problems. The rapid pace of scientific progress offers the promise of better health, nutrition, and opportunity for the world's children, and although more children are enrolled in school, many still face obstacles in reaching their potential. School social workers have a unique role to play in helping overcome these obstacles to ensure a brighter future for all children. The international challenge for this profession is to extend its reach to all countries and every child who needs help accessing and benefiting from education.

School Social Work Companion Website

Please be sure to check out our companion website at www.thomsonedu.com/social_work/bye, where you will find relevant materials for each chapter, including flashcards, online practice quizzes, and PowerPoint slides.

REFERENCES

Aguirre, L. (1995). California's efforts towards school-linked, integrated, comprehensive services. *Social Work in Education, 17,* 217–225.

Al-Garni, M. (2002). The impact of family structure and family function factors on the deviant behaviors of high school students in Mecca City, Saudi Arabia. *Journal of School Social Work, 12*(2), 47–61.

Allen-Meares, P. (2003). *Social Work Services in Schools.* Needham Heights, MA: Allyn and Bacon.

Anderson, G., Pösö, T., Väisänen, E., & Wallin, A. (2002). School social work in Finland and other Nordic countries: Cooperative professionalism in schools. In M. Huxtable & E. Blyth (Eds.), *School social work worldwide* (pp. 77–92). Washington, DC: NASW Press.

Annan, K. (2000). *We the peoples: The role of the United Nations in the 21st century* (Millennium Report of the Secretary-General of the United Nations). Retrieved March 13, 2005 from www.un.org/millennium/sg/report/full.htm

Blyth, E., & Cooper, H. (2002). School social work in the United Kingdom: A key role in social inclusion. In M. Huxtable & E. Blyth (Eds.), *School social work worldwide* (pp. 15–32). Washington, DC: NASW Press.

Briar-Lawson, K., Lawson, H., Collier, C., & Joseph, A. (1997). School-linked comprehensive services: Promising beginnings, lessons learned, and future challenges. *Social
Work in Education, 19,* 136–148.

Caldas, S. J. (1993). Reexamination of input and process factor effects in public school
achievement. *Journal of Educational Research,* 86(4), 206–214.

Commonwealth Fund. (1927). *The Commonwealth Fund eighth annual report for the
year 1925–1926.* New York: Author.

Constable, R., Flynn, J., & McDonald, S. (Eds.). (1999). *School social work: Practice
and research perspectives.* Chicago: Lyceum.

Corrigan, D., & Bishop, K. (1997). Creating family-centered integrated service systems
and interprofessional educational programs to implement them. *Social Work in
Education, 19,* 149–163.

Costin, L. (1969). A historical review of school social work. *Social Casework, 50,*
439–453.

Council on Social Work Education. (2001). *Proposed educational policy and accreditation standards.* Retrieved November 2003 from www.cswe.org/accreditation/EPAS/
EPAS_start.htm

Cousins, L., Jackson, K., & Till, M. (1997). Portrait of a school-based health center: An
ecosystems perspective. *Social Work in Education, 19,* 189–202.

Dupper, D. (2002). *School social work: Skills and interventions for effective practice.*
Indianapolis, IN: Wiley.

Han, I., Hong, S., Kim, H., & Kim, K. (1997). *School and social welfare: Theories and
practice of school social work.* Seoul: Hakmunsa.

Han, I., & Kim, M. (2002). A pilot project for school social work in Korea. *Journal of
School Social Work,* 12(2), 35–46.

Hokenstad, M. C., Khinduka, S. K., & Midgley, J. (Eds.). (1992). *Profiles in international
social work.* Washington, DC: NASW Press.

Hokenstad, M. C., & Midgley, J. (Eds.). (1997). *Issues in international social work:
Global challenges for a new century.* Washington, DC: NASW Press.

Huxtable, M. (2003). *Status of school social work: Results of 2003 questionnaire.*
Unpublished manuscript.

Huxtable, M., & Blyth, E. (Eds.). (2002). *School social work worldwide.* Washington,
DC: NASW Press.

Kelen, J. (2003, October). Faces and voices of refugee youth. *SSWAA Bell.*

Kim, K. (2002). School social work in Korea: Current status and future direction. In M.
Huxtable & E. Blyth (Eds.), *School social work worldwide* (pp. 201–216).
Washington, DC: NASW Press.

Labath, V., & Siroky, B. (2002). Concept, experience and dilemmas of school social
work: A message from Slovakia. *Journal of School Social Work, 12*(2), 8–18.

Loughborough, J., Shera, W., & Wilhelm, J. (2002). School social work in Canada:
Historical themes and current challenges. In M. Huxtable & E. Blyth (Eds.),
School social work worldwide (pp. 57–75). Washington, DC: NASW Press.

Shanedling, P. (2003, November). Going Ghanaian, training school social workers in
West Africa. *SSWAA Bell.*

Socrates-Erasmus: The European Community programme in the field of higher education. (2000). Retrieved November 2003 from europa.eu.Int/comm/education/
socrates/erasmus/home.html

Sossou, M., & Daniels, T. (2002). School social work practice in Ghana: A hope for the
future. In M. Huxtable & E. Blyth (Eds.), *School social work worldwide* (pp.
93–108). Washington, DC: NASW Press.

Tapper, D., Kleinman, P., & Nakashian, M. (1997). An inter-agency collaboration strategy for linking schools with social and criminal justice services. *Social Work in Education, 19,* 176–188.

Tonon, G. (2002). School social work in Argentina: The challenge of state reform. In M. Huxtable & E. Blyth (Eds.), *School social work worldwide* (pp. 109–119). Washington, DC: NASW Press.

United Nations Children's Fund. (2000). *The state of the world's children.* Retrieved November 2003 from www.unicef.org/sowc00

Vyslouzil, M., & Weissensteiner, M. (2001). *Schulsozialarbeit in Österreich: Projekte mit Zukunft.* Wien, Austria: OG Bverlag.

Werner, E., & Smith, R. (1989). *Vulnerable but invincible.* New York: Adams, Bannister, Cox.

World Factbook—Saudi Arabia. (2003). Retrieved November 2003 from www.cia.gov/cia/publications/factbook/geos/sa.html

Yamashita, E. (2002). School social work in Japan: A partner for education in the 21st century. In M. Huxtable & E. Blyth (Eds.), *School social work worldwide* (pp. 217–231). Washington, DC: NASW Press.

Index